# MEANING AND VALUE IN WESTERN THOU

## A History of Ideas in Western Culture
## Volume I: The Ancient Foundations

## J. William Angell
## Robert M. Helm

UNIVERSITY
PRESS OF
AMERICA

LANHAM • NEW YORK • LONDON

Copyright © 1981 by

University Press of America,™ Inc.

4720 Boston Way
Lanham, MD 20706

3 Henrietta Street
London WC2E 8LU England

Printed in the United States of America

Library of Congress Cataloging in Publication Data

Angell, John William.
    Meaning and value in Western thought.

    Includes index.
    CONTENTS: v. 1. The ancient foundations.
    1. Values–History. 2. Meaning (Philosophy) –
History. 3. Philosophy–History. 4. Civilization,
Occidental. I. Helm, Robert Meredith, joint author. II.
Title.
BD232.A5                      190              80–67174
ISBN 0–8191–1368–9
ISBN 0–8191–1369–7 (pbk)

To

John Allen Easley

and

Albert Clayton Reid

Great Teachers of Meaning and Value

## Acknowledgements

it goes without saying that this work is only incidentally ours. What is recorded has been gathered from countless sources and we acknowledge our debt to all who have taught us, by voice and in print.

We appreciate permission to quote material from:

ARISTOTLE, translated by Philip Wheelwright, copyright (c) 1935, 1951, by the Odyssey Press, Inc., reprinted by permission of the Bobbs-Merrill Co., Inc.

THE PRESOCRATICS, edited by Philip Wheelwright, copyright (c) 1966 by the Odyssey Press, reprinted by permission of the Bobbs-Merrill Co., Inc.

The Revised Standard Version of the Bible, copyright 1946, 1952 (c) 1971, 1973.

THE TROJAN WOMEN, translated by Gilbert Murray, copyright (c) 1915 by George Allen and Unwin, Ltd.

We are especially grateful to Marjorie S. Angell and Alma J. Helm for their constant encouragement and support from the beginning of the project.

We wish to thank Dean Henry S. Stroupe and the Graduate School of Wake Forest University for financial assistance; Provost Edwin G. Wilson and Dean Thomas E. Mullen for making research leaves possible; and our colleagues in the Departments of Religion and Philosophy for their cooperation.

We record our gratitude to Mrs. Ann F. Francis and Mrs. Mary C. Reid for their excellent typing and editorial assistance in the preparation of the manuscript, and to Ms. Janet Middlebrooks of Mercer University Press for setting the type.

# CONTENTS

## Preface

This two-volume work is intended to describe the origins and development of the philosophical and religious heritage of Western civilization. The first volume presents the foundations as they appeared in the ancient Near East, especially as they were given form and substance by the Hebrews and the Greeks and as they were then fused in Roman culture and early Christianity. The second traces the development of Western thought from those beginnings in antiquity to its varied expressions in modern times.

In both volumes the emphasis is upon those aspects of culture which reflect concern with meaning and value, usually considered as the disciplines of philosophy and religion. The result is a survey of Western cultural history which is purposely selective in its content, seeking only to identify and clarify those formative motifs and discernable directions that lie beneath contemporary experience.

This study is our response to several concerns which we have shared since our undergraduate days and through a quarter-century as academic colleagues. We believe that there is a widespread and continuing need for interdisciplinary synthesis, not only in academia but also in the lives of thoughtful people of society in general. We are convinced, also, that the curriculum of higher education should be centered in the examination and weighing of meaning and the discovery and acceptance of values. The condition of mankind throughout the world demonstrates the inevitable confusion and danger which result from knowledge and training without wisdom and morality. Further, we have found an eager excitement, both in our classrooms and off the campus, when a course of reading and study of this nature is made available.

This is our attempt to respond to those concerns and observations. The two volumes are the product of our thought and study, and the material has taken this form because of its repeated presentation in our classes and in lectures in other communities. We actually designed the original course which this material represents while we enjoyed a visit together in London, in the summer of 1971. We have taught a two-semester course on the subject every year since, and our classes have been responsive and encouraging.

The two volumes, though treating a continuous historical development, have been written so that they are independent of each other. Each may be read or used as a text without the other.

They have been constructed so as to be convenient for class-room use, but we believe they will also be of equal interest to the thoughtful general reader.

The work is intended to be introductory, neither assuming a previous knowledge of the subjects nor attempting to deal with the critical and historical problems of detail which will often appear. We have also attempted to avoid as much as possible the scholarly notations which might complicate the reading. The primary sources, to which constant reference will be made, should be read along with this commentary whenever possible, and we hope eventually to collect and edit a book of such appropriate readings.

J. William Angell and Robert M. Helm

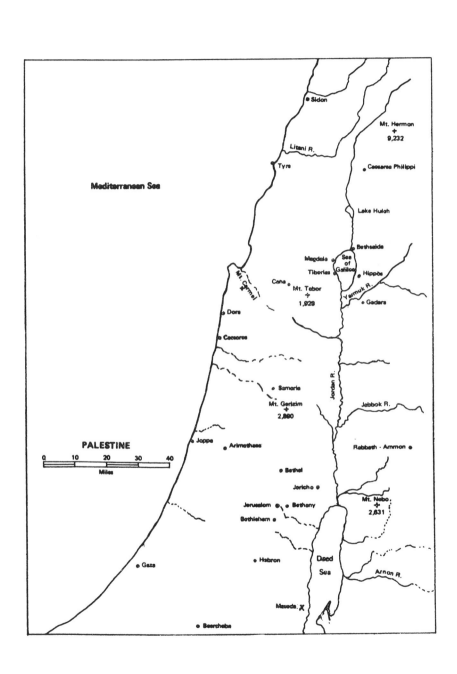

Mediterranean Sea

Sidon

Litani R.

Tyre

Mt. Herman
+
9,232

Caesarea Philippi

Lake Hulah

Bethsaida

Magdala
Sea
of
Galilee

Tiberias

Hippos

Cana

Mt. Tabor
+
1,929

Yarmuk R.

Gadara

Mt. Carmel

Dora

Caesarea

Samaria

Mt. Gerizim
+
2,880

Jebbok R.

PALESTINE

0    10    20    30    40

Miles

Joppe

Arimathesa

Rabbeth - Ammon

Bethel

Jericho

Jordan R.

Jerusalem

Bethany

Mt. Nebo
+
2,631

Bethlehem

Habron

Dead
Sea

Gaza

Arnon R.

Maseda X

Beersheba

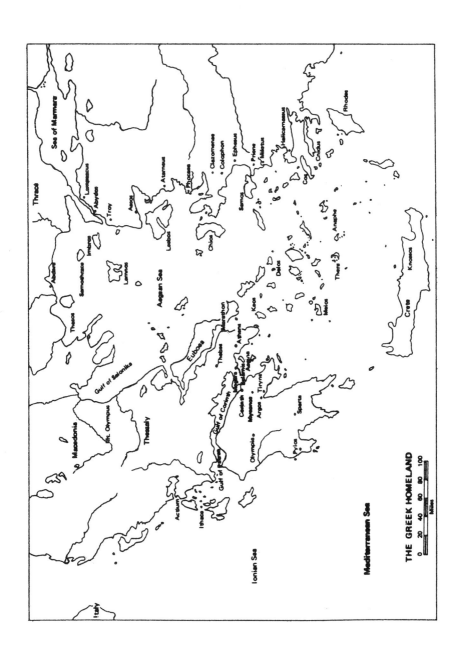

THE GREEK HOMELAND

Sea of Marmara

Thrace

Lampsacus
Abydos
Troy
Assos

Akamas

Phocaea
Clazomenae
Colophon
Ephesus
Priene
Miletus
Samos
Halicarnassus

Cos
Cnidus

Rhodes

Abdera
Samothrace
Imbros
Lemnos
Lesbos
Chios

Aegean Sea

Thasos

Anaphe
Delos
Thera
Melos
Kaos

Knossos
Crete

Macedonia
Mt. Olympus
Gulf of Salonika

Euboea

Marathon

Thebes

Thessaly

Corinth
Gulf of Corinth
Gulf of Patras
Eleusis
Athens
Aegina
Megara
Mycenae
Tiryns
Argos
Sparta

Olympia
Pylos

Actium
Ithaca

Ionian Sea

Mediterranean Sea

Italy

0  20  40  60  80  100
Miles

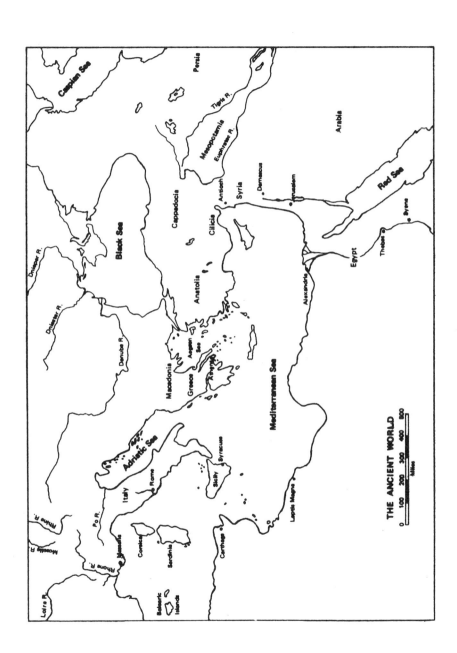

THE ANCIENT WORLD

0  100  200  300  400  500
Miles

# I.
# WESTERN ORIGINS IN THE ANCIENT EAST

# Chapter 1

## *The Drama of Western Culture*

The civilization of the Western world is like a broad stream with many tributaries which continues to flow through the valleys of space and time. Within the last century, expecially, it has overflowed its more narrow course of the previous millenia and spread out in a floodtide that has inundated nearly all of the earth, bringing refreshing blessings and deadly curses alike to the arid deserts and sterile pools into which its rushing waters have flowed. Both those who live in the mainstream of this culture and those who live in the vast outlands and yet find themselves affected by it, for good and evil, may find orientation and enrichment in a better knowledge of the nature and history of this ancient, powerful, and dominant civilization.

The last quarter of the twentieth century is a particularly appropriate time for an analysis and evaluation of Western culture, for several urgent reasons. One is that this culture has come to dominate all other cultures of the world and therefore needs to be well understood. Another is that some of the most perceptive observers of the culture, both from within and without, are expressing grave concern about the health of the culture. Many suggest that Western man has grown so corrupt and irresponsible, and at the same time so powerful and dangerous, that he may have brought himself and his conquered world to a spent, polluted, and explosive end.

A third reason for taking a new and careful look at the whole stream of Western civilization is that renewal and direction may thus be discovered. When a man is disoriented, he finds healing in the familiar. When a man is lost, he needs to retrace his steps. And when a man is beset by doubt and uncertainty, he will find wisdom and strength by consulting the sages. Western man and all the people of the earth, living in a time of unparalleled stress and with the very threat of extinction, may find meaning and value for the future by looking first to the past for courage and wisdom.

This book proposes a backward look as a preparation for going forward. It is a cultural history, a searching for roots. We shall begin at the headwaters of the broad stream, indentifying the earliest sources of our culture and tracing their major developments. The main concern will be to discover the conceptions of meaning and the standards of value which Western man has developed, expressed, and preserved, since these are the central elements of culture for which there is the greatest need in the modern age.

### The Stage of the Drama

We may gain added insights for understanding by changing the figure from a stream to a drama. There are many characteristics of the dramatic in the history of Western culture, and it remains "the greatest show on earth." The scenes are numerous and constantly shifting, the action is always exciting, and there is a multitude of actors and actresses, both famous and unsung. Whether the drama is seen as a comedy or a tragedy remains undetermined; that judgment must be made by those on the stage. Life is what we make of it, and the final critique has yet to be written.

A drama requires a stage, and we must know this one well if we are to follow the action. Therefore we must begin by noting that the great drama of Western civilization began in a propitious location, where the three continents of Asia, Africa, and Europe meet. That fact alone provided adequate resources, opportunity for expansion, and a reasonably favorable climate. The first long scenes were played out on the land bordered by five familiar bodies of water—the Mediterranean Sea, the Black Sea, the Caspian Sea, the Persian Gulf, and the Red Sea.

Two great river valleys, at the center of this land, were the cradles of Western culture. The first, called Mesopotamia, is given life by the Euphrates and the Tigris Rivers. The earliest stirrings of civilization may have begun there, as will be discussed in the next chapter. The second valley, of course, is Egypt, "the gift of the Nile." Its history and ancient culture will be the subject of the chapter to follow. But there are other, smaller rivers in the area which have often been of great significance in the affairs of man, and they should be noted. The Jordan, though short and small by world standards, has been important to man since the dawn of history, and it still "rolls on" at the center of the stage. The careful observer should also locate on the map the Rivers Halys, Orontes, Litanni, Yarmuk, and Jabbok. There are also the Oxus, the Indus, the Abana, and even the tiny Kishon. Later we shall learn about the

Tiber, the Danube, the Po, the Rhine, the Rhone, the Seine, and the Thames.

Why are the seas and rivers of so great importance? First, because they represent water, without which life itself is impossible. We shall hear constant reference to water in the most ancient myths and historical records. The earth is surrounded by water and rests on water, it was believed, and the sacred writings frequently spoke of water as the symbol of vitality and refreshment (cf. Psalm 1). Moreover, rivers and seas were avenues of travel, commerce, and conquest; and most of the earliest communities were built beside rivers and streams. Some early philosophers, as we shall see, even identified water as the basic substance from which all things were derived.

"The Fertile Crescent" is a familiar designation for that long, crescent-shaped stretch of well-watered land which begins at the head of the Persian Gulf, runs northwestward through Mesopotamia, and then curves west and south through the arable lands of Syria and Palestine. Along with the valley of the Nile, it is the main stage for the action of our drama. However, as the scenes and the centuries pass, the stage will become enlarged until its center will finally move inexorably toward the west, first in the area of the Aegean Sea, surrounded by the Greeks, and finally, in this volume, to Italy and Rome.

The stage of our drama will usually be centered in cities. After all, even the word "civilization" is derived from the Latin "civitas," *city*, and the etymology indicates what civilization means: the creation of human communities for the sustaining and enrichment of life. The history of Western civilization is a tale of many cities, from the Sumerian city of Ur to the mighty mistress, Rome. Along the way we shall see scenes in the drama set in such creative communities as Babylon and Nineveh, Jerusalem and Athens, Damascus and Alexandria, Sparta and Syracuse, Antioch and Carthage. Observers of the drama will need to consult their maps in advance of the action so as to be thoroughly familiar with these and scores of other cities and towns.

Geography is the description of the stage for the drama of man. So often, as will become evident in this study, the stage determines the action. There is a decisive relation between the affairs of mankind and the physical context of those affairs. Hence it is crucial for the stage to be well known before the drama can be understood.

## The Actors in the Drama

Who are the heroes and heroines—and villains—of this master drama? There has been a vast array of individuals and groups crossing this stage, and one of the enriching benefits to the observer is becoming well acquainted with his intellectual and spiritual ancestors. We who seek enlightenment and guidance in the confusing conditions of the twentieth century may find models to emulate and errors to avoid in the lives and choices of those who have gone before. There is wisdom in the famous maxim of Santayana that he who does not know the mistakes of the past is condemned to repeat them. Further, an intimate knowledge of the giants of the past can be an antidote to boredom and emptiness, two ever-present enemies to modern peace of mind; for we can have the constant companionship of such challenging persons as Plato and Job, Moses and Hesiod, Socrates and Jesus.

The opening scenes of Western cultural history bring before our eyes the nameless multitudes in Mesopotamia and Egypt who toiled and suffered through unimaginable hardships to understand and control nature and to rise above the other animals in acceptance and cooperation, as they constructed the first foundations of civilized living. Then, among those multitudes we shall begin to make out the forms of creative leaders such as Sargon the Great, Akhenaten, and Abraham. And with the passing of time we shall see Homer on the stage, telling again of the profoundly representative struggles of Odysseus in his journey home from Troy; we shall witness Jeremiah, warning his fellow-citizens of Jerusalem of the consequences of injustice and infidelity; and we shall walk, in imagination, around the Acropolis in Athens, listening in on the provocative conversations of Socrates and the demanding lectures of Aristotle. We shall follow Alexander across the Fertile Crescent to central Asia and back, and we shall accompany Jesus from Galilee to his crucifixion in Jerusalem.

We shall travel swiftly through the centuries, as in a time-machine, following the course of culture from the marshes in the delta of the Tigris and Euphrates to the borders of the Nile to the basin of the Aegean Sea, and then, finally to Rome and northwards across the Alps. One scene displays the pageantry of Nebuchadnezzar leading a procession of priests and warriors through the Ishtar Gate of ancient Babylon, with the king "taking the hand" of the great god Marduk, in celebration of the promising

New Year. Another scene presents the Forum of Rome, flanked by the Capitoline Hill adorned with the gleaming columns of the Temple of Jupiter. Marching through the Forum, the Legions of the victorious Titus pass beneath the new arch of their commander, son of the Emperor Vespasian, who has just returned to the Eternal City from capturing and destroying ancient Jerusalem, the vaunted city of the Jewish people. Such scenes and characters are commonplace in this drama of Western cultural history.

## The Scope of the Drama

The drama which lies before us is vast in scope and played by all the great actors in history. We are invited to see them individually and to hear their voices. It can be a liberating and instructive experience. There is no more adequate way for us to understand where and who we are, and to determine where we should go and what we should do, than to rediscover our cultural heritage. Standing on that platform of accomplishment, we may find meaning and value for the present and the future.

It has been well said that Western culture is the child of a Hebrew mother and a Greek father, born and reared in Rome. That simplistic epigram summarizes significant truth though it is not, of course, the whole truth. The ancestors of the child came also from wider lands, to the east, north, and south; and the family has been steadily enlarged through the millenia by mixture with many strangers. Those of us in northern and central Europe and in the Americas, for example, must remember that the culture we enjoy, from the Mediterranean world, was not our creation but became ours by adoption and absorption, since we are physically descendants, at least in part, of the diverse barbarian and northern peoples who invaded the Roman Empire and medieval Europe.

Nevertheless, it is in truth our culture, the source of our language, religion, philosophy, science, law, art, literature—the elements, in short, of meaningful life. It is ours to enjoy, to improve, and to pass on.

Returning, then, to the original figure of speech, introduced at the beginning of this chapter, let us go at once to the headwaters of this great, broad stream. The mighty river first appeared, so far as the records show, in Mesopotamia and Egypt. Let us go there and discover the sources of meaning and value.

# Chapter 2

# *Mesopotamian Sources*

The Tigris and Euphrates rivers rise in the mountains of eastern Turkey, in the region of Lake Van and Lake Urmia, and their volume increases as they flow mostly in a southeasterly direction until they dissipate into the swamps at the head of the Persian Gulf. To the east of the rivers stands the wall of the Zagros Mountains; to the west lie the vast Syrian and Arabian deserts. The two rivers, with their tributaries, give life to the broad plain through which they flow, creating arable land from what would otherwise be an extension of the desert. That fertile plain, now occupied by Iraq, is known to history by the name Mesopotamia, "the land between the rivers."

Mesopotamia and the lands which border it, along with the valley of the Nile in Egypt, are the ultimate cradles of Western civilization. Man may have developed the rudiments of culture earlier at other places on the earth, such as in central Asia, central Africa, or in the Western Hemisphere; but the evidence discovered so far, and it is considerable, indicates that civilization *per se* had its birth and early development in and around those hospitable valleys about 10,000 years ago. It was there that men took the major step from hunting and gathering food to producing and preserving food. That primary activity, accompanied by the domestication of animals, led swiftly and inevitably to cultivation and ownership of fields, the accumulation of herds, the building of permanent housing, and the beginnings of structured communities far more inclusive and complicated than family and tribe.

The technological, urban, and economic revolutions were the creative causes out of which civilization arose. They began with the making of tools, the building of communities, and the ownership and exchange of commodities. The process, even on the most primitive level, probably took place over thousands of years. It was sporadic in some areas and more rapid and continuous in others. Furthermore, the results of these fundamental elements of civilization were of mixed value, providing not only the blessings of comfort, leisure, and security, but also the dangers of conflict, anxiety, and selfishness. Civilization has always been morally ambiguous, producing proportionate amounts of good and evil.

The beginnings are obscure. There are no written records and descriptions of the earliest times, since language and the art of writing are themselves both a part and the product of civilization. Only the artifacts tell the story. Nevertheless, there is sufficient evidence to sketch the main stages of the history of the many peoples, cities, kingdoms, and empires of the ancient and ultimate source of Western culture in Mesopotamia.

### Successive Peoples

Archeologists have demonstrated that the sedentary revolution had already occurred as early as 8000 B.C. among the people who lived on the western slopes of the Zagros Mountains of upper Mesopotamia. Excavated sites such as the mounds of Jarmo and Karim Shahir, northeast of present-day Baghdad, have yielded evidence that farming, stone tool-making, house-building, and even cloth-making, were well advanced by that early date. Similar progress had clearly been made by various inhabitants of other locations throughout the area, though the climate and topography of some sites were more favorable than others for the preservation of man-made materials. One of the most ancient cities was Jericho, in the Jordan Valley just north of the Dead Sea. Extensive investigation of the mound there has uncovered the remains of advanced pre-ceramic cultures which existed long before 8000 B.C.

About 6000 B.C., the people known as the Hassuna, after a mound on the upper Tigris River, began to make significant advances which marked the end of the Stone Age and the beginning of the use of metal. They became more settled, dwelled in multi-roomed adobe houses of logical design, stored grain in large clay containers, and painted their pottery with intricate decorations. There is even evidence that considerable commerce had already begun, with such commodities as pottery and excess grain being traded among diverse communities from the mountains of the north to the Persian Gulf. And after the so-called Hassuna, there appeared another people, known especially from Tell Halaf in northern Syria, who brought farming, herding, city-building, and trade to even higher levels of development. They were among the earliest to use copper decorations and implements.

For reasons that remain obscure, the farmers and artisans of northern Mesopotamia migrated south toward the delta, beginning about 5000 B.C., and there they built the first extensive civilization known from linguistic evidence. As a group, these people are called the Ubaidians because much information about them has come from Tell al-Ubaid, near the ancient city of Ur in the delta of the two rivers. Within a millenium they built a complex, far-reaching culture, scattered in organized communities throughout the lands stretching from the Caspian Sea to the ends of the Fertile Crescent. They were successful and energetic farmers and builders. They were carpenters, metal-workers, and weavers, making plows and developing herds. They made bricks of baked clay and built houses, temples, and walled towns. Their highly-developed skills of organization and technology lasted at least until they were absorbed into the great Sumerian civilization, around 3500 B.C., which in turn left written, clay-tablet descriptions of the Ubaidian accomplishments.

Incursions of Mesopotamia have been constant through the ages, and they have frequently been in the form of waves of nomadic migrants from the deserts in the south and the mountains in the north. Families and tribes have regularly drifted into the "sown land" along the great rivers in search of sustenance and security. Larger invasions have occurred sporadically during the millenia because of shifting populations, economic pressures, and natural calamities. Thus the whole Fertile Crescent, especially Mesopotamia, has been like a vast, concave beach upon which the waves constantly wash and to which the storms often bring the flotsam and jetsam of the restless seas. Thus it was, for example, that the Sumerians came, around 3500 B.C., probably from central Asia via the highlands of Iran, to merge with the Ubaidians and other inhabitants of southern Mesopotamia. The resultant fusion of beginnings produced what has been called the first true civilization. The Sumerian hegemony was to last for a millenium and a half, achieving heights of power and development previously unknown; and the foundation stones of that highly developed culture have remained throughout history as major elements of Western civilization.

The Sumerians were centered in southern Mesopotamia, between Baghdad and the Gulf. There they built the great cities of Eridu, Kish, Ur, Erech, Lagash, and Nippur. The fields around the towns were watered by irrigation canals and protected by levees, and they produced an abundance of food and large herds of cattle. The cities grew large and interdependent, with alliances, bureaucracies, and social systems created to meet rising needs.

Problems of ownership and control, social order, economic rivalry, and political struggle increasingly brought warfare, attempts to establish justice and peace, and the dynastic and despotic concentration of power. The remains of that complex and productive civilization reveal not only remarkable material accomplishments but also astounding and permanent contributions of art, literature and religion. The Sumerians constructed ziggurats and temples, highways and palaces. They also composed hymns and prayers and developed sacred rituals and festivals. *The Epic of Gilgamesh*, one of the religious and philosophical classics of antiquity, was composed about the Sumerian king of Erech, who reigned about 2700 B.C.

The Sumerians were rivalled by the Akkadians, who established a powerful kingdom in the northern half of Mesopotamia by 2300 B.C. The greatest of the Akkadian rulers was Sargon the Great, who conquered both Sumer and the Elamites to the east, a people who frequently invaded the great river valley. Other groups also, such as the Gutians from the region of the Caspian Sea, made temporary conquests into Sumer and finally caused the decline of the Sumerian rule.

The Amorites, a Semitic people from the western reaches of the Fertile Crescent and the desert, brought about the downfall of the Sumerian empire around the beginning of the Second Millenium B.C. Their most famous leader was Hammurabi, who ruled over the first great Babylonian Empire from about 1750 until his death in 1708 B.C. The Amorites did not destroy the ancient culture of the Sumerians; rather they absorbed and modified it. Hammurabi is probably best known because of his Code of Law, found engraved on a stone shaft which may be observed today in the Louvre, in Paris. In the name of his god, Marduk, he administered justice and order throughout a vast kingdom which spread a common civilization throughout most of the Fertile Crescent. Since this time of the Amorites coincides with the stories of the Hebrew Patriarchs, the conditions of Hammurabi's reign, relatively well-known from the Code and his extant letters, shed significant light on the earliest parts of the Bible.

Several centuries of social and political turmoil followed the decline of the Babylonian Empire. The Hittites from Anatolia wrought havoc in Mesopotamia as well as down to the borders of Egypt beginning around 1600 B.C. Then another non-Semitic people, the Kassites from beyond the Zagros Mountains, invaded and ruled Babylonia for more than four centuries. They are well known because of the Letters of Tell el-Amarna, a vast collection of clay-tablet correspondence discovered near a village of that name in Egypt in 1887. Finally, the Elamites also made another conquest of Babylonia in 1170 B.C

Gradually, at first, the Assyrians gained domination of Mesopotamia, beginning around 1100 B.C. A ruthless and warlike people from the region of Nineveh and Assur on the upper Tigris River, the Assyrians first gained widespread power under their ruler, Tiglath-Pileser I, who conquered and ruled over the homeland as well as Syria and Phoenicia in the southwest and Babylonia in the southeast. He built Nineveh, the capital, into an impressive city, with temples, bridges, parks, and libraries; and he provided the benefits of security and prosperity to the people of the land. However, the record also reveals that he began the policy of extreme military barbarism which has been ever since a synonym for Assyria. The Hebrews, like many other conquered enemies of Assyria, were to experience the ferocious butchery and merciless terror of the people from Nineveh (cf. Nahum). Assyria was the first nation from Mesopotamia to invade and conquer Egypt (in 671 B.C.), and in the process she overran and annexed Damascus (732 B.C.) and the northern Hebrew kingdom, Israel (722 B.C.), and she made a frightened vassal of the kingdom of Judah (cf. Isaiah 36-39).

The mighty Assyrian Empire became senile and corrupt after the unprecedented conquests by Esarhaddon and Ashurbanapal, who ruled the whole Fertile Crescent and Egypt. Its decline was rapid following the death of Ashurbanapal, in 633 B.C., and Nineveh itself was destroyed by the combined forces of the Medes and Babylonians in 612 B.C. The death of Assyria occurred at the historically decisive battle at Carchemish, on the Euphrates, in 605 B.C., when the Babylonians under Nebuchadnezzar defeated both the remnants of the Assyrian forces and their new allies, the revived Egyptians. Now the land between the rivers and the western areas to the borders of Egypt, including Judah, became the Neo-Babylonian, or Chaldean, Empire.

It is a commonplace of history that Nebuchadnezzar's Empire did not last long. His death in 562 B.C. marked the beginning of a rapid decline in Babylonian stability, and the end came with the defeat of the army at Opis on the Tigris and the capture of Babylon by Cyrus and the Persians in 539 B.C. The Persians, having already defeated and annexed both the empires of the Medes, in the north and east, and of the Lydians, west of the Halys River in Anatolia, soon conquered Egypt also, thus building the largest empire the world had yet seen. At its height, the Persian rule extended from the Aegean Sea and the deserts of Libya to the Indus River and central Asia. And, in addition to its vast size, the Persian Empire provided the multitudes of ethnic groups under its domination with two centuries of enlightened rule, effective administration, and relative peace and security.

Mesopotamia and its environs came under foreign rule and cultural influence with the coming of the Hellenists led by Alexander the Great and his successors. During the decade preceding his untimely death at Babylon, in 323 B.C., Alexander made a personal conquest of the entire Persian Empire, and, in the process, introduced the brilliant new culture of the Greeks to the ancient lands. However, the bargain was reciprocal, and the ideas and practices of the past were exported also to the growing cultures of southern Europe. Hence, during the long centuries of development and control by the Greeks and the Romans, there was a continuing fusion of the civilizations which may be traced to the beginnings of the process itself in pre-historic Mesopotamia.

### Religious, Deities, Myths

Religion was a major aspect of all the successive cultures in the long history of Mesopotamia, as indeed it has been in every civilization known to man. That is inevitable and probably necessary because religion, in its various forms, is the whole response of mankind to the awesome mystery of being and to the threats that arise from the experiences of existence. Religion has often been gross and primitive, and even immoral, but it has always been present because at every stage of civilization man has been aware of the givenness of reality, of his obvious finitude, and of the certainty of suffering and death. The most ancient cultures recognized these ever-present and undeniable realities in life and thought, and their responses may be seen in the earliest development of religion and its twin, philosophy.

The ancient Sumerians, building on the ideas and practices of the cultures which had preceded them, explained the facts and characteristics of reality by reference to anthropomorphic, cosmic persons called the gods. They recognized a hierarchical family of such beings, and a considerable number of records have survived concerning their beliefs about the origins and functions of the gods. There were, apparently, four primary gods, representing the four major realms of the universe: An, the god of the heavens; Enlil, the god of the air; Enki, the god of the waters; and Ninhursag, the mother goddess of the earth. Many other gods and goddesses occupied the Sumerian pantheon, and the names, realms, and works of the gods changed with the rise and fall of successive civilizations and empires. Assyrian and Babylonian records, along with the Hebrew Scriptures, show that the great national god of the Babylonians was Marduk, supposedly the son of the water god, Enki; and Marduk became the chief god, by the decision of all the other gods, because he had heroically defeated Tiamat, the chaotic sea goddess, who had threatened to destroy all of the other gods and their created domains. The Assyrians called Marduk by the name Ashur.

Like the later, similar gods and goddesses of the Greeks and Romans, the deities of the Mesopotamian cultures often displayed all the foibles of their human counterparts. They married and bore offspring, they were born and they died, and they experienced all the joys and sorrows of humankind. The stories of the gods told of their passions, crimes, intrigues, and sufferings. And they, like men, were not ultimate in power. The Sumerian mythology referred to the divine *me* (pronounced "may") which were apparently similar to the Hellenic idea of *moira*; they were cosmic principles, or universal laws, which controlled the nature of all reality and by which all conduct could be judged. There were hundreds of *me*, given, according to one version, by Enlil, the god of the upper air; but, when Enlil broke the sacred order, as when he raped the beautiful young goddess, Ninlil, he was himself punished by banishment to the netherworld.

The netherworld was believed to be a vast space beneath the earth, just as the heavens are above the flat disk of man's abode. Gods and men alike must go there when they die, being ferried across the river by the boatman of the dead. Two gods, Nergal and Ereshkigal, were the rulers of the dark and gloomy realm, and they were assisted by a whole troupe of terrible deities, including the seven Anunnaki, the dead gods who were judges of all who entered. There were also hosts of *galla*, evil spirits who patrolled the underworld and often made forays into the earth in order to seek and torture evildoers.

Mesopotamian religion developed all the usual trappings of temples, priestcraft, rituals, and sacred festivals. The *ziggurat*, or temple platform, was a large, man-made hill, or "tell," built, in all probability, to break the monotonous plain of the great valley, and to elevate the holy places above the cities surrounding them. Some have survived the ravages of time and may still be seen in the ancient land. Many scholars believe that the Hebrew story of the Tower of Babel (Genesis 11) was composed in part as a reaction against the paganism out of which Hebrew religion arose. The temples were the scene of regular ceremonies, led by the priests, who appeased the gods and provided guidance and security for the people. There were many kinds of rituals, sacrifices, and incantations, and the role of the people was to support and attend them. They were apparently intended to achieve the major goals of fertility and immortality, since life itself depends upon the continued fecundity of the family, the flock, and the field; and, since life is perceptibly short, there was always the yearning for assurance that death is not the end.

The most significant festival, especially among the Babylonians, was the New Year celebration. Occurring in the spring, at the time of the vernal equinox, it lasted for eleven days and involved a renewal of the marriage vows between Dumuzi (the Biblical Tammuz), represented by the king, and the goddess Inanna, Queen of Heaven, represented by the high priestess. There was also a grand procession of the gods, who renewed their subservience to Marduk; and the creation epic, the *Enuma Elish*, was recited, chanted, and dramatized for the faithful.

The *Enuma Elish* takes its familiar name from the opening words, in Akkadian, meaning "when above." The great epic, which lies behind so much later Western thought, religion, and literature, has been discovered in various texts older than 1000 B.C., but its material may be traced back to the culture of the Sumerians, at least. It contains the explanatory myths of the relationships between the gods, the creation of the earth, the struggles between order and chaos, and the origin and duties of man. It was clearly intended not only to account for the beginnings of all things but also to give legitimacy to the structures of society. The reader is struck repeatedly by similarities between the epic and later literature, particularly the early portions of the Hebrew Scriptures and the writings of Homer and Hesiod.

The *Gilgamesh Epic* is one of the most ancient and significant classics of world literature. It presents the culture and thought of the Mesopotamian peoples from the mists of prehistoric times, and it is known to have been inscribed in cuneiform writing no later than 2000 B.C. It was known in Palestine before the Hebrews arrived, and its influence is clear on much of the later thought and literature of the area, including the Bible. Along with the *Enuma Elish* and the Code of Hammurabi, *The Gilgamesh Epic* reveals that the intellectual, moral, and spiritual sources of Western civilization must be traced to the ancient land between the rivers as well as to Egypt and the narrow land bridge between them.

Gilgamesh was the hero-king of Erech, one of the cities of the Sumerians. He was the son of the goddess Ninsun and a human father. The story begins with an account of his passionate friendship with Enkidu, a human animal who had been made from clay by the goddess Aruru. After Gilgamesh has achieved the "civilization" of Enkidu, the two enjoy several exciting exploits together, but eventually Enkidu is killed because he insulted the prostitute goddess, Ishtar. Gilgamesh is then filled with unrelieved grief, and he vows to search for immortality. His seeking brings him to the immortal Utnapishtim, the wise old man who long before escaped the great Flood (cf. Genesis 6-9). Utnapishtim tells him about the Flood but cannot give him the secret of immortality. However, Utnapishtim does direct Gilgamesh to a plant which grows at the bottom of the sea. The plant, when eaten, reportedly has the power to restore youth. Gilgamesh dives to the depths and procures the plant, only to have it stolen by a serpent. Finally, Gilgamesh accepts his mortality, with bitter tears, and returns to his city with both the resignation and confidence of his humanity.

## The Quest for Meaning and Value

The *Enuma Elish* describes man's early and profoundly meaningful thoughts concerning how things came to be, how they are, and how they ought to be. *The Gilgamesh Epic* represents wonder, protest, and the suggestion of defiance. Both show that from the most ancient beginnings Western civilization has dealt at the deepest levels with the issues of life.

This all-too-brief sketch of the progression of cultures in ancient Mesopotamia reveals to the perceptive student that certain fundamental questions were present even from the beginning. Those questions and the changing answers given to them have provided the form and substance of all civilizations at every stage. It is well to conceptualize the questions as clearly as possible at the beginning of this study so that they may throw light on the remainder of our journey through the centuries.

The first and constant problem of existence is that of survival. The question takes many forms, and it is frequently below the level of consciousness; but it is always present since, obviously, without survival no other question may even be asked. Along with the other animals, man has always responded to the unspoken questions: how do I find food, water, and protection from the threats of a hostile environment? How do I escape, even if temporarily, discomforts, disease, injury, and death? Such questions lead inevitably to the securing of regular supplies of water and food. Shelter and companionship follow. Communities are built, involving increasingly complex social structures. Then, with sophisticated language and abstract thought, the question of survival is projected into the future, not only until inevitable death but even beyond. The instinctive desire for survival thus provides the primary cause for the development of civilization.

A second question asks about reality. What *is*, and how did everything begin? It is the question of ultimacy, and the answers given to that question provide the foundations for living and acting. In the formal language of philosophy, it is the *ontological* question, and it determines the prior ground for morality. Man immediately discovers that everything he experiences is transitory. Change is constant and everywhere. And yet there appears to be a regularity to change, and being itself is always present in existence. Thus there must be some permanent reality underlying appearance and change. If that unchanging reality, that substance which provides stability and security, can be found and grasped, then man will have found the secret of being itself. He will thereby have escaped all anxiety and, in traditional language, will be like the gods. Theology, ontology, and ethics are the products of such searching.

Closely related to the question of reality is that of morality. What ought to be? Since change is constant and apparently inevitable, what controls change and brings the changing back to its original status? In like manner, must there not be standards of conduct just as there are ultimate forms of being? As man has sought to answer these questions, he has sought to formulate ideas about right and wrong, about how they may be determined and established. Every level of culture has been concerned with the knowledge of right and the control and defeat of wrong. The result has been the theories of both religion and philosophy, in which men have looked to the transcendent gods for guidance and grace while at the same time using their own resources of reason as means for directing life.

Thus, finally, the question of virtue has been the constant, unresolved problem of civilization. Perhaps more difficult than the question of what is right is the problem of how to achieve it. There may be a consensus regarding the nature of justice, and excellent codes of law may be composed, but greed and power will always override them. The self is by nature selfish since it is its own center around which everything else in existence seems to be peripheral and therefore of less value; and the group, whether it is family, tribe, or nation, becomes also a center of interest which seeks first its own security and power. Hence man has always found it necessary to construct means to control selfishness and power, and to establish the primacy of virtue in spite of them. The history of civilization, therefore, from its beginnings in the mountains and valleys of Mesopotamia and Egypt, discloses a continuing attempt, not always successful, to discover and establish the good for the benefit of both the individual and the group.

# Chapter 3

## *Egyptian Sources*

The impact of Egypt on Western civilization has been no less significant than that of Mesopotamia, and its history is of almost as great an antiquity. The land of Kemet, as its early inhabitants called it, was becoming civilized by 3,800 B.C., but its pre-history can be glimpsed in relics dating from as far in the past as 13,000 B.C., in the late African Paleolithic period. At that time the land enjoyed plentiful rains and readily supported nomadic tribes with an economy based on hunting. About 12,000 B.C., however, the rains began to fail, and the plains which had supported a large animal population began to turn into desert. The people of the region were forced to settle in the Nile Valley and the Delta area, where they became farmers.

During the Neolithic period, beginning about 5,000 B.C., they made rapid strides in the development of the arts and crafts possible to an agricultural people, and the date usually given for the beginning of Egyptian civilization as it is known to history really marks no sharply defined change in the way of life of the inhabitants of the region. The growth of their culture was, in great measure, made possible by the Nile, which for some 750 miles between Nubia and the Mediterranean provides a quiet highroad for commerce and a reliable annual source for the irrigation of the lands bordering the river. The Oracle of the God Amon succinctly defined the dependence of the land on the sacred river when it declared, "Egypt is the land watered by the Nile in its course, and those who dwell below the city Elephantine and drink that river's waters are Egyptians."

By 3,800 B.C., the country probably had already beome organized into about forty "nomes," ruled by "nomarchs." In the succeeding several hundred years, these political divisions became consolidated into two states: the Kingdom of Upper Egypt, stretching along the Nile Valley, and the Kingdom of Lower Egypt, spreading across the Delta. During this period, great advances were made in the manufacture of metal tools and weapons, as well as in the production of a great variety of articles for use and ornament.

About 3,200 B.C., hostility between the two kingdoms resulted in sporadic warfare, which lasted for some two hundred years and ended with the subjugation of lower Egypt by its southern neighbor. The King of Upper Egypt, officially known as Na'r and probably indentifiable as the legendary hero Menes, became the first monarch of a united land which was destined to maintain its political integrity for nearly three millenia. To symbolize the unification of the two kingdoms, he set the tall white crown of Upper Egypt into the red wicker-work crown of the Lower Kingdom and wore them together, thus establishing a precedent which endured throughout the history of the monarchy. The familiar term *Pharaoh*, often applied to Egyptian rulers is derived from a term meaning "Great House" and was apparently used to avoid the presumption of speaking too directly of a ruler who claimed not only to rule by divine sanction but to be a god himself.

With union an accomplished fact, Na'r founded the great city called "White Wall" — later to be known in the West by its Greek name, "Memphis" — to serve as a capital, and the "Protodynastic Period" of the preceding two hundred years gave way to what is known as the Early Dynastic Period.

It must not be supposed that the Egyptians themselves used these terms at the time their history was unfolding. Indeed, it was not until the third century B.C. that a Graeco-Egyptian historian named Manetho divided the monarchial period into thirty dynasties, establishing a basis for the system still in general use.

## The Old Kingdom

The two hundred and twenty years of the Early Dynastic Period saw two Dynasties, which were succeeded in 2,780 B.C. by the first dynasty of what is called the Old Kingdom. The reign of Djoser, the first monarch of this period, is significant for the history of thought primarily because of the attainments of his chief counselor, a man named I-em-hotep. Famed as a magician, physician, architect, priest, and writer, he so impressed the Greeks who later discovered Egyptian culture that they promptly identified him with Asklepios, their god of healing.

A little more than a hundred years after Djoser's accession, the Egyptians were engaged in building a structure which would one day hold the remains of their king Khufu, called Cheops by the Greeks. The resultant tomb, the Great Pyramid, measuring seven hundred and sixty-seven feet on each side of the base and rising to a point four hundred and seventy-nine feet above the ground, required two million, three hundred thousand blocks of stone for its construction.

During the latter years of the Old Kingdom, the landed nobility gained power which threatened the authority of the central government, and in what is known as the First Intermediate Period, lasting from about 2270 to 2160 B.C., a condition of disorder prevailed. The defeat of the Herakleopolitan Confederacy by the Theban nomarchs resulted in the re-establishment of stability and the beginning of the second great age of the Dynastic Period.

## The Middle Kingdom

In the early years of the Middle Kingdom, as it is now called, the rulers of the Eleventh and Twelfth Dynasties gradually gained the loyalty of the powerful nomarchs, and the Egyptians profited from their political stability to develop a new appreciation of reflective thought. A papyrus surviving in mutilated form from the period, which may, however, be a copy of a work composed in the troubled time of transition, presents an argument between a man and his soul over the desirability of life as opposed to death.

The sharp distinction made between the two states in his discussion runs counter to Egyptian popular thought, which generally regarded life as eminently delightful and the hereafter as a state in which the pleasures of earth could be enjoyed in even more gratifying degree. The writer of the treatise on suicide, however, found the world around him filled with evil. "There are no righteous men," he complained. "The land is left over to workers of iniquity. To whom shall I speak today? I am laden with misery through lack of an intimate." The position taken by the writer's soul, in contrast, though not without ambiguity, seems to have favored life. "If thou recallest burial, it is a sad matter. It is the bringing of tears, making a man sad. It is dragging a man from his house and casting him on the hillside. Thou shalt never go up that thou mayest see the sun."

How the author resolved his problem is not known, but in the literary form of his reflection he anticipated by considerably more than a millenium the sort of discursive treatment of the meaning and value of human life found in the book of Job.

Beginning in 1788 B.C., with the passing of the Twelfth Dynasty, the order which had prevailed for nearly four centuries gave way to a period of turmoil known as the Second Intermediate Period. Weak rulers permitted Egypt's defenses to be undermined until, in 1730 B.C., the northern part of the Kingdom was lost to the Hyksos, a Semitic people who entered Egypt from Palestine.

In the long run, the results of the invasion, however traumatic it may have been for the Egyptians, seem to have been more beneficial than otherwise. The Hyksos were a highly civilized people, who introduced into the life of the native population a number of valuable innovations, not the least of which was the horse, an animal with which the Egyptians appear not to have been familiar prior to that time. The chariot corps, which later enabled Egypt to become an imperial nation, owed its origin to the invaders. The Hyksos lords, classified as the Fifteenth and Sixteenth Dynasties of Egypt, reduced the native rulers of the south to vassalage and controlled the country with little opposition for more than a century. It is possible that this temporary dominance of a Semitic dynasty paved the way for the acceptance of Hebrews as residents of Egypt, and even as high officials.

### The New Kingdom

A little before 1600 B.C., an aggressive line of Theban rulers began to contest the Hyksos suzerainty. Kamose and the brother who succeeded him, Ahmose, inflicted serious damage on the armies of their overlords, and, in 1580 B.C., Ahmose was at last successful in driving them back to Palestine, assuring himself of a place in history as founder of the Eighteenth Dynasty and the New Kingdom, sometimes known as the New Empire.

Five generations of Pharaohs addressed themselves to the task of expanding Egypt's territory, and under their able rule, the power of the nation was extended in Africa to the Fourth Cataract of the Nile and in Asia as far as the Euphrates. Rich in gold, they succeeded in establishing the metal as the standard medium for trade throughout the Near East. Conservative by tradition, the Egyptians nevertheless proved capable of profiting technologically and culturally from their contacts with other societies. The monarchs of the Eighteenth Dynasty completely suppressed the power of the landed nobles and administered the affairs of the country through two viziers, one for Upper and one for Lower Egypt. All land belonged to the Crown except that specifically ceded to Amon, who was now the chief deity in the complex

Egyptian pantheon. To honor the god, the rulers of the New Kingdom lavished immense wealth on his temple at El Karnak which, at the close of a two-thousand-year construction period was the largest structure ever built for religious purposes—a record unbroken to this day. The priests of Amon gained control of enormous riches in money and property, and organized religion in Egypt achieved a power and a complexity unprecedented in earlier days. It was during this peiod that Thutmose I started the funerary excavations in the cliffs at Thebes which were to become known as the "Valley of the Kings."

From very early times, the Egyptians, a people who loved life in the sun, had tried to insure the continuation of a pleasant existence after death by an elaborate process of mummification, followed by an interment which, to as great an extent as their resources permitted, provided the traveler to the abode of the dead with useful articles and representations of everyday life which, in some magical fashion, might furnish him with an environment of comfort and entertainment in the other world. In the New Kingdom,the methods prescribed for the achievement of perpetual felicity were codified in a collection of writings known as the "Book of the Dead." Readers of the book learned that the soul facing judgment was entitled to greater optimism concerning his fate if his life on earth had been virtuous, but, as in later times, the purchase of a dispensation could cancel out the effects of moral lapses which might otherwise threaten his happiness.

Thutmose I died about 1520 B.C. and became the first occupant of his new necropolis. He was succeeded on the throne by several able monarchs, including the militant feminist Hatshep-sut, who, as co-ruler with her young nephew Thutmose III, had herself proclaimed "King" and apparently made use of all the royal regalia, including the ceremonial false beard. After her death, Thutmose III became one of Egypt's greatest monarchs.

### The Rule of Aten

In 1375 B.C., Amenhotep III named his son and namesake co-regent. The young man promptly began to assert himself in affairs of the kingdom and, on his father's death, presided over an attempt to alter the worship of the Egyptians in ways which faced the priests of Amon and the other ancient gods with a threat to their power which could not be ignored. The victim in youth of a condition identified in modern times as Fröhlich's Syndrome, which produced some bodily and facial deformity, young Amenhotep IV was a single-minded devotee of a deity known as the Aten—a god often represented as the solar disk, with life-giving rays terminating in hands.

Obsessed with his desire to induce his people to acknowledge the Aten as the one true god, Amenhotep left Thebes, a city dominated by the oppressive power of Amon, and moved his court some two hundred miles down the Nile to Tell-el-Amarna, where he presided over the building of a magnificent new city called Akhetaten, "Horizon of Aten." His own name, flawed by its reference to the hated Amon, he changed to Akhenaten, "Spirit of Aten." His adventure of the spirit, characterized by his insistence on "living in truth" resulted in striking artistic and religious innovations and was to gain for Akehnaten, more than three thousand years later, recognition as "the world's first monotheist"—a title which would be disputed by those who would prefer to call him a henotheist or a monolater, one who, while not denying the existence of other gods, ascribes to his own the exclusive right to be worshipped. Unfortunately, the more immediate outcome was the virtual dissolution of the empire during his reign, a result of his neglect of the national defense and the hostility engendered among his people by his fanatical adherence to the new faith. He was finally separated from his wife, the beautiful Nefertiti, and it is highly probable that he met a violent end at the hands of assassins.

The most eloquent surviving testimony to Akhenaten's faith is the celebrated Hymn to Aten, found in hieroglyphic carving on the wall of a royal tomb at Tell-el-Amarna. Its content indicates vividly the extent to which the heretic-king's religious revolution was rooted not so much in moral reform as in intellectual and aesthetic appreciation of the divine as manifested in nature. It hails the god— the living Aten—as maker of earth and source of light and life. The reign of Aten extends to the most distant foreign lands, for whose people he has "set a Nile in the sky" to water their fields as the great river waters the fields of Egypt. Specifically, the Hymn declares him to be the father of Akhenaten, who, unlike his subjects, who directed their prayers to the king, was, with his family, privileged to commune directly with the god.

Under Akhenaten's successor, the worship of Amon was restored, and young Tutankhaten was induced or compelled to change his name to Tutankhamon and move the capital back to Thebes. When he died at the age of eighteen, he was succeeded for a short time by an elder statesman named Ay and then, about 1340 B.C., by a soldier-king named Horemheb, who apparently worked with single-minded zeal to eradicate every trace of Akhenaten's reign and the religious revolution which had destroyed it. That he was not entirely successful is shown by the obvious influence of the Hymn to the Sun on the Hundred and Fourth Psalm, and it is not unlikely that the seed of monotheism planted by the heretic monarch had other effects in the development of the Hebrew religion.

To Horemheb's credit, it must be acknowledged that during his twenty-year reign, he restored Egypt's power and prosperity. When he died without an obvious heir, the throne went to a General Pa-Ramessu, who became Ramses I, the founder of the Nineteenth Dynasty. He, in turn, was succeeded by Sethy I and, twenty-one years later, by Sethy's son, Ramses II, who reigned for sixty-seven years.

### The Later Pharaohs

Was Ramses II the Pharaoh of the Exodus? It has been widely held that he was, and what is known of his character would have fitted him admirably for the role. He was a man of imposing appearance and considerable vanity, as is proved by the colossal statues of himself which were his most conspicuous contribution to the art of Egypt. He was probably a popular monarch, and during his reign, the nation undoubtedly seemed to its people to be at the summit of its greatness. It was, however, under constant attack from neighboring countries, and the cheerful optimism characteristic of the Egyptians became increasingly moderated by questionings about the relationship between suffering and guilt not unlike those found in Hebrew literature. During the reign of Ramses II, a craftsman named Nebre erected a stele inscribed with a poetic text as an expression of gratitude for the recovery of his son from a sickness brought about by some offense given to Amon-Re "because of his cow," presumably one of the temple herd. It read:

"The servant was bent on doing wrong
Yet the Lord is bent on being merciful.
The Lord of Thebes does not spend a whole day angry;
As for his anger, in the completion of a moment nothing is left.

The wind is turned back to us in mercy;
Amon has returned with his breezes.
As thy soul endures, thou wilt be merciful,
We shall not repeat what has been averted."

The New Kingdom also produced a good deal of love poetry,
probably originally set to music and sung to an instrumental
accompaniment. In many of the verses, the beloved is spoken of as
"my brother" or "my sister." This convention and the sensitive
appreciation of the beauties of nature found in the Egyptian poems
testify to the influence they must have had on later Hebrew love
poems like those which survive in the collection known as the Song
of Songs.

Egypt was to endure for several centuries after Ramses II under
monarchs bearing the ancient titles, but many of them were
invaders, and none of them, native or foreign, were to attain the
eminence from which the Ramessids surveyed the world. The
country fell in 525 B.C. to King Cambyses of Persia and remained
under Persian control until it was conquered by Alexander of
Macedon in 332 B.C. On Alexander's death in 323 B.C., one of his
generals, Ptolemy, became ruler of Egypt and founded the last
dynasty of the Pharaohs. Cleopatra VI was the last of the reigning
Ptolemies, and at her death in 30 B.C., Egypt became a Roman
province.

### Egypt and the West

The cultural contributions of Egypt to the Western world are
not easy to evaluate fairly because they lack the direct and obvious
connection with the modern world which exists in the case of the
Hebrews, the Greeks, and the Romans. With few exceptions,
Europeans and Americans are not surrounded by churches, banks,
government buildings, and railway stations built in the Egyptian
fashion. We offer up no prayers to Egyptian deities, and our
languages contain few recognizably Egyptian words. Egyptian
poetry is rarely taught in Western schools, and we do not look to
Egyptian philosophers for our metaphysical and ethical concepts.

Nevertheless, the contributions were very real, though they
reached the modern world by somewhat indirect routes. The culture
of Egypt clearly affected that of the Minoan civilization, one of the
two principal formative influences on the Hellenic world, and there
is ample evidence that the Greeks had a respect for the antiquity and

wisdom of Egypt unusual in a people prone to treat with disdain any folk ignorant of the Greek language. Plato told of a visit to Egypt by Solon, who accepted with good grace the remark by one of his hosts, "Solon, Solon, all you Greeks are children."

In innumerable ways, the Egyptians, through sometimes devious channels, left their mark on the West, and it is not surprising that when we are confronted in museums or books with the many reminders they left us of their daily lives, we feel a kinship with them that defies the ages which have gone by since their civilization was at its height. Their graceful ornaments and household furnishings often impress us as unexpectedly "modern." Their sports and games, as depicted on tomb walls, are pastimes in which we can readily imagine ourselves as participants. In their spacious, columned buildings, we see the forerunners of the Greek and Roman structures which gave rise to much of our own architecture. Their musical instruments were, through their influence on other Mediterranean cultures, the ancestors of our own brass, woodwind, string, and percussion instruments. The toys with which their children played show a striking resemblance to those which catch the fancy of modern girls and boys.

There is much in their recorded thought too which strikes a sympathetic chord in modern times. In a country ruled by a monarch regarded as a god, there yet developed a curious sort of democracy of merit, in which the accident of birth played little or no part in defining the role which a man might play in Egyptian society. The idea of *ma'at*, or justice, as a social ideal grounded in religious conviction, may be seen as a forerunner of the concept of natural law, which has played a continuing and, arguably, an essential part in the moral and political thought of the West. In their love lyrics, Egyptian poets caught the essence of the emotions which have similarly motivated other poets in many lands to express what they felt for those they loved.

Finally, their religion was not as alien as we might think it at a first bewildered encounter when we find ourselves in the midst of a fantastic array of gods with animal heads, performing improbable functions in the worlds of the living and the dead. Underlying the whole priestly theology were certain enduring convictions of paramount importance: that man is composed of body and spirit; that his life, meaningful here and now, continues beyond the grave and that the quality of his living here determines his ultimate destiny; and that the ultimate criterion of truth, goodness, and beauty lies not in the flux of opinion, but in the enduring realm of which the stability which the Egyptians sought for their own land was a reflection.

# II.
# GOD AND MAN
# IN EARLY
# HEBREW RELIGION

# Chapter 4

# *The Seed of Abraham*

A cursory reading of Genesis, the first book in the Bible, seems to provide a reasonably uncomplicated account of the origins of the Hebrews and of their earliest religious beliefs and practices. The story begins with Abraham, a citizen of the city of Ur in the lower Mesopotamian valley, who migrated first to Haran, in the northwest, and then to Canaan, a land bordering on the Mediterranean, northeast of Egypt. After a brief visit to Egypt, Abraham settled among the people of Canaan. All this apparently occurred during the time of Amorite ascendancy, probably around the time of Hammurabi (c. 1700 B.C.).

Most of the book of Genesis is composed of stories about Abraham and his immediate progeny, Isaac, the son of Abraham, is presented for the most part in relation either to Abraham or to the next generation, especially Jacob. The three generations lived in Canaan but maintained close relations with their Semitic kinsmen in the area of Haran. However, Jacob and his large family finally migrated to Egypt, apparently to escape a famine in Canaan, and they settled there under the favorable protection of the Pharaoh, who had elevated one of Jacob's sons, Joseph, to a position of great influence. Thus the Hebrews, having their origins among the Semitic peoples of the Fertile Crescent, established themselves in the narrow, arable land-bridge which joins Asia to Africa. The stage was set, at the end of Genesis, for the dramatic story of the Exodus.

However, the familiar and apparently uncomplicated stories of the Patriarchs may be deceptive in their simplicity. A closer study reveals that these are not merely narratives about individuals and families in the distant past but that rather they are a literary deposit of epic proportions, loaded with significance not only for religion but for information about Western culture in general. Genesis becomes much more profound and intelligible when read in the light of all the other sources of information which are available concerning ancient history, religion, and the beginnings of all things human.

## The Sources of Information

Generally speaking, there are four categories of source material for information about the ancient Hebrews. They are the canonical Scriptures, non-canonical Hebrew literature, relevant historical writing from other peoples, and the great mass of archeological material.

The canonical Scriptures are usually referred to as the Old Testament, though that phrase, of course, carries a Christian bias since it implies that the complete Bible is composed of both the Old and New Testaments, an opinion not shared by Jews, to whom the Scriptures owe both their origin and preservation. These writings are called "canonical" because of the special sacredness and authority attributed to them. The word "canon" came into English by way of Greek from the ancient Semitic languages. It was derived from "cane," or "reed," and meant a standard of measure; hence the word came to designate a collection of writings which were considered to be both of divine origin (sacred) and the final standard of judgment in matters of religion (authoritative).

The Hebrew Scriptures are divided into three parts. This is a matter of fundamental importance for their accurate understanding and interpretation which, unfortunately, has been obscured and usually ignored because of the Christian rearrangement of the canon. The first and earliest division is the *Torah*, a Hebrew word meaning "teaching," though often rendered as "law." There are five books of Torah, thus leading to the designation Pentateuch, which is a Greek word meaning "five scrolls": Genesis, Exodus, Leviticus, Numbers and Deuteronomy. A quick glance at the five books will show that they are not merely a code of law but rather that they contain a great deal of narrative and religious teaching. Hence the Torah is really a collection of Hebrew theological teaching, the foundation and center of Jewish religion.

The second division is called *Nebi'im*, the Prophets. This contains two sub-groups of four books each, the Former Prophets and the Latter Prophets. The four Former Prophets are Joshua, Judges, Samuel and Kings. Because of their length and for the sake of convenience, the last two were separated into two volumes for each and hence are familiarly known as I and II Samuel and I and II Kings. In the Christian canon, these four Former Prophets have been considered to be books of history, and the tragic result has been a gross misunderstanding of their nature and purpose. The

Latter Prophets are the books of Isaiah, Jeremiah, Ezekiel, and the Book of the Twelve. Again, the last of these has been sub-divided into the twelve small books that are known as "the twelve minor prophets." It was probably St. Augustine (c. 400. A.D.) who first used the Latin term *minor* to indicate the brevity of these books rather than their relative value.

The third division of the canon is the *Kethubim*, meaning "Writings." This is an anthology of eleven books representing a variety of literary types: Psalms, Proverbs, Job, Song of Solomon, Ruth, Lamentations, Ecclesiastes, Esther, Daniel, Ezra-Nehemiah, and Chronicles. Again, the last two were transmitted in separate volumes. A striking and significant feature of this group is the inclusion of Daniel, an apocalyptic writing from early Judaism which has been mistakenly counted among the prophetic books in the Christian canon, leading to unnecessary and unfortunate misunderstanding.

This Canon of Hebrew Scriptures, thus divided into three parts, originally contained twenty-four books. Sometimes the number was reduced to twenty-two (the number of letters in the Hebrew alphabet) by combining Lamentations with Jeremiah and Ruth with Judges. The three parts had a long history of development and canonization, but the Torah has always been considered of primary significance and value. It was apparently completed and recognized as "the written Word of God" by 400 B.C., the Prophets by 200 B.C., and the Writings by the end of the first century after Christ.

The fact that canonization was a long process of inclusion and exclusion suggests that there must have been a great deal of contemporary Hebrew literature which was finally rejected from the Scriptures. Much of that literature has nonetheless survived, and that is what we are designating as non-canonical Hebrew literature. There are two main collections which belong to this category: the *Apocrypha* and the *Pseudepigrapha*. In addition to these there is also a vast collection of Jewish theological material called the *Talmud*, a varied body of rabbinical commentary, interpretation and exposition which originated in post-biblical Judaism, some as late as the early Middle Ages. The *Apocrypha* ("hidden," of unknown origin) is composed of fifteen books (or fourteen when two are sometimes combined). Some of these are included in the canon of the Old Testament by Roman Catholics and Orthodox Christians, though, not, of course, by Jews or Protestants. The

*Pseudepigrapha* ("false writings," that is, by pseudonyms) is an even
more uncertain and indefinite collection of ancient Jewish writings,
comprising more than a dozen books of uneven value. However, all
three of these collections are useful for the understanding of early
Jewish life and thought. They provide an invaluable source of
information in addition to the canonical Scriptures.

A third source for a knowledge of Hebrew religion is the
historical literature of antiquity written among other peoples, such
as the Greeks and Romans. As would be expected, little is found
concerning the Hebrews in this material; but there are significant
incidents recorded in the works of Herodotus, Thucydides,
Manetho, Tacitus, Pliny and others which are both corroborative
and explanatory, and hence useful to the serious student. The
writings of Josephus should also be included in this category,
although he was a Jew like the writers of the above-mentioned non-
canonical literature, for he wrote in the first century after Christ as a
Roman in an attempt to give a helpful and favorable explanation of
the history and religion of the Jews.

Finally, a fourth source for study are the increasingly numerous
and instructive materials continuously being discovered in the field
of archeology. The libraries and museums of the world are filled
with artifacts, translations and explanations from this source, and
the supply grows larger every year. It is sufficient merely to mention
such examples as the Dead Sea Scrolls, the Nag Hammadi
documents, the Rosetta Stone, and the Stele of Hammurabi to
illustrate the incalculable value derived for modern scholarship by
the methods and research of archeology and related fields of study.

## Hebrew Stories of Beginnings

Abraham was not *sui generis*, of course. The Hebrew Scriptures
consciously provide a description of the background for the
Patriarchs, tying them to the peoples and cultures of greater
antiquity and, indeed, sketching in a background explanation for
the condition and existence of all men and all things. This
significant fact stands as a constant reminder that Biblical religion
has always been concerned with ultimacy—with all history and all
mankind, conceived against the mysterious background of God's
eternal nature and purpose. Genesis begins the process of presenting
in human languages (no other vehicle is available or useful) the
revelation given in time and space, as seen by the eyes of faith, of
that mysterious and ultimate meaning and value.

How may mystery be known and communicated? How is it possible to describe and explain what is believed by faith rather than known by experience? There are means, of course, and they are the marks of mankind's grand gifts of self-transcendence and creativity. Language itself is the primary means, and there are others such as expressive acts, gestures, art and music. In terms of literature, language employs the forms of prose and poetry, fact and imagination, record and myth, literal description and picturesque vision; all these and other forms are the tools of language used to communicate the thoughts of the mind and the feelings of the heart. And all are perfectly legitimate means of expression.

The Hebrew Scriptures, using many of the devices of literature, begin with magnificent stories about the beginnings. The first eleven chapters of Genesis are composed in the main of four epic stories which present, in unparalleled simplicity and beauty, the explanations of Hebrew faith concerning the beginnings of creation, of mankind, of evil, of human divisions, and of the principles of judgment and redemption.

The term *myth* may be useful in categorizing these stories, but only if it is understood that myth is not fiction but truth, one of the forms of literature that is most useful in the attempt to communicate ultimate meaning. Myth is language's most appropriate way of expressing the truth that is finally inexpressible precisely because it is mysterious and beyond cognitive knowledge. It is the category of literature which is particularly useful to religious expression because it is, by definition, a way of presenting the dealings of God, or the gods, with men. The stories of Genesis, therefore, are not only myth; they are *etiological* myth, because their purpose is to speak of faith's conceptions about how things came to be as they are, tracing origins all the way back to their source. The stories are truth in the language of faith.

The first story is that of the Garden of Paradise (chapters 1-3). The earliest edition of the story, beginning with 2:4b, in an introductory, dependent clause, speaks of the creation of the earth and the heavens, and then goes directly to the unique formation of mankind. The dual nature of man is given explicit expression: he was formed "of dust from the ground," and thus is a part of nature, subject to all its characteristics of causality and temporality; but he was also given "the breath of life," the spiritual nature of the Creator, and thus became "a living being." Such a contingent being could not be expected to exist on its own, separated from the Power that so graciously constituted it. The vain attempt to do so led immediately to both evil and the fruit of evil, which is death, the estrangement from the source of being. Hence the first brief story tells of Paradise given and Paradise lost. With stark and profound simplicity, it describes the nature of being, the condition of existence and the necessity of re-creative reconciliation which only the power of Creative Being, God, can accomplish.

The second story is the tragedy of the Two Brothers (chapters 4-5). The fatal flaw in all mankind, caused by man's attempt to be self-sufficient, resulted in hate and murder. Cain, the first child of mankind, despised and killed his brother, Abel; and the immediate consequence was the burning pain of guilt which was not merely the result of remorse and social displeasure but, more inescapably, of the condemnation of the all-knowing and righteous God. Cain, the son of mankind (Adam), could henceforth do nothing but wander (note the derivation of Nod) over the earth, seeking such temporary tasks and pleasures as he could discover. The Hebrew epic simply suggests, with forlorn brevity, that after Adam and Cain the destiny of man upon the earth is the cycle of birth and death, creation and decay, and seeking without satisfaction. The epilogue of the story remains: *sic transit gloria mundi.*

The third story, that of Noah and the Flood, carries further the truth and consequences of the second. Chapters 6-10 contain the Hebrew version of a common heritage in many ancient cultures, the memory of a frightening calamity in the form of a deluge which threatened the very existence of all men. The Hebrew account, however, unlike all similar stories in other literature of a universal flood, reflects the theological and moral principles of the developing religion of Israel. Edited no earlier than during the time of the prophets, the story of Noah assumes both God's righteousness and man's sinfulness; and it therefore portrays the terror of retributive justice, the reward of faithfulness, and the finality of hope. The sign of the rainbow remains for all time as a promise that judgment is never the last word from God. The storm clouds may be dark and threatening but the rainbow is the guarantee that the light of the sun will return. The story ends in hope, therefore, as the three sons of Noah go out into the various parts of the earth; "and from these the nations spread abroad on the earth after the flood" (10:32).

The fourth story (chapter 11) is short but profound and with continuing significance. It is the well-known story of Babel, the Tower of Confusion. In the light of the conditions of mankind which the first three epics had portrayed, the editors of Genesis completed the backgound for the introduction of God's purpose through the seed of Abraham by adding the Prometheus-like myth of man's direct revolt against heaven. Men dared even to challenge God. The creature, having come of age, in his own estimation, determined to become his own creator; and so he began to build "a city, and a tower with its top in the heavens," (11:4) intending thereby to gain security, dominance, and self-control. The results, predictably, were disastrous and permanent. The myth is the vehicle of universal truth—that rebellion against God inevitably produces misunderstanding and social fragmentation in every form. The variety of languages on the earth is symbolic of all the elements of separation between individuals and groups which lead to suspicion, hostility, violence and death. The only antidote is in the initiative of the Creator who, by his patience and grace, may reverse Babel by the healing of spiritual unity.

## The Patriarchs and Their Faith

The gracious and redemptive initiative of the Almighty, the end of which would be the defeat of evil and the restoration of Paradise, began with the call of Abraham. In the inscrutable ways of God, a particular people were chosen to be the channel of grace and truth. The major portion of Genesis (chapters 12-50) is comprised of the lives and times of the Patriarchs of Israel—Abraham, Isaac, Jacob, and Joseph and his brothers. The familiar and fascinating stories are correctly counted among the greatest literature of all cultures, not only because of their inherent beauty but also because of their universal truth and historical reference.

Three of the stories about Abraham must be given special emphasis here precisely because they bear the seeds of ideas which are to grow to major proportions in the subsequent development of Hebrew religion and thus become important deposits in the foundations of Western culture.

40

The first story (chapters 11-17) is about the call of Abraham in Ur of Chaldea, and later in Haran, both cities in the ancient civilizations of Mesopotamia. History and archeology confirm the Biblical implication that there was a certain cultural homogeneity throughout the vast plain between the Tigris and Euphrates rivers, and, indeed, in the whole Fertile Crescent. It was a highly developed culture characterized by polytheistic paganism, religiously sanctioned codes of law and social mores, and prescriptive practices designed to control a capricious nature and an uncertain destiny. Abraham heard the mysterious call of the one he believed to be the Almighty, commanding him to separate himself and his family from such a milieu and to seek a new beginning in the land of Canaan. So he went; and so he began the pilgrimage of faith which has been the essence of religion in the Western world ever since.

The faithful response of Abraham culminated in the making of a covenant between him and the God who spoke to him. Continuing obedience and trust were required of Abraham, and in return he and his offspring would receive the blessings of God forever. The promise was specific: "I will make of you a great nation, and I will bless you, and make your name great, so that you will be a blessing. I will bless those who bless you, and him who curses you I will curse; and by you all the families of the earth will bless themselves" (12:2-3). The covenant, a binding moral and spiritual agreement, was sealed by the rite of circumcision, by which Abraham and all his descendants would understand that those who came from their loins would be marked as a people set apart for the service of the Almighty One. Therefore, when the son, Isaac, was born to Abraham and his wife, Sarah, in their old age, the process was begun which has been interpreted since as the redemptive purpose of God.

The second story (chapter 18-19) signifies a principle which is of the greatest importance, a major contribution of Hebrew religion to Western thought. It is the story of Sodom and Gomorrah, the Canaanite cities which were destroyed because of their blatant wickedness. The modern reader should not be deterred by the primitive form of the story from seeing beneath the surface the golden principle, which is that authentic religion and morality are inseparable twins, neither of which is valid or vital without the other. This principle has become so thoroughly imbedded in the subsequent culture of the Western world that often the result has been the mistaken notion that therefore morality *is* religion, as though a coin could have one side without the other. The sense of righteousness discerned in Abraham and his children was the direct product of their growing vision of the character and commandments of the Almighty God, and of their faithfulness to him.

The third story of Abraham (chapters 20-22) wich we must consider here is that of the sacrifice of Isaac. This strange and poignant event also serves to illustrate a major Hebrew religious teaching, one that has not been even yet fully understood or applied. For at the heart of this familiar story lies the essential idea that true and acceptable sacrifice is not a ritual by which offending or supplicant man may appease a wrathful god or gain merit for reward; rather, authentic sacrifice is a way of worship in which the sinner is reconciled to the God from whom he has been estranged, and life is restored by its return, renewal and dedication.

Abraham was not doing anything new, or even unusual, when he prepared, so sadly and reluctantly, to offer his only son to the Almighty. The Scriptures and archeology alike show that human sacrifice was a commonplace feature of ancient religion, both before and long after the age of the Patriarchs. Offering the first born son was an especially pious and propitious act of worship, and the giving of the first fruits of the flock and field was a major means of guaranteeing continued fertility and favor. What is new and of fundamental significance in this story is not the intention to slay Isaac, but, rather, the transformation of the idea of sacrifice. Thenceforth the children of Abraham were reminded again and again, especially by the great prophets, that their convenant God desires obedience and not ritual sacrifice; he requires faithful living, not the attempted appeasement believed to be purchased by suffering and death.

These three prominent events in the life of Abraham, therefore, are clearly pregnant with meaning for the future of Hebrew religion, and hence for Western culture. Thenceforth, Abraham was to be known uniformly as "the father of the faithful." His place and role in the history of religion is nowhere described with greater depth and power than in the little book, *Fear and Trembling*, by Soren Kierkegaard.

There are many other stories of the Patriarchs in addition to these. That of Joseph and his brothers, occupying chapters 37-50, is

42

one of the best-known masterpieces in literature. In it we are told how and why the children of Abraham, the Israelites, came to be enslaved in Egypt; and that fact, obviously, was the necessary condition which served as a prelude to the Exodus from Egypt.

# Chapter 5

# *Covenant, Community and Cult*

Two primary factors must be considered with regard to the earliest Hebrew experiences with Egypt. Both of them are at the same time problematic and pivotal. The first factor has to do with the event itself: what are the facts, the evidences, the causes, the probable conjectures? The student finds that there is an enormous amount of scholarly opinion on all of these, and no final conclusion is likely. The Biblical record explains how the Hebrews happened to be in Egypt, as we saw at the end of the preceding chapter; and it also tells, in dramatic detail, how they were led out of Egypt, through the wilderness of Sinai, and finally into the promised land of Canaan. But there are large gaps in the account, and many questions about history and geography are left unanswered. Although archeology throws some light on the subject, it seems to raise as many problems as it solves.

The second factor concerns the significance and consequences of the event, whatever the facts may be. There can be no doubt about this factor: the Exodus is *the* event of paramount significance for all future Hebrew thought and existence. Like the birth of a child, the Exodus is for Israel the event *sine qua non*. It has been celebrated ever since as the birthday of Israel; and her traditions, cultic practices, and religious teachings have revolved around that ancient event as the fixed center. Moreover, the relation of these two factors—the event and its significance—may illustrate a fundamental characteristic of Biblical religion, which is that events may be the source of truth as perceived by the eyes of faith, even though the events themselves may be dimly seen and poorly or incompletely recorded. It is the faithful interpretation of the events and not the later perfect knowledge of the events which is vital. Further, Israel recognized the risks of faith, since faith is by nature precarious; but even though her memory of her birth and infancy was clouded and incomplete, she was constantly reminded that her existence as the People of God was ample proof that she had been born, and that not of herself.

## Moses: Prophet of Yahweh

Moses is the dominant figure in Hebrew religion. He is the Deliverer from Egyptian enslavement, the constitutive Lawgiver of the Hebrew nation and its religion, and the Mediator between the Israelites and their God. During the more than three thousand years since he lived, Moses has remained the human Alpha-point of Hebrew life and thought.

This being true, it is ironic that the Father of Hebrew religion bore an Egyptian name, and apparently a nickname at that. In spite of the Hebrew explanation (Exodus 2:10) that his name was derived from the word *mashah*, "to draw" (as from the waters of the Nile), it seems clear that *Moses* (Hebrew, *Mosheh*) is from the Egyptian root meaning "to be born." Hence the Hebrew son of a Levite family who was adopted by the daughter of the Pharaoh became known simply as "son," just as Ramses means "son of Ra," and Thutmose means "son of Thut."

The story recorded in Exodus 1-6, of Moses' infancy, early manhood, and call to be the Deliverer, may be usefully supplemented by references to geography, to the evidences of archeology, and to available historical knowledge about the contemporary Near East. For example, it has been suggested that the migration of the Hebrews into Egypt during the time of the Patriarchs may be better understood in the light of our knowledge of the conquest of Egypt by the Hyksos, just prior to 1700 B.C. The Hyksos were a partially Semitic people from Canaan and Syria who invaded Egypt in a time of internal decline, and with their horse-drawn chariots of war they were able to conquer and rule the land of the Nile for a century and a half. They were finally expelled by a native revolt around 1580 B.C. These facts clarify the story in Exodus. The tribes of Israel are thus understood as fellow-travelers of the Hyksos, their ethnic kinsmen, who made possible the settlement in Egypt during the time of Joseph and his brothers. And the enslavement which followed the rise of a Pharaoh "who did not know Joseph" (1:8) may be seen as a natural consequence of the expulsion of the Hyksos.

If Moses was a child of the despised and oppressed Hebrews who nonetheless was reared as a member of the royal family in the court of the Pharaoh, how much of his thought and later teaching may be traced to Egyptian cultural influence? Did he know, for example, of the revolutionary Akhenaten, the mysterious Pharaoh of the previous century who had instituted for a brief period a monotheistic cult of Aten, a god represented by the Solar Disk? There are important differences between Atenism and the religion of Moses, but if Moses was aware of the older, short-lived attempt at reform in Egyptian religion, this would not be the last time that Hebrew teaching received creative impetus from foreign sources which it radically changed, developed, and theologically purified. Some Egyptian influence on Moses and the Israelite tribes in Egypt would appear to have been inevitable.

The reputed long sojourn of the exiled Moses among the probably kindred Midianite tribes of Sinai and the Negeb also suggests some of the likely sources of Hebrew social and religious practices. According to the account in Exodus, Moses fled eastward from Egypt and lived for forty years among the Kenite tribe of the nomadic Midianites, even marrying Zipporah, the daughter of the priest, Jethro (or Reuel, according to another tradition). These tribes, who were later absorbed by the Israelites after the settlement of Canaan (cf. Judges 1:16), appear to have lived in the region of the oasis of 'Ain El-Qudeirat (Kadesh-barnea?), which is surrounded by a forbidding wilderness of barren mountains, one of which may have become later known as Sinai, or Horeb. The so-called Kenite or Midianite Hypothesis claims that several central elements of Hebrew religion had their origins in the Hebrew contact with the Kenite-Midianites, especially the sacred name of Israel's God, Yahweh, as well as the organizational structure of the incipient nation, and the beginnings of their cultic practices associated with sacred places.

Like his ancestor Abraham in the cities of Ur and Haran, Moses heard the mysterious and undeniable call of the Almighty to be his instrument and servant. He was reluctant to accept the commission, and he used every argument of reason in his attempt to avoid the dangers of duty and the possible illusions of an imagined revelation. But he found every question answered and every way of escape blocked. One especially significant reply came to him when he pleaded to be excused on the grounds that he was not an eloquent speaker. Recognizing his limitations, his God declared that Aaron, the brother of Moses, would be his mouthpiece. "He shall speak for you to the people; and he shall be a mouth for you, and you shall be to him as God" (Exodus 4:16). Thus the nature of prophecy was defined as a man serving as the spokesman for God. As Aaron was to Moses, so Moses was to Yahweh—Moses, the prophet of God.

## Exodus: Birthday of Israel

The dramatic events related to the Israelite escape from Egypt are recorded in chapters 7 through 18 of Exodus. There are the stories of the confrontations between Moses and Aaron on the one side and the forces of the Pharaoh on the other, and in the background may be seen the victorious struggle of Yahweh, the Lord of nature and history, with the impotent nature gods of the Egyptians. The plagues mark the defeat of those gods, one by one, Then followed the escape itself, highlighted by the unforgettable deliverance from the armies of the Pharaoh at the Reed Sea. Finally, by the providential care of their God, the disorganized and grumbling people were led by Moses through the threatening wilderness of Sinai to be united with the family of Jethro, in the land of the Midianites. The descendants of Abraham, Isaac and Jacob appeared to be ready to fulfill the promises to their forefathers by entering and occupying the land of Canaan immediately; but they remained unprepared, and the road would be long indeed before their children would drink the milk and eat the honey of homeland and nationhood.

Three features of this story call for emphasis. The first is the Hebraic view of history, to which we have alluded earlier. Is it not strange that an event of such magnitude as the Exodus is reported to have been in the Scriptures is nonetheless passed over in silence in the records of Egypt? It is true, of course, that there are small references in a few of the remains to the effect that nomadic shepherds came and went on the northeastern borders of Egypt; and some of the recorded Egyptian concerns with the "Habiru" in Canaan may be considered as corroborative evidence. However, the affair was obviously much more significant in the traditions of the Hebrews than in those of the Egyptians.

The explanation may be found in the Biblical perspective of historical events. Whereas the Exodus may have been for the Egyptians a commonplace occurrence, the unfortunate escape of some useful, migratory tribes, it was for the Hebrews a mighty work of Yahweh in which he called and redeemed his people. The Hebrews looked upon history as the realm in which God acts and reveals both himself and his purpose.

This distinguishing characteristic of Biblical religion points to a second significant feature of the Exodus story: the operative principle of election and response. The prophets and sages of the future constantly reminded Israel that she who had been no people was made to be a people by the gracious election of the God who called her out of Egypt. It was always mystery beyond understanding, but it was the primary fact of Hebrew existence that Israel came into being as the people of God whose initiative was evident, to the eyes of faith, in the deliverance from Egypt. Her response, therefore, should be one of gratitude and obedience, made manifest in faithfulness. The original sign of that dedication was the blood of sacrifice. The mark of separation between Hebrew and Egyptian was the blood of the slain lamb, smeared on the doorposts and lintels of their houses, at the first Passover. As we have seen in the previous chapter with regard to Abraham's sacrifice of Isaac, the blood was not a means of appeasement or a sign of suffering and death; rather the blood of sacrifice was a symbol of response in faithful dedication of life to the gracious and redemptive election of God.

The initial celebration of the Passover festival is a third feature of the Exodus which must be emphasized because of its importance for the future. This became one of the most prominent practices in Hebrew life and worship, and it has continued to be celebrated as a memorial of the grace and presence of God among his people, both in historic Judaism and, in transformed manner, in Christianity. As they prepared to depart quickly from the land of their enslavement, the Hebrews were instructed to take a lamb "without blemish, a male a year old" (Exodus 12:5); and, after using its blood as a sign of their identity as the people of Yahweh, they were to roast and eat it, with unleavened bread and bitter herbs. The manner and the meaning of the celebration were clearly specified: "In this manner you shall eat it: your loins girded, your sandals on your feet, and your staff in your hand; and you shall eat it in haste. It is the Lord's passover. For I will pass through the land of Egypt that night, and I will smite all the first-born in the land of Egypt, both man and beast; and on all the gods of Egypt I will execute judgment: I am the Lord. The blood shall be a sign for you, upon the houses where you are; and when I see the blood, I will pass over you, and no plague shall fall upon you to destroy you when I smite the land of Egypt. This day shall be for you a memorable day, and you shall keep it as a feast unto the Lord...." (12:11-14).

Modern research has indicated that the Passover festival probably had its origins in ancient nature festivals, possibly celebrating the fertility of the flocks or the beginning of a new year. If that is true, then the Passover as it came to be observed by the Hebrews serves to illustrate a favorite means by which Biblical religion both remembered and expressed the truths which it believed were revealed in the mighty acts of God in nature and history. The Exodus for Israel was not a commonplace event. It was her birthday, made possible by the power and grace of Yahweh. Therefore it must be celebrated, year after year, forever, so that the memory of grace might be refreshed and the frailty of faith might be renewed in strength.

### Sinai: Foundations for the Future

If the Exodus was the birthday of Israel, the period of wandering in the wilderness of Sinai was the time of her moral and spiritual formation. The lessons and experiences of that hard school provided the foundations of her future life and faith. We do not need to be concerned here with the perplexing problems of geography and history which are encountered in a careful study of this "forty years" between Egypt and Canaan. A voluminous literature is available to the student who wishes to investigate the facts and probabilities, and it is a fascinating and rewarding study. However, our purpose is to observe this formative period in order to discover the beginnings of the religious faith and practice which have been preserved and developed since that time in such a way as to become a major source of Western culture.

The experiences of Sinai are recorded at unusual length in the Torah, along with a large deposit of laws, directives and exhortations. The account of the Exodus from Egypt concludes with the arrival at Sinai, in Exodus 19:1; and the remainder of the book of Exodus, the whole of Leviticus, and the first ten chapters of Numbers, are given to a discussion of what may be called the time of Yahweh's instruction of Israel in the wilderness of Sinai. In fact, the rest of the Pentateuch may be included, since the last part of Numbers contains additional laws and an account of events which occurred as the Hebrews approached Canaan just prior to the entrance; and Deuteronomy is composed for the most part of recapitulative addresses to Israel, purportedly given by Moses at the conclusion of his career.

Four foundation stones were set in place at Sinai, and the magnificent edifice of the future Biblical faith has been constructed upon them.

1. The first was the controlling concept of God. The nature and character of the God of Israel were so clearly and irrevocably delineated during the wilderness period that the traditions of Moses remained for centuries as the theological norm to which erring times were called to return. This is not to say, of course, that the conceptions of God in this early period did not need correction and expansion; to the contrary, the Hebrews remained polytheistic, or henotheistic at best, and they often returned to pagan practices. A full universal, ethical monotheism would have to wait many centuries for expression, until the pain of national judgment had brought a purging of idolatry. Nevertheless, the essential elements of the Biblical doctrine of God were established at the beginning, and the fundamental conceptions needed only to be deepened and enlarged rather than replaced.

The name of Israel's God is of crucial significance in this regard. The record clearly shows that the Hebrews used the name Yahweh for their God at least from the time of Moses. The evidence is ambiguous concerning whether the name was known and used in earlier times, and modern scholarship is divided on the question as, apparently, are the traditions which lie behind the Scriptures. The Priestly Tradition (P), the last of the major sources of the finally edited Pentateuch (c. 500 B.C.), but not necessarily comprised of later materials, makes the explicit claim that the name Yahweh was first used in the period of Moses. According to that tradition, when God commissioned Moses to be the agent of deliverance from Egypt, and Moses inquired as to the identity of the deity, the reply came, "I am Yahweh. I appeared to Abraham, to Isaac, and to Jacob, as God Almighty [El Shaddai], but by my name Yahweh I did not make myself known to them" (Exodus 6:3). Furthermore, this tradition avoided the use of the sacred name in its narratives about earlier periods. However, the oldest of the Pentateuchal traditions, the Yahwist Epic (J), which is usually believed to have been compiled soon after the time of Solomon (c. 900 B.C.), states that the name of Yahweh was known from the beginning of human existence (Genesis 4:26). Other Biblical evidences do not contribute to any greater certainty. As we suggested above, the Kenite Hypothesis, popular among some scholars for more than a century, claims that the name Yahweh is of Kenite-Midianite derivation and that it was adopted by the Hebrews when they came under the tutelage of Jethro, the priestly father-in-law of Moses, after the Exodus.

Of far greater importance than the question of origin is that of meaning. What does the sacred tetragram (the Hebrew name has four letters: YHWH) signify? The Hebrew Scriptures everywhere emphasize that a name carries meaning and, further, gives being and presence to the person so identified. A name is much more than just a useful label, as though the person were an object needing merely to be distinguished from other objects. Thus the name, Yahweh, protected as it was by such unusual reverence, certainly bore particular and profound meaning for the Hebrews from the time of their earliest religious formation.

Both the etymology and the use of the name signify power and personhood. It may have been derived from the verbal roots meaning "to be," "to cause to be," or "to blow;" it certainly came to be identified with the God who had been, or was also, known as El Shaddai, "the Almighty God," or simple Elohim, "the strong god." It often appears in other forms, as Yah, or Yahu, or Adonai. Nevertheless, in all forms and cases, the basic reference is to awesome power, and the implication—the Hebrews seem given to little abstraction—is that Yahweh is the source and sustainer of his people and of their environment. Here, then, is the basis for the later idea of universal monotheism, a theological concept expressed in terms of Yahweh as the Creator of the heavens and the earth. Furthermore, the name itself, along with the anthropmorphic attributes of God which elucidate it, unquestionably implies the category of personhood. Yahweh is the Almighty One, the source of all that is, who calls, directs, and judges his people; thus he is the God of purpose and grace, directing the affairs of nature and history, demanding obedience to his commandments, and overcoming every obstacle, human or divine, for the ultimate fulfillment of his redemptive intention.

2. The second fundamental concept of Hebrew religion which was given permanent and controlling form at Sinai is the idea of the covenant between Yahweh and Israel. We should note the important fact that here again is an example of the Hebrews' habit of taking a commonplace idea or practice from their environment or background to be used as the vehicle of great meaning in their religion. We have seen already how Abraham responded to the call of his God, the Almighty, by accepting the covenant of faithfulness, which was signified by circumcision. Furthermore, archeological remains show the common social and political use of covenant-

making among many of the people of the ancient Middle East, especially the Hittites. Such religiously-sanctioned agreements were both convenient and necessary in a time when social stability was rare and the structures and powers of government were tenuous at all levels. No greater surety was to be found than in the binding power of a covenant, whether it was between individuals, tribes, or nations; and this was especially true when the covenant was made in the name and presence of the gods and then sealed by the solemn ceremonies of sacrifice and the performative words of blessings and curses.

Modern research has revealed that there were two distinct types of covenants among the people of antiquity. On the one hand, there were covenants between equals, in which bargaining took place and the results were of mutual benefit. This is called the parity type. On the other hand, there were suzerainty covenants. These were means of grace by which a sovereign, or the greater participant, shared his abundance, without duty or compulsion, with his subjects, or vassals, the lesser participants. Clearly, the Covenant of Sinai, between Yahweh and Israel, was of the latter type, Yahweh owed nothing and needed nothing; out of his freely-given grace alone, he chose the weakest of all people, who were no people, in order that, as he said to Abraham, he might bless all nations through them.

This element of gracious choice must not be overlooked, in a consideration of the Covenant. It points to the understanding, increasingly clarified by later Hebrew prophets and sages, of Yahweh's transcendence and purposefulness—essential marks of personhood; and it provides the nexus from which were derived all the teachings about Yahweh's righteousness and consequent moral demands on his people. Further, at this precise point may be discerned a decisive distinction between the Yahwism of Sinai and the other religions of the surrounding peoples: whereas the other tribes and nations believed themselves to be in some sense the natural offspring of their gods, sustained by an unbreakable relation, Israel was constantly reminded that she was a chosen child with no necessary or unbreakable claim on her God. The Covenant of Sinai was given out of gracious, inscrutable love. Therefore, the response of gratitude should be greater, and the possibilities of faithfulness or rejection always remained.

3. Closely related to the idea of the Covenant was the giving of the Law of Sinai. If Israel asked what it meant to be faithful to her

Covenant with Yahweh, the answer was that she should live by the Law. In modern, commercial terms, the Covenant was the contract and the Law was the specifications. Thus these two foundational elements of Hebrew religion appear in close proximity; Exodus 19 announces the making of the Covenant, and Exodus 20 specifies the essential moral Law, given in terms of the Decalogue.

As was the case with respect to all other elements of Hebrew religion, the Law was not without social and historical antecedents. A well known example may be seen in the Code of Hammurabi (c. 1700 B.C.), the discovery and translation of which at the beginning of the twentieth century caused a great stir among Biblical scholars. There are striking similarities between that Code and many of the laws of the Pentateuch. Furthermore, several other great codes of law from Middle Eastern cultures of great antiquity have been discovered more recently. However, there are also obvious and important differences between the laws of the Pentateuch and the laws of the other codes. Perhaps the greatest distinction may be found in the nature and character of the God who is said to be the source of the Law of Sinai. He is the only God (at least for Israel) and he is righteous. The resultant lesson, to be made increasingly plain, is that he will therefore permit no idolatry, injustice or immorality; hence theology, covenant, and law were bound together from the beginning in the structure of Israel's religion.

The function of law is to provide norms for individual and social behavior, to contribute to the unity and cooperation of social groups, and to make sanctions available for the judgments of reward and punishment. In a word, laws are necessary to give concreteness to the abstract ideal of justice. Hence, the Law of Yahweh, given to Israel at Sinai, helped to constitute the varied tribes into a people, a nation. It related religion to life, thereby giving value and consistency to creedal profession by requiring that orthodoxy bear fruit in personal and social practice. And, finally, it served to remind all future generations of what their God was like, therefore how they should live as his people, and, frequently, of the failures in their obedience and the fact of their unfaithfulness. The Law was the plumb line of Yahweh in Israel.

4. The fourth cornerstone of Israel's faith which was established during the Mosaic period was the Cult, the custodian of the foregoing three elements. Content requires form if it is to be preserved, and ideas must touch ground if they are to be useful. In

the field of religion, spirit must take on flesh, if it is to be redemptive. Recognizing that principle—it may well be called the principle of incarnation—Moses and the other leaders of Israel developed the ways and means of a cult so that the religion of Yahweh might be celebrated, regulated, and preserved. Several major aspects of the cult apparently had their origin during the period of the wilderness, though others were added, and all developed in form and direction as needs and conditions required.

Three prominent and lasting elements of the cult are sufficient for special notice here. The first is the priesthood. All of the religions of history have found it necessary and convenient to set aside certain members of the group who have as their particular function the representation of all the faithful before the god, or gods. The Hebrews were not unlike all the others. Thus a priesthood was ordained and given the care of the cult, Moses himself being the leader. The records of the Pentateuch contain detailed descriptions of the dress, the sacred instruments, and all the paraphernalia of the priests. The tribe of Levi, to which Moses and Aaron belonged, became the priestly tribe; and when, upon settling in Canaan, the tribes apportioned the land among themselves, the Levites were spread among the others, with designated cities in which to dwell. Research has raised difficult problems in this connection, especially with regard to the role of Aaron and the place of bull worship among the Hebrews (cf. Exodus 32). Nevertheless, the fact of the early establishment of an official priesthood seems to be certain, and we shall see the historical consequences.

A second significant aspect of the cult was the Tent of Meeting. The Hebrews had a nomadic background, as we have observed, and they were now a people in transit. It is to be expected, therefore, that among their tents there should be a special one to symbolize the dwelling place of Yahweh among them. The Pentateuch, again, gives detailed descriptions of its construction (cf. Exodus 26). Two factors concerning this Tent of Meeting deserve special comment. The first is that its very construction indicates a remarkable insight regarding what is called, in sophisticated terms, the omnipresence of Yahweh. He was not a localized god; he called Abraham in Mesopotamia, he overcame the Pharaoh and gods of Egypt, and now he was present with them in their travels. That view was the germ of transcendent universality. A second factor relates to the Temple which was to be constructed later in Jerusalem. The Tent of

Meeting was the portable temple which would later be replaced by the grandiose Temple of Solomon. Would that development represent progress, or create a problem?

The third element of the cult which we may mention was the Ark of the Covenant (cf. Exodus 25). This ornate object was apparently both a large portable chest which contained other cultic objects and, also, a glorious throne for the sovereign Lord among his people. It did not survive the final collapse of the Hebrew nation, but it did play an important role in the religious practices of the people during the intervening years which followed its creation in the wilderness. Perhaps its chief importance was its remarkable symbolizing of the protective presence of Yahweh among his people. When the Ark was lost, and the Temple was destroyed, the Covenant people were scattered in terrible judgment.

Thus Israel was born, formed, and equipped under the leadership of her greatest prophet, Moses. The beginnings made at Sinai would determine the future, and the ideas would grow through the succeeding ages; but the seeds would grow in harrowing times, as our next chapter will begin to show.

# Chapter 6

# An Experiment in Theocracy

The purpose of this chapter is to observe the further formation and development of permanent religious ideas among the Hebrew people during a period of more than four centuries. In the two foregoing chapters we have discussed the beginnings of the Hebrews and their religious principles and practices during the times of the Patriarchs and in the wilderness of Sinai. That process required more than half a millenium, ending around 1200 B.C. Now we shall describe the major developments which occurred during the next four centuries, from the settlement in Canaan following the Exodus until the last days of the Kingdom of Israel, in the middle of the eighth century B.C.

This long period, during which Israel abandoned the innocence of her infancy and became a rebellious adolescent, marked the rise of new ideas and institutions which were to remain as lasting features of Hebrew religion. The seeds that had been nurtured in the wilderness were now planted in the dry and rocky soil of the Promised Land. Some produced a rich harvest for the future, but others were perverted and poisoned by the environment so that the bitter fruit of evil, division, and death were the result.

## Land, Nation, Division

The question of the composition of Israel into a unified people who achieved nationhood is one of the most complex problems in early Hebrew history. The available sources of information, both Biblical and archeological, cause the confusion by their insufficiency of detail and apparent ambiguity.

Were all of the Hebrews in Egypt and at Sinai; or were the Israelites of the Exodus only the creative minority that became the nucleus of a larger "mixed multitude" which later formed a tribal confederacy and ultimately became a powerful nation, the center of an empire stretching all the way from Egypt to the Euphrates? Were the "Joseph tribes" of the north a separate group of Hebraic peoples who settled earlier in Canaan; and were the Exodus-Sinai tribes later arrivals who eventually achieved religious and political dominance? Was there a quick and concerted conquest of Canaan, as Joshua indicates; or was there rather a gradual migration and settlement, as Judges suggests? Were the various ethnic groups, who lived in Canaan prior to the coming of the Hebrews, driven out or destroyed; or were they absorbed, becoming finally a part of the Covenant People of Yahweh? These are only a few of the major questions which arise from a study of Hebrew history from Moses to the "writing prophets."

The familiar story may be read in deceptive simplicity in the books of the Former Prophets—Joshua, Judges, Samuel and Kings. According to the story, the twelve tribes, which were descended from Jacob-Israel, finally emerged from the wilderness of Sinai and quickly overran the small, sedentary kingdoms east of the Jordan River. There Moses mysteriously passed from the scene, after delivering the final directives and warnings which were later recorded in the book of Deuteronomy. Joshua, who is presented as a pale copy of Moses, then took up the leadership and led the fighting men of all Israel in a series of devasting campaigns west of the Jordan, conquering the center, the south, and the north of Canaan in rapid succession. The land was then apportioned to the tribes, and a great tribal assembly was held at Shechem, where the Covenant was renewed and a tribal confederacy was formed.

For nearly two centuries following the death of Moses, the Hebrews lived in Canaan as a twelve-tribe amphictyony, a loosely-organized confederacy bound together by a common religious commitment and practice. They had no king but Yahweh; they were therefore a theocracy. When they were threatened or oppressed by their enemies, the Spirit of Yahweh inspired a leader (judge, *shophet*) to rally the tribes in a battle for deliverance. These tribal leaders were temporary and non-hereditary; they exercised both political-military and religious functions; and their only authority was derived from Yahweh, who called them and gave them his spiritual power (*charisma*).

Restive under such a spiritually demanding arrangement and threatened with extinction by the culturally more advanced Philistines (the Sea Peoples who settled on the coast of Canaan at the same time that the Hebrews invaded from the eastern desert), the Hebrews demanded a king so that they might be like the other nations. Reluctantly, the judge-priest-prophet, Samuel, granted their wish and chose Saul, of the small tribe of Benjamin, to be their first king. When Saul failed to stem the tide of Philistine conquest,

Samuel anointed a new king, the young David, of Judah. His long reign was crowned with glorious success. The tribes were united into a strong kingdom, and, through alliance and conquest, an empire was built which represented for all time the height of Hebrew worldly power.

Nevertheless, the glory soon passed. Solomon succeeded his father, David, and during his reign the Covenant People, whose true king was Yahweh, were forced to endure the tyranny of an absolute monarchy characterized by injustice and idolatry. After the death of Solomon, the nation was divided into two kingdoms, Israel in the north and Judah in the south. Both were infected with the deadly disease of moral weakness, and both finally succumbed to the rapacious power of the great empires which rose and fell in the ancient Fertile Crescent.

This, in sweeping generalities, is the story of the Hebrew experience of nationhood that is recorded in the Former Prophets. Although many details of the history are cloudy and confused, it remains one of the best records of individual lives and national events that have survived from antiquity. Second Samuel, in particular, deserves praise and recognition for its eye-witness detail, fascinating narrative, and excellent literary quality. Furthermore, the main outlines of the story are substantiated by a mass of archeological evidence.

The uncertainties and confusions which remain after a study of the sources may be explained, at least to some degree, by a consideration of the literary and religious purpose which apparently lay behind the composition of the Former Prophets. And it is precisely at this point that our present interests may be found. For the redactors of the books which we know as the Former Prophets were not concerned with the facts and events, primarily, but with the ideas and principles which they chose to illustrate by using the traditions of the past. They were theologians and not historians; thus they used the oral and written materials available to them in such a way as to accomplish their purpose, without particular regard for details. This is an important principle of methodology which should always be kept in mind by the reader of the Bible, for it is a necessary assumption for accurate interpretation of the Hebrew and Christian Scriptures.

What is the religious principle which the Former Prophets illustrate? It may be called the Doctrine of Two Ways. According to that teaching, Yahweh is the God of righteousness and power; he requires obedience to the moral law, and he executes judgment over the affairs of history. Goodness will receive its reward, but wickedness will be punished. Furthermore, the equation may be reversed: those who prosper are clearly the righteous, and those who suffer may be judged as sinners in the sight of God. Thus, the story of Israel serves as a grand illustration of this moral truth, for it clearly shows the blessings that came in the times of faithfulness and the curses that befell the people when they forsook Yahweh. The Former Prophets reveal the regular rhythm of apostasy, oppression, repentance, and deliverance which was repeated in the whole history of Israel.

That fundamental principle of moral judgment became through the years a touchstone of interpretation in Hebrew religion and, later, in Judaism. It became, also, a dominant moral principle in Christianity, as we shall see, and thus profoundly affected the ethical teachings of Western culture. It did not take long, of course, for flaws to become apparent in the application of the principle, and we shall observe how the question which resulted gave impetus to some of the most searching thought to be found in Jewish and Christian literature.

There is another legacy which has remained in subsequent history as a result of the ancient Hebrew settlement in the land of Canaan, a legacy which lies at the root of one of the most perplexing social and political problems of the twentieth century. It is the tenacious attachment of Israel to that particular land itself. The modern Jewish philosophy of Zionism, which came to overt expression primarily among the persecuted Jews of Europe during the nineteenth century, has always been grounded in the ancient promise of the land to Abraham and his seed, forever, and in the historical fact of Hebrew presence in the land ever since. The reestablishment of the state of Israel in 1948 has been explained and justified as a legitimate realization of the right of the Covenant People of God, based upon both the divine promise and a continuous occupation for more than 3,000 years.

The history of the Middle East during this century, and the daily news alike, demonstrate the consequences of that principle, that devotion to the Promised Land. A long series of foreign powers have exercised control over the land during most of the three millenia, and most of the descendants of the ancient Hebrews were scattered among the nations of the earth. But in spite of the dispersion, there have remained everywhere a devoted memory of the beloved and barren land, and a yearning for return. The incredible Holocaust in Europe during the Nazi era aroused an undeniable motivation among the Jews of the world to reclaim the fatherland and to reestablish the nation. The dream has been realized to a remarkable degree; but the story remains incomplete.

## Yahwism versus Baalism

When the Hebrews entered the land of Canaan, whether in concert under Moses and Joshua or, as is more likely, in a gradual migration of various groups over a period of centuries, they were primarily a nomadic people. Some of them may have been semi-sedentary in their recent past, as, for example, those who had lived in Egypt and had escaped in the Exodus; but most had been tent-dwellers and followers of their flocks, wandering from oasis to oasis, seeking water and grazing. Both their traditions and archeology demonstrate this fact; and even the name, Hebrew, was probably first applied to a class of wanderers (the *Habiru*), primarily of Amorite stock, who gradually migrated into the sown land of the Fertile Crescent from the desert during the second millenium B.C.

The passage of the Hebrews from nomadism to the agrarian life involved social change of enormous proportions. Their total way of existence was affected, especially their religious faith and practice. They underwent a titanic struggle in the realm of the spirit, and in the process they cast new light on the dangers that humanity must always face; but they also discovered new means for the guidance and safety of mankind in spite of the corruptions of selfishness and power.

When the Israelites migrated into Canaan and settled there, they did not enter an empty land. The various Canaanite people who are so often mentioned in the books of Joshua and Judges were already living there, and most of them were far more culturally advanced than the Hebrews. In addition to the Canaanites, the Hebrews also soon confronted the Philistines, who were the remnants of an older Aegean civilization and thus were far advanced over both the Canaanites and the Hebrews. Furthermore, it should not be imagined that the Canaanites and Philistines were without religion and that the Hebrews, on the other hand, possessed a highly developed religion to which they were fanatically devoted. The people who lived in Canaan prior to the coming of the Hebrews were not simple-minded pagans who looked upon the Hebrews as heaven-sent missionaries and hence fell on their knees in eager acceptance of Yahweh.

The Hebrews found in Canaan a culture superior to their own. They had to abandon their tents and build houses. They ceased to share the whole desert, and every man began to draw a boundary around his own property. The natural equality among those who can own no more than they can carry gave way to the social inequality that results from acquisition, ownership, power and exploitation. The freedom of the wanderer was replaced by the structures and tyrannies of social regulation and control. And, most shockingly of all, doubts began to arise as to the adequacy of the nomadic deity of the wilderness, the Yahweh of Sinai, with his stringent requirements of justice and sobriety. Yahweh was a shepherd, but the Baals were farmers. How could a young Hebrew be expected to remain loyal to the old God of his fathers when the worship of the Baals, the gods of fertility, seemed so much more appropriate and practical—and certainly more fun?

The story of Israel which is recorded in the Former Prophets provides a description of that radical social change. Furthermore, that story has become paradigmatic for succeeding generations and for the modern world because, by being incorporated in the Scriptures, it has revealed both the dangers inherent in the inevitable changes of history and the sources of guidance and stability which can control and derive benefit from such changes. In its broadest ramifications, the struggle between Yahwism and Baalism in early Israel represents the timeless problems faced by mankind always and everywhere as he becomes increasingly sophisticated and civilized. Those crucial problems have to do with nature, man, and God. What is man's responsibility with respect to his total natural environment, of which he is a part and yet in some sense in charge? How is justice to be achieved and maintained in all the cross-currents of shifting social structures? In view of the pluralities of existence and the uncertainties of human knowledge, what is the proper balance between religious conviction and tolerance?

During the period under consideration here, the Hebrews did not develop fully satisfactory solutions to any of these fundamental human problems, of course; but they did illuminate the questions and point in the direction of some of the answers. That historically significant and remarkable accomplishment was made possible by the appearance of several unique persons and by the development of the incalculably powerful and influential institution which we know as Hebrew prophecy.

Aside from the great prophets, who will occupy our thought in several succeeding chapters, there were other creative leaders among the Hebrews, particularly in the period being considered here, who contributed to the survival and development of the religious ideas which have left their mark on Western thought. The judges and certain priests and kings are the major ones who can hardly escape our notice. The distinctive nature and role of the judges were described earlier in this chapter, and a reading of the book of Judges reveals their function as that of charismatic leaders who led the tribes temporarily during the time of settlement in Canaan, helping to preserve Yahwism and Hebrew identity. The priests were primarily the custodians of the religious institutions, and that is a vital function; for religious values and ideas cannot survive without institutions, in spite of the obvious dangers of sterility and self-serving power which are involved in the very nature of institutions. As for the importance of the kings, it is sufficient to record the name of David, the great creator of the nation, and even an empire, who has had no equal in all of Israel's history and is thus still considered the ideal king of the past and the future.

### The Hebrew Prophet: Theologian and Moralist

The Hebrew prophets and the Greek philosophers are the two most significant creative sources of our Western spiritual and intellectual heritage. The phrase "Moses and the prophets" has been used since ancient times to symbolize and summarize the essence of Hebrew religion. This is the copious spring, indeed, from which have flowed the broad and successive streams of Judaism, Christianity, and Islam; and the spring first bubbled forth from the numinous mystery of eternal purpose during the historical period described in the Scriptural books of the Former Prophets.

Prophecy, as a religious function, did not originate among the Hebrews, though it did receive its most distinguished expression there. As in many other instances, the Hebrews adopted a common thing from other peoples and cultures, and then polished it to special brilliance in order to reflect the light of truth. Such roles as shaman, oracle, and ecstatic were certainly common in the whole Mediterranean world long before the rise of prophecy among the Hebrews, and such phenomena have continued through the ages. However, there seems to have been a distinctive character to Hebrew prophecy from its earliest beginnings. That fact is probably due to the unique nature of Hebrew religious ideas, as we have observed them being formed in the time of the Patriarchs and Moses.

Prophecy in Israel apparently developed, historically, from the role and function of the priests and, especially, the judges. The priests were supposed to be ordained by God; they therefore possessed special powers of grace and insight, and they occupied a unique place between God and other men. The specific role of the priests was to be representatives of the people before God, in worship and all other cultic practices, such as sacrifice; but that role enabled them also to be the channel of the power and word of God to the people. Nevertheless, the duties and privileges of the priests inevitably led to their primary concern with personal position and the preservation of the cult as such. Form became dominant over spirit. Only those among the priests who maintained the particularly spiritual concern, despising the vested interests, were able to continue to hear God and to speak for him authentically. They then ceased to be priests and instead became prophets.

Moreover, the rise of prophecy may be seen even more clearly in the decline of the charismatic judges among the tribes of Israel. We have observed above that the judges were temporary but powerful leaders in the amphictyonic tribal confederacy who claimed to be given the spiritual power (*charisma*) of Yahweh in fulfillment of a task which was both political-military (to rally the tribes in war against their enemies) and religious (to rescue Israel from idolatry and thus to preserve Yahwism). When the confederacy failed at the time of the Philistine crisis, and the tribes were welded into a monarchial nation under Saul, David, and Solomon, the office of judge became divided between king and prophet. The kings assumed the political and military functions of the judges, enhancing the role by adding the characteristics of dynastic heritage, secular emphasis, and totalitarian power; but the prophets kept alive the religious functions of the judges, receiving the *charisma* and, without apparent authority, proclaiming the demands and judgments of Yahweh.

The nature of Hebrew prophecy may be further illuminated by reference to the words used to designate the office. Apparently the oldest Hebrew word so used is *ro'eh*, usually translated "seer," and derived from the verb *ra'ah*, "to see." Another kindred word is *hozeh*, from the verb *hazah*, which also means "to see," but carries the special meaning of "to see in a vision, or ecstatically." Thus the central idea is one of perception, experience, and privileged knowledge, which would be the basis for speaking of God, and for God, to the people, both in judgment and for salvation. However, the word which became most common is *nabi'*, derived from the Akkadian term for "to call, or speak out." This word was translated into Greek as *prophetes*, "one who speaks for another." Hence, all three terms, especially the later, indicate that a prophet is one whose calling is to be a spokesman for God. (Cf. Exodus 4:16 and 7:1, as noted in the last chapter, relative to Aaron's relation to Moses before the Pharaoh.)

In the crucial time of Israel's growth to adulthood, after Moses, and before the great "writing prophets" who witnessed her decline and death, there was a long series of these mouthpieces of Yahweh. It is significant that they always appeared and delivered their memorable oracles in times of special pain and tragedy. They may be designated as "oral prophets" because no book has survived bearing their names and preserving their messages. Rather, what is known of them is found in the well-named books of the Former Prophets. Seven of them are given special attention: Samuel, Nathan , Gad, Ahijah, Micaiah, Elijah, and Elisha. It is well worth noting that their main arena of operation was the public realm. They believed that Israel was called to be a special people, a holy nation, the Covenant People of Yahweh, a theocracy; and thus they dared, without fear or apology, to introduce religion into the political life of the nation. They spoke to all the people, but they proclaimed the word of God with particular force to the kings and queens.

Among all the prophets, Elijah became the symbol of prophecy *par excellence* in later Hebrew religion and in Judaism. Even in modern Jewish life, he is the prophet who is expected to appear at the Passover meal, and a place is reserved for him. It is noteworthy also that among the earliest Christians, Elijah was associated with the ministry of John the Baptist; and in the mystical experience of the Transfiguration of Jesus, just prior to his death, the Apostles saw Moses and Elijah appearing with Jesus on the mountain, probably thereby signifying the culmination of God's work among men in the giving of the Gospel along with the Law and the Prophets.

The stories about Elijah which are recorded in I Kings provide beautiful illustrations of the primary functions of Hebrew prophecy. What were those functions? The answer to that question may be given by reference here to an implied promise made earlier in this chapter which may appear to have been forgotten. For we suggested there that the Hebrew prophets, more than anyone else, pointed toward solutions to the crucial problems which bewilder mankind at every stage, especially under the conditions of an increasingly complex civilization. They are the problems that have to do with nature, man, and God—questions about environment, justice, and faith. The prophet Elijah cast helpful light on all three.

One of the best-known stories in the Scriptures is that of the contest on Mt. Carmel between Elijah and the prophets of Ba'al, or between Yahweh and the Phoenician god, Melkart (I Kings 18-19). Ahab, son of Omri, the strong monarch of Israel, had sealed an alliance with Phoenicia by marriage to Jezebel, princess of that neighboring kingdom. Jezebel was a dedicated advocate of the god, Melkart, whose priest her father, Ethba'al of Sidon, had been before he gained the throne of Phoenicia. Therefore, there was danger that Jezebel's particular fertility cult might actually replace the worship of Yahweh in Israel. However, the rough-hewn prophet from the eastern desert, Elijah, became the nemesis of Ahab and Jezebel. He challenged them to a trial by fire between the two opposing deities; and when Yahweh defeated Melkart, the people were persuaded to reject Ba'alism, proclaiming, "Yahweh is God!" (Elijah itself means precisely that.) At the same time, a long drought in Israel was broken by torrential rain, showing again that nature itself remains under the control of the creator God, Yahweh.

Another of the famous incidents in the life of Elijah concerns the murder of the Hebrew citizen, Naboth of Jezreel, and the appropriation of his coveted property by Ahab and Jezebel (I Kings 21). Such cruel and unjust behavior was accepted practice among the all-powerful tyrants of antiquity, and it is too often of modern times also; but it could not be tolerated by the just and righteous

God of the Covenant. Elijah thus spoke the terrible words of Yahweh's judgment, not only upon the king and queen but also upon their whole house: they would all be wiped from the face of the earth.

These stories clearly illustrate that the prophets were essentially theologians and moralists. They struggled to preserve and purify the ancient faith of Moses and the Covenant of Sinai; and they proclaimed the moral consequences of that faith in terms of social justice and personal righteousness.

The prophets taught that the land belongs to God, not man. Nature has been given to man for his use and enjoyment, but it is a temporary, fragile gift, involving responsibility. Man is a steward of his possessions, and he must recognize their source and use them prudently. Ahab was not allowed to take Naboth's land because it belonged even to Naboth only for his lifetime, and then it became the inheritance of his children. In like manner, David was to be the servant of Yahweh and the people, not the miser-like counter of *his* gold and *his* people; therefore he was condemned by the prophet, Gad, for "numbering Israel."

The prophets pointed to the perennial pitfalls of man's so-called progress and inevitable civilization. In the face of ownership, with its attendant evils of greed, violence and exploitation, they asked for human kindness and humble responsibility. Against social injustice, they proclaimed the temporary judgments of history and the final judgment of God. They required that men live by the moral law, and they planted the seeds of later political theories of freedom by implying the essential equality of all men before God and the resultant responsibility for respect and tolerance. Nevertheless, the prophets affirmed uncompromising conviction in their religious beliefs, and they clearly displayed an intolerance toward what they considered to be false. Thus, while making invaluable contributions to the moral and spiritual tutelage of man, they left further work to be done by their successors.

# III.
# GODS AND MEN
# IN EARLY GREEK
# THOUGHT

# Chapter 7

# Hellenes and Olympians

In Greek mythology, the three major divisions of Hellenic culture—Dorian, Ionian, and Aeolian—were held to be descendants of three sons of Hellen, whose parents, Deucalion and Pyrrha, repopulated the earth after the great flood not only with their natural progeny but by turning stones into those men and women who did not have the good fortune to be Hellenes.

Be this it may, what bound the Greeks together in historic times was not so much a tie of blood as the use of a common language. People who spoke Greek as their native tongue were Hellenes. Those who did not were barbarians—speakers of unintelligible nonsense which sounded to a cultivated Hellene like "bar-bar-bar." At the height of its influence, Hellas embraced areas extending from beyond the Black Sea in the east to the coasts of Spain in the west.

The origins of the Greeks, though somewhat obscure, certainly involved a fusion of peoples native to the Mediterranean area with invaders from the north. In the area of the Great Sea itself, the most prominent forerunners of the Greeks were the inhabitants of Crete, now known as Minoans, from the name *Minos*, traditionally given to their kings. These people attained a remarkably high level of culture, characterized by refined taste, superbly executed art, and superior technology.

Cretan civilization probably was developing by 4,000 B.C., but it received considerable inpetus about 2,800 B.C., when the Minoans began to fashion tools and weapons in bronze. Masters of a powerful navy, they disdained fortifications for their islands while at the same time maintaining a flourishing trade with Egypt. Their religion was complex, apparently being centered around the Great Goddess, who was sometimes represented as holding serpents in both hands, but it also involved rituals associated with bulls. It was the story of the Minotaur, a half-human, half-taurine creature, inhabiting a maze-like structure in the Cretan capital and killed at last by the Athenian Theseus, which provided the modern world with most of its imagery of the Minoans until almost the end of the nineteenth century.

Then, in 1893, Arthur John Evans, a graduate of Harrow, Oxford, and Göttingen, and Keeper of the Ashmolean Museum at Oxford, began excavations in Crete to discover the source of some little milkstone seals bearing curious symbols, which he had found in Athenian shops. On the second day of digging, he discovered a Bronze Age palace. Several years later, he bought the site of Knossos and devoted much of the rest of his life to bringing the Cretan culture to the light of day. In the intricate network of chambers and passageways of the great palaces of the Minoan kings, he uncovered a plausible basis for the description of the abode of the Minotaur, and the discovery of representations of a double-edged axe, a *labrys*, provided an explanation for the origin of the name of the maze—the *Labyrinth.*

Sir Arthur—he was knighted in 1911—gave a lecture in London in 1936 on the subject of some clay tablets dug up in the course of his excavations. Most of them bore inscriptions in characters designated as "Linear B" to distinguish it from the earlier "Linear A," but the tablets had baffled all attempts to decipher them.

A schoolboy named Michael Ventris heard the lecture and determined to solve the mystery of the language. Some sixteen years later, he was able to announce that he had fulfilled his childhood ambition. Linear B consisted of eighty-eight signs, too many for an alphabet, too few for ideographs. They must, Ventris had decided, stand for syllables. Linear B, he had concluded after further investigation, could be identified as a way of writing archaic Greek. His theory was confirmed by later finds, and the discovery led to the conclusion that as early as 1300 years before Christ, Knossos had come under the rule of Greek-speaking invaders who, in appropriating many of the customs and institutions of their victims, had adapted Cretan script to their own language. Apparently, it was only after the destruction of the Minoan civilization and that of its conquerors that later Greeks, possibly after a long period of virtual illiteracy, adapted the Phoenician alphabet to their native tongue to produce the written language of the classical period.

### The Mycenaeans and the Dorians

Who were these invaders? They appear to have been Ionian and Achaean warriors from the Greek mainland, and their presence in Crete may have been a result of the weakening of Minoan power after the cataclysmic explosion about 1500 B.C. of the volcanic island of Thera, which sent tidal waves a hundred and sixty feet high crashing over the Cretan coast, seventy miles away.

Conquest and assimilation were no new experiences for these Bronze Age warriors, Indo-Europeans who had originally made their home in the Danube basin and later had swept down over the Greek peninsula, absorbing the culture of the native Mediterranean population in the process. Their conquest of Crete must have provided them with many of the cultural accomplishments which converted them into the Greeks of the Homeric epics.

Stories of their exploits which, over three millennia, had come to be regarded as legends resting on an obscure foundation were given substance in the nineteenth century by a self-educated German archeologist named Heinrich Schliemann. Born in poverty, he survived an adventurous boyhood to become rich in a variety of daring commercial enterprises. Becoming obsessed early in life with Greece, he never wavered from his resolve to verify the old stories. He even justified his marriage to a Greek girl, arranged by mail, on the ground that he and his bride "could excavate together and share our common love of Homer."

The excavations for which he is best known were conducted at the site of Troy in the years 1871 to 1873. Before that time, the location of the city of Priam had not been definitely established. Schliemann insisted that any site worthy of consideration must satisfy the strictest Homeric requirements. Achilles must have been able to chase Hector around the walls, and the Greeks must have been able to move from the sea to the city eight times a day. A mound at Bunarbashi in Asia Minor, believed by some to be the spot where Troy had stood, was rejected because it was too far from the sea and had a river which would have brought Hector's flight to a premature conclusion. Schliemann elected to excavate at another mound at Hissarlik, which met the demands of his faith in Homer. He dug down through several layers of ruins, erroneously identifying ruins now believed to date from 2500 B.C. to 2200 B.C. as the city which was the object of his search. He had, however, gone right down through the layer which is now recognized as the twelfth-century city of the *Iliad* and, by uncovering older ruins, had added several thousand gold artifacts to the archeological treasures discovered during the course of the excavation. At Homer's Mycenae in 1876 and Tiryns in 1884 he was equally fortunate. Digging behind the Lion Gate at Mycenae, he found, along with other priceless gold objects, skeletons clad in the precious metal, and a golden mask which led him to telegraph the King of Greece—again missing the mark by several centuries—"I have gazed on the face of Agamemnon."

The importance of the find at Mycenae has led to the use of the term *Mycenaean* to designate the whole culture which flourished between the time of the fashioning of the treasures which so delighted Schliemann and the century following the Trojan War. It was an age dominated by luxury-loving nobles who built great fortified palaces, delighted in beautiful and costly objects fashioned in the Cretan style, and had an impartial enthusiasm for feasting and fighting. Aristocratic elegance and opulence rested on a relatively uncomplicated economy of agriculture, craftsmanship, foreign trade, and pillage.

Some combination of circumstances brought about the twilight of the heroic age at the close of the twelfth century B.C. Its final demise probably occurred at the hands of the Dorians, Greek-speaking invaders, little affected by the civilizing influences which had altered the lives of their Ionian and Achaean predecessors. They conquered the Peloponnesus, where they founded the city of Sparta. A number of cities on the Greek mainland were destroyed and their surviving inhabitants subjected to Dorian rule. Athens survived the invasion and proudly continued to assert her Ionian heritage. Greeks from other areas fled to Asia Minor and established new Ionian cities such as Miletus and Ephesus. The Dorian invasion thus was initially responsible for the Greek colonial movement, which was to play an important part in the development of Western culture. It also marked the beginning of a Hellenic dark age in which little of literary or artistic importance seems to have been produced.

### The Gods of the Greeks

A revival of Greek culture came in the ninth century B.C., a century especially notable for the production of two of the most important literary works in the history of the West: the *Iliad* and the *Odyssey*. Attributed to a blind poet named Homer, the first of the epics tells of a few weeks in the protracted Trojan War, and the second, probably by the same author, tells of the wanderings of the Achaean hero Ulysses, or Odysseus, while he is attempting to return to his native Ithaca after the fall of Troy.

More importantly, the two works, though written some two hundred and fifty years after the end of the Mycenaean culture, seem to express its spirit with remarkable fidelity and, as Schliemann claimed, to do so with more than a modicum of historical accuracy, once allowance is made for the introduction of a number of supernatural elements foreign to twentieth-century concepts of history. Those elements of the stories, however, provide an especially valuable service in furnishing us with an important source of our knowledge of Greek religion.

The society of the gods, as described in these and other works, was an amalgam of the beings worshipped by the various peoples of Hellas. There were spirits of nature to whom the indigenous inhabitants of the mainland offered bucolic sacrifices. There were Minoan goddesses from Crete, closely associated with the life-giving earth, and Mycenaean gods who made their home in the sky. These varied deities and demi-deities retained their ancient roles in the fully developed religion of the Greeks, but an aristocracy of a dozen gods and goddesses assumed a dominant position in the official religion of the Greek city-states, as well as in the best of Greek literature.

Mount Olympus, in Thessaly, was the home of the pantheon. There, Zeus Cronion, "cloud-gatherer" and "Father of Gods and Men," held his court. He was not the first ruler of the universe, having been preceded by a race of Titans, produced by the mating of Uranus (Heaven) and Ge, or Gaea (Earth). The Titans deposed their father, and one of them, Cronus, assumed the throne, married his sister Rhea, and fathered children, whom he swallowed to avert the fulfillment of a prophecy that one of them would overthrow him. Only one, Zeus, escaped that fate. He grew to mature godhood, forced Cronus to disgorge his offspring, and imprisoned the Titans in the depths of the earth. Having become lord of the sky and produced a number of divinities by union with a succession of goddesses, he at last married his sister Hera, noted for her fine wide eyes and her understandable suspicions concerning her husband's amours, which continued with distressing frequency after their marriage. Hera, a goddess of great antiquity and the patroness of marriage and motherhood, was a model of feminine virtue.

As Zeus ruled the sky, so his brother Poseidon reigned over the sea, lashing with storms those who met with his disfavor. His power was not limited to salt water. He controlled streams, rivers, and underground watercourses, and, through his power to produce earthquakes and tidal waves, controlled the fate of men and women who lived far from any sea. Hades, another brother, was the dark god who presided over the underworld, and a sister, Hestia, was the goddess of the sacred fires which burned on Greek hearths.

Hermes, whose worship originated in the cult of sacred stones, was the herald of the gods, traveling on winged sandals and delivering messages so effectively that he was recognized as the god of eloquence. As a young godling, he stretched strings across a tortoise shell to produce the first lyre. He was also the patron of wayfarers, thieves, embezzlers, and perjurers, the latter duties apparently not having aroused serious question about his trustworthiness as the guarantor of scales and measures.

Apollo, son of Zeus and Leto, was god of light, truth, and beauty. He drove the chariot of the sun across the sky, and art, poetry, and music were under his patronage. He was concerned with all the disciplines in which reason and order are dominant and so even shared in the supervision of wars. He was god of healing and father of Asklepios, patron of physicians. No darkness clouded his worship, and he was universally loved and honored. His twin sister Artemis, virgin goddess of youth and the hunt, was equally admirable, representing an ideal of athletic girlhood and symbolizing the love the Greeks had for the woods and hills and meadows of their homeland. She was also goddess of the moon as her brother was god of the sun. In Asia Minor, her maiden status suffered some compromise, for she was identified with an Asian goddess of motherhood and fertility. Her statue in the great temple erected in her honor at Ephesus seems to have emphasized this side of her nature.

Aphrodite, a goddess of Near-Eastern and Cyprian origin. sprang from sea foam (*aphros*) in the Greek tradition. She was the patroness of sacred and profane love and the ideal of feminine beauty. Paris gave her the prize of the golden apple in her contest with Athena and Hera, and Greek sculptors sought out the most celebrated beauties of their day—usually courtesans—to serve as models for their representations of the goddess. She was married to Hephaestus, a son of Zeus and Hera or, according to another story, of Hera alone. Born weak and unattractive, Hephaestus was rejected by his mother and expelled from Olympus. He came back, built the splendid dwellings of the gods, and generously defended his mother in one of her disputes with Zeus with such enthusiasm that the enraged Cloudgatherer flung him earthward. He fell for a whole day and suffered an injury to his ankle which crippled him—if, indeed, he was not already lame, as Homer claimed. Returning to Olympus with commendable perseverance, he served as armorer and artificer to the gods. He was, among his other accomplishments, said to have constructed the first robots. He was patron of all craftsmen.

Aphrodite, alas, was not faithful to her talented husband. Her most celebrated affair was with Ares, god of war, another son of Zeus and Hera, a deity somewhat lacking in refinement, called by Homer "the curse of men." Their liason, according to one version of the story, produced Eros, the young god of love. There was, however, an unresolved mystery about his paternity. Other stories named Zeus or Hermes, and another myth denied that Eros was the youngest of the gods and credited him with being one of the oldest. At any rate, he was to play an important part not only in poetry, but in philosophy.

Gray-eyed Athena, who, under curious circumstances, sprang from the head of Zeus, was, like Artemis, a maiden goddess and had as her spheres of influence, wisdom and war. She was the patron deity of Athens, and the most beautiful temple of antiquity, the Parthenon, was built in her honor.

These Olympian gods and goddesses, a host of lesser supernatural personages, and a few other deities of high rank—notably Pan, Dionysus, and Demeter—though not omnipotent, were extremely powerful. They exercised a considerable measure of control over nature, hurling thunderbolts, stirring up storms at sea, and controlling the cycle of the seasons. Toward these shining beings, the attitude of the Greeks was somewhat ambiguous. On the one hand, the awesome power of the gods caused them to be regarded with reverence not unmixed with terror; the word *panic* — *panikos* in Greek — is itself descriptive of the feeling appropriate to mortals who may encounter great Pan in the lonely places of the earth. On the other hand, many legends, and even some parts of the Homeric epics, treated them with the sort of familiarity proper to domestic drama. Thus, we see Zeus Cronion as a henpecked husband, vainly trying to hide his flirtations and infidelities from his jealous wife, and, in the *Iliad*, when Hector is being chased around the walls of Troy by Achilles and the gods are interestedly watching the progres, of the race, Zeus is tempted to change his mind about the predestined outcome in order to save Hector, who has been diligent in offering him oxen in sacrificial ceremonies. His suggestion horrifies wise Athena, who reminds him that Hector is "a mortal man, long doomed by fate," and that the rest of the gods cannot approve his being saved from death. The introduction of Fate or *Moira* into the discussion brings in an element of Greek theology which defines a limit to the power of the gods. Recognizing that even he could be guilty of *hubris*—the overstepping of the bounds set by the unseen power, or powers, guiding the destiny of gods and men, Zeus answers, "Never mind, Tritogeneia, my love. I did not really mean it."

The mood of the work turns solemn at this point.

"See now, the Father laid out his golden scales and placed in them two fates of death, one for Achilles and one for Hector. He grasped the balance and lifted it: Hector's doom sank down, sank down to Hades, and Apollo left him."

The year of the first Olympic Games, 776 B.C., is a convenient date for marking the beginning of what is called the Hellenic period, and the century in which they were first held was also marked by political and economic ills in Greece which forced small farmers to emigrate or become serfs on lands they had formerly owned. One of the victims of injustice was a farmer and poet named Hesiod, who lived in the little village of Ascra, near Thespiae, a place which the poet himself described as "miserable in winter, insufferable in summer, and never good." In a book entitled *Works and Days*, the writer told how his brother Perses bribed an unjust noble to assist him in defrauding Hesiod of his father's inheritance. Outraged by the theft and unable to find redress for his grievance from an earthly power, Hesiod looked to the divine order. Homer, while emphasizing the power of Zeus more than his moral qualities, had associated him with *Dike*, or Justice, and Hesiod based his hope on that connection. For him, the greatest wrong was seen as the oppression of the defenseless, and he looked to a day when the Father of Gods and Men would balance the scales. His interest in the gods was genealogical as well as moral and his *Theogony*, together with his *Works and Days* and Homer's *Iliad* and *Odyssey*, were to become the core of the literary curriculum for generations of Greek schoolboys.

On the whole, however, the influence of the Olympian religion on the popular mind resided less in its ethical content than in its recognition of the gods as superhumanly powerful and therefore to be placated with sacrifices and ritual observances. As guardians of cities, they performed a useful political and military service. As idealizations of the classical conception of humanity, they have had an enduring effect on Western culture. Encounters between gods and men were, however, rather to be dreaded than sought, and the religion was ill prepared to deal with the higher personal concerns of redemption from suffering and salvation from sin. For these, the Greeks were obliged to turn to the mystery religions, to be considered in the next chapter.

## The Sixth Century

By the beginning of the next century, Greeks, wherever they might be found and despite differing national loyalties, regarded themselves as a single people. By this period too, the city-state had developed as the characteristic political institution of the Greek world, preserving its character even in colonial cities which, bound to parent governments in most cases only by sentiment and common interest, conducted their affairs as independent sovereignties. The colonial movement, probably receiving early impetus from the Dorian invasion, had flourished since that time, due to a variety of personal, political, and economic motives. Prosperous Greek city-states had sprung up all over the shores of the Mediterranean, never extending far inland, but influencing and being influenced by a variety of other cultures. With a high degree of prosperity and leisure for speculative thought and artistic creation, talented Hellenes laid an increasingly solid foundation for the golden age which was to follow.

On the mainland, the Dorian and Ionian ways of life were sharply contrasted in the two states which were to symbolize the Greek spirit to subsequent generations. Sparta was, in effect, a military garrison, dedicated to the arts of war and the cultivation of heroic virtues which earned the Spartans the admiration even of their enemies. Their entire educational system was designed to produce citizen-soldiers, who needed only that degree of literacy which would enable them to perform their duties to the state. The Spartans, in fact, suspicious of speech, cultivated a terseness which has given us the word *Laconic*, from *Lakon*, a native of Laconia, or Sparta. As a result, although the deeds of the Spartans provided a wealth of material for heroic treatment in literature, the society was incapable of producing the poets who might have sung those deeds or the philosophers who might have reflected on the nature of the courage which made them possible. The more liberal society of Athens was as favorable a breeding ground for the arts as the Lacedaemonian state was for the martial spirit. If its citizens were not the originators of all the varied forms of literature and art which were the glory of Greece, they were so hospitable to them that Athens was able to make itself the cultural center of the Hellenic world, with results which will be explored in later chapters.

# Chapter 8

## *Oracle and Mystery*

Long ago, when the world was young, Zeus wished to determine the center of the earth. He dispatched two eagles, one from the place of the rising sun and one from the place of its setting. Flying toward each other, presumably at the same speed, they met at Delphi, in a region tortured and twisted by Poseidon in his role as Earthshaker. The point of their encounter was designated as the *omphalos*, the navel of the world and marked by an egg-shaped stone. There Ge, or Gaea, the Earth Goddess, and her daughter Themis held sway before the Dorian invasion, protected by a great serpent, the Python. With the ascendency of the Olympians, Apollo ranged through the earth, searching for a place to establish an oracle. Traveling through the Greek mainland, he came upon the spot previously determined by the meeting of the eagles and slew the serpent. A clear spring, the Castalia, sprang up upon the site of his victory, and Apollo built a shrine there at which he dispensed counsel to troubled pilgrims for more than a thousand years, interrupting his service only for an annual three-month winter vacation, during which the Oracle was silent while Dionysus took the Sun God's place at Delphi.

The temple held a small sunken chamber, the *adyton*, containing a golden statue of Apollo and the primeval *omphalos*, mounted on a rectangular base and flanked by golden effigies of the two eagles released by Zeus. In front of the *omphalos* stood a tall bronze tripod, official seat of the Pythia, the priestess of Apollo. The paving stone on which the tripod rested contained a hole through which vapor from burning herbs in a chamber below the *adyton*, or perhaps a less material *pneuma* from the god himself, may have risen into the chamber.

A visitor to the Delphic Oracle would walk up the Sacred Way, lined with "treasuries" built to house the rich offerings to the god which came from all over the Hellenic world. In accommodations provided for him on the grounds, he would wash and ritually purify himself. Summoned at last to the temple, he would pause outside to offer, on the main altar, a sacred cake, the cost of which bore no relationship to the price of the ingredients of which it was composed. Proceeding into the *cella* of the temple, he would make a sacrifice of a sheep or a goat on a hearth containing a perpetual fire. Summoned at last to the *adyton*, presumably mindful of an admonition to "think pure thoughts and speak well-omened words," he would seat himself at the end of the room. The chief priest, provided with the enquirer's question, would put it to the Pythia, seated on her tripod and already under Apollo's influence. She would respond with an incoherent outcry, sometimes, in her frenzy, shaking bronze laurel branches which flanked her seat of prophecy on either side. The priests in attendance claimed to be able to understand Apollo's message, delivered through his votary, and would provide the questioner with a written translation of it, subject to his perusal if he were acting on his own behalf and sealed if he were acting as agent for someone else. Though the answers were sometimes cryptic enough to insure that, whatever the outcome, the Oracle could not be shown to be wrong, they had sufficient substance to make the Pythian Apollo the most highly regarded source of advice in the Greek lands.

The Oracle was a major factor in the colonial movement which resulted in the establishment of Greek states over a widespread area. According to a Cyrenaean story recorded by Herodotus, a young man named Battus, a citizen of Thera, traveled to the shrine to ask how he could overcome a stammer.

"Battus," the Pythia replied, "You have come for a voice, but King Phoebus Apollo sends you as a founder of a colony to Libya, the nurse of flocks."

A colony? Nothing could have been more foreign to Battus' plans. He argued that he had no capacity for such an enterprise and took no immediate steps to carry out the command of the god. Apollo responded to his temporizing by visiting a famine on his native land and announcing through the Pythia that the Therans could end it only by sending Battus to do his bidding. Reluctantly, the stammerer set out, but shortly lost his nerve and tried to return. His fellow citizens forced him to take ship again, and this time he accomplished his mission, established the colony of Cyrene, and became its first king. In the process, he is said to have lost the speech impediment which had sent him to Delphi in the first place.

Locrus, another visitor to the Oracle, was ordered to build a city in a place where he would be bitten by a wooden dog. Undoubtedly feeling secure from the necessity of performing a task contingent on such an unlikely occurrence, he one day pricked his foot on a brier. It turned out that the Greek name for the plant was "dog-bush" (*kynobaton*), and Locrus established on the spot the city which was to bear his name.

In at least one celebrated instance, the ambiguity of which the Oracle was occasionally capable produced far-reaching consequences. Croesus, King of Lydia, a member of a dynasty with a long history of cordial relations with Delphi, was contemplating a war against Cyrus of Persia. He dispatched ambassadors to consult the Pythia about the advisability of executing his plan. They returned with an answer which seemed highly encouraging: "Croesus, having crossed the Halys, will destroy a great empire."

Elated, the King sent a gift of two gold staters for each Delphian, along with another question. Would his monarchy be long lasting?" The Oracle replied: ".... when a mule shall have become King of the Medes, then, soft footed Lydian, flee by the pebbly Hermas, do not linger, nor feel shame at being a coward."

Clearly a mule would never rule over Media. The message could only mean that Croesus' throne was safe. Accepting another counsel of the Pythia, he formed an alliance with the Spartans and led his army across the Halys. Cyrus defeated the invaders soundly, captured Croesus, and, after frightening him with the threat of burning, relented and accorded his royal captive treatment suitable to his rank. Croesus, feeling cheated by the Oracle, sent his chains to Delphi with a sharp complaint. The Pythia informed the King through his emissaries that he had no reason to think himself ill-used. He had indeed destroyed a great empire—his own. The mule? That was Cyrus, hybrid offspring of a Persian father and a Median mother.

Parmeniscus, a philosopher of Metapontum, went to Delphi troubled because he had lost the power of laughter. Putting a question about his difficulty to the Pythia, he received the cryptic response, "You ask me about soothing laughter, O unsoothable one. Mother at home will give it to you. Pay her special honor."

Parmeniscus went back to Metapontum, but found his mother as unamusing as she had been before his absence. Some time later, presumably convinced that the Oracle had, for once, been in error, he embarked on a journey which took him at last to Delos, where he visited the temple of Leto, the mother of Apollo. There, in the sanctuary, he found himself in the presence of a primitive wooden statue of the goddess, shapeless and ridiculous. Bursting into laughter, the philosopher realized that Apollo had been recommending his own mother's image as a cure for his petitioner's melancholy.

The Oracle survived the decline of the Greek city-states, but it ceased to play an important role in the Mediterranean world during the early centuries of the Christian era. A story was widely circulated that shortly after the birth of Jesus, the Roman Emperor Augustus addressed an enquiry to Delphi to ask who should be his successor. Confronted with the awesome question, the Pythia remained dumb. Why, Apollo was asked through his prophetess, did he not reply? The god answered:

"A Hebrew boy (he who rules as god among the blessed) bids that I leave this house and go to Hades. Depart therefore from our halls and tell it not in the future."

By the time of Constantine, the Oracle, after sporadic attempts by its followers to revive its authority, had fallen silent, never to speak again.

### *Personal Religion*

One important function of religion found little support from Olympus or Delphi. A man or woman wracked by guilt or oppressed by a sense of meaninglessness was unlikely to gain much satisfaction from an appeal to Zeus or Apollo, who had little to do with redemption from suffering or salvation from sin. The official religion, in fact, was almost completely unconcerned with individual values transcending these to be found in daily experience. Hesiod's recognition of Zeus as the guarantor of justice was not widespread in a culture steeped in legends showing the father of gods and man in quite a different light. In any case, whatever the Cloudgatherer's character, it was evident that justice does not always prevail on earth, and the state religions gave their devotees no hope that the manifest inequities experienced in this life might be redressed in a future one. In fact, early Greek literature presented an unattractive prospect for life after death, as did the Hebrew Scriptures. With the exception of a handful of heroes who might find a more or less tolerable quasi-existence in the Elysian Fields, the fate of the departed soul—which, at best, was a mere shadow of the real self—was unenviable. Even those who did not undergo actual torment like the punishments of Tantalus or Sisyphus faced the perpetual boredom of a gray half-life in Hades. The eleventh book of the *Odyssey* contains an account of Odysseus' visit with the pale, bloodless ghosts in the abode of the dead. There he encountered the ghost of Achilles and, in an attempt to cheer up his old comrade in arms, urged him not to grieve because he was dead.

"Nay, speak not comfortably to me of death, O great Odysseus," the shade replied. "Rather would I live on ground as the hireling of another, with a landless man who had not great livelihood, than bear sway among all the dead that be departed."

Regarding death as an unmitigated disaster, the Greeks reveled in life and light, but they could not banish from their consciousness images of the fate which awaited the poor remnant of the self when, after paying Charon the fee placed in the mouth of the dead, he would be ferried across the Styx into a realm of shadows.

During the sixth century B.C., the Hellenes began to revive and purify certain ancient beliefs and practices which compensated for the unsatisfactory conception of human destiny found in the official cult. From elements found in various forms throughout the Mediterranean lands and the Middle East, there emerged in Greece two principal sets of "mysteries"—the Eleusinian and the Orphic. These mystery religions, as the name suggests, involved secret rituals and dogmas, which were not to be revealed to anyone who had not been purified by initiatory rites.

### The Eleusinian Mysteries

The Eleusinian cult derived its name from the town of Eleusis, on the Rharian plain near Athens. The rites originated there, and initiation was at first restricted to townspeople, but when Eleusis became a part of the Athenian city-state, the cult was placed under the general supervision of the *Archon Basileus* and given official Athenian patronage. It remained a voluntary society, however, and its membership was opened not only to citizens of Athens, but to women, slaves, other Greeks, and, in later days, foreigners of every land, provided only that they could speak Greek. Associated rites were established in various parts of the world, honoring Demeter Eleusinia.

The myth on which the mysteries were based was well known in Greece. Demeter, or Ceres, "giver of goodly crops," had a daughter named Persephone. While picking flowers one day, Persephone was snatched up by Hades, Lord of the underworld, and carried through an opening in the earth to his dark realm. For nine days, Demeter wandered over the earth, mad with grief, searching, torch in hand, for her missing daughter. At the end of that time, she learned from Helios, the sun, that Zeus had given her child to his brother Hades to be his bride. Demeter, presumably to cloak herself in anonymity while considering her next move, disguised herself as an old woman and continued her travels until she came to a well in "fragrant Eleusis," where she sat down to rest. There the daughter of Celeus, a local prince, found the stranger and invited her to her father's house, where she refreshed herself with meal and water and pennyroyal tea. She accepted a position in the household as a nursemaid.

There are conflicting versions of the subsequent events in Celeus' house, but a boy named Triptolemus figures prominently in both of the best known accounts as the recipient of instruction in the art of agriculture, given by the goddess herself. They also agree in attributing the building of the temple at Eleusis and the establishment of the sacred rites to an injunction of the goddess.

Demeter, still distressed over Persephone's absence, brought a famine on the earth. Her action apparently upset Olympus, for, without crops, men were making no offerings to the gods. Zeus induced the other deities to try to persuade Demeter to abandon her strike. Failing in this, he turned to Hades and urged him to restore Demeter's child to her. Hades agreed, and Persephone returned to the upper world, only to learn that, because she had eaten a sweet pomegranate seed in the abode of the dead, she must spend a third of each year there. Demeter restored fertility to the land, but during the winter months, when Persephone returnes to her husband, the earth becomes cold and barren again.

This is the story which provided the substance of the Eleusinian rites. They celebrated both a nature myth relating to the cycles of the seasons and, more importantly, a dramatization of humanity's fundamental fears and hopes. The dark lord had carried his captive into the realm from which no return was believed to be possible, but Demeter's love had been so great that she had brought about the resurrection of her child. If Persephone had died and come to life again, might not others do the same if they could avail themselves of the power of the goddess? By Demeter's own instituion, a way to triumph over death had been offered in the mysteries. To become identified with the divine nature through ritual reenactment of the drama would bring about that miracle.

The initiatory ceremonies for candidates for regeneration seem to have been spread over a considerable period. The Lesser Mysteries, celebrated in the spring at Agrae, an Athenian suburb, were more or less public and provided the candidates with ir struction, purification, and preparation for the more important rites to follow. The Greater Mysteries began in September, and the initiation proper lasted several days. It began with a solemn warning to depart, addressed to anyone present who might not be "pure in hand and soul and of Hellenic speech." The next day, the *Mystae* bathed in the sea and then were sprinkled with the blood of sacrificed pigs. Some days later, they marched along the Sacred way from Athens to Eleusis in a torchlight procession, arriving in time for some sort of midnight ceremony.

The final event of the Greater Mysteries took place a year later in the *telesterion* at Eleusis, and the rites were so secret that their specific nature is still unknown. There is a piece of evidence, though, which gives a hint concerning some of the participants. Alcibiades, a friend of Socrates who earned a bad reputation in Athens on several counts, was charged with impiety for presenting a mock version of the sacred mysteries at a drunken revel. According to the allegation, Alcibiades took the role of the chief priest, two of the other guests played the herald and the torch-bearer, and the rest of the party were the initiates. Later writers suggested that the ceremony was in the form of a religious play, representing the story of Demeter and Persephone. However that may be, it is clear that something was done which had a powerful effect on the initiates, convincing them that they had entered into mystical communion with the goddess and undergone a redemptive experience which had purified them and given them promise of a blissful future life.

## Dionysus and Orpheus

As did the cult of Eleusis, the Orphic Mysteries had their origin in the worship of a deity with strong ties to the earth. Dionysus, or Bacchus, god of animal life and vegetation, especially the vine, came to Greece from Thrace. Son of Zeus and Semele, he lost his mother at birth, when Hera successfully plotted the destruction of Semele by her husband's lightning. Zeus, however, succeeded in hiding his infant son from his jealous consort, and the child survived to become one of the most important of the gods. So close to nature that he was actually thought on occasion to be present in the wine used in his worship, he was ideally suited to become the center of a religious movement dedicated to the translation of earthbound devotees to a higher plane of existence.

Originally the cult of Dionysus had little about it to suggest the elevating effect it was ultimately to have on religion in the classical period. The presence of Dionysus was originally felt most strongly by worshippers who, after consuming large quantities of wine, worked themselves into a frenzied ecstasy in which they felt themselves possessed by the god. Recognizing his identification with the animal world, they also invoked him by orgiastic feasting on the raw and bleeding flesh of a sacrificial victim—probably in early times a human being, but in later days a goat, a fawn, or a bull. These mad festivities, which also involved wild dancing to the accompaniment of wind and percussion instruments, were usually nocturnal affairs, lighted by burning torches. Especially subject to the divinely inspired frenzy were the female devotees, the *Maenads*, who would become possessed to such an extent that they would tear to pieces and devour any living being they encountered. This fate, according to one tradition, befell Orpheus, the purifier of the rites, when he interrupted an unreformed Bacchanalian revel.

Horrifying as these practices seem to the modern Western mind, and, indeed, to that of the classical Hellenic world, there was a high degree of religious significance in the sacramental relationship between Dionysus and the food and drink in which he was held to be present. In consuming them, the Bacchant freed himself from the restraints of convention, incorporated himself into the life of the deity, assured himself of a desirable form of immortality, and, in popular belief, acquired the power to work miracles.

It cannot have been easy for the more orderly residents of the Greek mainland to accustom themselves to the incursion of the disruptive and terrifying god from the north, but among others, starved for a religion with personal significance, the worship of Dionysus spread like wildfire during the sixth century, and the astute custodians of the official religion realized that if it was to be controlled, it must be given respectability. Dionysus joined Apollo at Delphi in alternating control of the shrine, and at Athens he led Demeter's procession along the sacred way to Eleusis. His public worship gave rise to Greek drama, and two states—Teos and Naxos—named him their official protector. It was, however, under the sobering influence of Orphism that the worship of the wine-god made its most significant contribution to Greek religion.

Orpheus, a legendary figure who may have also been a historical personage, was a teacher, a theologian, and a musician of such power that his playing and singing charmed wild beasts and savage men. Himself, at last, a victim of the excesses of the Dionysian spirit, he was credited by members of the cult which bore his name with having preserved the truths embodied in Dionysus-worship while stripping away the elements of intemperance and license which made it unpalatable to Greeks unwilling to reject the motto "Nothing in excess."

The cult had its own form of the Dionysian myth, expressed in several forms, but emphasizing in all of them the essential element of divine immanence as a path to human transcendence. According to a common version of the story, Persephone bore Zeus a son, Dionysus Zagreus, "the hunter." Zeus favored the child and intended for him to become the ruler of the cosmos. Hera, however, was jealous of him and conspired with the brutal Titans to bring about his death. The Titans collected some attractive toys and lured the little god away from the Curetes, his guardians. Having seized him, they tore him to pieces, which they then cooked and ate. Athena, however, managed to save the child's heart and conveyed it to Zeus, who swallowed it, in that way preserving his son's identity, so that the child he later had by Semele was, in fact, Dionysus Zagreus reborn. Zeus, directing his terrible wrath against the Titans, destroyed them with his thunderbolts, and man was created out of their ashes. Earthy as the Titans were, they had nevertheless eaten the divine child, and so man is of two natures, the lower testifying to his Titan origin and the higher to his kinship with Dionysus. "I am a child of Earth and Starry Heaven," a third century B.C. gold tablet quotes a soul as saying, "but my race is of Heaven."

For Orphic devotees, throughout the history of the cult, the soul represented the divine element in man. Its lodgment in the body is a sort of death, from which the soul is obligated to seek deliverance. This must be done in a series of lives in which one is united to body after body through rebirth (*palingenesis*) until, through ritual purification and ethical action, the soul frees itself from its carnal nature and, in Pindar's words, can "pass by the highway of Zeus into the tower of Cronus where the ocean breezes blow around the Islands of the Blest."

The similiarity between the Orphic doctrine of transmigration of souls, known as *metempsychosis*, and the Hindu idea of reincarnation, associated with the concept of *karma*, suggests a common origin. Such Orphic features as vegetarianism and the characterization of the cycle of rebirths as a wheel from which escape must be sought are found in several Oriental religions. The specific rituals of the cult, though, appear to have been directly based on the Dionysian legend. The feast of raw meat was preserved, and initiates were daubed with clay, not only as an act of purification, but to recall the story that the Titans, in order to avoid being identified when they dismembered little Zagreus, had smeared themselves with gypsum.

The principal significance of the Orphic movement lay in the personal disciplines practiced by its members. They wore white garments and guarded themselves rigorously against defilement with dead bodies. After the single initiatory meal of raw flesh, they abstained from meat altogether. They opposed suicide, on the ground that since the soul's incarnation is a penance for past misdeeds, it has no right to leave the body until its appointed time. Even after it has purified itself and completed its appointed rounds, it is obligated to perform certain acts after death. On entering Hades, it must avoid Lethe, the spring of forgetfulness, appropriate for souls passing from one incarnation to another, and ask instead to drink from the wellspring flowing from the Lake of Memory, using the formula, "I am a child of Earth and Starry Heaven." Then the soul faces Persephone, assuring the goddess that the applicant for perpetual bliss is of her blessed race. The response, "Happy and blessed one, you shall be god instead of mortal," assures the successful pilgrim that he has attained his goal.

The importance of the mystery religions in the making of the Western mind can hardly be overestimated. Co-existing with an official religion which was in great measure insitutional and this-worldly, they called attention to the importance of the individual and his transcendent and permanent value. They emphasized the often neglected matters of redemption from suffering and salvation from sin, and, in the more mystical aspects of their theology, they moved in the direction of a recognition of unity underlying the multiple facets of experience. In these and other ways, the mysteries were destined to exercise incalculable influence on the thought of a succession of Greek philosophers—notably Pythagoras,

Heraclitus, Empedocles, Parmenides, Socrates, and Plato—and through them the overall world view of the West.

# Chapter 9

# *The Mirror and the Mask*

Homer and Hesiod had worthy literary successors in the centuries which separated their times from the onset of what came to be known as the golden age of Greece. In the seventh century, Aesop wrote the popular fables which left an enduring imprint on the everyday thought of the West, and poets like Archilochus, Tyrtaeus, and Alcman mirrored a variety of aspects of Greek culture in lyric verse. In the sixth, Alcaeus and Theognis continued in their tradition, and Sappho of Lesbos proved that poetic talent of a high order was not limited to men.

The sort of poetry produced during that period found its most enduring expression in the work of Pindar, a poet who reached maturity at the beginning of the fifth century, when significant signs of change were already becoming evident in the city states of Greece. Cleisthenes, a political liberal of aristocratic lineage, had come to power in Athens and instituted electoral reforms which laid the foundations for the democratic society which would reach its height some years later under the leadership of Pericles.

Pindar, a citizen of Thebes, was unaffected by the winds of social change blowing from the south. The unsullied conservatism of his thought was characteristic of an earlier generation. His was the poetry of a self-confident aristocrat, and his uncomplicated conception of virtue was derived from the *noblesse oblige* proper to a caste free of doubt concerning its divinely instituted right and duty to set the standards by which its society should live. His poetry, more than that of any other Greek writer, has the reputation of being untranslatable in any way which would preserve the quality of the original language. The difficulty is due partly to the fact that the music to which the odes were sung has been lost and partly to the fact that the excellence of his poetry is in no small measure due to intricacies of metre which cannot successfully be suggested in English verse.

Of the many poems he composed in honor of a variety of persons and events, forty-five survive, named after the games in which the heroes honored in the odes triumphed. Despite their ostensibly athletic theme, they have little to say about the contests themselves, being devoted rather to praise of the victor, religious reflection, and moral counsel, all couched in the noblest of language. Unfortunately, he lived in a time when the way of life he celebrated was already giving way to a new age—the age of Marathon and Salamis and Athenian ascendency, which played no part in his lofty conception of the world. He died in 442 B.C., an honored anachronism in a world of change from which he had steadfastly averted his gaze.

## Aeschylus

One day late in the sixth century, it is said, a boy asleep in his father's vineyard was confronted in a vision by the god Dionysus, who commanded him to write a drama in the form which was to provide the wings on which the Greek spirit would soar to its greatest heights of artistic expression. On that day, if we may credit the story, the great age of Greek tragedy began.

Aeschylus, the boy in the vineyard, was born in the year 525 B.C., in Eleusis. His father, Euphorion, was a member of the *Eupatridai*, the Athenian nobility, and we may suppose that the boy was given an education appropriate to his rank. From his childhood in Eleusis, he undoubtedly absorbed the pervasive atmosphere of concern for the problems of life, death, and judgment celebrated in Demeter's mysteries. He served Athens as a soldier in the war against Persia, and was present at Marathon, Artemisium, Salamis, and Plataea.

His first plays were presented at Athens in 499 B.C., and of the ninety tragedies he wrote during the next forty-one years, seven survive in their entirety. The dramatic tradition which he inherited had originated in the singing and dancing of Dionysian revelers dressed in the costume of goats, and its very name — *tragoidia* — means "goat song." In Athens, the performances had been given a formal character in a theatre dedicated to Dionysus, and the dancing had assumed a quasi-dramatic quality. One Thespis of Icaria, an instructor in the sacred dance, had, in the sixth century B.C., set himself apart from the chorus as an individual performer playing a variety of roles. When his troupe appeared at Athens, no less a dignitary than Solon had denounced the innovation as deceptive and immoral, but the new dramatic art had proved too popular to suppress, and within a generation had resulted in regular dramatic competition at the Dionysian festival, using a chorus and a single actor.

By Aeschylus' day, certain theatrical traditions were well established. The plays were performed by daylight in outdoor theatres. The actor—the *hypokrites* or "answerer"—played all the personal roles in the drama, wearing appropriate masks with exaggerated features and brass mouthpieces to enhance the resonance of the voice. His height was increased by *kothornoi*, or thick-soled shoes, and by a headpiece known as an *onkos*. The chorus, all male, danced, sang, and provided a running interpretation of the significance of the action. Subject matter for the plays was usually provided by well-known Greek legends, many of them relating to characters involved in the Trojan War and its aftermath.

Aeschylus altered the character of tragedy by the addition of a second actor. This change, while not increasing the number of roles which could be represented, permitted dialogue between two principal characters in the same scene and was, therefore, a significant step in the direction of drama in the modern sense. There was apparently no restriction on the number of incidental characters who might be present on the stage.

The earliest of his surviving plays was probably the *Supplices*, or *Suppliant Women*, a work which, in the predominant role of the chorus, was closely related to the earlier form of Attic drama. It deals with the fifty daughters of Danaus, played by the chorus, who, with their father, flee to Argos to avoid marriage to the fifty sons of their uncle Aegyptus. The play, in order to be properly appreciated, would have to be seen as one element of a traditional trilogy, the other two parts of which unfortunately were lost. The second work, a historical drama called the *Persae*, or *Persian Women*, describes the battle of Salamis. In the *Supplices*, the playwright failed to scale the heights of the fully developed tragic drama, and produced a work more choral than dramatic in form. In *Seven against Thebes*, Aeschylus moved cautiously toward the dramatic maturity which was to characterize his later works. The last play of a trilogy dealing with the ill-fated Theban royal house, it specifically introduced the theme of undeserved suffering which was to recur in subsequent works of Greek tragedy and, a century or so later, in the Jewish book of Job.

The surviving *Prometheus Bound* may have been a part of a trilogy, the other plays of which were *Prometheus the Fire Bringer* and *Prometheus Unbound*. In this work, if not in earlier ones now lost, Aeschylus attained maturity as a poet and playwright. In his treatment of the Titan chained to a rock at the command of Zeus for his presumption in teaching men how to use fire, he presented a character who, though divine, is in every other respect, the archetypal tragic hero, unconquered in spirit by the inexorable forces which bring about his downfall and crying out, "Behold me, I am wronged!"

It was, however, in the *Oresteia*, produced two years before his death, that Aeschylus reached the peak of his dramatic genius. The three plays that compose the trilogy — *Agamemnon, Choephoroe*, and *Eumenides* —are based on one of the most widely exploited Greek stories — the fate of the house of Atreus, whose brother, Aegisthus, has sworn vengeance against him for the murder of Aegisthus' children. Aeschylus began the first play of the trilogy with the return from Troy of Atreus' son Agamemnon, who has alienated his wife Clytaemnestra when embarking for Troy, by sacrificing their daughter Iphigenia to secure favorable winds for the voyage. The drama continues with the ax murder by Clytaemnestra, in collusion with Aegisthus, of Agamemnon and the prophetess Cassandra, brought to Mycenae as a prisoner of war. In the *Choephoroe*, or *Libation Bearers*, Agamemnon's son Orestes, sent to Phocis as a boy by his mother, returns to Argos and, under the influence of his unforgiving sister Electra, murders their mother and Aegisthus to avenge their father's death. The third play tells of Orestes' flight over the face of the earth, pursued by the Eumenides, or "Well-Wishers," as the Erinyes, or Furies, were euphemistically called, and of the trial before the Athenian Areopagus in which Athena, breaking a tied vote, frees Orestes from the consequences of his act and thus confirms the primacy of law over blood vengeance.

Aeschylus was a volcanic poet in whom the fires of creativity burned with unsurpassed brightness. The horror of the actions of many characters in his plays is elevated from sordidness into tragedy by the greatness of their suffering and by a grandeur of conception which lifts their crimes into a realm which inspires awe at their magnitude and convinces the reader or spectator that the drama is being played on a cosmic stage in which inexorable forces transcending human nature—personified in the gods who appeared liberally throughout the plays—hold the reins of destiny. It is the affirmation of human dignity in the face of these forces which gave that tragedy its peculiar power in the Greek world and which has enabled it to speak to the Western mind for two millenia and more.

Underlying his clear-eyed recognition of the inevitability of human suffering was a deep-seated religious conviction which transcended the popular theology of his day to such an extent that the quality of his faith was not always evident to his contemporaries. On one occasion, in fact, he was charged with impiety when, as an actor in one of his own plays, he made a reference to Demeter which his audience interpreted as a violation of the secrets of Eleusis. In the ensuing riot, he saved his life by fleeing to the altar of Dionysus in the orchestra of the theatre. Brought before the Areopagus, he affirmed "that he did not know that what he said was secret." His brother Ameinias, speaking in the poet's defense, reminded the Assembly of the patriotism of the brothers by baring the wounds he had received at Salamis, and Aeschylus was acquitted. Actually, Aeschylus was not entirely orthodox in his piety. The attack leveled against the gods by his Prometheus was a devastating one, and only by moving into another dimension of faith was he able to preserve any confidence in the ultimate rightness of the universe. He did this by suggesting that the name of Zeus, applied in the *Prometheus* to a vengeful deity, might better be used to refer to a good beyond the gods—"the Law that is Fate and the Father and All-comprehending." In the *Agamemnon*, he called on the one God in an eloquent passage:

Zeus, Zeus, whate'er He be,
If this name He love to hear,
This He shall be called of me.
Searching earth and sea and air.

After the first performance of the *Oresteia*, he went to Sicily, where, in 456 B.C., according to a popular story, an eagle, holding in its claws a tortoise whose shell it had been unable to penetrate, killed the poet by dropping its carapaced prey on the bald head which the bird had mistaken for a stone.

## Sophocles

It does not stretch the bounds of probability to suppose that Aeschylus, returning to Athens after the destruction of the Persian fleet at Salamis, may have been present at the public celebration of the victory and, with his fellow citizens, looked on with benevolent approval as a chorus of boys, the flower of the city's youth, honored their elders' prowess with song and ritual dance. He would likely have known most of the young celebrants from their infancy and might well have taken a special interest in the principal chorister, a handsome boy of about fifteen, selected by the city to lead the group in recognition of his outstanding qualities of mind and body. The forty-five year old Aeschylus, watching young Sophocles, lyre in hand, dance around the trophies of battle, flushed with excitement at the high honor accorded him and the admiration of his elders, might well have predicted a brilliant future for the lad, but unless Dionysus favored him with a second vision, he could hardly have foreseen that the happy boy would one day secure a place beside Aeschylus himself as one of the supreme playwrights of the Western world.

Few men have been favored by nature and circumstance with greater gifts than Sophocles, and few have accepted with greater serenity the tragic reality which he saw as lying beneath the brightness with which his own life was flooded. He was a member of a well-to-do family and never knew the pinch of poverty. In his youth, he was renowned as an athlete and won the double prize for wrestling and music. He had great charm, a ready wit, and a becoming modesty. Despite a taste for pleasure, he had a strong sense of civic and religious duty. He held high office under Pericles and, in 440-439 B.C., served as a general in the Samian war.

Of the hundred and twenty odd plays he wrote, only seven survive, and the order in which they were produced is uncertain. At the age of twenty-five, he won the first of the many prizes he was to be awarded for best play in the Dionysian and Lenaean festivals. Like his predecessors, he acted in his own plays until a weakness of voice made it inexpedient for him to do so, and he made a significant contribution to the theatre by increasing the number of principals to three. He also enlarged the chorus from twelve to fifteen members and introduced painted stage scenery. Although Greek tradition required that plays be composed in trilogies, Sophocles was looser than Aeschylus in his observance of the convention, and his surviving dramas stand quite successfully as independent works.

The oldest of the plays, *Ajax*, deals with the self-willed and headstrong Greek warrior who, after the death of Achilles, has expected to be given the armor made for Achilles by Hephaestus. When it is awarded to Odysseus instead, Ajax resolves to murder the Greek generals. Athena throws him into a confusion in which he thinks the army's sheep and cattle are the offending chieftains. He deals death to some of them and, after binding some of the survivors together, proceeds to torment them preparatory to their execution. When he learns that he has made a fool of himself, he determines on suicide, and, despite an apparent change of heart, ultimately carries out his resolve and falls on his sword, receiving proper burial only at the insistence of Odysseus, whom he sought to kill.

The *Electra* of Sophocles is a re-telling of the familiar story of the murder of Clytaemnestra by her son. Unlike Aeschylus, who was fascinated by the appalling moral implications of the series of crimes which stained the house of Atreus, Sophocles found his principal interest in the exploration of the personalities of the characters, especially that of Electra, whose passionate hatred of her mother the poet developed with telling force. In Sophocles' play, the vengeful brother and sister are capable of performing the fatal act without soul-searching and of speaking of it afterwards with chilling good humor. "All is well within the house," Orestes reports on emerging from the room where he has killed his mother, and when Aegisthus, not knowing Pylades' or Orestes' identity, asks Electra where "the strangers" might be, she replies, "Inside. They have found a way to the heart of their hostess."

A psychological interest is similarly manifest in *The Trachinian Women*, which concentrates on the feelings of Deianeira, who sends her husband Heracles a robe which, unbeknownst to her, is poisoned and so brings about his death and her subsequent suicide. In the *Philoctetes* too, Sophocles explored a complex psychological problem, albeit one with moral implications, through a drama with much talk and little action about the efforts of a son of Achilles to induce a man earlier marooned by the Greeks on a desert island to rejoin his former comrades in the siege of Troy.

In *Oedipus the King*, Sophocles attained the summit of his art in producing one of the greatest of all tragedies. He based it on a legend familiar to all Athenians—the story of the son of Laius and Jocasta, doomed, according to an oracle, to kill his father and marry his mother. Exposed in infancy in an attempt by his parents to avoid their fate, he was found by a shepherd, who gave him to the king and queen of Corinth to be brought up as their own child. He learned of the prophecy from the oracle after growing to manhood and fled from Corinth, believing his foster parents to be his own. On the way to Thebes, he got into a quarrel with an older man and killed him, not knowing that the victim was his father. Later, he was confronted by the Sphinx, a winged creature with the head of a woman and the body of a lion. The monster had the unpleasant habit of killing travelers unable to answer a riddle it posed for them but, in a sporting gesture, had promised to kill itself if anyone solved the riddle. The Thebans, subjected to a reign of terror by the creature, had promised to acknowledge as heir to the throne anyone who could bring about their deliverance.

To the Sphinx's question as to what walks on four legs in the morning, two at noon and three in the evening, Oedipus answered correctly that it is a man, who crawls as a baby, walks erect in maturity, and uses a cane as an old man. The Sphinx, as good as its word, committed suicide, and when Oedipus turned up in Thebes, and Laius did not, they made him king. According to custom, he married the queen, Jocasta, and fathered two sons and two daughters.

It is at this point, that Oedipus makes his first appearance in Sophocles' tragedy. The city is suffering from a plague, and an oracle has said that it can be cleansed by the banishment or death of Laius' killer. Through revelation piled on revelation, Oedipus is forced to face the knowledge that he was, in fact, the slayer of his father and the husband of his mother. Jocasta, horrified at learning of her part in the fulfilment of the prophecy, hangs herself, and Oedipus, in anguish, tears the gold brooches from her clothing and puts out his eyes with them, exclaiming that they should never again witness such horrors. After commending his two daughters to Creon, his uncle—and brother in law—, he accepts exile

Years after the production of *Oedipus the King*, Sophocles took up the story again in *Oedipus at Colonus*, telling how the blind old king comes to a grove sacred to the Eumenides in the Athenian suburb. He is accompanied in his wanderings by his daughter Antigone, who has somehow managed to share his exile, and is joined at Colonus by his other daughter Ismene. After some encounters with Theseus, King of Athens, Polyneices, Oedipus' older son, and Creon, regent of Thebes, he hears the voice of a god calling him, says farewell to his daughters, and walks into the grove, accompanied by Theseus. Shortly afterwards, Oedipus has vanished, and the king alone is visible, "holding his hand before his face to screen his eyes, as if some dread sight had been seen, and such as none might endure to behold."

*Antigone*, which may have been written at an earlier date than the other two members of what is acutally a trilogy, carries on the story of the ill-fated family, with Oedipus' dutiful daughter as the principal character. She returns to Thebes to try to end a civil war between her brothers Polyneices and Eteocles. She is unsuccessful, the brothers are killed, and Creon, previously a supporter of Eteocles, becomes king. He decrees that Polyneices may not be give proper burial, and Antigone, deliberately disobeying his command, is asked by Creon if she has dared to transgress the law.

"Yes," she answers, "for it was not Zeus that had published that edict; not such are the laws set among men by the Justice who dwells with the gods below. Nor did I deem that your decrees were of such force that a mortal could override the unwritten and unfailing statutes of heaven. For their life is not of today or yesterday, but from all time; no man knows when they were first put forth."

Creon condemns her to be buried alive. His son Haemon, betrothed to Antigone, protests the sentence, and when his counsel is rejected, tells his father that he will never look on his face again. After a further series of events, the play reaches its climax with Antigone and Haemon both dead in the rocky tomb prepared for her, Haemon by his own hand. Creon's wife, learning of her son's fate, commits suicide.

Sophocles created dramas with a polished perfection of structure and language unmatched by any other Greek playwright. More orthodox in his religious views than other poets of the golden age, he found little to promote easy optimism in the relation of man to the gods, but behind the seeming injustice of Heaven, he, like Aeschylus, sensed a moral order which must ultimately triumph. In the meantime, while men must suffer, it is clear that Sophocles thought it best for them to suffer with the sort of grandeur which inspires great art.

Approaching the age of ninety, he was enjoying a liason with a hetaira named Theoris and busying himself with the writing of *Oedipus at Colonus* and the equally powerful *Philoctetes.* His legitimate son, Iophon, perhaps concerned lest his father might leave his considerable estate to Theoris' child, went to court to try to have Sophocles declared incompetent. To prove the clarity of his mind, the poet read the court passages from the play on which he was working, whereupon, he was promptly awarded a favorable judgment in the suit and escorted home in triumph by the judges. He died in 406 B.C and was accorded divine honors by his fellow countrymen.

## Euripides

While the middle-aged Aeschylus and the youthful Sophocles were celebrating the battle of Salamis, Euripides, who was to be the next great torchbearer of Athenian tragedy, was lying in his crib in the swaddling bands of infancy, probably on the island of Salamis itself, where he is said to have been born in the year—and, according to some accounts, on the day—of the battle. His parents, people of substance, had fled their home in Phyla to escape the invading Median army. As a young man, Euripides was a pupil of the great metaphysician Anaxagoras of Clazomenae and the Sophist Prodicus of Ceos. He was a close friend of Socrates and so sympathetic to the questioning spirit of the new philosophy that hostile critics branded him as one of the murderers of the tragic outlook. No less an authority than Aristotle, however, while not judging Euripides to be as great a master of dramatic technique as Aeschylus or Socrates, nevertheless called him "with all his faults the most tragic of the poets." Showing just enough respect for the state religion to avoid disaster, he was skeptical of the gods. On one occasion he was indicted unsuccessfully for impiety, and in one of his plays, now lost, he drew the audience to its feet in protest with the words, "O Zeus, if there be a Zeus, for I know of him only by report." A thoroughgoing "modern" in the perennial sense of the word, he assailed social injustice, war, slavery, and personal cruelty. He lacked Sophocles' easy conviviality and was not averse to a quiet life, spending much time in his later years on his native isle.

He wrote seventy-five plays, eighteen of which survive in their entirety. Many of them—his *Electra* and *Orestes*, for instance— were re-workings of plots already superbly exploited by Aeschylus and Sophocles. In Euripides' hands, however, they took on a new dimension. No poet has ever expressed more vividly the full nature of human grief or of the capacity of human beings to inflict suffering on their fellows.

In his *Electra*, the murder of Clytaemnestra by her children, though, by Greek tradition, not performed before the audience, is given overpowering emotional force by the cries of the victim offstage and by the harrowing account of the crime given by the matricides when they emerge from the house. A similar device was

80479

employed in the *Medea* to give awful immediacy to the murder by the jilted princess of her two children.

It was in *The Trojan Women*, though, that Euripides reached the most nearly unbearable heights of poignancy and—if unnecessarily arbitrary restrictions are not placed on the use of the word—of tragedy.

Troy has fallen, and the women of the city's chieftains are about to be carried off into slavery by the victorious Greeks. Talthybius, herald of the Greek army, reluctantly informs Andromache, Hector's widow, that the leaders of the conquerors have ruled that her little boy Astyanax must die by being dashed from the "crested wall of Troy." If she wishes the child to be properly buried, he tells her, she must refrain from cursing her captors and bear the fortunes of war as best she may. Andromache addresses the child:

> Go, die, my best-loved, my cherished one,
> In fierce men's hands, leaving me here alone.
> Thy father was too valiant: that is why
> They slay thee! Other children, like to die,
> Might have been spared for that. But on thy head
> His good is turned to evil . . . . . . . . . . . . . . . .
> . . . . . . . . . . . . . . . . . . . Weepest thou?
> Nay, why, my little one? Thou canst not know.
> And Father will not come; he will not come;
> Not once, the great spear flashing, and the tomb
> Riven to set thee free! Not one of all!
> His brethren, not the might of Ilion's wall.
> How shall it be? One horrible spring . . . deep, deep
> Down. And thy neck . . . Ah God, so cometh sleep!
> And none to pity thee! . . . Thou little thing
> That curlest in my arms, what sweet scents cling
> All round thy neck! Beloved; can it be
> All nothing, that this bosom cradled thee
> And fostered, all the weary nights, wherethrough
> I watched upon thy sickness, till I grew
> Wasted with watching? Kiss me. This one time;
> Not ever again. Put up thine arms, and climb
> About my neck: now kiss me, lips to lips . . . . . . . .
> . . . . . . . . . . . . . . . . . . . . . . . . . . . . . . . . . . . . .

Quick! take him: drag him: cast him from the wall,
If cast ye will! Tear him, ye beasts, be swift!
God has undone me, and I cannot lift
One hand, one hand to save my child from death . . ."

Talthybius bends over Andromache and gently separates the little boy from his mother.

Come, Child: let be that clasp of love
    Outwearied! Walk thy ways with me,
Up to the crested tower, above
    Thy father's wall . . . Where they decree
Thy soul shall perish.—hold him: hold!—
    Would God some other man might ply
These charges, one of duller mould,
    And nearer to the iron than I.

The child is taken away to the city wall and the mother to the Greek ships. Later in the play, Talthybius returns and leaves the dead child in the arms of his grandmother Hecuba, widow of King Priam and mother of the slain Hector. She says:

Ah, what a death hath found thee, little one!
Hadst thou but fallen fighting, hadst thou known
Strong youth and love and all the majesty
Of godlike kings, then had we spoken of thee
As of one blessed . . . . . . could in any wise
These days know blessedness. But now thine eyes
Have seen, thy lips have tasted, but thy soul
No knowledge had nor usage of the whole
Rich life that lapt thee round . . . . . Poor little child!
Was it our ancient wall, the circuit piled
By loving Gods, so savagely hath rent
Thy curls, these little flowers innocent
That were thy mother's garden, where she laid
Her kisses; here, just where the bone-edged-frayed
Grins white above—Ah heaven, I will not see!

Ye tender arms, the same dear mould have ye
As his; how from the shoulder loose ye drop
And weak! And dear proud lips, so full of hope
And closed for ever! What false words ye said
At daybreak, when he crept into my bed,
Called me kind names, and promised: 'Grandmother,
When thou art dead I will cut close my hair

And lead out all the captains to ride by
Thy tomb.' Why didst thou cheat me so? 'Tis I,
Old, homeless, childless, that for thee must shed
Cold tears, so young, so miserably dead.
    Dear God, the pattering welcomes of thy feet.
The nursing in my lap; and O, the sweet
Falling asleep together! All is gone.
How should a poet carve the funeral stone
To tell thy story true? 'There lieth here
A babe whom the Greeks feared, and in their fear
Slew him.' Aye, Greece will bless the tale it tells!

In these, as in countless other passages, Euripides united the literary skill of a great tragedian with the moral fervor of an Old Testament prophet. If he shared with Socrates the role of gadfly to an Athens needing to be aroused from its lethargy, he has also, with his great contemporary, proved to be one of those extraordinary thinkers who can speak with immediacy and authority to an age separated from his own by the gulf of more than two millenia. It was only after his death in 406 B.C., however, that his greatness was given full recognition in Athens. A gadfly is better appreciated when time has dulled the memory of his sting.

### Aristophanes

If it is profitable to look to the tragic poets for a timeless view of the profoundest depths of the human spirit, it is to the writers of comedy that one must turn for an understanding of the surface of the society which created the golden age of Athens.

Greek tragedy had little comic relief, but the tragic poets occasionally produced "satyr" plays in which wit and humor were given free rein. In time, as the writing of comic plays came to be recognized as a distinct and legitimate form of artistic activity, a separate prize was awarded for comedy at the Dionysian festivals. The democratic society of Athens allowed an almost unlimited range of freedom for personal and political satire, and the comic dramatists took full advantage of their immunity from censorship. Satiric comedy by its very nature implies some measure of opposition to the persons, customs, and institutions being satirized, and the liberalized character of the Periclean government led the comic playwrights to adopt a conservative stance, from which they poked fun at the radical innovations of the new age and established themselves as defenders of aristocratic conservatism. Socrates and

Euripides were favorite targets for their barbs, and Cratinus, one of the less restrained of the writers of comedy, went so far as to refer to Pericles himself as "the squill-headed God Almighty." Restraint, in fact, was not a notable characteristic of Athenian comedy. Broad, rowdy, vulgar, and uproariously funny, it held up a mirror to Hellenic society in which it could contemplate its own foibles, exaggerated by the curvature of the glass, like figures seen in a house of mirrors at a carnival.

Most notable of the satirists on all counts was Aristophanes, whose very name—"The best made manifest"—eminently suited him for his role as defender of the values of the nobility. Born about 448 B.C. into a cultivated family of Aeginan landowners, he moved to Athens as a young man when the Spartans invaded Attica. Aristophanes opposed the war. He also detested the government of a prosperous tanner named Cleon, who came to power in Athens after the death of Pericles in 429 B.C. In a lost play, *The Babylonians*, for which he was prosecuted and fined, he presented an unflattering picture of the chief of state, and two years later, in *The Knights*, he himself had to play the part of a character called "the Tanner" because no other actor would touch the role. In that play, he voiced some of his most biting criticisms of popular government. A general is trying to persuade a sausage seller to act to fulfill a prophecy that a practitioner of his trade will be the next ruler of the house of Demos (the people), whose major domo is the Tanner.

> Sausage Seller. Tell me this, how can I, a sausage-seller, be a big man like that?
>
> General. The easiest thing in the world. You've got all the qualifications: low birth, marketplace training, insolence.
>
> Sausage Seller. I don't think I deserve it.
>
> General. Not deserve it? It looks to me as if you've got too good a conscience. Was your father a gentleman?
>
> Sausage Seller. By the gods, no! My folks were scoundrels.
>
> General. Lucky man! What a good start you've got for public life!
>
> Sausage Seller. But I can hardly read.
>
> General. The only trouble is that you know anything. To be a leader of the people isn't for learned men, or honest

men, but for the ignorant and vile. Don't miss this golden opportunity.

In play after play, he mercilessly held up his fellow citizens and their institutions to public ridicule, sometimes even to the enjoyment of certain of his distinguished victims who, like many Englishmen of later centuries, were able to laugh at their own foibles as seen through the eyes of a witty critic. From forty-three to fifty-four comedies were ascribed to Aristophanes, of which eleven survive: *The Acharnians, The Knights, The Clouds, The Wasps, The Peace, The Birds, The Lysistrata, The Thesmophoriazusae* (Priestesses of Demeter) *The Frogs, The Ecclesiazusae* (women in the Assembly), and *The Plutus* (Wealth).

Master of hyperbole and ribaldry, Aristophanes showed a growing restraint and subtlety as he grew older. Throughout his career, he injected into his comedies wonderful passages of lyric poetry like the chant of the Dionysian Initiated in *The Frogs* and the chorus of the feathered inhabitants of Cloud-Cuckoo-Land in *The Birds*, who, in addressing mankind, say:

Ye children of man, whose life is a span,
Protracted with sorrow from day to day,
Naked and featherless, feeble and querulous,
Sickly calamatous creatures of clay,
Attend to the words of the sovereign birds,
Immortal, illustrious lords of the air,
Who survey from on high, with a merciful eye,
Your struggles of misery, labor, and care.

The date of his death is uncertain. It may have been about 385 B.C., and with his passing one of the most impressive chapters in the history of literature came to an end.

# IV.
# THEOLOGY AND
# JUSTICE
# IN HEBREW
# PROPHECY

# Chapter 10

# *"Do Justice and Love Kindness"*

Hebrew religion came to full bloom in the two centuries which followed the rise of the Assyrian Empire in the middle of the eighth century B.C. That flowering may be seen in the recorded oracles of the great prophets for whom books were named, especially Amos and Hosea, Isaiah and Jeremiah, Ezekiel and Second Isaiah. Those two centuries witnessed an unparalleled succession of great empires dominating the stage of history and rapidly falling into impotent decay. Assyria was conquered by Babylonia which was in turn replaced by Persia, and all three were constantly faced with the threat of opposition on their southwestern flank by Egypt and the small nations between them. Among those small nations which thus found themselves continually between the hammer of conquest and the anvil of exploitation were the twin Hebrew kingdoms, Israel and Judah.

The history of those two centuries, therefore, provides a clear exhibition of one of the most profound ideas in Western culture: that truth may be the product of tragedy, and that meaning and value are more often the fruit of suffering than of prosperity. The prophets lived through fire and storm. They were almost always unpopular, rejected and persecuted. They knew pain and loss in their personal experiences, and they, along with their beloved people, drank the bitter cup of judgment, filled with the dregs of apparent hopelessness. It was out of that suffering, that fire and hopelessness, that they spoke the "Word of Yahweh" which provided subsequent generations with their greatest source of moral teaching and undying hope.

Tiglath-pileser III came to the throne of Assyria about 745 B.C. and began the expansion of the empire toward the southwestern reaches of the Fertile Crescent. He was succeeded by five other powerful monarchs who, during the following century, swept over every nation between Mesopotamia and the Nile, finally realizing the ultimate goal of conquering Egypt and making it a province of the Assyrian Empire. Israel and Judah were among the "little peoples" who became subjects of Nineveh, and vassals of Assyria were always raided for slaves, emptied of treasure, and required to abandon their native culture, especially their religion, in favor of the ways of the conqueror.

Coincidental with the beginning of Assyrian expansion, Israel and Judah reached their peak of prosperity and power. With the deaths of Jeroboam II of Israel (746) and Uzziah of Judah (742), the two Hebrew nations were poised for rapid decline. The loss of strong leadership led immediately to confusion, decay, and what has been called a "delirious dance of death." The binding power of the Covenant was broken, resulting in social fragmentation. The Law of Moses was ignored and forgotten, leaving no guide for social justice and personal righteousness. And when idolatry became the chosen way of worship, the power of the Spirit was abandoned, or the Spirit reluctantly abandoned them, and the nations became empty shells of frenzied, frightened and selfish people. Their end was inevitable.

### Amos, the Prophet of Justice

Amos, the shepherd of Tekoa in Judah, stands at the head of the list of Hebrew preachers who are known as "the writing prophets" because their sermons were remembered, recorded and finally included among the books of the written canon. But Amos heads the list also in the sense that he apparently gave initial expression to some of the principles and positions which were to become fundamentally characteristic of Hebrew prophecy. Many of his bare suggestions were given stronger emphasis and broader development by later prophets and sages. Thus Amos deserves to be studied with care as one of the creative teachers of mankind.

Very little is known about the man apart from his message. He went to Bethel, the major sanctuary city of the northern kingdom, Israel, from his home in the wilderness of Judah, apparently during the last days of Jeroboam II. He alternately pleased, shocked and angered the people, including their chief priest, Amaziah. Without welcome or authority, he delivered a series of stinging oracles, indicting their ways and threatening cataclysmic judgment. He suggested that is was too late for repentance, announcing instead the horrors of impending doom. Then, threatened with the more visible power of priest and king, he turned away from the sick society and disappeared, leaving his thundering words to echo through all the years to come.

The unforgettable oracles of Amos are preserved in the little book that bears his name, a part of the Book of the Twelve in the Hebrew Scriptures. There are four sermons, three psalms, an apocalypse and a short narrative. The student of Hebrew thought should read the nine chapters with special care, enjoying their literary beauty as well as their moral power. A brief analysis of the structure of the book may be helpful here.

The first sermon (1:3 - 2:16) is a model of rhetorical acumen and psychological skill. Daring to speak for Yahweh, even at the sanctuary in Bethel and in the presence of the priest, the prophet gained immediate attention by roaring like a lion which had come from the estranged sister kingdom, Judah, and from the authentic temple in Jerusalem. He probably delighted his audience, however, by announcing the impending judgment of God upon all the surrounding nations, including even Judah among them. The seven nations were denounced—Syria, Philistia, Phoenicia, Edom, Ammon, Moab and Judah—and in each case a specific and historically typical sin was cited as the cause for the punishment which Yahweh would no longer withhold. But then, having pleased his hearers by arousing the natural instinct for vengeance, Amos delivered a scathing attack upon the people of Israel also. While they no doubt listened with shocked surprise at his impudence and severity, he proclaimed their indictment also by Yahweh and unmercifully predicted that the nation would soon be crushed like a bug under the wheels of a heavily-loaded cart.

The second sermon (3:1 - 15) is an enlargement of the same message, as is, indeed, the remainder of the book. Everything is a variation on the same theme, encompassing the essence of all Hebrew prophecy, that returning to Yahweh (teshubah, repentance) is the only way to escape the fatal consequences of idolatry, hypocrisy and injustice. The particular emphasis of the second sermon is upon the unique responsibility incumbent upon the people of God because of their privileged relationship in the Covenant. Thus Egypt and Assyria are summoned to be the instruments of Israel's destructive punishment.

The third sermon (4:1 - 12) raises the pitch of indictment to a higher key. The edge of sarcasm cuts without pity. Amos addressed the rich women as "cows of Bashan," well-fed and splendidly dressed dowagers whose only concern was for parties and pleasure: "who say to their husbands, 'Bring, that we may drink!' " He mimicked their falsely imagined hearing of an invitation from God to practice an empty ritual at their holy places, "for so you love to do, O people of Israel!" Then he attacked with a litany of past calamities—famine, drought, blight, pestilence and defeat—none of which had brought the intended repentance ad faithfulness. "Therefore," he commanded, with a voice of despair and disgust, "prepare to meet your God, O Israel!" It is a summons to trial for a capital offense.

The fourth sermon (5:1 - 6:14) continues the moral intensity of the third, beginning with a dramatic dirge over a fallen Israel, as though she were already overrun and slaughtered. Amos offered a flickering hope ("Seek me and live...Seek the Lord and live....") but quickly turned away from that possibility with utter resignation. Then he delivered a lengthy homily which comprises one of the greatest statements in all literature concerning the inseparable relation of religion and morality. It is another classic principle bequeathed to subsequent culture by Hebrew religion. Set like a diamond in a cluster of precious stones is the summary: "But let justice roll down like waters, and righteousness like an everflowing stream" (5:24).

In addition to the four sermons, the book contains three psalm-like passages (4:13, 5:8 - 9, 9:5 - 6) which present the majesty, power and presence of Yahweh, the Covenant God of Israel. But, perhaps more significantly, the book records a long passage (chapters 7 - 9) which suggests the beginning of apocalypticism at least as early as the eighth century B.C. The preacher-prophet becomes a seer, using the vehicle of vision as a device for prediction, warning and judgment. There is a description of five visions, all signifying agents of doom. The first two, a plague of locusts and a burning drought, are mercifully withheld because of the intercession of the seer. But the other three become inevitable, possibly because the third, the testing of Israel with a plumb line, reveals the moral crookedness and spiritual instability of the people who find even their temple collapsing upon them and who discover to their horror that there is no place to hide, either in Sheol or in heaven.

A short narrative completes the book (7:10 - 17). It clearly illuminates the opposing roles of prophet and priest. The priest, Amaziah, with his vested interests and religious authority, disdainfully challenged the authenticity of Amos as a prophet. But Amos responded with the prophet's unsubstantiated claim of

Yahweh's commission. Then, with words of terrible judgment upon the priest and his whole family, Amos turned away from Bethel and walked off the stage of history.

Many have claimed a special stature for Amos because he stood at the head of the line, the earliest of the "writing prophets." It was stated above that he was an initiator, one of the greatest creative teachers of mankind. What, then, were his seminal teachings? What were the ideas which he contributed to the prophetic tradition of Israel, which have been laid as foundation stones for the edifice of Western culture?

At least six major themes from the prophet Amos may be given particular notice:

1. The special responsibility of Israel as the "chosen people" of Yahweh. This is a fundamental assumption which runs through all Hebrew religion. It may be traced back explicitly to the call of the Patriarch Abraham, and it reappears with increasing clarity at every stage of the story. Later prophets, as we shall see, made it a matter of central concern. It also provided the basis for theological debate and development in later Judaism and Christianity. Amos stated the truth and its consequences with unequivocal starkness: "You only have I known of all the families of the earth; therefore I will punish you for all your iniquities" (3:2).

2. The concept of a faithful, redeemed remnant. This pregnant notion had already been suggested, of course, on various occasions in Hebrew history. One example may be found in the well-known story of Elijah's flight to Horeb when Yahweh reminded him, "Yet I will leave seven thousand in Israel, all the knees that have not bowed to Baal, and every mouth that has not kissed him" (I Kings 19:18). Here, indeed, is the seed that will grow into a large plant with many branches. One thinks immediately of the *Qahal* (cf. Isaiah, later), the New Covenant (cf. Jeremiah), the synagogue, and even the coming Christian Church. The idea was expressed picturesquely by Amos: "Thus says the Lord: 'As the shepherd rescues from the mouth of the lion two legs, or a piece of an ear, so shall the people of Israel who dwell in Samaria be rescued, with the corner of a couch or a part of a bed' " (3:12).

3. The Day of the Lord as a time of judgment. Much has been written by modern scholars concerning the origin and meaning of the phrase, *Yom Yahweh*. It appears to be accurate to say that Amos adopted a familiar idea and used it as a club of judgment

rather than as an expression of hope. "Woe to you who desire the day of the Lord! Why would you have the day of the Lord? It is darkness, and not light; as if a man fled from a lion, and a bear met him; or went into the house and leaned with his hand against the wall, and a serpent bit him" (5:18 - 19). At least it is certain that many future speakers and writers took up the same theme, warning that false hope would be turned to despair.

4. A more refined, implicit monotheism. It is impossible, of course, to derive adequate details from the few extant oracles of Amos to know with any certainty what eighth-century Hebrews in general or Amos in particular believed in terms of a doctrine of God. The evidence seems to suggest that all Hebrews were at best henotheists until after the Babylonian Exile. However, the three brief psalms in Amos point to a theological development that was moving inevitably from polytheism to monotheism.

5. The prophetic antipathy toward the cult. Amos gave one of the earliest warnings on record of the inherent danger that religious form always tends to become rigid, perverted and empty of content. True prophets ever since have warned that the subtle, fatal disease of all piety is ritual for its own sake. The very appearance of the judgmental Amos at the sanctuary of Bethel, as well as the confrontation with Amaziah, are dramatic signs of these truths. But, as we shall see, the estrangement between prophet and cult becomes more pronounced with every passing generation. Amos gave classic form to the assessment by Yahweh: "I hate, I despise your feasts, and I take no delight in your solemn assemblies... I will not accept them... I will not look... I will not listen...."(5:21 - 23).

6. The use of apocalypticism as an expression of both judgment and hope. We shall reserve our discussion of the nature of apocalypticism for a later chapter concerned with the period when it becomes dominant in Jewish life and literature. However, notice should be taken here of the presence of this genre even as early as Amos. The presentation of the five visions in the last three chapters of the book gives undeniable evidence that apocalyptic did not appear *de novo* in post-exilic Judaism but rather had its origins at least among the early prophets. The prophets were primarily moral preachers calling for repentance and faithfulness in their own times, but, as early as Amos, they artistically used lurid colors and harsh sounds to depict both an awful judgment to come and an undying hope in the ultimate victory of God and goodness.

## Hosea, the Man Who Discovered God

The prophet Hosea was a contemporary of Amos, though his work was apparently extended longer into the last days of Israel's death. He was the only prophet native to Israel whose recorded oracles have survived. There is no real evidence that he ever heard or knew of Amos, but the possibility cannot be denied. There are similarities as well as differences between their oracles and they certainly shared a common perspective with regard to the nation and its inevitable fall in consequence of its unfaithfulness to Yahweh. They were like two musicians playing the same symphony; Amos played a blaring brass and a crashing cymbal while Hosea accompanied on the strings, especially with the sad tones of the cello. The coming terror which Amos described in visions, Hosea saw before his own eyes and suffered in his own heart.

Little more is known about the life of Hosea than about that of Amos. What can be surmised has been the subject of much doubt and debate, especially the story of his personal tragedy with Gomer, his unfaithful but beloved and forgiven wife. It does seem evident, however, that Hosea prophesied in Israel during most if not all of the quarter of a century following the death of Jeroboam II in 746 B.C. They were days of instability in a desperate nation, wracked with civil war and torn by frantic attempts to stave off the inexorable catastrophe approaching with the armies of Assyria. Hosea could only weep and hope, like Jeremiah a century later in Judah.

The surviving book of Hosea accurately symbolizes the conditions of the time of its origin by its corrupted text and jumbled, disorganized structure. The ancient Hebrew text contains an unusual number of words and constructions which are difficult and uncertain, and the oracles are strung together with little if any regard to temporal order or topical logic. The only clear division that may be found in the book is that separating chapters 1 - 3 from 4 - 14. Any other outline of the material must be arbitrarily imposed.

The first of these parts contains the account of the prophet's marriage to Gomer, the birth and naming of their three children, and the pain that both broke the heart and opened the eyes of Hosea as a result of the unfaithfulness of his beloved. Volumes have been written since ancient times by both Jewish and Christian interpreters in an attempt to explain what actually happened and why. Were there two women involved, or only one? Was Hosea commanded by God to marry a prostitute? Were the children illegitimate? Did Gomer, after her marriage to Hosea and the birth of the children, only then become an adultress? Is the whole story to be taken as a literal account of personal experience, or is it better interpreted as an allegory, a means of expressing Hosea's central idea but never intended to be understood literally?

The answers to these questions can never be given with certainty. Fortunately, that is not a matter of primary importance. Whatever the facts, a moral and theological truth of first magnitude was given expression in the passage, and that is what should not be missed. Let it be noted, however, that the usual order in Hebrew religious experience is to go from event to truth, rather than from truth to story as simply a means of elucidation, though that is certainly not always the case.

The essential story is that Hosea married Gomer and she bore him three children. The first, a son, was given the name "Jezreel," intended to point to the judgment of Yahweh upon the "house of Jehu," to which the king, Jeroboam II, belonged, because of its historic cruelty and injustice. The royal house would reap what it had sown ("Jezreel" is from the word "to reap"). The second child, a daughter, was called Loruhamah, "Not-pitied," a clear sign that Yahweh would no longer withhold punishment. The third, another son, was similarly named Loammi, "Not-my-people," as a symbol of rejection. Then follows the mysterious account of Gomer's harlotry and eventual enslavement, culminating in her unimaginable ransom, forgiveness and restoration by her husband. Could a righteous Hebrew go beyond all human nature, expectation and social convention to do such a thing? Is *that* the nature of love?

The second part of the book, chapters 4-14, is composed of poetic oracles that are unsurpassed in power and pathos. They remind the reader of the ocean, rising and falling from the depths, sometimes gentle and soothing but often frothy with anger and terrifying by the continual beating of their sweeping, irresistible waves. Memorable words are found here, phrases that have become an indelible part of subsequent culture.

Those oracles have bequeathed a legacy of meaning and value to all mankind. They stand as irrefutable testimony that pain may be redemptive, that tears may function as microscopes enabling vision to become magnified, and aiding sight to gain insight to truths otherwise never known. Four of Hosea's major teachings may be listed as follows:

1. The root of all evil is covenant-breaking. Hosea, of course, thought in the context of Israel's covenant with Yahweh; however, the same essential truth may be applied to any human condition. He learned the lesson from his experience with Gomer, and the parallel with Israel as the chosen, beloved bride of Yahweh was immediately evident. That is the unmistakable truth at the center of the first three chapters. There is an inevitable order in human sinfulness: first, the rejection of God, the separation of the self from the ground that constituted it; second, the alienation from other persons, the breakdown of all sustaining human relationships; and, finally, the schizophrenic fragmentation of the person into lonely misery, despair and death.

2. A vital knowledge of God is not cognitive but existential. "There is no faithfulness or kindness, and no knowledge of God in the land. . . My people are destroyed for lack of knowledge. . . . Let us know, let us press on to know the Lord. . ." (4:1, 6; 6:3). In consistent Hebrew fashion, Hosea spoke of knowledge as an intimate, spiritual relation between persons. He did not mean that the Israelites needed merely improved instruction or a more orthodox creed; rather they were not committed and faithful, and hence their religion provided no vitality.

3. The essential characteristic of God is love. This is the teaching of Hosea which was suggested by our heading, above, that Hosea was "the man who discovered God." He was the first to put *primary* emphasis upon Yahweh's everlasting love and faithfulness to his people, even in spite of their rejection of him. The Hebrew term, so important to Hosea, is *chesed*. It is the love that forgives and restores with creative power. Yahweh says: "When Israel was a child, I loved him, and out of Egypt I called my son. . . . How can I give you up, O Ephraim! How can I hand you over, O Israel!"(11:1, 8). The claim may be made that out of his tragic experience with Gomer, culminating in her forgiveness and restoration, Hosea came to understand that he could so love only because God does so first and supremely.

4. The way out of sin and death is found in returning. The heart of all prophecy is the call to repentance, *teshubah*. "Come, let us return to the Lord; for he has torn, that he may heal us; he has stricken, and he will bind us up" (6:1). Hosea illustrated the idea by

the return of his wife, showing, more profoundly, the necessary initiative of graceful forgiveness. This idea of return as the means of reconstitution was expressed, though differently, in the literature and philosophy of Greece, and it has become a major theme in modern psychology and theology. But we should not overlook the necessary condition made explicit by Hosea, that the power of restoration lies with the forgiver, not the forgiven. Herein lies a fountainhead of the grand teaching of prevenient, irresistible grace.

# Chapter 11

# *"Walk Humbly With Your God"*

The prophet Isaiah was a contemporary of Amos and Hosea, but whereas their sermons were directed to the northern Hebrew kingdom, Israel, his work was apparently in Judah exclusively. He has often been called "the prince of the prophets" because many have suggested that he may have been in some way related to the reigning family of Judah, the House of David. At any rate he appears to have had easy access to the kings who ruled during his long lifetime, and he lived in the capital city of Jerusalem.

Isaiah began his prophetic work "in the year that King Uzziah died," 742 B.C. That event marked the end of an era for Judah, as was the case nearly simultaneously for Israel with the death of Jeroboam II in 746. The following half-century was to be a period of horror, conquest and enslavement for many of the small nations between Mesopotamia and Egypt, including both Israel and Judah, as Assyria suddenly awakened from her lion's den on the Tigris and went on a bloody rampage throughout the west. Amos warned of its coming, Hosea suffered its beginnings, and Isaiah experienced the agony of its reality.

The armies of Assyria under their new monarch, Tiglath-pileser III, the "Pul" of the Hebrew Scriptures (II Kings 15:19), first protected their eastern flank by conquering Babylonia and annexing it into their empire. Then, wheeling west and south, they rapidly overran the small city-states and kingdoms along the coast of the Mediterranean, defeating Syria and making it a province of Assyria in 732 B.C. Israel was next, and Judah would be sure to follow. However, the inevitable was postponed for a few years by Israel's submission. Galilee and Gilead were ceded to the conqueror, a large annual tribute was paid, and, in 732, an Assyrian puppet, Hoshea, was placed on the throne of Israel at Samaria.

The costly respite did not last long for Israel. It should be noted that the merciless cruelty and crushing power of Assyria made attempts to revolt inevitable at every opportunity. Such times seemed to appear when the death of every Assyrian ruler was followed by a period of necessary consolidation by the next king.

Therefore, when "Pul" died, in 727 B.C., to be succeeded by Shalmaneser V, Hosea of Israel seized the apparent chance to regain independence. Israel withheld tribute and sought an alliance with Egypt against Assyria. "Then the king of Assyria invaded all the land and came to Samaria, and for three years he besieged it. In the ninth year of Hoshea the king of Assyria captured Samaria, and he carried the Israelites away to Assyria, and placed them in Halah, and on the Habor, the river of Gozan, and in the cities of the Medes" (II Kings 17: 5-6). The catastrophe that Amos had predicted came to pass. Israel, conquered and scattered, disappeared from the stage of history.

Isaiah's small, mountain homeland, Judah, survived, though just barely. It was no match for Assyria, as Isaiah very well knew. The question now was how to survive. There appeared to be only two options: to resist, with the help of Egypt, and thus perhaps to thwart the historic expansionistic ambitions of Assyria; or to capitulate, becoming another humiliated vassal of Nineveh. Ahaz, the Davidic king of Judah, chose the latter, cowardly course, making thereby a "covenant with death." But Isaiah, with prophetic vision, saw another way.

### The Authentic Oracles of Isaiah

It is probably wise at this point to pause for an investigation of the book of Isaiah to determine the limits of the authentic oracles of the prophet. The student will observe that Isaiah is a big book of sixty-six chapters. However, all this contains a complex anthology of prophetic material, much of it from other hands and later times, which ultimately came to be collected and written on one scroll of the Hebrew canon by later editors. It is probable that the extant oracles of the eighth-century prophet are so limited in scope as to make little more material than we have seen in Hosea.

Most scholars have long agreed that chapters 40 through 66 contain a variety of prophetic materials which came from a later time, probably in the sixth century B.C. and beyond. That leaves only thirty-nine chapters to be considered here. The evidence for this judgment is weighty and convincing and may be found in any good introduction or commentary. It is sufficient to say here only that the second half of the book bears witness to its later origin by its historical references, its literary distinctiveness, and its obviously more developed theology.

For convenience in study, the first thirty-nine chapters may be divided into four parts. First, chapters 1-12 contain most of the authentic sermons of the prophet and his essential message. Second, 13-23 is a series of oracles against the nations, probably of later composition by other writers. Third, 24-35 is a collection of apocalyptic utterances, probably also from later seers, mixed with a few passages from the last years of Isaiah's ministry. And, finally, 36-39 is narrative history about current events, clearly borrowed by the editor from II Kings, or from a common source.

## Creative Events in the Career of Isaiah

The story of Isaiah's life illustrates the formation of all Hebrew prophecy. The prophets were active participants in the affairs of their times and their messages were forged on the anvil of public affairs. They reacted to tragedy by interpreting its meaning; they overcame pain and loss by appreciating joy and understanding value. Even more than his contemporaries, Amos and Hosea, Isaiah endured the shocking anarchy of the second half of the eighth century B.C., and it was precisely out of that crucible that he produced the insights that have been considered ever since to be the purest gold of prophecy. At least five critical events may be observed as creative causes of his religious insight and inspiration.

Isaiah's prophetic career began with his transforming vision, recorded, with such memorable power and mystery, in the sixth chapter. It is a brief and rare page of autobiography, bequeathing to posterity the intimate experience of true mysticism in which a finite man stands naked and dependent before the terrifying light of holiness, suddenly aware of his creatureliness and sinfulness but also sustained by the redemption and strength that come through confession, forgiveness and acceptance. The man with unclean lips is healed and commissioned as a messenger of God.

The message of the young prophet is found in the collection of oracles comprising the first twelve chapters of the book. The words are similar to those of Amos and Hosea. They are also paralleled by the prophecies of Micah, another contemporary, who lived in the rural areas to the southeast of Jerusalem which felt the pillaging devastation of the Assyrian troops while the people of Jerusalem remained relatively secure in their walled, mountain fortress. It should at least be noticed here, in passing, that the one best known statement of Micah (6:8) is a splendid summary of the essential teaching of the other three eighth-century prophets whose sermons are extant:

> He has showed you, O man, what is good;
> and what does the Lord require of you
> but to do justice [Amos], and to love kindness [Hosea],
> and to walk humbly with your God? [Isaiah]

The message of Isaiah is the familiar one of unremitting judgment upon the people of God, but the tenor is different from the others in that the point of departure is more transcendent. Like all the prophets, Isaiah spoke for God. However, he preached as one who stood, in all humility, by the throne of him who is "high and lifted up" (6:1). He delivered Yahweh's condemnation upon specific groups, especially the priests (1:10-17), the wealthy (3:18 - 4:1), and the national leaders (notice the seven "woes" in 5:8 - 24 and 10:1 - 4). And one of his oracles, the unforgettable "Song of the Vineyard" (5:1 - 7), is a fearful indictment of the whole Covenant People. The poetic parable accuses both Israel and Judah of producing "bad fruit," summarizing Yahweh's judgment in the classic passage:

> and he looked for justice [mishpat],
> but behold, bloodshed [mishpah];
> for righteousness [sedhaqah],
> but behold, a cry [se'aqah]! (5:7b)

After the call and commission to prophesy determined the career of the young Isaiah, probably triggered by the death of the great king, Uzziah, another event occurred on the international scene which gave form to the message of the prophet. The approaching threat of Assyrian power caused Syria and Israel, around 734 B.C., to form a coalition among the small western states in a vain attempt to protect themselves. Their kings, Rezin and Pekah, sought to force the participation of Ahaz of Judah. (The event is recorded in II Kings 15-17 and in Isaiah 7-8.) Isaiah counseled Ahaz not to join the alliance, and thereby Judah escaped the subsequent destruction of her two northern neighbors. Probably the most significant result of the crisis relative to Isaiah's role in it was the giving of the "sign of Immanuel" (7:14). Endless and sometimes vitriolic debate has ensued concerning the meaning of the prophecy, with reference both to its application to later Messianic teachings and, in Christian theology, regarding the claim to "virgin motherhood." That debate aside, Isaiah was clearly giving a message to Ahaz and Judah by a sign from Yahweh that they need have no fear of Rezin and Pekah because God's protective presence is his gracious response to faithfulness in every crisis of life and history. God would be with them (Immanuel, "God with us") even in spite of their unfaithfulness; and "the River," Assyria, that would destroy their enemies, though flooding them also, would not bring death (8:5 - 8).

A closely related creative event during the life of Isaiah was the fawning capitulation of Ahaz to Tiglath-pileser III at their meeting in Damascus (II Kings 16:7 - 18). Not only did Ahaz, following Isaiah's wise counsel, refuse to join the Syro-Israelite coalition against Assyria; he even became the apparently willing vassal of Assyria, going so far as to procure a model of the pagan altar of the Assyrians so that a copy could be built before the Temple of Yahweh in Jerusalem, replacing the ancient cultic symbols there. Isaiah, of course, reacted with dismay to this adoption of idolatry. His words and deeds supplied both judgment and hope to the people, providing symbols and ideas which were to become major components of future Hebrew, Jewish and Christian faith and theology. He named one son She'ar-jashub, meaning "a remnant shall return," thereby expressing confidence in the preservation of God's people beyond judgment. He named another son Maher-shalal-hash-baz, "the spoil speeds, the prey hastes," pointing to the cutting cruelty of Assyria, the "hired razor" of Yahweh (7:20). He had already spoken to the king about the child, Immanuel, who, even as an infant, was a constant reminder of the presence of God— to protect *or* to punish. And, finally, he demonstrated the way in which God's work and purpose would be accomplished in the future by calling together a faithful group of disciples who would insure both the preservation of his message and the ultimate triumph of righteousness (8:16).

One of the memorable poetic oracles of Isaiah, probably growing out of the Syro-Israelite affair, was the charge that the people of Judah, including their cowardly king, Ahaz, failed to appreciate the value of Yahweh's gentle care and providence. They "refused the waters of Shilo'ah that flow gently" (8:6). Isaiah by these words pointed to the aqueduct which carried vital water to Jerusalem from the Spring of Gihon. It was because they had no faith that they lacked stability (7:9b).

A fourth international crisis which contributed to the insights of Isaiah took place during his later years. He may have withdrawn temporarily from the public arena because of the open paganism of Ahaz, giving attention for a while to the instruction of a creative minority. However, Ahaz was succeeded in 715 B.C. by Hezekiah, a strong king who was much praised by the Deuteronomic editor of II Kings for his Yahwistic reforms. Isaiah apparently became the confidant and counselor of Hezekiah. Shortly thereafter, the government of Egypt instigated a rebellion by several of Judah's neighbors, centered in the ancient Philistine city of Ashdod, against their overlord, Assyria, whose emperor now was Sargon II. Egypt, of course, promised help in the rebellion. Isaiah had nothing but contempt for such promises by Egypt because he knew they were empty and dangerous. The Pharaohs of the Nile were simply playing their cheap game of urging the small nations to fight Egypt's battles with Assyria. Isaiah therefore ridiculed Egypt and urged Hezekiah not to become involved in the rebellion.

The prophet again resorted to signs as well as words to dramatize his message. Already clothed in sackcloth, a symbol of repentance and mourning, Isaiah put off his shoes and donned the bare loincloth of a slave, thus walking around Jerusalem "naked and barefoot for three years" (20:3) in demonstration of the certain enslavement of its people if they participated in the futile conspiracy against Assyria. Fortunately, Hezekiah heeded the advice and Judah was saved for a little longer.

Nevertheless, the respite was short-lived. Sargon II died in 705 B.C. and, as noted above, there was the usual turmoil throughout the empire as the suppressed nations seized the opportunity for freedom during the interim of uncertainty. This time the revolt was unusually widespread; Babylonia, to the southeast of Assyria's heartland, attempted to regain its independence. The vassal king of Babylonia, the Merodach-baladan of II Kings 20 and Isaiah 39:1, joined forces with Egypt and enlisted the participation of the small nations of the west. This time Hezekiah ignored the advice of Isaiah and became openly involved in the conspiracy, even taking Padi, king of the Philistine city of Ekron, as a prisoner in order to force solidarity against Assyria. Since the new emperor, Sennacherib, had hardly settled on the throne in Nineveh, such a widespread revolution appeared to be certain to succeed. National deliverance was in sight.

Confident as they were, Babylonia, Egypt and Judah did not adequately estimate the genius of Sennacherib. With a rapid series of campaigns, he led the Assyrian armies to crush the Babylonian rebellion and, having secured his eastern flank, marched inexorably through the west, devastating the countryside and conquering the conspirators one by one. The Egyptians were defeated in the Philistine plain and fled home to lick their wounds, weak and cowardly as Isaiah had predicted.

The account of Sennacherib's punishment of Hezekiah is one of the most dramatic in ancient history. Reported with great bravura in the Taylor Prism and substantiated in both II Kings 18-19 and Isaiah 36-37, the story is told in remarkable detail of the Assyrians' strangling conquest of Lachish, the Philistine center of revolt, and of how Sennacherib's chief deputy, "The Rabshakeh," beseiged Jerusalem, shutting up Hezekiah "like a caged bird." The Rabshakeh, backed by his powerful army, strutted before the walls and teased the frightened emissaries of Hezekiah as well as all the defenders of the city. When requested to speak quietly and in Aramaic, so as not to alarm the people listening on the walls, he only became more mocking and threatening. "On what do you rest this confidence of yours? Do you think that mere words are strategy and power for war?. . . ." (Isaiah 36:4 - 6). He scornfully reminded them of their unfaithfulness to their God, and claimed that Yahweh had sent Assyria to punish them. He even challenged them to a contest, offering to provide Judah with two thousand horses of war if they could furnish riders! It was a terrifying day for Judah, when defeat and extinction stood at the gate.

Within the city, Isaiah counseled Hezekiah with apparent nonsense. He advised calm and confidence. He claimed that Jerusalem would be saved by the power and will of Yahweh, who would protect his Zion so that Sennacherib would not "come into this city, or shoot an arrow there, or come before it with a shield, or cast up a seige-mound against it. . . . For I will defend this city to save it, for my own sake and for the sake of my servant David" (Isaiah 37:33 - 35). And that is what happened. For reasons that are obscure, the Assyrian army withdrew at the last moment. The record, both that of the Scriptures and other sources, hints at plague in the enemy camp as well as "a rumor" of serious rebellion at home in Nineveh. Whatever the explanation, Jerusalem was saved, Isaiah was vindicated, and Judah was to survive for more than a century.

This dramatic and unexpected rescue may have been the occasion for a Hebrew poet to compose the 46th Psalm:

Come, behold the works of the Lord,
How he has wrought desolations in the earth.
He makes wars cease to the end of the earth;
He breaks the bow, and shatters the spear,
He burns the chariot with fire!
Be still and know that I am God.
I am exalted among the nations,
I am exalter in the earth!

And with the same sense of triumph and security, the prophet Isaiah appears to have come to the end of his ministry. His last days are not recorded, though they may have lasted until the dark reign of Manasseh.

### The Lasting Legacy of Isaiah

The claim was made, above, that Isaiah produced golden insights out of the searing heat of suffering, thus fulfilling his prophetic character. Undoubtedly, his teachings have been both preserved and developed in such a manner as to contribute major themes to the religious and even political history of the West. He took some of the ideas of the past and recast them, adding also the Word of the Lord as he heard it in the catastrophic noises of his own time. We will briefly examine a few major examples of his legacy.

First, Isaiah was apparently the original theologian of the holiness of God. That emphasis upon the majesty and transcendence of Yahweh is heard in the account of his transforming call (chapter 6). From that point on, he habitually referred to Yahweh as "the Holy One." The idea of holiness had been an important aspect of Hebrew religion at least since the experience at Sinai, as we have observed earlier; but it remained for Isaiah to apply the concept in a more precise and descriptive sense to the very nature of Israel's God. His emphasis on God's "otherness" gave impetus to the historic development in Israel of the conscious and fundamentally uncompromising monotheism which probably began with the henotheism of the Patriarchs and Moses, received nurture in the work of the oral prophets (especially Elijah), and reached full expression in the lyric oracles of the later prophet of the Exile whose teachings were finally incorporated in the second half of the scroll of Isaiah. The teaching was also the centripetal force which, more than any other, was to bind together the Covenant People even in the coming diaspora. The passing of time would of necessity lead to the logic: if Yahweh is truly *holy* he is therefore *only*; and if he is both holy and only, he is *creator* and *sustainer*, which means he is Lord of both nature and history. With a faith like that, Israel would survive any trial that history might bring. And the moral consequences of that faith would become increasingly demanding. In a word, with his emphasis upon the holiness of God, Isaiah sowed the seeds of the deepest theology and the highest ethic.

Closely related to Isaiah's idea of the holiness of Yahweh was his constant reference to history as the realm of Yahweh's Lordship. For him, God's transcendence by no means meant the absence of God from the affairs of men and nations. As suggested above, Isaiah claimed, repeatedly and explicitly, that the events of history, whether they are the birth of a child or the struggles of great nations, are directed by the hand of the Almighty. Assyria was the rod of his anger and the staff of his fury (10:5) and he used it as a hired razor to cut down the nations he would punish (7:20); but no one should confuse the instrument with its wielder. "Shall the ax vaunt itself over him who hews with it, or the saw magnify itself against him who wields it? As if a rod should wield him who lifts it, or as if a staff should lift him who is not wood!" (10:15) Yahweh directs the course of history, according to Isaiah, and he is the source of both rewards and punishments. It is both wicked and foolish to disobey him since his purpose cannot be thwarted. The golden age of peace and righteousness is sure to come (2:2-4; 9:1-7).

Such sweeping claims for Yahweh raised a plethora of moral and theological questions in the future. Not least among them was that of Israel's consequent relation to the other peoples of the world. And what of an adequate theodicy: how can the fact of evil, in all forms in the world, be explained if God is both righteous and almighty? We shall see these and similar issues in the thoughtful struggle of later men of faith. It is sufficient here to take note of Isaiah's part in creating the questions.

A third significant contribution of Isaiah may be seen in his recasting of the idea of the Remnant. Amos had spoken of the providential preservation of a faithful minority, at least in his metaphorical reference to "a piece of an ear" and "the corner of a couch and part of a bed" (Amos 3:12), and it was possibly a frequent expression of hope amid judgment in Israel. The idea received concrete form in the perilous time of Ahaz when Judah became the willing vassal of Assyria. In the face of the resultant adoption of paganism in Jerusalem, Isaiah gathered a small coterie of disciples and entrusted to them a faithful witness to the historic faith of Israel. He also spoke in several oracles of the near and distant future when the faithful would survive all adversity and share the final triumph of their God. As we shall see, this optimism in disaster was to be developed further by later prophets and apocalyptists, particularly Jeremiah and Ezekiel, becoming part of the content and structure of Biblical religion.

Again, one of the most familiar and characteristic themes in the prophecy of Isaiah was his so-called "royal theology" about the covenant with David and the messianic age to come. This was the center pole of Isaiah's vision of the future and around it were clustered his related teachings concerning Yahweh's mighty deeds in history, the saving of the Remnant, and the protection of Zion, the city of David. The evidence indicates that there had been a common belief among the Hebrews since the days of the United Monarchy that Yahweh had given an irrevocable promise to David that his House would survive along with his city, Jerusalem (cf. II Samuel 7 and I Kings 11:34-36). Thus in the midst of decay and disaster, Isaiah sustained a stubborn hope that a bright future was assured. "The Day of Yahweh" would bring woes beyond description but ultimately there would appear a new David, from "the stump of Jesse," upon whom the Spirit of Yahweh would rest. He would thus be the Davidic heir, the Anointed One (Hebrew, "messiah"). He would judge the earth with righteousness and bring perfect peace to nature and men (chapters 9 and 11). We hardly need to be reminded of the historic significance of these grand passages in later Judaism and especially in Christianity.

Finally, Isaiah added a dimension to the role of Jerusalem in the history of mankind. We noticed earlier that Isaiah assured King Hezekiah, during the seige of Jerusalem by the armies of Sennacherib, that Yahweh would protect the city "for my own sake and for the sake of my servant David." The same conviction is found expressed in various forms in many oracles of the prophet. "Like birds hovering, so the Lord of hosts will protect Jerusalem; he will protect and deliver it, he will spare and rescue it" (31:5).

From such teachings there arose what is called Isaiah's doctrine of "the inviolability of Jerusalem." The record of history since

Isaiah's time shows the significance of that special place in the faith, the passion and the struggles of men and nations. Often conquered and destroyed, it has been repeatedly rebuilt. Jerusalem remains the holy city of Jews, Christians and Muslems, and it stands as a symbol of God's presence in the past and his final abode in the unseen age to come. Jews cry out, "next year in Jerusalem." Muslems revere it as the holy city of the Patriarchs and the site of the Prophet's ascent into heaven. And Christians make it a place of pilgrimage, the place of Jesus' crucifixion and resurrection and the promise of the New Jerusalem of the eternal Kingdom of God.

# Chapter 12

# *"To Pluck Up . . . and To Plant"*

The very name of Jeremiah has become a symbol of grief and despair. The word "jeremiad," meaning a lament, a complaint, a tirade, has become a part of the language, and Jeremiah is most commonly known as the "weeping prophet." The story of his life gives ample evidence for the appropriateness of that characterization and the reasons for it. However, that is not the whole truth. Sad though he was, Jeremiah was not entirely, or finally tenebrific. He was also full of hope. No prophet had greater confidence in the future of God's purpose and people than he, and Jeremiah described the structure and conditions of that future with remarkable accuracy. It was his unwanted vocation "to pluck up," but it was also his privilege "to plant" the seeds of the religion of the spirit.

## *The Last Days of Judah*

We have seen in the two previous chapters how Assyria became the dominant power of the Fertile Crescent during the second half of the eighth century B.C. By the beginning of the seventh century, Syria and Israel, along with several smaller states in the area, were defeated and incorporated as provinces of the empire; and Judah remained with little independence, a tribute-paying vassal kingdom required even to worship the gods of her master. Egypt was finally conquered and occupied by her ancient enemy in 671 B.C., crowning Assyria's ascendency.

Judah's reforming king, Hezekiah, died in 687, and his successor, Manasseh, apparently purchased a moribund peace for his kingdom during a long reign of nearly half a century by remaining the willing puppet of Assyria. There is an ancient tradition that the prophet Isaiah was silenced by martyrdom early in the rule of Manasseh, the so-called "villain of Judah." At any rate, the religion of Moses and the prophets reached its lowest ebb during the bleak period. The Temple seems to have been largely abandoned and allowed to fall into disrepair. The Law of Moses was forgotten. Sacrifice ceased, the holy days were not observed, and the voice of prophecy was not heard, probably by royal proscription. Yahwism came close to extinction.

Jeremiah was born about the time of Manasseh's death. His birthplace was the little known town of Anathoth, in the previous territory of the tribe of Benjamin, just four miles north of Jerusalem. The town was remembered as the place to which Solomon had banished one of the chief priests, Abiathar, when he seized control of David's realm in the struggle with his brother, Adonijah, after their father's death. Jeremiah was a member of that proud and bitter family of Benjamite priests-in-exile. The facts of his birth may thus help in the understanding of his career and teaching: a priest banished from the Temple, an outsider amid the circles of power in the capital, and a loyal Benjamite within the kingdom of Judah.

Manasseh's death in 642 B.C. brought a period of political anarchy in Judah and paralleled the series of events which culminated in the rapid decline of Assyria. His son, Amon, who continued the pagan practices of his father, was assassinated by palace enemies after ruling for only two years. But "the people of the land," the leading citizens who doubtless wished to maintain social stability even at the expense of foreign control and imposed paganism, put the eight-year-old Josiah, son of Amon, on the throne. However, Assyria's domination was fading. Egypt had already revolted successfully against her (663 B.C.) and, in 652, Babylonia began the struggle for independence which would ultimately bring about the demise of Assyria and her replacement by Babylonia as the mistress of the Fertile Crescent (605 B.C.). Thus Jeremiah was to live and speak during a period of fast-changing international affairs when the fortunes of Judah would be at stake in every reaction.

Ashurbanapal, the last powerful monarch of the Assyrian Empire, died in 633 B.C., signalling the momentous events which were to follow in rapid succession. The Scythians and other pillaging hordes from the lands to the north of the Black Sea poured into the empire around 625, bringing widespread fear and devastation. All of the conquered peoples began to throw off their yokes, symbolized, for example, in Judah by a return to the faith of the ancestors. The Babylonians, in temporary alliance with the Medes, captured Nineveh, the Assyrian capital, in 612. Although the rulers of what remained of Assyria fled westward to Haran, the ancient city between the Tigris and the Euphrates, they were finally caught and destroyed at Carchemish in a historic battle in 605 B.C. Egypt, now revitalized, attempted to win the western horn of the Fertile Crescent by going to the aid of Assyria, but after Carchemish she retired home, defeated again. During the uncertainty of battle, Judah sought a means of freedom for herself and thus experienced an internal struggle between pro-Egyptian, pro-Assyrian and pro-Babylonian parties. But in the end she found herself a vassal still, now subject to Babylon instead of Nineveh.

Josiah, during whose reign occurred the political-religious reformation which attempted to manifest national freedom, was killed in 609 at Megiddo as he tried to favor Babylonia by blocking Egypt's march north to aid Assyria at Carchemish. He was succeeded in rapid order by three sons and a grandson before Judah was finally punished for her repeated rebellions. Nebuchadnezzar, ruler of Babylonia, lost patience with his vassal and brought an end to Judah's long life, sacking Jerusalem in 586 B.C. The last son of Josiah, Zedekiah, was blinded and taken captive to Babylonia, along with the leaders of Judah. The Temple was destroyed and the walls of Jerusalem were pulled down. The battle-shocked, impotent people, Jeremiah among them, were left to survive as best they could under the watchful eyes of Babylonian troops. In desperation some fled to Egypt, dragging the unwilling Jeremiah with them. The end had apparently come with a whimper of complete finality.

## The Book of Jeremiah

The life and though of Jeremiah are well known, when compared with the other Hebrew prophets, because of the extensive information recorded in the book bearing his name. It is one of the longest books in the Hebrew canon, containing 52 chapters in its surviving edition. Fortunately, we are given not only lengthy examples of the oracles delivered by the prophet during the last, terrible days of Judah, but we are also privileged to witness the internal conflicts which he endured. Here is a man in the "dark night of the soul" stubbornly fighting for light amid self-doubt, rejection, overwhelming grief for the people, personal suffering, and national disaster. Jeremiah's spiritual triumph over all opposition, as recorded in this book, has scarcely been rivaled in any literature.

The first twenty-five chapters contain most of the extant oracles, with a small amount of narrative about the life and times of the prophet. The order is uncertain, perhaps because the original record, made by Baruch, the faithful scribe of Jeremiah, was destroyed disdainfully by the king, Jehoiakim, to whom it was presented (cf. chapter 36). Most of the remainder of the book, chapters 26-45, is composed of biographical materials, sometimes called the Memoirs of Baruch. This part contains fascinating accounts of Jeremiah's prophetic career, including his frequent confrontations with other prophets, the priests, and all of the last five kings of Judah. The remaining section of the present book consists of a group of oracles against other nations (46-51), which are believed to be of later origin, and a brief conclusion concerning the fall of Jerusalem (52) taken from II Kings 24-25.

## Event and Word in Jeremiah

Three events stand out with special significance during the life of Jeremiah. First, there was the personal call from Yahweh, coming to the young man from despised Anathoth and setting him unwillingly "over nations and over kingdoms, to pluck up and to break down, to destroy and to overthrow, to build and to plant" (1:10). Second, there was the great reformation of Mosaic religion, based upon the re-publication and adoption of the ancient Law of Sinai, which symbolized the determination of Josiah to secure and declare the new freedom of Judah from foreign control. Jeremiah's reaction to that revival is completely unexpected. And, third, there was, of course, the final seige and capture of Jerusalem, first in 598/97 and then in 587/86, resulting in the enslavement of the people of Judah, "the Jews," as they were now called, and the apparent end of their nation's existence. Jeremiah lived in the midst of the tragedy and felt every throbbing pain of it.

Jeremiah heard the strange and undeniable call of Yahweh "in the thirteenth year" of the reign of Josiah. That would have been about 626 B.C., when he was certainly less than twenty years of age. "I am only a youth," he protested, but the Lord refused to accept his excuse (1:6-7). Instead, he was told that he had been predestined by Yahweh to be a prophet from the time of his conception. He was assured of protection and deliverance, a promise he often had reason to question. His commission was to continue the kind of harsh condemnation and dire warning which had been the burden of former prophets in Israel, except that he would also see, through unstaunched tears, the terrors of the judgment which they and he had proclaimed.

Two illustrative visions accompanied the call Jeremiah received, reminding the reader of the visions of Amos. The first was of a budding almond bush, and in typical Hebraic literary form, brought its message by a play on words: *shaqed*, an almond sprout, the harbinger of spring's awakening, is similar to *shoqed*, the word for "watching;" hence Yahweh's active involvement in the events of history was indicated. And, again, the vision of an overturned cauldron, in the north, spilling its scalding contents toward the south, portrayed the flood of continuing conquest from that direction by the Scythians and the coming Babylonians.

The essential message of Jeremiah, delivered during the subsequent years with such sad reluctance, was similar to that of the eighth-century prophets, especially Hosea. A constant theme was the marriage of Yahweh and Israel in the days of the Exodus. Yahweh's protection, providence and constancy were compared with Israel's amazing and obscene unfaithfulness. Alternating between shrill accusation and broken-hearted appeals to return, the prophet evidently did not expect repentance and hence announced that Yahweh had issued a bill of divorcement from his adulterous bride.

There was, however, a national return to faithfulness. The weakening of Assyrian control over Judah following the death of Ashurbanapal was accompanied by a great revival of Yahwism in Jerusalem. The centerpiece of the reformation was the re-publication of the Torah, in the eighteenth year of Josiah's reign, 621 B.C. (II Kings 22-23). Now generally believed to be the major part of what came to be called Deuteronomy (*deuteros*, second; *nomos*, law), the newly edited material was in the form of addresses to Israel by Moses just before his death east of the Jordan. It contained a ringing call to faithfulness, and it repeatedly presented the Two Ways: to choose obedience to God's Law is the Way of Blessing and Life, but to choose disobedience is the Way of Curses and Death. That decisive principle was to become increasingly in later years the fundamental principle of Jewish moral theology. Along with the Torah, the ancient traditions were also edited and published in such a way as to illustrate how the Doctrine of Two Ways had operated inexorably in Israel's past history. That material, the so-called Deuteronomic History, is essentially the Former Prophets of the Hebrew canon—Joshua, Judges, Samuel and Kings.

Josiah led all Judah in a grandiose reaffirmation of faith, based upon this newly discovered Torah, and the ancient liturgies were renewed with a great display of piety. It would have been expected that Jeremiah would rejoice; instead, after a possible initial endorsement (11:1-8), he denounced the whole affair in the sharpest terms. The oracle contained in chapter 7, called the Temple Sermon, was his reply to what he saw to be a veneer of meaningless ritual and empty worship. With seething indignation reminiscent of Amos, he ridiculed the hypocrisy of the outwardly religious people and called for deep spirituality proved by the fruit of moral action. Because it was not forthcoming, he predicted that Jerusalem with its Temple would be destroyed as ancient Shiloh had been.

Such a shocking response to revival by a professed prophet of Yahweh brought continuing and increased rejection, ridicule and temporary imprisonment to Jeremiah. He was accused of false prophecy and even of treason. Despair and darkness closed in upon both him and the nation after Carchemish, when the stranglehold of Babylonia made it clear that no independence was likely for Judah. Expectation of help from the "weak reed" of Egypt was as foolish and perverse as it had been a century earlier in Isaiah's time. Jeremiah saw that there was no escape from the judgment of God upon his people. He watched the nation go through its dying agony. It had chosen the Way of Disobedience and Death: "Then the Lord said to me, 'Though Moses and Samuel stood before me, yet my heart would not turn toward this people. Send them out of my sight, and let them go! And when they ask you, "Where shall we go?" you shall say to them, "Thus says the Lord: Those who are for pestilence, to pestilence, and those who are for the sword, to the sword; those who are for famine, to famine, and those who are for captivity, to captivity." I will appoint over them four kinds of destroyers, says the Lord: the sword to slay, the dogs to tear, and the birds of the air and the beasts of the earth to devour and destroy. And I will make them a horror to all the kingdoms of the earth because of what Manasseh the son of Hezekiah, king of Judah, did in Jerusalem' " (15:1-4).

When judgment had come and darkness was deepest, Jeremiah began to preach a message of hope. There are several oracles of hope scattered through the book, but it will be sufficient to mention only two here as illustrations. The first is found in chapter 24, recording a vision of two baskets of figs. The occasion was the first capture of

Jerusalem by Nebuchadnezzar, in 597 B.C., when the city was spared but the next-to-last king, Jehoiachin, was taken captive to Babylonia along with many leaders of the nation. Jeremiah therefore spoke of the captives in Babylonia as "good figs" and of his remaining fellow-countrymen in Judah as "bad figs." Concerning the captives in exile, he spoke for Yahweh, saying, "I will set my eyes upon them for good, and I will bring them back to this land. I will build them up, and not tear them down; I will plant them, and not uproot them. I will give them a heart to know that I am the Lord; and they shall be my people and I will be their God, for they shall return to me with their whole heart" (24:6-7).

A second optimistic oracle is in the form of a letter written by Jeremiah to the same people in exile. Evidently there were false prophets and magicians among them who continued to advise insurrection, claiming that their yokes could be broken and the fortunes of Judah restored. Jeremiah realized that worse punishment must come before restoration was possible. He even claimed that the Babylonians were the instrument of Yahweh's correction of his people and therefore rebellion against Babylon was rebellion against God. Thus he wrote to the exiles, urging acceptance of their condition. He advised them to settle down, marry and raise families, and even to pray for the welfare of the Babylonians; "for thus says the Lord: When seventy years are completed for Babylon, I will visit you, and I will fulfill to you my promise and bring you back to this place" (29:10). There is hope, but it is in the future and it is in what God will do.

## Jeremiah's Special Contributions

The prophet Jeremiah should probably be listed among the ten most profound and influential teachers in all history. Instead of an exaggeration, that may be an understatement, as many scholars have testified. A man of such unusual perception and enormous influence, therefore, will have left a rich and varied legacy in the history of ideas. We must limit our discussion here, however, to three of his special contributions.

First, Jeremiah as much as anyone defined the character of authentic religion. He described it in terms of fidelity to commitment, unyielding struggle with spiritual mystery, and stern morality under all conditions. No one has ever voiced a more severe indictment of hypocrisy. Yet he knew firsthand the subtle enervation of abiding doubt. He often felt forsaken and misled, even by God, and he like Job went so far as to question God's fairness and steadfastness. But he would neither abandon his faith nor turn from his painful task. His loneliness and suffering resulted from obedience, not disobedience; and his doubt sprang from the deep struggles of the spirit rather than from a fragile and shallow confession. He discovered the character of authentic religion by testing it in the fires of trial and tragedy.

The core of Jeremiah's understanding of genuine religion was his emphasis upon spirit. His assumption that God is spirit was made manifest in his teaching that Yahweh is everywhere and within, beyond nature and history and yet the master of both, known and dealt with by every man within the secrets of the self. This was the basis of his ridicule of every form of idolatry; it was the source of his assurance that the future must be controlled by the purposes of God. Assuming also that man is spirit, he therefore insisted upon the necessity of direct communion with God. For the same reason he required utter sincerity in every form of worship as well as both personal and social morality consistent with an honest recognition of God's command and God's all-seeing watchfulness. Jeremiah refined the gold of pure, spiritual religion with such simplicity and clarity that he provided thereby a standard for all future generations.

Second, Jeremiah supplied both questions and answers to the perennial problem of authority in religion. How does one distinguish between truth and falsity? How can one know whether he is hearing the call of God or merely responding to an acoustical illusion? Is there any dependable standard by which to distinguish a true prophet from a false prophet? Upon what adequate basis can one stand, even at the cost of possible persecution and death, when opposed by consensus and custom, by the highest religious and civil authorities, by family and friends, and often even by one's own best reasoning and inclination?

Jeremiah wrestled with these precise questions as have few people in recorded history. His most intimate thoughts are revealed in the book that bears his name. There we see him, and hear his meditations within himself, as he challenged his people even in their intended revival of religion, as he opposed the recognized prophets and ordained priests, and as he castigated the kings, the anointed of Yahweh, who held the power of death over him. He dared to debate with God, accusing Yahweh of misusing and misleading him. Yet, through the most painful struggles, he stood by his conviction that he *did* hear God correctly and that he *did* see truth clearly. He apparently believed that if he could not trust his own experience of reality then he could never know reality. And he clearly believed that the best evidence that his vision of righteousness was authentic could be found in the character of his opponents. Jeremiah taught that true religion may be judged by its fruit and by its alternatives.

Finally, Jeremiah gave substance to his hope by supplying the structure of its future realization. He was the prophet of the New Covenant. Looking beyond his own time and the inevitable catastrophes that befell the Covenant People of God, he insisted that a new day was coming when the Good Shepherd would gather his people and make a New Covenant with them (chapter 31). Judgment had come, but it could never be the last word because of the nature and purpose of God.

The concept of a New Covenant provided the ideological foundation for the restoration of the faithful community which was born during and after the Exile, becoming the religion of the People of God, Judaism. Though they were scattered among the nations, never again to be one nation in one place, they developed and maintained a new faith, in continuity with the old, which preserved the traditions of the fathers and became a bond of unity. The sufferings caused by the loss of the Temple, the city, and the nation were the birthpangs of a deeper spiritual relationship between Yahweh and all mankind.

Seven centuries after this historic insight and foresight of Jeremiah, in the restored city of Jerusalem, a new prophet arose among the Jews who took up the teaching of the New Covenant. Jesus of Nazareth interpreted his message as the proclamation of the New Covenant realized by his own sacrifice. He celebrated the Passover with his friends, commemorating the establishment of the Covenant of the Exodus; and he anticipated his imminent death with the words: "this cup is the new covenant in my blood" (I Corinthians 11:25). The new universal religion later designated as Christianity, born among Jews and retaining the Law and the Prophets, has always claimed to be the fulfillment of Jeremiah's vision of the New Covenant between God and his people (cf. Hebrews 8:8-13).

# V.
# BEING
# AND KNOWING:
# PRE-SOCRATIC
# PHILOSOPHY

# Chapter 13

# *Thinking About What Really Is*

The sixth century before Christ was characterized by a remarkable surge of intellectual activity in widely separated parts of the civilized world. Among the Hebrews, it was the century of Ezekiel and the prophet responsible for later portions of the Book of Isaiah. In India, Gautama the Buddha and Mahavira, founder or, as he maintained, reviver of the religion of the Jains, left enduring marks on the cultures of the East. In China, Confucius and Lao-tse propounded systems of thought which for more than two millennia were to reign as the dominant influences in the life of that country. In the second decade of that same century, the western coast of Asia Minor was the scene of one of the most significant events in the history of thought—the birth of Greek philosophy.

## *Thales, Father of Greek Philosophy*

A specific if somewhat arbitrary date has been assigned to that event. In the year 585 B.C., an eclipse of the sun created a panic sufficiently great to stop a pitched battle between the Lydians and the Medes. The year if not the month of its occurrence seems to have been accurately predicted by Thales, a citizen of Miletus, traditionally regarded as the father of formal philosophy in the West.

A versatile man, Thales, in addition to demonstrating his ability as an astronomer and philosopher, showed considerable talent as an army engineer, businessman, and practical scientist. Among his last writings was a nautical star guide, and he is reputed to have devised a method for measuring the distance between an observer and a ship at sea.

His greatest importance, however, lies in his having initiated a tradition of inquiry into the ultimate nature of reality—the *physis* which is the basis of all phenomena. Unfortunately, no coherent fragments of his writings have survived, and the statements attributed to him by later authorities, if taken at their face value, do little to help us understand why he was once regarded with reverential awe as one of the Seven Sages of Greece.

Aristotle cited four propositions of Thales. Briefly stated, they assert that the fundamental nature of all things is water, that the earth floats on water, that all things are full of gods, and that a lodestone has a soul, as evidenced by the fact that it sets iron in motion.

In Aristotle's view, the first proposition may have had its origin in ancient myths. "There are some," he wrote, "who think that men of olden times—those who long before the present era, first began to speculate about the gods—held similar views about basic nature. For they represented basic Oceanus and Tethys as the parents of creation, and the gods as swearing their oaths by the River Styx, which is to say by water, the oldest and most honorable thing by which man swears." Mythic considerations aside, the first proposition is, perhaps, more readily understandable if one reflects that of all the substances which appear at various times in the three forms in which we ordinarily apprehend the physical world—solid, liquid, and gas—water is the one which has its transformations effected within the most commonly experienced range of temperature. It can, moreover, readily be seen that it constitutes the major bulk of the substance of living organisms. Lacking a developed scientific vocabulary, Thales is hardly to be faulted for using the term *water* to designate the one reality which can differentiate itself into the many.

The earth does not, of course, float on a sea of water in the same way that a block of wood floats on the surface of a pond, but if, indeed, *water* is the name given the primordial cosmic reality, Thales' view that the earth is supported by it is, in essence, eminently reasonable. As for his contention that all things are full of gods, it is not unlikely that he was suggesting metaphorically that in nature, even seemingly inert objects are permeated by some sort of force or energy—a notion which is further supported by his observation about the lodestone.

Aëtius, a later writer, credited Thales with a high degree of astronomical sophistication—a not surprising characterization of a man capable of predicting a solar eclipse. "Thales and certain others agree with the astronomers of our day," Aëtius wrote, "that the monthly phases of the moon indicate that it is lighted by the sun and travels in relation to it. Lunar eclipses he explained as caused by the earth's shadow, in that the earth cuts off the sun's light from the moon when it is directly between the two orbs. . . . And he says that eclipses of the sun occur when the moon passes directly in front of it; explaining that the moon is of an earthy nature, even though it gives the appearance of a disc laid across the disc of the sun."

Another intriguing suggestion by Aëtius gives ground for seeing Thales as having anticipated later philosophers in identifying God as universal mind, presumably immanent in the primal water which is the universal *physis.*

## Anaximander

Thales had a pupil named Anaximander, another Milesian who, like his teacher, excelled in scientific pursuits. He constructed instruments for measuring hours and used the gnomon, of which he was the inventor, for determining solstices and equinoxes. He drew a complete map of the known world and constructed a global chart of the heavens.

Anaximander, with considerable daring, suggested that the *physis* at the heart of nature cannot be anything which is, in essence, a specific part of nature. It is, rather, the *Apeiron*—the Infinite or Boundless—a substantial but originally undifferentiated reality which becomes transformed into the objects which constitute the world apprehended by the senses. Although the term *Apeiron* undoubtedly refers in part to qualitative unlimitedness, Anaximander seems to have been singularly free of the common Greek discomfort occasioned by the difficult notion of spatial and temporal infinity, and his universe contains a limitless number of worlds, coming into being and ceasing to be throughout infinite time. The entire cosmic process rests on a law according to which each existing thing, having "committed injustice" by denying existence to its opposite, must make "reparation" by returning to the *Apeiron.* This concept marks the first appearance in formal Greek philosophy of a dialectic of opposing qualities, which has been a persistent element of Western thought. Anaximander was also apparently the earliest thinker to anticipate later theories of evolution by the suggestion that man's forebears originated in the sea. His reasoning, as described by Plutarch, was impressive: "He says. . . . . that in earliest times men were generated from various kinds of animals. For whereas the other animals can quickly get food for themselves, the human infant requires careful feeding for a long while after birth; so that if he had originated suddenly he could not have preserved his own existence."

## Anaximenes

Anaximander, in turn, was the teacher of the third celebrated Milesian, a man named Anaximenes, born in the year of the eclipse which Thales so successfully predicted. In some respects, his characterization of the cosmos as being essentially composed of air seems to have been a backward step, but the importance of air, or breath, in the symbolism of many societies must not be overlooked. As the principle of life, it was associated in antiquity with the soul of man, and it could be imagined without too much difficulty to be sufficiently variable in density to produce fire, water, and earth. Specifically, he made a real contribution to the development of metaphysics in his theory that the primal reality assumes varied forms as a result of two opposing forces, rarefaction and condensation, which determine the degree of density possessed by any particular substance.

He is said to have maintained that even the gods are products of air and that the stars were originally produced by exhalations rising from earth. His inaccuracy in this respect is consistent with the rest of his cosmology. He thought the stars to be fixed like nails in a crystalline sky, revolving around the outer edge of a flat earth like a cap turned around on a head. The stars are pushed around in their courses by compressed air, and rainbows—a subject of intense interest to philosophers for two millenia—are caused by diffraction of the sun's rays falling on compressed air.

## The Pythagoreans

An important Greek settlement farther to the west than the Ionian communities was Crotona, in southern Italy. There, a native of Samos named Pythagoras, a few years younger than Anaximenes, founded a society destined to have profound influence on the course of the development of European thought. Essentially a religious organization based on earlier mystery cults, it was dedicated to the quest for the release of souls from the chain of successive incarnations by which they are bound. The daily life of the Pythagorean community was directed toward the end of making its members increasingly conscious of their true natures and of the divine reality in which they were said to have their being.

Some of the maxims by which the Pythagoreans were governed are difficult to understand without a clearer view of their origin and meaning than is now possible. Others are more amenable to symbolic interpretation. Among the more familiar maxims are:

"Do not poke the fire with a sword."

"Abstain from beans."

"Do not turn back in the middle of a journey."

"On rising from bed obliterate the print of your body."

"Leave no mark of the pot on the ashes."

"Wear no rings containing the images of the gods."

In addition to its emphasis on ritual and morality, the Brotherhood stressed the importance of the attainment of a proper intellectual grasp of the nature of reality. The result was an attention to mathematical and scientific disciplines which led to the formation of many of the molds in which subsequent European thought has been cast.

Number, the Pythagoreans taught, is at the heart of truth. The cosmos is to be understood in terms of relationships rather than things. Numbers, conceived in geometrical fashion as patterns of dots, are of three basic sorts: triangular, square, and oblong.

Triangular numbers are generated by the addition of successive integers. Three, the smallest, results from adding one and two. The addition of one, two, three, and four generates ten, the sacred tetraktys, a figure of great holiness by which the Pythagoreans swore their oath of loyalty and secrecy:

.

. .

. . .

. . . .

The addition of successive odd numbers regarded as masculine, produces square numbers. A dot is fixed, and other points representing the sequence of masculine numbers are arranged around L-shaped gnomons in this manner:

Thus,  1 + 3 = 4, or $2^2$
       1 + 3 + 5 = 9, or $3^2$
       1 + 3 + 5 + 7 = 16, or $4^2$
       1 + 3 + 5 + 7 + 9 = 25, or $5^2$

Oblong numbers, conceived as feminine, are similarly generated by the addition of successive even integers:

Thus,  2 + 4 = 6
        2 + 4 + 6 = 12
        2 + 4 + 6 + 8 = 20
        2 + 4 + 6 + 8 + 10 = 30

In the case of square numbers, a straight line can be drawn diagonally through the gnomons, and the shape of the figure generated remains constant through any degree of expansion. Neither is the case with oblong numbers, which, accordingly, suggest infinitude and indefiniteness in Pythagorean thought.

Pythagoras is credited with the theorem which bears his name, affirming the equality of the square of the hypotenuse of a right triangle with the sum of the squares of the other two sides. In relating the lengths of the two sides to the length of the hypotenuse by the use of whole numbers, no difficulty arises in the case of right triangles which have a ratio like 3:4:5, but a serious problem arose for the Pythagoreans when they turned their attention to isosceles right triangles, in which two of the sides are the same length. They discovered to their dismay that no whole-numbered relationship can exist between the hypotenuse of such a triangle and either of the other sides—a fact so upsetting to a school dedicated to the proposition that number is the ground of intelligible reality that the information was sealed under the vow of silence. One Hippasus violated his oath and revealed the dread secret to others, whereupon he was excommunicated from the Brotherhood and, to add injury to insult, was alledgedly drowned in a shipwreck by the outraged gods.

According to an authority cited by Diogenes Laertius, "The first-principle of all things is the monad. From the monad there arises the indeterminate dyad, which then serves as passive material to the monad, while the monad serves as active cause. From the monad and the indeterminate dyad there arise numbers; from numbers, points; from points, lines; from lines, plane figures; from plane figures, solid figures; from solid figures, perceivable bodies compounded of the four elements, fire, water, earth, air. These elements undergo full transformations into one another; they combine to produce a universe that is animate, intelligent, and spherical."

In the tension of opposites found in the processes which generate the world, square, straight, right, male, and the like are on the credit side of the ledger, so to speak, whereas oblong, crooked, left, female, and so on, while equally necessary, are regarded more or less negatively. It is not difficult to point to ways in which notions of this sort have survived in the popular thought of the Western world. An upright man is, or at any rate used to be, a "square shooter." *Dexter* and *sinister*—right and left in the Latin language—are the source of adjectives bearing complimentary connotations for the right side and pejorative ones for the left, a source of continuing discomfort for left-handed persons and liberal politicians. As for male and female, the sides of the coin assigned to each simply reflect the relative status of men and women in the Greek world, as, indeed, in other societies of the time.

The Pythagoreans are given primary credit for the theoretical development of Western music, a result of their interest in the mathematical properties of the vibrations of plucked strings. Interested in astronomy, they postulated a "music of the spheres," produced by the harmonious movements of the celestial bodies, and were led by certain ideal mathematical considerations to develop a theory of the earth's revolving with the other heavenly bodies around a central fire, which, unfortunately for any claim which might be urged on their behalf to authorship of the heliocentric theory, is not the sun. Aristotle's account of their thought emphasizes the influence which their preoccupation with number exercised on their cosmology.

"Accordingly," he said in the *Metaphysics*, "they collected and employed all the analogies they could find which would represent the relation of numbers and harmonies to the properties or parts of the visible heavens and even to the entire universe; and if they came up against any gaps in such analogies they would snatch at whatever additional notion they could find to bring an orderly connection into their total explanation. For example, since the decad is believed to be perfect, and to embrace the essential nature of the whole system of numbers, they conclude that the number of things existing in the sky must therefore be ten; but since in actuality there are only nine that are visible, they postulate the existence of a counterearth as the tenth."

Always actively concerned with politics and frequently rising to high positions in government, the Pythagoreans devoted some thought to political theory. They saw society as consisting of three groups, analogous to vendors, participants, and enlightened spectators at the Olympic games. When translated into political terms, they represented seekers of gain, the lowest class, seekers of honor, at a somewhat higher level, and seekers of wisdom, who are qualified to rule.

### Heraclitus of Ephesus

Heraclitus, a citizen of the Ionian city of Ephesus in Asia Minor, was born about 540 B.C., and his life extended well into the following century. An eldest son in an aristocratic family, he inherited the office of *Basileus* of the city, a religious post which imposed on him the duty of supervising public sacrifices. He relinquished the position to his younger brother and devoted himself to philosophy. Embittered by the exile of his friend Hermadorus by the ruling party, he declined to play an active role in politics, and his aversion to popular government found expression in an angry outburst: "the Ephesians had better go hang themselves, every man of them, and leave their city to be governed by youngsters, for they have banished Hermadorus, the finest man among them, declaring: 'Let us not have anyone among us who excels the rest; if there should be such a one, let him go and live elsewhere.' "

Heraclitus wrote in a style which has been characterized as obscure but which is, more importantly, charged with meaning at more than one level and, accordingly, challenging to thoughtful readers. A generation or two later than Pythagoras and an avowed opponent of the school, he nevertheless shared the Pythagorean view that reality is not essentially a permanent, unchanging stuff. For him, however, it is not number, but rather ceaseless change, or process, symbolized by fire. "This universe," he said, "which is the same for all, has not been made by any god or man, but it always has been, is, and will be—an ever-living fire, kindling itself by regular measures."

Change, however, occurs in ordered patterns, and Heraclitus attributed the order to divine Reason, which he called *Logos* or *Word*, a term which was later to have a significant use in Christian doctrine. When one conforms oneself to the Logos, he is thinking correctly and objectively. "We should let ourselves be guided by what is common to all," he said. "Yet although the Logos is common to all, most men live as if each of them had a private intelligence of his own."

Such strength and stability as may be found in the cosmos are the result of a balance of opposing forces, a circumstance which led Heraclitus to exalt that tension of opposites which he called "war" as "father of all and king of all." The dynamic quality of Heraclitus' thought is evident in his ready acceptance of conflict as inevitable in nature and in human life. "It should be understood," he said, "that war is the common condition, that strife is justice, and that all things come to pass through the compulsion of strife." It is, indeed, the very ground of existence. "Homer was wrong in saying, 'Would that strife might perish from amongst gods and men,' " Heraclitus asserted, "For if that were to occur, then all things would cease to exist."

Many of his aphorisms have a paradoxical quality. "The way up and the way down are one and the same," he said, and "Into the same rivers we step and do not step." Aspects of reality which may seem to lead to contradiction when viewed at one level of observation are reconciled when contemplated from a higher point of view. All paradoxes are, in fact, resolved in the nature of God, who is "day and night, winter and summer, war and peace, satiety and want."

# Chapter 14

## *Thinking about Permanence and Change*

Xenophanes (570-480 B.C.), a native of the Ionian city of Colophon, turned the principal focus of his attention from problems of substance and process to a consideration of theology. He rejected the popular gods, holding that they are no more than fictions resulting from the representation of human traits on an Olympian scale. Such deities, he said, are invariably endowed with the sort of features most often found among their worshipers—gray eyes and red hair for Thracian gods, snub noses and black hair for those of the Ethiopians. If horses or oxen or lions had gods, he suggested, the divine forms would be correspondingly equine, bovine, or leonine.

The one true God, however, has no physical form at all. Immanent in the world, he is not dependent upon special sense organs for his experience. "It is the whole that sees, the whole that thinks, the whole that hears." He is not, however, to be identified with the processes of nature. He is, rather, the intelligent orderer of those processes. "Without effort he sets everything in motion by the thought of his mind."

Xenophanes' attack on anthropomorphism was directed against the attribution to the divine nature not only of manlike physical qualities but of human moral defects as well. "Homer and Hesiod," he said, "attributed to the gods all sorts of actions which when done by men are disreputable and deserving of blame—such lawless deeds as theft, adultery, and mutual deception."

Xenophanes has been called a pantheist and a monist, but it is doubtful that he can properly be assigned to either of these categories. He may more plausibly be described as a monotheist, crediting the one God with these characteristics of awareness and purpose which are ascribed to him by the Hebrews while denying the limitations implicit in the representation of the divine nature in human form. It may be argued that he underestimated the difficulty of thinking without some sort of symbolic imagery, but he at least provided a useful reminder of the dangers of inappropriate symbols or of symbols which become substitutes for the reality to which they properly refer. That knowledge about the divine nature is not easily acquired, he readily acknowledged. "No man has existed, nor will exist," he said, "who has plain knowledge about the gods and the questions I discuss. For even if someone happened by chance to say what is true, he still would not know that he did so. Yet everybody thinks he knows." As for himself, he claimed only that what he had presented had seemed to him "resemblances of what is true."

## The Eleatics

Xenophanes may have had some influence on the development, in the Greek colony of Elea in southern Italy, of a group of philosophers who came to be known by the name of that city. At any rate, the founder of the school, Parmenides, is said to have studied under Xenophanes, although there is not a great deal in the Eleatic philosophy which can be attributed directly to the older man. The three principal sages of Elea seem rather to have been led by the accomplishments of Greek geometers to suggest an account of the nature of reality based on reason alone.

Parmenides, who flourished during the early part of the fifth century B.C., composed a poem *On Nature*, beginning with an imaginative account of his journey from the realm of seeming into the presence of a goddess who enlightened him concerning "the unshaken heart of well-rounded truth and the opinions of mortals which lack true belief." Her teaching, which goes to the heart of the ontological question of the ultimate nature of Being is the core of the Eleatic philosophy.

Of whatever may be thought, Parmenides learned from the goddess, one must say, "It is,"or, more precisely in Greek, simply "Is." To affirm that "it is not" is nonsensical,for there can be no intelligible content associated with the term "non-being." It is similarly unintelligible to say, "It came into being" or "It will cease to be," for such statements entail the notion of passage from being to not-being or from not-being to being, and, in either case, the not-being is unthinkable. It must, moreover, be unchanging, for any change would involve cessation and origination of being, forbidden by Parmenidean logic. Plurality is similarly excluded by the exercise of pure reason.

The result of this line of logic—the "way of truth"—is that if the physical world is to be thought of as having real existence at all, it must be conceived in a way which excludes every datum of sense experience. It must be one homogeneous, undifferentiated mass—a finite sphere, as Parmenides described it, which, nevertheless, cannot be imagined as surrounded by anything or by nothing. Such a picture of physical reality cannot fail to suggest the finite but unbounded model of the universe proposed by some twentieth-century cosmologists.

But how real did such a world actually seem to Parmenides? Did he regard ultimate being as physical at all? One short surviving fragment of his writings says, "Thought and being are the same," and again we find him saying, "Thinking and the object of thought are the same. For you will not find thought apart from being, nor either of them apart from utterance." These observations would seem to suggest that his position may have anticipated that of later idealists who regard the nature of reality as essentially mental, but the idea was not further developed in the fragments of his work which have survived.

What of the world of experience? It is apprehended not by the way of truth, but by the way of seeming. It is a sort of phantasm, no more susceptible to rational treatment than the content of a dream. Nevertheless, Parmenides apparently thought it necessary to include in his poem accounts of the ways in which inorganic and organic objects are alleged to come into being by those who take phenomena seriously. His treatment of these matters shows him to have been well acquainted with the speculative works of other philosophers, but it is not easy to determine what role the concepts he enunciated played in his own thought other than as convenient ways of dealing with the senses in response to the goddess's observation that "it is needful that by passing everything under review you should learn this also—how to judge of mere seeming."

Zeno (c. 530-490 B.C.) was a pupil of Parmenides and, according to Plato, visited Athens with his teacher when Socrates was a young man and Zeno about forty years of age. His philosophy, his appearance, and his personality all seem to have made a favorable impression on the Athenians, and some twenty years later, the manner of his death earned him a hero's fame when he refused under torture to reveal the names of his confederates in a plot against the tyrant Nearchus of Elea.

Zeno devoted himself to a defense of Parmenides' position by attempting to demonstrate that the assertion of the reality of the world of the many entails contradictions which make it logically untenable. His method of doing this involved a series of "attacks" (*epicheiremata*), which take the form of *reductiones ad absurdum*. This form of argument employs the postulate it is designed to refute as the antecedent of an implicative proposition, in order to show that its assertion would necessitate the acceptance of a pair of contradictory statements. As a self-contradictory consequent must be rejected, it is concluded that the proposition in question must be false. Thus; if a proposition $p$ implies $q$ and *not-q*, $p$ is not true.

Zeno used this sort of argument with considerable skill to bring out the paradoxes inherent in the Pythagorean picture of a universe containing a multiplicity of objects. If there is such multiplicity, he maintained, the many things must be both finite and infinite in number—finite because there can be no more nor fewer of them than there are, and infinite because any two things that exist must have other things between them. As the two propositions contradict each other, there cannot be many things. Again, any existent thing does or does not have magnitude. If it has no magnitude, it would not increase the size of anything to which it might be added or decrease the size of anything from which it might be taken away. That, however, is equivalent to saying that it is nothing—that it does not exist. If something exists, its parts must have size and bulk and be at some distance from one another. But then, the same must be true of the parts of the parts and of the parts of the parts of the parts and so on. No part can ever be the ultimate, and any object composed of an infinite number of extended parts must be infinitely large. Zeno concluded that multiplicity cannot be thought.

His most celebrated arguments, though, are the four directed against the idea of motion. According to the first of these, as described by Aristotle, motion would entail passing through an infinite series of half-distances before the space between any two points could be traversed, a clear impossibility according to Zeno's conception of motion.

The second, and perhaps most interesting, is that dealing with a foot race traditionally attributed to Achilles and a tortoise. Achilles, who begins the race from point $A$, being a sporting man, gives his opponent a head start at a point $B$. Assuming both to be mobile and the distance between them finite, Achilles should be able to overtake the tortoise. But where?

Not at $B$, for by the time Achilles reaches that point, the tortoise would be some distance ahead, at $C$. Nor will he catch his adversary at any point between $B$ and $C$ or at $C$ itself, for the tortoise would be moving from $C$ to $D$ and so on. The result is that if motion be thought possible, Achilles, though he must overtake the tortoise, can never do so. Thus, the impossibility of motion is demonstrated.

The third paradox, that of the arrow in flight, seems to suggest that a moving object could occupy only the space in which it rests at any given instant and thus cannot have the sort of ambiguous extension implied in the concept of motion.

The fourth—the case of the moving columns—is more complicated and, indeed, its meaning is the subject of some dispute. Zeno imagined three equally spaced columns of men in a stadium, two of them marching at equal speeds but in opposite directions, and the third standing still. As the two moving columns pass each other and the stationary column, each man passes every man in the moving column in half the time that it takes him to pass a man in the stationary column. This, Zeno concluded, is to say that the half is equal to the whole, which is absurd. Whether or not the fourth argument in its original form, now lost, was impressive as a refutation of the idea of motion, it certainly suggested that if the concept is to be entertained at all, it must be thought of in relative rather than absolute terms. It is of interest to note that somewhat similar paradoxes which can be formulated on the basis of the premises posited in twentieth-century relativity theory are not thought to necessitate the conclusion that motion is merely phenomenal. Rather they are held to preclude any description of the movement of an object which does not involve a prior specification of the coordinate system from which the movement is observed. For Zeno, however, a proof that absolute motion is unintelligible would be sufficient to establish the thesis that reality must be static.

Aristotle, anticipating several modern efforts, undertook a refutation of Zeno's arguments by pointing out that the Eleatic conception of infinity is not unambiguous and that an infinite number of points on a line can be traversed in a finite time if the time itself is divisible into a similarly infinite number of instants. Zeno would undoubtedly maintain that such criticisms, rather than attacking his position head-on, attempt to evade its consequences by showing ways in which motion can be described without contradiction. This, the sage of Elea could readily admit, for, if by one description motion can occur and by another equally authentic account it cannot, his *reductio ad absurdum* could still be upheld.

The third of the "Eleatics," Melissus of Samos, was an admiral in the Samian fleet which was victorious over the Athenian navy in 440 B.C. He wrote a poem entitled *On Being*, in which, with a single exception, he agreed with all of Parmenides' conclusions based on the axiom that not-being is not. It is this exception which has assured him a place in the history of thought. Being, he held, cannot be limited in space or time, for any limit would necessarily imply the existence of the not-being bounding it. Being, therefore, must be spatially and temporally infinite.

### Empedocles

The radical monism of the Eleatic school was rejected by Empedocles, a native of the Sicilian city of Acragas. He was the son of a man of noble birth whose name was probably Meton and the grandson of another Empedocles, whose victory in the Olympic games was erroneously attributed by later writers to the philosopher himself. Active in politics, he is said to have turned down an opportunity to become king after saving his native city from tyranny and to have induced the citizens to adopt a democratic form of government. This story, like most of the accounts of event in his life, has been challenged, and his reputation rests largely, not on his role in the political life of the Greek world, but on his writings. It does seem, however, that his skill in various sciences, especially medicine, together with a dramatic personality, made him a celebrity in his own time. Spectacular legends clustered around his name, and even the manner of his death is uncertain, due to the creativity of the story-tellers who elevated him to a semi-divine status—not, it may be remarked, without prior encouragement from Empedocles himself. He was the author of two important poems, *On Nature* and *Purifications*, and all the surviving fragments of his work are from these books.

In *On Nature*, he identified four mythological beings who symbolize the primary substances which constitute reality: Zeus, Hera, Aidoneus, and Nestis. It is apparent that Empedocles used these names poetically to refer to the four traditional elements, Earth, Water, Air, and Fire, Zeus and Hera probably being Fire and Air, Aidoneus Earth, and "tearful Nestis," as Empedocles called her, clearly representing Water.

The Four Elements are eternal and appear to consist of infinitesimal particles which somehow intermix and separate, although, in Eleatic fashion, Empedocles denied that there can be any empty spaces between them. The process is governed by two forces—Love (*Philia*) and Hate (*Neikos*), which, as their names might indicate, have a role in psychology and ethics, but which are also the attraction and repulsion by which the physical world is formed.

The cosmos follows a cyclical pattern. In one age, Love progressively overcomes Hate, and the universe becomes increasingly homogeneous as the four elements come together. In a succeeding one, Hate stirs the mixture, and forms develop with ever greater diversity until the pendulum has swung sufficiently far for Love to begin asserting its dominance again. The present state of things falls somewhere in that portion of a cycle in which Love is being overcome by Hate, a circumstance which explains the growing disharmony in human affairs and provides a rationale for the classic Greek myths of a golden age.

Love is the source of all good, and so ethical conduct in the current age presumably could be directed toward a retarding of the inexorable march of events toward the dissolution which will end the cycle, or, if a less personal and more cosmic view were taken, toward an acceleration of the process in order that Love might more quickly begin its resurgence. In the latter case, however, Empedocles would find himself in the position of advocating that evil be done in order that good might result, and, from the general tenor of the fragments of his work which have moral significance, such a course would be repugnant to him.

The cyclical theory of the universe so widely accepted by the Greeks has had an enduring history in Western thought. In twentieth-century cosmology, the theory that the universe is alternately expanding and contracting is reminiscent of Empedocles' version of the doctrine.

His religious beliefs seem to have been drawn from several sources. Like the Pythagoreans, he expressed a belief in metempsychosis, claiming knowledge of past lives in which he was a boy, a girl, a bush, a bird, and a fish. His image of God as "purely mind, holy and ineffable, flashing through the world with swift thoughts" is reminiscent of Xenophanes.

### Anaxagoras

The pluralistic view of reality developed by Empedocles was presented in a somewhat different form by Anaxagoras of

Clazomenae (c. 500-429 B.C.). After leaving his native Asia Minor, he lived in Athens for some thirty years, in the course of which he had considerable influence on Pericles, as well as on Euripides and Archelaus. He was finally impeached on a charge of impiety which must have seemed frivolous to educated Athenians, based as it was on his contention that the sun and the moon are material bodies rather than gods. As a result of the accusation, but under undetermined circumstances, he left Athens and spent the remainder of his life at Lampsacus in Asia Minor, where he was remembered by schoolchildren for a long time because the magistrates of the city carried out his dying request that they be given a holiday each year during the month of his death.

Anaxagoras was the first of the Greek philosophers to confront the West with a clear-cut dualism of Mind and Matter. His conception of the latter is even more pluralistic than that of Empedocles, involving the notion of infinitesimal particles which he called "seeds," infinite in number and all, in some measure, qualitatively different from one another. Like the Eleatics, Anaxagoras rejected the idea of absolute change if the change must be defined as the coming into existence or the passing out of existence of qualities. But if motion can be admitted, the seeds can retain their distinguishing characteristics perpetually without entailing a denial of change as it is observed in our experience, for as seeds of different sorts move into and out of a compound substance, it assumes the sensory characteristics of the particles which are dominant. "In everything," however, "there is a little bit of everything else." This notion, that no matter how small an object may be, it must contain seeds of every sort of substance, led to the difficult idea of infinite divisibililty and the conclusion that the seeds must be infinitesimal. "Of the small there is not least, but always a lesser."

Unlike Matter, Mind (*Nous*) is all of one piece. It is, on the cosmic level, the divine principle which separates different qualities from one another to produce an ordered universe. Originally, the world is a sort of undefined mush, with all the seeds so thoroughly intermingled that no qualities are dominant and, in consequence, no objects exist. Then *Nous*, present in the mixture, sets it into rotary motion so that lighter particles are thrown off from heavy ones as cream is from milk in a separator. Through its capacity for discrimination, Mind forms the previously amorphous Matter into specific forms and produces the world of sense.

# Chapter 15

# *Thinking About Structure and Value*

With the Atomists, Leucippus and Democritus, there was a movement from qualitative to quantitative pluralism, for the particles which they posited as the basis of reality are not distinguished by differences in what philosophers of a later age were to call "secondary" properties — color, sound, taste, and the like — but only in the "primary" attributes of size and shape. Their system marked the first emergence in Western thought of a philosophy which was at once genuinely materialistic and mechanistic.

Leucippus, probably a student of Zeno,. was, by various accounts, a native of Miletus, Elea, Melos, or Abdera. Little is known of his life except the significant fact that he founded at Abdera the school which brought fame to him and to his disciple, Democritus.

The influence of his Eleatic training is shown in his acceptance of the argument that true Being must be a *plenum*. The contention that it cannot involve empty space reinforced the Parmenidean contention that motion cannot exist because there are no "chinks" in Being into which objects can move. Recognizing the force of the argument, Leucippus, nevertheless, affirmed the existence of motion and adjusted his rational account of reality to accommodate the concept.

He did this by contending that there are an infinite number of *plena* rather than just one and that they move in a void, which, though it is not Being, is truly existent. Each of the tiny particles which constitute Being is, in a sense, an Eleatic universe, eternal, homogeneous, and unchanging, but the whole of which it is a part is subject to alteration because of the interaction of the various particles.

It is impossible to determine how much of the Atomists' doctrine is attributable to Leucippus and how much to elaboration by Democritus. Because of Democritus' success in publicizing his theory, he attracted more attention from classical writers, notably Aristotle, and his work is therefore better known than that of Leucippus.

A native of Abdera, Democritus is said to have been forty years younger than Anaxagoras, a circumstance which would make the date of his birth about 460 B.C. He is reported to have been instructed in childhood by Chaldean Magi and to have continued his studies later in Babylon, Egypt, India, and Ethiopia. A prolific writer, he was interested in a variety of subjects, some of which undoubtedly would have caused him difficulty as a mechanistic materialist if he had attempted to preserve a greater degree of consistency than is evident in the fragments and accounts of his work now extant.

The general nature of his metaphysics is clear. Like Leucippus, he recognized only two aspects of reality: atoms and the void. The void is an actual vacuum with spatial extension, but presumably with no other properties. As the Greek word *atomos*—"indivisible" or "uncuttable"—suggests, each atom is an irreducible *plenum*, and the atoms are infinite in number, differing from one another in size and shape. From eternity, they have been flying about through the void, colliding with one another and, through the variety of their shapes, combining together and separating in unceasing motion. When the atoms collide, a vortex is set up, and atoms which resemble one another in size or shape or both tend to be separated off into objects which are the constituents of an infinite number of worlds.

On the atomic level qualitative distinctions do not exist. Such differences have a sort of secondary or derived reality in the world of complex things as experienced by observers who, "by custom," identify objects through sensory differentiation which somehow emerges in the relationship between subject and object. The minds of men are themselves formed of light, smooth, mobile atoms, which are as material as the atoms composing their bodies.

The atomism of Democritus exhibits essential features common to the several forms of mechanistic materialism which have enjoyed perennial popularity in Western thought. On the credit side, it has offered a single, relatively uncomplicated explanatory principle for nature, requiring no cosmic intelligence or purpose to account for the ceaseless flux of matter. On the debit side, Greek Atomism and its more modern variants have encountered serious difficulties in trying to extend that principle to cover certain features of human experience which cannot easily be dismissed or reduced to the fortuitous concurrence of insensate atoms.

The first of these is the fact of experience itself. It is not immediately evident that particles having no consciousness can, through collision, become organized into objects which, merely by virtue of their complexity, can experience colors, sounds, tastes, smells, and touch, qualities which exist neither in the component atoms of the experiencing mind nor in those of the object experienced.

The second difficulty relates to the nature of knowledge itself. The only account the Atomists were able to give of the process of knowing is a purely mechanical one involving the collision of one particle with another. Unless it can be said that simply in being knocked into a corner pocket, a billiard ball can be said to "know" the cue ball which struck it, it is difficult to form a definition of knowledge which fits neatly into the framework of Democritan Atomism. A material reaction is what it is, and it makes little sense to say that one is "correct" and the other "incorrect." Yet it is precisely the notion of criteria of correctness which is essential to any coherent epistemological theory. If the philosophical materialist wishes seriously to maintain that all psychological processes are nothing more than physical movements induced by the impact of external or internal stimuli, his contention may prove fatal to any theory of verification by which his own position might be known to be true.

There is some evidence in the surviving fragments of Democritus' work that he recognized the difficulty faced by the atomist in elaborating a theory of knowledge. Man, he admitted, is "divorced from reality." He can have no authentic knowledge about anything, for every man's opinion is "simply what flows into him." Faced with the consequences of a skepticism which would undermine his own philosophy, he tried to make a distinction between genuine and obscure knowledge, relegating to the obscure category all the data of the senses and advocating "a finer means of knowing." The "finer means," presumably a rational or intellectual sort of knowing, could not, however, withstand critical scrutiny, for it had no real basis in his philosophy, a fact which Democritus ruefully acknowledged in a brief exchange between the intellect and the senses. The intellect declares, "It is by convention that color exists, by convention sweet, by convention bitter."

"Ah, wretched intellect," the senses reply, "You get your evidence only as we give it to you, and yet you try to overthrow us. That overthrow will be your downfall."

The third problem is one of value. Like the rest of the world, materialists make value judgements which seem to themselves and others to be something more than conditioned responses. They are, therefore, in their evaluation of such judgments, under the necessity of regarding their apparent objectivity as illusory — and illusion itself is not easily explained in atomistic terms — or of watering down their materialism to accommodate real values which are not composed of atoms. Democritus, without admitting that he was doing so, may have been following the latter course in the development of a moral philosophy which permitted him to write, "Justice is to do what should be done; injustice is to fail to do what should be done, and to put it aside."

In constructing a model of the universe which could reasonably be interpreted as excluding intelligibility, and value, the Atomists brought into question the whole process by which the great systems of the early period of Greek philosophy had been developed and opened the way to serious questions about man's capacity to know. It was to these questions that the Sophists addressed themselves.

### The Age of Pericles

By the time the principal figures of this movement came into prominence, the political structure of the Greek world had undergone considerable change. Miletus had been destroyed by the Persians, who had then moved against the Greek cities of the European mainland. Held back for a time at Marathon and Thermopylae, the had amassed enough power by 480 B.C. to capture and burn Athens, almost an empty city at the time due to a prior withdrawal of the citizens. The Persian triumph was short-lived, for before long the Persian king Xerxes — the Ahasuerus of the Book of Esther—suffered the humiliation of watching the destruction of his fleet by the Athenian navy at Salamis and, within two years, was forced to withdraw all his forces from Europe.

During the latter years of the war, the city-states of Greece entered into a confederacy, with Athens as the principal member. Growing in political and economic power, she arbitrarily moved the treasury of the confederacy from Delos to Athens and, in time, became the capital of what was, in effect, an empire. Her growing success inaugurated the greatest period in Greek history.

Pericles, the outstanding statesman of the time, replaced the Athens destroyed by the Persians with the city of marble which, in ruin, still retains its hold on the mind of Western man. Under his administration, wealth poured into the expanding metropolis, and there was an unprecedented flowering of all the arts.

The Golden Age ended with the beginning of the Peloponnesian War, in which the Greek cities aligned themselves on the side of one or the other of the two principal combatants, Athens and Sparta, in a fratricidal conflict which, after twenty-seven years, resulted in the destruction of the Athenian navy and the walls of the city.

## The Rise of Sophism

The prosperity of the Periclean era and the subsequent rigors of war contributed to the intellectual climate which altered the attitudes of the Athenians. The old religious faith and the amibitious world systems of the Ionian and Italian schools were regarded with increasing suspicion—a suspicion which made the city a fertile ground for the spreading movement of Sophism.

The word *sophistes* means variously "expert," "wise man," or "clever man." The Sophists, who presented themselves to the public as professional teachers, gave the term the narrower meaning of one who offers to sell wisdom for money. Like the earlier Greek philosophers, many of the Sophists were colonials, but the fame and wealth of Athens lured the best of them to the city at one time or another. Their principal instruction was in the art of rhetoric, or persuasion, by means of which their students might hope to succeed in such practical activities as lawsuits and political campaigns. Their association with rich clients earned them the condemnation of those who could not afford their services, and their conception of wisdom as a practical commodity of the market place brought them into conflict with serious seekers of truth like Socrates. However, some of them became quite rich, and for many of their admirers, the name "Sophist" remained an honorific one. Certainly, later Western thinkers must acknowledge a debt to members of the school who challenged their predecessors' unexamined assumptions about human cognition in a way which brought into sharp relief the central problem of knowledge.

## Protagoras

Protagoras (ca. 480-411 B.C.), was a native of the Thracian city of Abdera. He became an intinerant professional teacher at the age of thirty and charged high fees for his teaching, with the proviso, however, that a student who thought he had not received his money's worth could take an oath to that effect and pay only what he thought proper. That he was generally thought not to have overvalued his instruction is suggested by the fact that he amassed a large fortune.

It is said that he once made an agreement with a pupil named Euathlus that the unreasonably high fee he was charging for the instruction was to be paid only if the student should be successful in pleading his first case in court. Euathlus, reluctant to put the matter to a test, put off going to court, but he would neither pay the fee nor refuse to pay it. At last, Protagoras sued him for the money, explained the nature of the agreement to the judges, and confronted Euathlus with a dilemma.

"If I win the case you will have to pay me by the decision of the judges," he said, "and if you win you will still have to pay me because of the terms of our agreement; thus win or lose you are equally condemned. So what are you expecting to gain?"

Euathlus, an apt pupil of his master, blandly replied, "Whatever the outcome of the suit, I am freed of having to pay what you demand. For either I win the case and thus am cleared by the court's decree, or I am beaten and thus am cleared."

Protagoras became famous in his own time. He visited Athens several times, discussed legal matters with Pericles, and, according to Plato, participated in the celebrated Socratic dialogue which bears his name and also in the *Theatetus*. In these, as in the extant fragments of his writings, the relativistic character of his teaching is clear.

"Man," he maintained, "is the measure of all things: of things that are, that they are; of things that are not, that they are not." By "man," it is clear, he meant any individual rather than mankind, and his statement constitutes a denial of any universal standard accessible to mankind as a whole by which truth might be ascertained. Any quest for ultimate truths is doomed to failure, due to obstacles which include "the obscurity of the matter and the brevity of human life." The wisdom attainable by men is of a practical variety, and, in view of the fact that every human being experiences the world from his own point of view, no one can judge another's experience to be less well authenticated than his own. It follows that every opinion is "true" in the Sophistic sense.

Some opinions prove in experience, however, to be "better" if not "truer" than others, and the business of the teacher is to cultivate ideas which are conducive to the best possible adjustment of his pupil to the particular circumstances in which he finds himself. To conform successfully to one's own society is an accomplishment of practical wisdom, and in this conformity lies the true virtue (*arete*) which, like any other art, can be taught.

## Gorgias

If all propositions are, in Protagoras' view, true, they are all false as seen by his contemporary Gorgias. A native of Leontini in Sicily, Gorgias was an ambassador to Athens in 427 B.C. and, like Protagoras, became the subject of one of Plato's dialogues, which, however, reportedly led him to remark, "What a clever satirist Plato is." He remained unmarried, earned enormous fees from teaching in many lands, and remained in good health for more than a hundred years. He wrote a textbook of rhetoric, but is best remembered for his philosophical argument about being and knowing, presented in his treatise *On Being*, or *On Nature*.

Gorgias' first startling assertion is, "Nothing exists." He justified it by pointing out that if anything existed, it would necessarily be either being or not-being or both. Through use of the Eleatic method, he demonstrated that all three options involve self-contradiction and therefore must be rejected, leaving only the denial of all existence as a possibility.

His second proposition is that if anything exists, it cannot be comprehended. Concepts of the mind are not realities. Neither the senses nor the imagination provide any guarantee of any reality outside themselves, and "pure mind" is a fiction.

The third proposition is that if anything can be comprehended, it cannot be communicated. Admitting the existence of "perceptibles," the different senses still cannot communicate with one another. Sight cannot be translated into hearing. In our intercourse with one another, we are even more limited, for we are confined to speech, which, composed from perceptibles, can never be equated with that which might exist outside ourselves, or even with the perceptibles to which it is professed to refer. Therefore, even if something does exist and can be comprehended, it cannot be communicated.

It is clear that Gorgias, in his philosophy, was what would in a later day be called a dogmatic skeptic, denying not only the possibility of knowledge, but the very existence of any substrate reality to which knowledge or assertions based on knowledge could refer. The impossibility of giving an account of any universe of discourse accessible to all rational beings limits human intellectual effort to the individual and the practical, thus justifying, for Gorgias, his lucrative activity as a Sophist and explainining the fact that for him, speech was seen as largely manipulative in nature rather than expository.

### Other Sophists

Another Sophist who achieved some prominence in Athens, where he was a frequent visitor, was Prodicus, a native of the town of Ioulis on the Aegean island of Ceos. Never made the principal character in one of Plato's works, he is nevertheless often mentioned, having apparently intrigued Plato by his concern with the teaching of "correct terminology." He is said to have produced a work *On Nature*, or *On the Nature of Man*, and to have advocated a conventional morality based on a relativistic ethic not unlike that of Protagoras.

Antiphon, a contemporary of the other major Sophists, is a shadowy figure, sometimes confused with two others bearing the same name. He may have been a native of Athens. He taught for money, but was author of a work called *Truth*, which seems to have presented a philosophical position more closely akin to Eleatic thought than to the skepticism of his fellow Sophists.

Hippias of Elis, a district of southern Greece, is known primarily as an occasional character in Plato's dialogues, where his reputation is based in part on his claim to have made more money than any two other Sophists. He was reputed to be a man of great natural gifts and enormous learning, but none of his writings survive.

Critias of Athens, a member of a rich and distinguished family of that city, was a first cousin once removed of Plato and appears prominently in the dialogues, notably the one which bears his name. Execrated by Xenophon and other writers because of his later political career, in which his Spartan sympathies led him to accept the leadership of the Thirty Tyrants who governed Athens after the Peloponnesian War, he was given a more sympathetic treatment by his distinguished cousin, and his literary style, exhibited in a variety of writings, was highly praised by later writers.

Sometimes classified as a Sophist, Critias showed little kinship with others who bear that name except for his concern with practical statecraft and the everyday conditions of life. The few surviving fragments of that part of his writing of philosophic interest show a highly poetic mind, as in his description of Time as "unwearying, full, with everflowing stream, self begetting" and his apostrophe to the Creator, "self made, who hast woven the nature of all things in the aetherial whirl, round whom light and dusky shimmering night, and the innumerable throng of the stars for ever dance."

Thrasymachus, a native of Chalcedon in Asia Minor, was a prolific writer and an authority on rhetoric. He is best known, however, for the ethical views which he is represented as expressing with some heat in Plato's *Republic*. Justice, he maintained there, is nothing more than the advantage of the stronger. This position, though probably quite accurately represented, is not easy to reconcile with a speech cited by Hermeias in which Thrasymachus lamented the lack of justice in the affairs of men. The context of the latter statement is unknown, but it does not in itself provide sufficient grounds for rejecting his identification with the clearly Sophistic view with which he is credited by Plato.

# IV.
# UNIVERSALIZING HEBREW RELIGION

# Chapter 16

## *Confronting a New Situation*

Three decisive events in antiquity determined the life, thought, and destiny of the people of Israel. The first was the Exodus, which marked the birthday of Israel as a people. The second was the destruction of the nation by the Babylonians, followed by the exile of the leaders of Israel. The third was the decimation and scattering of the Jewish people by the Romans, in 70 A.D., which apparently brought down the final curtain on the drama of God's redemptive activity through the seed of Abraham. It may be, of course, that the perspective of history will add yet a fourth event from modern times to this list: the unspeakable Holocaust of the Jews in Europe perpetrated by the Nazis and their henchmen before and during the Second World War.

We observed earlier, in chapter 5, that the Exodus was a creative event, followed by the difficult times of wandering in the wilderness of Sinai and settlement in Canaan, times which, in spite of their difficulties, or, perhaps, because of them, provided the opportunity for laying the solid foundations of Israel's historic faith. Now we come to consider the second decisive event, the Babylonian Exile, in order to discover how it also proved to be creative in terms of religious faith and development. With the end of their national existence and their exile to strange lands, the Hebrews confronted a radically new situation; but out of that new situation there came a "new thing," Judaism, which, as we shall see, has supplied many of the most important ideas and institutions of subsequent Western culture.

We have described the last days of Judah, which Jeremiah first reluctantly predicted and then experienced with agony of soul. The Babylonians, new masters of the Fertile Crescent since their defeat of Assyria, captured Jerusalem in 597 B.C. and took Jehoiachin, the king of Judah, captive to Babylon, along with a large number of the nation's leaders. Judah survived for another decade as a vassal state under Zedekiah, the uncle of Jehoiachin; but when rebellion flared again, Nebuchadnezzar captured Jerusalem a second time, in 586, and the city was demolished beyond habitation. The Temple was burned, the walls of the city were pulled down, and all but a helpless remnant of the people were taken as exiled slaves to Babylon. To all appearances, the end had come. Nevertheless, the remarkable fact is that Israel and her faith did not disappear from the stage of history. The surprising survival and development of that faith was due to its radical transformation, and the transformation reflected the unstable world scene in which it occurred.

### Rapid Changes in Political Power

The powerful Babylonian Empire, which was built upon the ashes of Assyria by Nabopolassar and his son, Nebuchadnezzar, did not long endure. From the beginning it shared the region of the Middle East with its erstwhile ally, the empire of the Medes, as well as with the Egyptians and with the Lydians of western Asia Minor, who were now at the height of their power. Nebuchadnezzar was able to consolidate his hold upon nearly all of the Fertile Crescent, and he even succeeded in conquering Cilicia and making a successful punitive campaign against meddlesome Egypt. But, when he died, in 562, the Empire immediately began to crumble. His son, Amel-Marduk (the Evil-Merodach of II Kings 25:27), ruled for only two years before he was assassinated and replaced by his brother-in-law, Neriglissar, who, in turn, died after only four years and was succeeded by his minor son, Labashi-Marduk. The throne was then quickly seized by an Aramean nobleman, Nabonidus, who later exhibited more interest in history and archeology than in affairs of state. Nabonidus neglected the cult of Marduk, thereby angering the priests, and left the government in the hands of his incompetent son, Belshazzar (mistakenly referred to as Nebuchadnezzar's son in Daniel 5).

Meanwhile, events of epoch-making proportions were occurring in the territory of the Medes, a vast, crescent-shaped empire which then stretched across the lands north of the Fertile Crescent from the Halys River in central Asia Minor to the borders of India in the east. Cyaxares, king of the Medes, had been the ally of Nebuchadnezzar against the Assyrians. An uneasy peace continued with Babylonia when Cyaxares was succeeded, around 585 B.C., by his son, Astyages. However, the Babylonians made a fatal mistake by supporting Cyrus of Anshan, a petty vassal of Astyages, when Cyrus revolted against his Median overlord and began a seizure of power which soon led to his taking over the whole empire. Cyrus captured Ecbatana, the capital of the Medes, and dethroned Astyages, in 550. Then he marched westward against the

Lydians, and by 546 had defeated their king Croesus, and had captured Sardis, the capital of Lydia, thus enlarging his domain to the Aegean Sea. Nabonidus and the Babylonians had attempted to thwart the expansion of Cyrus by forming an alliance with Egypt and Lydia, but the effort failed. Babylonia for a brief period awaited inevitable defeat while Cyrus campaigned in the east, conquering new lands in the Afghan mountains and beyond, as far as the Aral Sea, the Oxus River, and the northwestern boundaries of India.

The end came quickly for Babylonia. Nabonidus attempted to rejuvenate the Babylonians by restoring the cultic practices of Marduk, especially the dramatic New Year's Festival, but it was too late. The handwriting was on the wall, and Babylonian rule was weighed in the balances and found wanting (cf. Daniel 5). The people of Babylon, including the exiled Jews, actually anticipated the coming of Cyrus and welcomed his Persians as liberators. Cilicia in the west and Elam in the east were already lost. A decisive battle was fought at Opis, on the Tigris River, and Babylon itself capitulated in the fall of 539 B.C. Cyrus was the master of the new Persian Empire, the largest the world had ever known.

A new epoch, indeed, began with the Persian Empire. The long dominance of the Middle East by Semitic peoples was ended. Aryan nations, first represented by the Persians, were to rule the Western world for millenia to come, and the star of empire would later march inexorably toward the west. Cyrus and his successors also introduced a new policy toward conquered cultures. Unlike the Assyrians and Babylonians, who ruled with crushing power and attempted to forestall revolt by forbidding ethnic identity and by scattering captured nations, the Persians encouraged indigenous cultures and permitted considerable ethnic autonomy. Cambyses, the son and successor of Cyrus, added Egypt to the empire. For two centuries, until the coming of Alexander the Great, the Persians ruled the vast region, governing with remarkable efficiency and leniency, and providing the people an unparalleled period of relative peace.

## Living in a Larger World

A lively imagination is required in order to understand the adjustments which inevitably occurred in Israelite religion during these times of rapid political and social change. The depth of the transformation is symbolized by the fact that it is no longer accurate to speak of the people as Hebrews, and of their faith as Hebrew religion; now they are Jews (from Judah) and their religion is Judaism. The former Covenant People of Yahweh were dispersed among the nations (goyim), never to be united politically again. The Diaspora had begun. The leaders of future Judaism lived as displaced persons, first as slaves and then as increasingly comfortable free citizens, in Babylonia; a small number remained as farmers and herders in the ravaged homeland; and still others built communities of fragile faithfulness in Egypt. The passing centuries and empires of the future were to witness an ever-widening dispersal of the worshippers of Yahweh who were descended from Abraham, Isaac, and Jacob-Israel.

The Exile brought culture shock difficult to imagine. An illustration from the twentieth century might help us to comprehend, even to feel, the confusion and temptation which must have assaulted the minds and spirits of the Jewish people when Jerusalem fell and they found themselves in strange lands. Consider, for example, what would happen to a simple Indian lad from an isolated tribe in Central America if he were suddenly removed from his home and people and taken overnight to a large metropolis such as New York City. Suppose, further, that the boy were to be kept in the city for the remainder of his life, to be educated, allowed to work, to marry, and to become thoroughly immersed in the cultural "melting pot" of modern society. Would he be expected to retain his old customs, ideas and, especially, primitive religious beliefs and practices? The obvious answer indicates what should have been expected of the Israelites from Judah as they suddenly faced a wider world, a world in which they were a tiny, defeated, and culturally undeveloped fragment.

The city of Babylon in the sixth century B.C. was an impressive metropolis, even by modern standards. It sat beside the life-giving Euphrates, which was spanned by a long bridge, constructed centuries before the Roman arch or modern steel. The people traveled on paved streets, enjoyed the security of high walls, and profited from a bustling commerce by barge and caravan. Nebuchadnezzar's Hanging Gardens broke the monotony of the flat landscape and were known as a wonder of the world. The Ishtar Gate, through which the pageantry of religious processions passed, has remained through the ages as a remarkable achievement of ancient construction. (It may be seen still in the German museum of East Berlin, where it was brought in the last century.) And, in addition, there were the other cities, and the splendor and power of Babylonia, to dazzle and humiliate the backward captives from Judah. How could one praise—or serve—Yahweh in such a foreign land?

The religion of Moses and the prophets survived these threatening conditions by discovering greater depth of meaning and wider measures of value. New leaders appeared to speak for Yahweh, and they revealed the universal dimensions of the old, apparently provincial faith. They interpreted the tragedies of the past as vindications of Yahweh's justice and truthfulness, and they began to develop structures of hope and redemption. The deprivation of Israel began to become a source of insight and strength. The Jews were taught, and increasingly believed, that just as Israel, the least and weakest of all people, had been called out of Egypt to be the redemptive people of God, so they were now chastised for their sins and scattered among the pagan nations so that they might further fulfill the historic vocation for which they had been created. God's instrument had been hardened and purified by fire so that it might become more useful for the eternal, divine purpose.

The transformation of Hebrew religion into Judaism was accomplished by the work of many new leaders of the people, some known by name and others remembered only from their work. Their task was to preserve the truth and value of the past but also to recast it so that it might be relevant to the new situation. The ideas and practices, literature and institutions of Judaism are the rich fruit of their labors.

### Judaism Taking Shape

One of the distinguishing characteristics of Judaism which has remained through the centuries is the special place given to sacred literature in faith and practice. In a later chapter, we shall discuss how and why the Jews have been known historically as "the people of the Book." Here we must note that the Exile was both the time and the cause of the beginning of this literary emphasis and development. Though dispersed, threatened, and cast down, the Jews began to listen to the Word of God from the past, in terms of written prophecy, as well as to hear the Word in their present, in terms of cultic worship and personal experience; and they began to believe and to teach that present religious experience must be judged and authenticated by past revelation. Thus sacred Scripture was born: a special corpus of writings began to be considered *sacred* (because it was believed to be the written record of the Word previously spoken by God) and *authoritative* (because it was the standard by which truth and righteousness could be judged).

At least four distinct groups of sacred writings began to take form during the general period of the Exile, though some had their oral or written beginnings in the distant past of Israel's history. One such was what has come to be known as the Deuteronomic History. This is the collection of ancient traditions, tribal stories, and monarchy records which was probably edited by the Yahweh loyalists who initiated the great reform which was attempted in the last days of the kingdom of Judah, when Josiah was king. The same prophetic voices who spoke for Yahweh through the words of Moses in the second giving of the Law—Deuteronomy—also used the available narrative material to illustrate the famous Doctrine of Two Ways which was so central to the theology of Deuteronomy (see chapter 12, above). Their work came to be called the Former Prophets—the books of Joshua, Judges, Samuel, and Kings.

A second collection of ancient traditions and written sources was made, according to modern scholarly opinion, by the priests of Israel. Their finished product became the centerpiece of Jewish piety, the Torah. Opinions vary as to the precise time of their work, the nature of their sources, and the extent of their contributions; but the general descriptive scheme worked out by the German theologian, Julius Wellhausen, in the nineteenth century, still appears to provide the best understanding of how the Pentateuch took its final form and was "canonized" by the end of the fifth century B.C. According to that familiar theory, four primary strands of material, or "documents," may be detected in the extant "five books of Moses," the Torah. They are, first, the Yahwist tradition, designated "J," believed to have been compiled in the Solomonic era, or by 850 B.C.; second, the Elohist ("E") tradition, originated around 750 B.C., and combined with "J" after the fall of Israel in 722; third, the Deuteronomic materials ("D"), edited about 625 B.C. as described above; and, fourth, the Priestly traditions ("P"), combined with JED during the Exile, or shortly thereafter, to complete the Pentateuch.

A third significant literary development in Judaism during the era of the Exile was the writing and collection of prophetic oracles. Two of Israel's greatest prophets, Ezekiel and the great theologian known as Second Isaiah, performed their creative task during the Exile. We shall devote the next two chapters to a discussion of their contributions. However, it is also probable that the oracles of the earlier prophets were treasured and subjected to restudy and redaction during this informative period. They certainly were carefully preserved, and, undoubtedly, began to receive the hearing which led, before too many centuries passed, to their canonization alongside the Torah. We know that, by the end of the third century B.C., both the Torah and the Nebi'im had achieved scriptural status among the Jews.

Finally, a fourth body of literature which seems to have had its origin among the exiles was the Chronicler's History (I, II Chronicles, Ezra-Nehemiah). Obviously, this sweeping review of the past, duplicating much that is found in the Former Prophets, could not have been completed early in the Exile, since it includes the materials in Ezra-Nehemiah which have to do with events which occurred during the Persian Period. However, it records important theological developments of the exilic and post-exilic periods, especially the tendency toward jingoism and the Jewish self-identification as a religious community rather than as a nation.

In addition to these permanently significant literary creations during the period of the Exile, a second, related characteristic of ancient Judaism may be seen in the increasingly prominent use of apocalypticism. We have already taken cognizance of its appearance as early as Amos. However, apocalyptic discourse, whether in oral or written form, did not come to full flower as a major vehicle of religious expression among the Jews until after the tragedy of the Babylonian Captivity. With that watershed event, prophecy began to decline and apocalyptic simultaneously began to replace it; and that process continued for centuries, until after the rise of Christianity. The influence of Jewish apocalypticism on Christian teaching and literature is so apparent that it has been said, not altogether in exaggeration, that Christianity is the only Jewish apocalyptic sect to survive the fall of Jerusalem to the Romans in 70 A.D.

Just what is meant by apocalypticism? It is a genre of religious expression, possibly oral but usually in written form, which arises out of suffering and despair. It is akin to prophecy, of course, though the two are clearly distinguishable, and it is one of the great tragedies of Biblical interpretation that many, with more fervor than information, have misunderstood the meaning of apolcalyptic materials in the Scriptures and have erroneously read them as their favorite prophecies. The two genres are different in style, content, and emphasis. As to *style*, prophecy is nearly always in the form of hortatory oracles: "thus saith Yahweh;" but apocalyptic characteristically appears in the form of visions or dreams, usually described in grotesque terms not common to nature and experience. As to *content*, prophecy displays particular concern with individual and social immorality; it thus calls for repentance, in the name of the Covenant God of Israel: "do justice, love mercy, turn from your wicked ways!" But apocalyptic foresees the coming judgment, apparently recognizing that repentance is not forthcoming; hence it describes the unimaginable terror of God's wrath, along with the indescribable felicity of the righteous, in the age to come. And, as to *emphasis*, prophecy is primarily concerned with the present, or with the immediate future, while the conditions of evil may yet be rectified; but apocalyptic discloses the distant, unknown future, under the conditions of another age, when the wicked will receive their deserved punishments and the righteous will enjoy the glories of heaven's rewards.

Although there was some use of apocalypticism before the Exile, it apparently first came to full expression in the oracles of Ezekiel. Some scholars have even described him as "the father of apocalypticism." The hopelessness of the people to whom he ministered explains his extensive use of this new mode. Later prophets also, such as Zechariah, were to use apocalyptic as an antidote to despair. As the darkening centuries passed and hope for restoration grew more dim, this became increasingly the chosen instrument of religious spokesmen among the Jews who attempted to assure the weary people that Yahweh will yet redeem his elect and finally triumph over all evil.

A third significant development during the period of the Exile which gave form to Judaism may be seen in the radical transformation of Israel's theology. In a word, the nature of Yahweh and of his moral relation to mankind required redefinition as a result of the trauma inflicted upon the Jewish mind by the fall of the nation and the shocking exposure to other cultures. The old theology was simply insufficient; indeed, it had apparently proved to be false. In the slave camps along the Chebar canal in Babylon, where was Yahweh? How could the old tribal God of Sinai and

Canaan be compared to the grand and victorious Marduk, mighty god of the Babylonians? Yahweh had failed to protect his people; his "inviolable Zion" had been sacked and burned; and his promise of reward for faithfulness was as empty as a broken cistern!

Such inevitable pessimism was undoubtedly the cause of widespread apostasy among the Jews in Babylon and Egypt after the fall of Judah. It is surprising that even a remnant remained faithful. The fact that they did is due to the work of a small group of inspired thinkers who created Judaism out of the chrysalis of a moribund though pregnant faith. They interpreted the tragedy of the past as proof of Yahweh's justice, since he had promised judgment if repentance were not forthcoming; and they elevated the older, inadequate conceptions of Yahweh as a local, tribal deity, expressing their deeper faith in universal proportions. The problem of theodicy remained, of course, as it always will in the mind of finite man; but the post-exilic literature of Judaism dealt with that theological problem with a grandeur and depth unequaled in any other culture.

Finally, a fourth characteristic of Judaism which appeared at this earliest stage was the institutional form which it has maintained throughout subsequent history. The former ways of worship and religious identity, associated with the tribal and nomadic past or tied to land and nation, were no longer possible for the dispersed people. New institutions and methods for the practice of holiness were required to match the cultural universalism which the Jews in exile began to experience. Living as a small minority with a strange and unique religion as their only uniting and identifying distinction, the Jews confronted a new situation in which their choice was between the death of amalgamation or the life which permits continuity only in the midst of change. The Jews chose the risks of life, as they have through all the ages, daring to retain the essence of their ancient faith through conserving institutions and rituals which bring the past and the other into the present.

We must confess that our knowledge of the religious developments among the Jews during the Exile is meager. The sources are limited, both in Scripture and in archeological materials. In fact, much more detailed information is available concerning the Hebrews from the time of Saul and David to the fall of Jerusalem, a period of more than four centuries, than there is from the exilic and Persian periods, which together lasted nearly three centuries. However, it is safe to conjecture that certain developments occurred during these centuries since institutions and practices were well established at the end of the period which were unknown, or nearly so, at the beginning.

One of the most important and permanent institutions in Judaism which had its beginning during the Exile is the *synagogue*. (Strangely, this is a term of Greek derivation which means "a coming together," which is practically the equivalent of the Latin "congregation.") Since the ancient Temple of Solomon no longer existed, and the cultic sacrifices there were no longer possible, the scattered Jews naturally gathered for study, guidance and worship, wherever they lived in the widening world. It was also natural and necessary that such groups should be led by trained and chosen leaders, especially those who retained copies of the written Law and the oracles of the prophets, and, furthermore, who possessed the increasingly rare ability to read the Hebrew language of their forebears. Thus arose the so-called *Tannaim*, the teachers and transmitters of the traditions; and from them arose the *Rabbis*, men who were not priests in the Levitical sense but rather were teachers of the Torah and leaders of worship in synagogue and community.

Three other distinctively Jewish institutions and practices which, though not originated in the exilic period, certainly received renewed emphasis then, are monotheism, Sabbath observance, and ritual circumcision. Belief in one, and only one, God was a strange and unusual religious position to be held in the vast, pagan sea of polytheism into which, like Jonah, Israel had been cast. Whatever may have been its older origins, keeping the last day in a seven-day week as a holy day for religious worship was peculiar to the Jews, and the practice clearly set them apart from their neighbors. And circumcision also became a required ritual sign that those who sprang from the loins of the Patriarchs were a separate people, "a holy nation" dedicated to Yahweh.

Other distinctive marks of Judaism were originated or began to occupy prominence during the post-exilic period. Holy days and seasons were celebrated, commemorating the events in the distant or recent past which the Jews believed had revealed Yahweh's deeds of redemption. The Passover annually reminded the people of the birth of the Covenant People by the Exodus from Egypt. Succoth similarly brought to mind the succor of Yahweh during the forty years in the wilderness of Sinai. Later, other special days were added to the calendar, all designed to preserve identity and to kindle faith.

Thus Judaism was born and formed in the fiery furnace of exile and in the dispersion among the lion's den of hostile nations. In spite of weakness and despair, the Jews creatively responded to the challenge and produced literature, ideas, and institutions which have survived the passing centuries and still remain as strong foundation stones in the culture of the West. Two of the creative giants in that remarkable process were the prophets Ezekiel and Second Isaiah. It is to their contributions that we now turn.

## Chapter 17

# Ezekiel and the Beginnings of Judaism

The prophet Ezekiel, and the book Ezekiel, present a matched enigma to the modern student. The unusually precise biographical detail provided about the former, and the apparently clear unity, provenance, and structure of the latter, both serve to illustrate the confused instability of their times and the apocalyptic style to which they gave impetus; for the biographical precision and the literary clarity are not what they seem. The truth is hidden in mystery, and the language seems designed to conceal as well as to reveal.

Ezekiel was a prophet who was also a priest, yet a priest without a temple, without the cultic necessities his religion required for worship, force to live in "an unclean land." He was a prophet, but his message was couched more in the mode of apocalyptic than of prophecy. He continued to proclaim a harsh judgment upon his own people, in words that were sharply unmerciful and often obscene, even after the judgment had come in terms of catastrophic human suffering and national humiliation. And then, when the glory of his angry God had departed from the smoking ashes of a rejected Zion, Ezekiel turned to the theme of hope, painting a picture of an ideal future when God's people would dwell in the new Zion, like contented sheep under the care of a good shepherd. Ezekiel reversed the direction of most of the prophets who had spoken before him: they looked backward to the golden age of the wilderness, to the youth of Israel, when she was chosen as the beloved bride of Yahweh, and they called upon her to repent of her later unfaithfulness; Ezekiel, on the other hand, accused Israel of harlotry from the beginning, and he looked in hope to a future state of virtue and love, made possible by the awesome and gracious power of Yahweh.

Moreover, the book is as enigmatic as the man. The ancient rabbis questioned whether it should even be included in the canon because of its numerous disagreements with the Torah (i.e., Ezekiel 46:6 and Numbers 28:11), and they would not allow the first chapter to be read in the synagogue. An ancient Jewish regulation went so far as to forbid anyone under thirty years of age to read some parts of the book! Later scholarship has raised innumerable questions concerning its authenticity, authorship, writing, date, place of origin, and, of course, interpretation. Probably no book of Scripture has been subjected to a wider range of opinion on these questions than Ezekiel. And yet it not only achieved and maintained its prominent place in the Hebrew Scriptures as one of the three "major prophets," but it has also exercised a powerful influence on the development of Judaism, and it has been a major source of ideas in Christian piety and thought as well.

## The Man and His Times

Ezekiel was a younger contemporary of Jeremiah, and he may have heard the sometimes harsh, sometimes hopeful oracles of the older prophet. Both were descendants of priestly families, and both suffered through the final, excruciating days of Judah's struggle against death. However, unlike Jeremiah, Ezekiel was among the leaders of Jerusalem, including the king, Jehoiachin, who were deported to Babylon in the first captivity of 597 B.C. There, in the first of history's many Jewish ghettos, ironically named Tel-Abib ("hill of fruitfulness"), Ezekiel lived among the displaced people, a priest without altar or legitimacy.

However, the priest, while remaining such, became also a prophet. In a manner reminiscent of the calls of Isaiah and Jeremiah, Ezekiel both saw and heard the summons of Yahweh to be his spokesman to the people. In the opening words of the book, the prophet described the setting and grandeur of his call: "In the thirtieth year, in the fourth month, on the fifth day of the month, as I was among the exiles by the river Chebar, the heavens were opened, and I saw visions of God" (1:1). There is a wide variety of scholarly opinion as to the meaning of "the thirtieth year," but the exact date of the vision is specified in the next verse: "it was the fifth year of the exile of King Jehoiachin" (1:2). That would date the call as having occurred on July 21, 592 or July 1, 593 B.C., depending upon whether the writer was using the Jewish or Babylonian calendar, since the former began a new year with the autumnal equinox and the latter with the vernal equinox. In any case, the call came in the form of a bizarre vision of the majestic God, and it required Ezekiel to prepare for his difficult task by first digesting the Torah. Then he was commanded to go to "the rebellious house of Israel" with unparalleled messages of judgment, reminding the people of their continuing sinfulness and announcing that "the end," "disaster," and "doom" had come upon the nation (7:1-13).

Ezekiel performed the task of condemnation without hint of mercy until the final blow fell with the destruction of Jerusalem in 586 B.C. He spoke both to the people who were in captivity with him and to the people who remained in Judah. He seems to have been transported back and forth between Babylon and Jerusalem. Did he, in fact, return to the native city? That is a perplexing question which has divided the scholars, and no certainty can be achieved. It is possible that he visited Jerusalem during those troubled days of Zedekiah's final reign, and the information he disclosed about conditions and events there would appear to make it likely. However, given his manner of speaking and his psychic character, it is just as possible that his visions of the Temple and of the growing paganism in Judah were symbolic and imaginary, based on facts available to him.

In either case, Ezekiel pronounced words of doom on the nation, just as the prophets before him had done, but with more immediacy and shrillness; and he delivered Yahweh's angry message in both word and deed. The method of revealing meaning by sign as well as speech was not new; we remember, for example, the naming of Hosea's and Isaiah's children, and the dramatic actions in Jerusalem by Isaiah and Jeremiah. But Ezekiel made greater use of dramatic signs, making them into a major vehicle of revelation.

Very little biographical detail is recorded for the years between the call of Ezekiel, in 593/92 B.C., and the fall of Jerusalem in 586. Apparently, the priest-prophet continued to live among the exiles in Babylonia, although, as indicated above, it is possible that he returned to Judah for a part of that time. Wherever he may have spent the years, he delivered his message of severe judgment, with word and sign, and the predominance of his burden was directed against the leaders of the people, especially those who remained in Judah. Like Jeremiah at the same time, Ezekiel evidently considered the people with Zedekiah, in the last days of Judah, to be "bad figs," although, unlike Jeremiah, he did not compliment his fellow-exiles as "good figs." His indictment fell upon both.

Finally, however, word came to Ezekiel in Babylonia that his prophecy had been authenticated, "In the twelfth year of our exile, in the tenth month, on the fifth day of the month, a man who had escaped from Jerusalem came to me and said, 'The city has fallen' "

(33:21). It was a debilitating message of death that had been predicted and was fully expected; and yet its shock and sorrow were no less real. Judgment, deserved though it may have been, was no less painful; there could be no advantage in continuing to remind the people of their guilt and of the previous warnings. Now another task must begin, that of comforting the hopeless people and discovering the way of restoration. The prophets of Israel, doleful Ezekiel included, never believed that judgment is the last word. Because God is gracious, his mercy endures forever, and there is always hope.

Beginning with that confirmation of catastrophe, therefore, Ezekiel began to speak in a new key. The remainder of his ministry, apparently, was devoted to the necessary message of hope. Again, almost no historical or biographical details are reported. We may only surmise that he continued to live in exile, where he contributed to the construction of the ideas and institutions of Judaism. Some of his oracles were preserved, probably by disciples, and they were compiled and edited, along with his earlier sermons and visions, to form what was finally to become the canonical Book of Ezekiel. The last portion of that material, chapters 40-48, provided an idealistic blueprint for the new Temple in the new Israel; it was dated "in the twenty-fifth year of our exile, at the beginning of the year, on the tenth day of the month, in the fourteenth year after the city was conquered..." (40:1). That was 572 B.C., the year of the last word heard from Ezekiel.

## The Book of Ezekiel

The Book of Ezekiel seems to fall naturally into four divisions. The first section is composed of the first 24 chapters, containing most of the authentic oracles of doom which the prophet spoke after his call, in 593/92 B.C., and before the fall of Jerusalem in 586 B.C. The second section, chapters 25-32, contains a series of prophecies against other nations; many scholars question whether they belong to Ezekiel, though there is no convincing reason to think otherwise. The third section, chapters 33-39, bears the mark of Ezekiel's style, and it begins his message of renewal after the nation had fallen. Finally, chapters 40-48 contain the detailed description of the restored community and have therefore been called "the priest's paradise," or a *civitas dei*. It may be that the two last sections should be considered together, reducing the divisions to three.

The first part of the book may be aptly designated Ezekiel's Book of Signs, anticipating the first half of the New Testament's Gospel of John, since it also is edited around the structure of seven signs. To follow that admittedly exaggerated comparison somewhat further, the first three chapters of Ezekiel may be considered a prologue, presenting an account of his vocational commission. Here is the famous vision of the "wheels, way up, in the middle of the air." It is clearly a vision of the throne-chariot of God, manifesting his power and mobility, by which the prophet sought to elevate the conception of Yahweh for the doubting Jews in exile. He skillfully used the imagery familiar in Canaanite and Assyrian religions, as well as in the mythology of the earlier Hebrews: the mighty throne of the deity, protected by winged cherubim and transported on massive wheels. The transcendent God of the Hebrews, Yahweh, now present with his people in Babylonia, spoke from the stormy heavens and commissioned Ezekiel to take the Torah, made incarnate by his eating, to the people in darkness that they might be enlightened to understand the cause of their punishment.

The seven signs follow, interspersed with the oracles of explanation and judgment. 1. The coming siege of Jerusalem was depicted by a diagram drawn on tile and by a model wall made from an iron plate or cooking griddle (4:1-3). 2. The prophet lay on his left side for 390 days and on his right side for 40 days, apparently illustrating the apostasy of the northern kingdom, Israel, and the coming exile of Judah (4:4-8). 3. The prophet prepared and ate mixed food in a limited manner in order to predict the famine of Judah's final days (4:9-17). 4. He trimmed his hair and beard with a sharp sword and then divided the hair into three equal parts, burning some, distributing some around the city, and scattering the remainder in the wind. A long series of oracles followed, explaining the action in terms of the scattering of the people of Judah in exile because of their persistent evil (5:1-11:25). 5. Ezekiel gathered his belongings and dug through the wall at night, again dramatizing the impending siege and capture (12:1-16). 6. He ate his food in trembling terror and attempted to convince those who would not acknowledge the fact of coming defeat (12:17-24:14). 7. Finally, Ezekiel accepted the death of his wife, "the delight of your eyes," without the customary mourning, attempting thereby to shock the people out of their complacency in the face of Judah's death (24:15-27).

By this structure and content, the pre-exilic portion of the Book of Ezekiel manifests a fundamental feature of Hebrew religion, which is, precisely, that the nature and purpose of God are revealed to the eyes of faith by the two means of personal disclosure: word and sign. How else can personal being (spirit) be known by other personal spirits, subject to subject? Ezekiel 1-24 illustrates the methodology of revelation and response; the one is by word and act, the other is by understanding and acceptance.

The last portion of the book contains three especially important oracles. The first one is the beautiful and influential portrait of God as the good shepherd, found in chapter 34. When spoken to the despairing Jews in exile, it must have been a tonic to the spirit, providing new vision and strength. The prophet announced that although the shepherds of Israel (prophets, priests, and kings) had miserably failed in their care of the flock, Yahweh himself would now be their guide and deliverer. "For thus says the Lord God: Behold I, I myself will search for my sheep, and will seek them out. As a shepherd seeks out his flock when some of his sheep have scattered abroad, so will I seek out my sheep; and I will rescue them from all places where they have been scattered on a day of clouds and thick darkness. And I will bring them out from the peoples, and gather them from the countries, and I will bring them into their own land; and I will feed them on the mountains of Israel, by the fountains, and in all the inhabited places of the country"(34:11-13). The figure of the good shepherd could never again fade from the image of God in the mind of Israel; thus despair could never be dominant or permanent among the people of Yahweh.

A second, unforgettable, oracle from the prophet in exile is that of the Valley of Dry Bones, in chapter 37. Greater assurance for the downcast people can hardly be imagined. Ezekiel saw Israel in death, separated from the creative and vitalizing power of the Spirit (*Ruach*) of Yahweh. The people were like scattered bones in the desert, parched, disoriented, and lifeless. But the Spirit, given through the word of the prophet, brought new spirit, life, and restoration to the dead. The promise of hope, thus dramatically delivered, included even the anticipation of the reunification of the divided nation and the reestablishment of the glorious reign of David. Out of such high vision would come major elements of future Jewish popular piety and messianic theology. God had promised a future, it was believed, that no suffering could diminish or deny.

Finally, we have already referred to the last nine chapters of the book as an idealized blueprint of the restored community. Ezekiel described a final vision given to him by Yahweh so that he might share with his fellow exiles the dimensions of a glorious future which would enable them to remain faithful against the ever-present threat of despair and apostasy. He delivered the detailed specifications for the reconstruction of the Temple, the reinstitution of priestly worship, and the settlement of the twelve tribes in their promised land. It was an inspiring preparation for the homecoming of the dispersed people of Israel. Most thrilling of all must have been the announcement that the glory of the angry God which had departed from the Temple before its destruction was now about to return. Judgment was past and forgiveness was offered. Ezekiel sowed the seeds of undying hope and passionate attachment to *that* land as he told of his vision: "And the vision I saw was like the vision which I had seen when he came to destroy the city, and like the vision which I had seen by the river Chebar; and I fell upon my face. As the glory of the Lord entered the temple by the gate facing east, the Spirit lifted me up, and brought me into the inner court; and behold, the glory of the Lord filled the temple....and he said to me, 'Son of man, this is the place of my throne and the place of the soles of my feet, where I will dwell in the midst of the people of Israel for ever' " (43:3-5, 7a).

## The Father of Judaism

Ezekiel has often been called "the Father of Judaism." That may be considered a fit appellation if only because he lived and taught at the crucial moment of Israel's history when the future was at stake, a time in her existence when, by usual historical standards, she might well have disappeared from the scene with scarcely an echo remaining. Undoubtedly, Ezekiel was one of those leaders, possibly the most important, who prevented that disappearance. There certainly were others, subsequently unknown and unsung, who contributed to the survival of Hebrew religion and participated in its transformation into the Judaism which incorporates the old views and values while purifying them and adding others; but we know and have in hand the work of Ezekiel, to a considerable degree, and we can see in that work the beginnings of the future faith. Therefore, he is properly praised as the Father of Judaism.

It is not enough, however, to accept that fact without further explanation. In addition to the decisiveness of his time in history and the fortunate preservation of his teachings, what was there, precisely, in his word and work which guaranteed the survival of the old and contributed to the formation of the new? We must press the question in order to assess the full magnitude of Ezekiel's legacy to future Western culture; for it must be remembered that the grandeur of pre-exilic Hebrew religion was transmuted into Judaism and that out of that moral and theological matrix were born both Christianity and Islam. Such creative and decisive significance should arouse careful inquiry as to its explanation.

We suggest, therefore, that Ezekiel was the Father of Judaism because he realized in his own experience and bequeathed to history a unique synthesis of the prophetic and priestly elements which are essential to adequate religion. The prophetic is primarily the moral emphasis. Its origin is in God, the gracious and righteous Creator. Hence,the prophet, who is a human spokesman for the Divine, declares the nature and will of God and calls the creature back from alienation to the source of being. The central word to man is the demand for repentance (*teshubah*, return) because, measured by the divine standard, man is evil—falling short of his possibilities, distorting truth and reality, transgressing the bounds of moral law. However, the demand for repentance is not to be heard, finally, as condemnation, but rather as gracious and loving invitation, an offer of acceptance, welcome, and blessing. The chastisement of God is always announced with tears and out of suffering love, with the intention of healing and reconciliation. Thus the prophet pleads for the return of rebellious children who are still beloved children nonetheless.

The priestly element of genuine religion, on the other hand, primarily celebrates, preserves, and transmits. Though ordained of God, it is directed from the side of man. Hence, the priest is one of his people, representing them to the Redeemer. He sits where the people sit, sharing their guilt and sorrow, but he goes continually on their behalf through the ways of worship to bring them again from their wanderings to the doorway of home. He leads their prayers, offers their reconciling sacrifices, and directs them to the sources of life. The priest creates and preserves the necessary forms and institutions which transmit and make relevant the grace and truth which the faithful community experiences and appropriates.

Because he was both prophet and priest at the moment of Israel's death and rebirth, Ezekiel combined the two elements with such remarkable balance that they have characterized the religion of the Jews through the subsequent ages. The result has been, on the one hand, a way of life which gives priority to morals and at the same time is lively, joyful and world-affirming. It is motivated by a vision of ultimate unity which finds expression in a stubbornly monotheistic theology. And it praises the Creator by acknowledging the goodness of his creation and revelling in it, like a happy child with a gift from its loving parents, eschewing both the pride of self-sufficiency and the blasphemous asceticism which calls unclean what God has made. On the other hand, the result of Ezekiel's priestly work has been a way of worship which has been maintained in a hostile world through the centuries by institutional form, social identity, and ritual enactment. He envisioned a glory-filled Temple in which Israel could meet her God in thankful praise and renewal; since that was not possible under the conditions of exile and dispersion, the synagogue came into being in order to meet the religious needs of the people of God wherever they went. Ezekiel called the people to holiness and drew a sharp line between them and the idolatrous nations outside the Covenant. That separateness has made possible the continued existence of Israel in spite of the constant temptation to a fatal tolerance and a religious indifference which inevitably result in a blurring of distinctions between truth and falsity, good and evil. And, finally, Ezekiel contributed to the development of Judaism as a way of faith which brings the past of revelation and redemption into the present by symbolic ritual and anticipates a future of blessedness by proleptic ceremony.

The two major portions of the Book of Ezekiel themselves illustrate the prophetic and priestly emphases which are joined in historic Judaism. The first part is primarily prophetic, speaking for Yahweh in judgment upon sin and calling for a moral turning. The second part is primarily priestly, showing the way to holiness through obedience and worship. Thus the God who is both Creator and Redeemer is presented as One, and Ezekiel, the pre-exilic prophet of doom, was last heard as a voice, crying in the wilderness of exile, giving comfort to the people.

# Chapter 18

## *The Creator Who Redeems*

One of Israel's most profound and influential prophets has remained completely hidden from the curious and searching eyes of scholars. Only his words have survived. That fortunate fact, however, is sufficient to make it apparent that a great, creative voice proclaimed the Word of Yahweh to the Jews in exile, probably around 540 B.C., when the end of Babylonia was at hand and the ascendency of Cyrus the Great and his Persians was beginning. The one who spoke is totally unknown, but his message has been repeated and heard through the succeeding ages, and his words of incomparable power and beauty have continued to bring joy and hope to the people of Yahweh as they must have when first uttered. The poetic oracles were preserved and edited, no doubt with loving care, and they found their place in the canon of Hebrew Scriptures by being added to the prophecies of Isaiah. Thus, for want of a better name, the unknown prophet is designated simply as Second Isaiah.

Whatever his name may have been, the prophet known as Second Isaiah is believed to have anticipated, and perhaps witnessed, the fall of Babylon to the Persians in 539 B.C. As we have already noted, that epoch-making event was accepted with joy by the citizens of Babylon, especially the priests of Marduk, who despised Nabonidus because of his neglect of the ancient cult. Even more jubilant, of course, were the nations held in subjugation by the Babylonians, including the Jews. The fires of hope for the eventual restoration of Israel, kept alive by the earlier promises of Jeremiah and Ezekiel, now burst forth in flames of lyric delight:

When the Lord restored the fortunes of Zion,
we were like those who dream.
Then our mouth was filled with laughter,
and our tongue with shouts of joy;
then they said among the nations,
"The Lord has done great things for them."
The Lord had done great things for us;
we are glad. (Psalm 126:1-3)

The mighty Cyrus did not disappoint them. He initiated a new policy which was very different from that practiced by the Assyrians and Babylonians, who crushed and scattered the nations under their domain. Cyrus encouraged cultural pluralism, allowing as much ethnic automony as the secure maintenance of his empire would permit. Although he worshipped the god of his people, Ahura-mazda, he also recognized the legitimacy of the gods of the other people under his rule, and he even supported the rebuilding of their shrines and the reinstitution of their cultic practices. The generous policy seems to have borne fruit, for most of the people of the vast empire, including the Jews, enjoyed an unparalleled period of relative peace and well-being which lasted for two centuries under the Persians. As might be expected, since the records of history contain more about war than peace, too little is known about the affairs of the Jews during that time.

The permissive policy of Cyrus is well documented both by Scripture and by archeological record. The famous Cyrus Cylinder, discovered at Babylon, reveals his apparently sincere generosity, not only to the Babylonians but to all the ethnic groups within his empire. The Jewish Chronicler also recorded an edict of Cyrus, issued in 538 B.C., both in the international language of the day, Aramaic (Ezra 6:3-5), and in Hebrew (Ezra 1:2-4). Accordingly, the Jews who were in Babylonia were allowed to return to Judah if they wished, to restore the walls of the city of Jersalem,and to rebuild the Temple. Furthermore, they were supported in their restoration by the Persian treasury and protected by Persian troops. Sheshbazzar, the son of the former Hebrew king-in-exile, Jehoiachin, was appointed to lead the return, thus restoring the line of David to a significant degree; and when he passed from the scene, being probably already an old man, his nephew, Zerubbabel, succeeded him as the Davidic heir-apparent. The small band of Jews who thus chose to return to the poverty-striken homeland immediately laid the foundation for a new Temple, and the traditional worship of Yahweh was begun upon the ancient site. Although economic and social conditions continued to make life difficult, and political freedom could be only a pious dream, the Jews had many reasons for joy and hope. That was the context in which the new prophet delivered his words of comfort and expectation.

## The Oracles of Second Isaiah

When we read the Book of Isaiah, whether in Hebrew or in English translation, in ancient manuscript or modern print, we find no separation into parts, some attributed to one prophet and some to another. It is all one book, and it has all been attributed to the eighth-century prophet, Isaiah of Jerusalem, since his name is given at the beginning and numerous times thereafter. Thus is was unanimously accepted as a unity by interpreters until near the end of the eighteenth century. Nevertheless, in 1782 the scholar Doederlein announced that a careful examination of the text demands a distinction between the first thirty-nine chapters and the remainder of the book. Since that time a majority of the students of the Hebrew Scriptures have accepted that conclusion, and there have been further refinements in the critical analysis of the Book of Isaiah so as to suggest the likelihood that chapters 56 through 66 were the work of yet another prophetic source, often designated as Third Isaiah. The generally-held view of modern scholarship, therefore, is that the authentic oracles of Second Isaiah ("Deutero-Isaiah") are found in chapters 40 through 55.

What is the basis of this hypothesis, now so widely accepted? This is not the place for a detailed account of the evidence, but the essential arguments are usually presented in three categories. First, and perhaps most persuasive, is the fact that the historical situation was obviously changed for the author of the material beginning with chapter 40 from what it had been for most of the oracles in the earlier part of the book. The first part frequently refers to Assyria, Sennacherib, Ahaz, Hezekiah, and other names of the eighth century; but the second part speaks of Cyrus and the conditions of the sixth century. The first part contains the oracles of Isaiah of Jerusalem which threaten punishment to come upon Israel and Judah because of their evil ways and disobedience to Yahweh; but the second part looks to a past calamity and now speaks joyously of forgiveness and restoration. The first Isaiah would be no more likely to have prophecied against "Chaldea" and to name Cyrus as Yahweh's "servant" than Benjamin Franklin would be to have published articles concerning Adolf Hitler or the Soviet Union. Second, the literary style of the second half of the book is markedly different from that of the first. This is not as easily seen as the historical references, but it is just as clear to the trained eye. Even a novice can detect a radical change in form and feeling as well as in language and spirit when he reads, in translation, chapter 40 immediately after having read chapter 39. Finally, the theological assumptions of the second part of the book are considerably developed beyond those of the earlier period. This fact becomes increasingly evident as one studies the history of Hebrew religion as a whole, taking into account all of the literature found in the canon and beyond. We shall see, for example, that a universal, ethical monotheism is found for the first time in Hebrew thought only in these oracles from the exilic period. In summary, then: it may be said that the hypothesis concerning a "Second Isaiah" can no longer be seriously disputed, in view of the evidence; only a nonbiblical, traditionalist dogmatism denies it.

### Good News to the Exiles

The sixteen chapters which are assigned to a Second Isaiah are composed of exhilarating poetry, except for two brief passages in prose: 44:9-20, a satire of idolatry; and 52:3-6, an assurance of redemption by Yahweh. The material as a whole displays an essential unity, the major theme being that Yahweh, the Covenant of God of Israel, is both Creator and Redeemer, the almighty Lord of nature and history who is also both just and gracious, active in the punishment of evil and yet determined to bring salvation not only to his chosen people, Israel, but also through Israel to all nations. That greatest possible Good News is proclaimed in a variety of modes and moods, and by a chorus of voices. The theme is not presented in a logical progression, or in didactic style; rather the structure may be compared to the sonata form of a triumphant symphony. The theme is stated by the opening oracle (chapter 40) in words of unforgettable power and beauty. The development follows in a series of poems (41-53), with the poignant portrait of the Servant of Yahweh as the centerpiece. And, finally, the recapitulation (54-55) uses every instrument and voice to sing and shout the invitation of Yahweh, the gentle Almighty One, for all nations to accept his loving gifts of mercy and pardon. The coda restates the theme:

> For you shall go out in joy,
> and be led forth in peace;
> the mountains and the hills before you
> shall break forth into singing,
> and all the trees of the hills shall clap their hands.
> Instead of the thorn shall come up the cypress;
> instead of the brier shall come up the myrtle;
> and it shall be to the Lord for a memorial,
> for an everlasting sign which shall not be cut off. (55:12-13)

The first poetic oracle (chapter 40) lifts Hebrew prophecy and religion to a new level of literary power and theological insight. Fully aware of the tragic past and the hopeless present of the Jews in Exile, and obviously alert to the impending political changes being realized by the rising power of Cyrus, the poet-prophet responds to the need of the time with a triumphant proclamation that announces not only pardon, release, and return for the captives but, much more than that, with a new description of Yahweh as the transcendent Creator of all things who, because he is Creator, will restore his threatened creation. The lyric oracle finally achieves the universalizing of Hebrew religion. Yahweh is no longer conceived to be a god among the gods, the god of the Hebrews as Marduk was the god of the Babylonians. He is the only God, the true God, and all others are pitiful, man-made idols. The tragic past and the imminent restoration are not mere accidents of history; they are part of the grand drama of the ages, directed from off-stage by the One who has ultimate and benevolent control.

The beauty and depth of the passage are much better seen and heard by reading than by description. Perhaps the oracle achieves its greatest emotional power when heard set to the gloriously matched music of Handel's *Messiah*. At any rate, it is sufficient here simply to urge the reader to attend to the words with care and imagination, trying if possible to hear them existentially as they were first heard by a people in despair. Something of the same burst of light in darkness might occur!

The remaining poems in the collection, through chapter 55, develop and restate the theme of certain redemption by Yahweh the Creator, with a variety of voices and instruments. Some passages are solo arias, frequently ecstatic with joy but occasionally in tones of mourning; other parts are sung by choruses, with strong declaration or in antiphonal dialogue. The unmistakable voice of Yahweh himself is often heard, and his words carry the power and authority which demand attention even when spoken with pastoral tenderness. And through it all there is a full range of irresistible emotion created by a full orchestra of strings, woodwinds, brass and percussion, played separately with soft sensitivity or together in overwhelming force. The prophet thus presented the word of God to the people in exile, and to all who anywhere experience the despair of alienation, in the form of a poetic symphony, using both chorus and orchestra to stir the emotions, persuade the will, and enlighten the darkened mind.

The central theme of these oracles is supported and accompanied by a number of original ideas. We may simply list five especially noteworthy ones here, with illustrations from the poems themselves:

1. Yahweh has chosen and anointed Cyrus to conquer the nations in preparation for Yahweh's gift of justice and blessing.

> Listen to me in silence, O coastlands;
> let the people renew their strength;
> let them approach, let them speak;
> let us together draw near for judgment.
> Who stirred up one from the east
> whom victory meets at every step?
> He gives up nations before him,
> so that he tramples kings under foot;
> he makes them like dust with his sword,
> and driven stubble with his bow.
> He pursues them and passes on safely,
> by paths his feet have not trod.
> Who has performed and done this,
> calling the generations from the beginning?
> I, the Lord, the first,
> and with the last; I am He. (41:1-4)
> Thus says the Lord, you Redeemer,
> who formed you from the womb;
> "I am the Lord, who made all things,
> who stretched out the heavens alone. . .
> who says of Cyrus, 'He is my shepherd,
> and he shall fulfill all my purpose';
> saying of Jerusalem, 'She shall be built,'
> and of the temple, 'Your foundation shall be laid.'" (44:24a, 28)
> "I have aroused him [Cyrus] in righteousness,
> and I will make straight all his ways;
> he shall build my city
> and set my exiles free,
> not for price or reward,"
> says the Lord of hosts. (45:13)

2. Yahweh repeatedly assures Israel that he will redeem and bless her in spite of her sins and obstinacy.

But now thus says the Lord,
he who created you, O Jacob,
he who formed you, O Israel:
"Fear not, for I have redeemed you;
I have called you by name, you are mine.
When you pass through the waters I will be with you;
and through the rivers, they shall not overwhelm you;
when you walk through fire you shall not be burned,
and the flames shall not consume you.
For I am the Lord your God,
the Holy One of Israel, your Savior." (44:1-3a)
Remember these things, O Jacob,
and Israel, for you are my servant;
I formed you, you are my servant;
O Israel, you will not be forgotten by me.
I have swept away your transgressions like a cloud,
and your sins like mist;
return to me, for I have redeemed you. (44:21-22)
But Zion said, "The Lord has forsaken me,
my Lord has forgotten me."
"Can a woman forget her sucking child,
that she may have no compassion on the son of her womb?"
Even these may forget,
yet I will not forget you.
Behold, I have graven you on the palms of my hands;
your walls are continually before me. (49:14-16)
"For a brief moment I forsook you,
but with great passion I will gather you.
In overflowing wrath for a moment I hid my face from you,
but with everlasting love I will have compassion on you,"
says the Lord, your Redeemer. (54: 7-8)

3. Yahweh is the Creator of all things in nature and the Providential Master of all things in history, expressing a constant disdain for idolatry.

Thus says God, the Lord,
who created the heavens and stretched them out,
who spread forth the earth and what comes from it,
who gives breath to the people upon it
and spirit to those who walk in it:
"I am the Lord, I have called you in righteousness,

I have taken you by the hand and kept you;
I have given you as a covenant to the people,
a light to the nations,
to open the eyes that are blind,
to bring out the prisoners from the dungeon,
from the prison those who sit in darkness." (42:5-7)
Thus says the Lord, the King of Israel
and his Redeemer, the Lord of hosts:
"I am the first and I am the last;
besides me there is no god.
Who is like me? Let him proclaim it,
let him declare and set it forth before me.
Who has announced from of old the things to come?
Let them tell us what is yet to be.
Fear not, nor be afraid;
have I not told you from of old and declared it?
And you are my witnesses!
Is there a God besides me?
There is no Rock; I know not any." (44:6-8)
I am the Lord, and there is no other.
I form light and create darkness,
I make weal and create woe,
I am the Lord, who do all these things. (45:6b-7)

4. Yahweh designates and describes his Servant, who will bring
redemption to all nations through his suffering and faithfulness.

Behold my servant, whom I uphold,
my chosen, in whom my soul delights;
I have put my spirit upon him,
he will bring forth justice to the nations.
He will not cry or lift up his voice,
or make it heard in the street;
a bruised reed he will not break,
and a dimly burning wick he will not quench;
he will faithfully bring forth justice.
He will not fail or be discouraged
till he has established justice in the earth;
and the coastlands wait for his law. (42:1-4)
He was despised and rejected by men;
a man of sorrows, and acquainted with grief;
and as one from whom men hide their faces

he was despised, and we esteemed him not.
Surely he has borne our grief
and carried our sorrows;
yet we esteemed him stricken,
smitten by God, and afflicted.
But he was wounded for our transgressions,
he was bruised for our iniquities;
upon him was the chastisement that made us whole,
and with his stripes we are healed.
All we like sheep have gone astray;
we have turned every one to his own way;
and the Lord has laid on him
the iniquity of us all. (53:3-6)

5. Yahweh offers salvation to all nations, demonstrating his promise by the restoration of Israel.

"Turn to me and be saved,
all the ends of the earth!
For I am God, and there is no other.
By myself I have sworn,
from my mouth has gone forth in righteousness
a word that shall not return:
'To me every knee shall bow
every tongue shall swear!' " (45:22-23)
And now the Lord says,
who formed me from the womb to be his servant,
to bring Jacob back to him,
and that Israel might be gathered to him,
for I am honored in the eyes of the Lord,
and my God has become my strength—
he says:
"It is too light a thing that you should be my servant
to raise up the tribes of Jacob
and to restore the preserved of Israel;
I will give you as a light to the nations,
that my salvation may reach to the end of the earth." (49:5-6)
Behold, you shall call nations that you know not,
and nations that knew you not shall run to you,
because of the Lord you God, and of the Holy One of Israel,
for he has glorified you. (55:5)

204

## The Creativity of Second Isaiah

We shall conclude this brief discussion of the work of the great unknown prophet of the Exile by highlighting three features in his prophecy which have left an influence of first magnitude on subsequent Western thought. The first has to do with what may be designated as the principle of incarnation; the second is the characteristic Western concept of deity, or ultimate reality; and the third is the pervasive interpretation of the necessary relation between suffering and redemption. Put more abstractly, they are specific ideas about revelation, monotheism, and atonement.

The phrase "principle of incarnation" is being used here to specify a particular characteristic of Biblical religion, namely, the use of the familiar, the ordinary, and the concrete, to communicate and to make relevant and effective the unknown, the transcendent, and the abstract. We have already observed this method in operation at earlier stages of Hebrew religious development and in the canonical Scriptures. For example, the idea of covenant was taken from common social and political usage, predating the origin of the Hebrews, and made into a primary category of Israel's relation to Yahweh; and the nomadic spring festival, perhaps first noting the new birth among the flocks, was transformed into the profoundly meaningful Passover celebration, annually commemorating the birth of Israel when she was delivered from Egypt by Yahweh.

Modern scholarship has often taken note of the influences of Assyrian and Babylonian culture to be found in the thought and imagery of Ezekiel and Second Isaiah. We are suggesting here, specifically, the apparent relation between the Babylonian New Year Festival and the ideas and structure of the oracles of Second Isaiah, particularly the opening poems. Details of the Babylonian celebration are well known, both from ancient historical accounts, for example, in Herodotus, and from archeological remains. It is hardly surprising that an alert and literate Jew, as Second Isaiah manifestly was, would have been familiar with the grand liturgy which occupied such an impressive place in the cultic and political life of the Babylonians. The prophet must, indeed, have been a witness to the great, public drama, probably on several occasions. He would have observed the ceremony of submission by the king to Marduk, the patron god; the assembling of all the lesser gods; the divining of the future year; the fertility-inducing union of Marduk and the great goddess, Ishtar; the chanting of the creation myth, *Enuma Elish*; and the dramatic account of Marduk's victory over death, culminating in resurrection. The procession of gods, royalty and priests through the beautiful Ishtar Gate to the sacred shrine outside the city must have been emotionally impressive to all witnesses, including the defeated and downcast Jews in captivity.

The prophet thus took the best and highest that he knew from the pagan culture of the all-powerful Babylonians and employed it as a vehicle by which to proclaim the sole reality and mighty power of Yahweh, and even to heap ridicule upon the bankruptcy of all idolatry. Who demands faithful submission by kings and people? Who controls the future year, and all the ages? Who causes the rain and the sunshine, bringing forth fruitfulness from family, flock and field? Who created the heavens and the earth, and sustains them every moment? Who gives life and is the true conqueror of death? Who prepares a grand procession to his temple, leading home his despairing people over a highway in the desert, a level road made smooth by grading down the mountains and filling in the valleys? Yahweh! He is the true God, and besides him there is no other.

> The glory of the Lord shall be revealed,
> and all flesh shall see it together,
> for the mouth of the Lord has spoken. (40:5)

By such an implied comparison between Marduk and Yahweh, between the vanity of man's futile seeking and God's gracious giving, the poet-prophet instilled new hope and determination in the people who had believed they were abandoned, dead like bleached bones in the desert.

This remarkable instance of the principle of incarnation was not its first use, as we have seen earlier, and it was by no means the last. It became increasingly a means of redemption, a method of revelation in the sense that truth in this way could be apprehended by the finite and distorted mind, and grace also could in this way be made available to all who would in faithfulness accept it. This is the principle by which Eternal Spirit redemptively anoints that which is flesh, and the created order becomes sacramental. In his majestic song, Second Isaiah was near the heart of meaningful truth, as passing ages have recognized.

The second feature of this prophecy which deserves special emphasis is its original and radical monotheism. The question of the origin of monotheism—who first believed and expressed the idea that there is only one God—has long been debated. Some would claim it for Elijah, or Moses, or Abraham...where does one stop? It is certainly true that the Hebrews were commanded to be at least henotheistic from the time of the Exodus, and passages in Amos, Jeremiah, and Ezekiel seem clearly to suggest the uniqueness of Yahweh. But the fact remains that full, universal and ethical monotheism was not explicitly and unequivocally stated until Second Isaiah gave the belief repeated and unmistakable expression during the time of exile. As we have seen, that is the fundamental assumption underlying all the oracles of joy and hope with which we are dealing. From the Babylonian Exile onward, nothing has been more doggedly characteristic of normative Judaism, and of the Christianity and Islam to which it gave birth, than insistence upon a belief in one, and only one God; and with that credo has gone an abhorrent revulsion from any appearance of polytheism and idolatry.

The effect of this most fundamental of all ideas, so originally and powerfully expressed by Second Isaiah, may readily be observed throughout the history of Western culture. It has been the accepted norm in all theologies, of course, but it has also driven nearly all philosophies to seek an ultimate unity in their ontologies and eschatologies. Moreover, the idea of monotheism, in its broadest ramifications, has supplied the most widely used and satisfactory prescription for meaning and value in Western philosophy and religion. That is to say, multitudes of thinkers and believers have sought, and many have claimed to find, courage for life, release from anxieties, and deliverance from alienation, by turning to God as the center and ground of being for all who are threatened by transient existence and fragmentation. As was true with the Jews who were with the prophet in exile, the way is not from speculative thought to theoretical unity, perhaps expressed in terms of theological monotheism; rather, the way is from need to fulfillment, from the experience of deliverance to the discovery that there must be a Deliverer. Israel's tragic pain and death, followed by unexpected and undeserved healing and new life, made necessary a new depth and universality for her old, inadequate faith.

A third feature of the teaching of Second Isaiah which has continued to exercise broad and permanent influence concerns the Servant of Yahweh. A host of questions have arisen since ancient times as to the proper interpretation of this teaching, and most of them remain unanswered; nevertheless, there is no question as to the centrality of the idea for Second Isaiah or concerning its crucial place in later religious thought, especially in Christianity. The specific identity of the Servant in the mind of the prophet has been widely debated. A voluminous literature on the subject is available for the reader to peruse with profit, and, in fact, the wide variety and massiveness of the scholarly discussion provide a clue to its significance. Many suggest that the Servant Songs of Second Isaiah present the apex of religion in the Hebrew Scriptures.

The scholar Bernard Duhm was apparently the first to isolate four specific passages among the poems of Second Isaiah as Servant Songs, and he even suggested that they were the work of another poet which had been incorporated into the text by editors. These four classic passages are as follows: 42:1-4; 49:1-6; 50:4-9; 52:13-53:12. Some would add a few verses to the first three of these; and others have gone further to claim a certain progressive structure for all of the poems taken together. All seem to agree, moreover, that the last of the poems presents the climactic culmination of the idea which had been variously developed in the first three. In it the Servant of Yahweh, who had brought truth and justice to the nations and had endured their rejection and persecution, became the redeemer of the nations precisely by means of his suffering and death. Thus suffering was for the first time interpreted as the necessary means of redemption from alienation and evil; it is not merely, as previously believed, the punishment justly resulting from sin. Using the familiar language of sacrifice, by which sinners are brought to atonement with God through representative suffering and death, the prophet set forth, in moving, unforgettable words, the idea of vicarious suffering:

Surely he has borne our griefs
and carried our sorrows;
yet we esteemed him stricken,
smitten by God, and afflicted.
But he was wounded for our transgressions,
he was wounded for our iniquities;
upon him was the chastisement that made us whole,
and with his stripes we are healed (53:4-5)

The key question, of course, is who was intended by Second Isaiah to be identified as "the Servant" who thus suffers and redeems? That is the question asked by the Ethiopian eunuch of

Philip the Evangelist in the earliest days of the Christian Church (Acts 8:34). Philip interpreted the passage as having been fulfilled in the person and work of Jesus, and that apparently was the view of Jesus himself, according to the Gospels, as well as of the early Christian community. (Cf. Oscar Cullmann, *The Christology of the New Testament*, chapter 3). It is instructive, however, to study the poems of the prophet as they stand, without preconceptions, in order to determine their original intent. Such scrutiny reveals, for example, that Duhm's four passages may be too exclusively drawn. The term *ebed* (servant) occurs 19 times in Second Isaiah, and in the plural form twice more. Only seven of those uses are in the four classic passages. Can it be that the idea of the *ebed Yahweh* is not, after all, an extraneous notion grafted into the authentic oracles by editors, but rather that we have here the central theme of all the oracles, namely, that Yahweh is Creator of all things and Redeemer of all nations, the only true God, whose justice and graciousness are manifest in his correcting and purifying of sinful Israel so that she, as the chosen, Covenant People, may by her suffering re-present all people in atonement with God? Such a view is not incompatible with the self-understanding of Jesus, himself a loyal Jew, or of the early Church, composed of Jews, who held the idea of "corporate personality," by which one person could stand for the total community, or who could see in the figure of the Servant of Yahweh the best model in the Scriptures for the role and work of Jesus.

We may be confident, at least, that Second Isaiah, the herald of hope to the Jews in exile, proclaimed the good news of restoration to the despairing people. He interpreted the grievous calamities of the past as more than the deserved chastisement which the earlier prophets had threatened, and he went far beyond the teaching of Ezekiel that the sufferings of Israel revealed the justice of Yahweh and were deserved even by every generation and individual. This unnamed poet-prophet comforted the chastened people by revealing new meaning for their misery and pain. He composed an incomparable symphony about Yahweh, the Holy and All-powerful God, whose eternal purpose may be seen in both his defeat of evil and in his redemption of his creation through the voluntarily accepted suffering of his chosen Servant. That seminal conception has provided meaning for suffering and death, as well as value for life, since it was first proclaimed by the waters of Babylon.

# VII.
# THE ATHENIAN VISION OF REALITY

# Chapter 19

# *The Quest for Meaning*

In about 470 B.C., some nine years after the decisive Greek victory over the Persians in the Battle of Plataea, Phaenarete, the wife of an Athenian named Sophroniscus, gave birth to a son. The boy, named Socrates by his parents, was destined to be the initiator of the greatest period of Greek speculative thought. The tradition that his father was a stone-carver, or maker of statues, and his mother a midwife has been doubted, but it has the sanction of several sources in antiquity. At any rate, both these occupations were apt models for the philosophical method which Socrates developed. With a sculptor's precision, he chipped away at unformed thoughts until only clearly formulated concepts remained. Seeing in the midwife's vocation an even closer affinity with his own, he held that knowledge, rather than being implanted in a person, must be drawn from him by a process analogous to bringing to birth.

His early life was passed in an Athens which was becoming the center of an empire and a magnet which drew to it at one time or another in their lives many of the greatest thinkers of the Hellenic world. In his later years, a war-induced depression and his own inattention to financial concerns were to reduce him to poverty, but there is no indication that he suffered in his youth from any serious lack of financial resources. He apparently enjoyed a leisured life and associated with the most distinguished citizens of Periclean Athens.

Physically and mentally, he stood out among other men of the city. In a culture which revered physical perfection, he walked the streets of Athens with a satyr's face and a gait compared by Aristophanes to that of a waterfowl, relying on the power of his intellect to move men to see in his soul the beauty which the gods had denied his body. He was, however, unusually hardy, wearing one garment the year round and walking barefoot throughout his distinguished service as a hoplite in the Athenian army. Temperate in food and drink, he paradoxically had a reputation for being able, without showing any sign of drunkenness, to hold prodigious quantities of the watered wine the Greeks drank in their *symposia,* and we have an account of a banquet at which, toward morning, he looked around, saw that his fellow diners had passed out, and went out to greet the new day, apparently none the worse for the drink and the loss of sleep.

According lip service to the joys of country life, he was, nevertheless, the quintessential city man, enjoying to the full the bustle of the market place, the activity of the gymnasium, the stimulation of the theatre, and the conviviality of the banquet table. From youth, he was addressed from time to time by a *daimon*, warning him against dangers, and at times he would go into a sort of trance, or state of intense concentration, which on at least one occasion during his military service, lasted for a day and a night.

During Socrates' formative years, the attention of the Greek philosophers was already beginning to turn from cosmology to an examination of man. By the time he reached maturity, the day of the Sophists had arrived, with its widespread doubt concerning the possibility of knowledge. Socrates, not satisfied with the sophistic decision to be content with the reduction of knowledge to the practical ability of each man to regulate his life in conformity to his own individual experiences, sought to find some ground for confidence in concepts which would be evident to any rational human being.

Anaxagoras' conception of *Nous*, or Mind, seemed promising, but a closer study of his work convinced Socrates that the idea had merely been introduced as a sort of *deus ex machina* to impart motion to the otherwise inert "seeds." Becoming convinced that he could never validate knowledge by speculation about nature, or, as he jokingly put it, that he "had no head for natural sciences," he turned his attention to the development of a new method. That method was called *dialectic*, a term which had appeared earlier in Greek philosophy in connection with Zeno's method of inquiry. As used by Socrates, it referred to the use of conversation to arrive at universal definitions of concepts. Armed with a philosophic technique which proved highly effective, he acquired, before he was forty years of age, a reputation for wisdom which extended well beyond the bounds of his native city.

Chaerophon, a good friend of the philosopher, went to Delphi and asked the Oracle whether any man living was wiser than Socrates. He received the unequivocal answer that no one was wiser. Socrates was puzzled. He knew that he was not wise. What, then, could the god mean? Clearly the question could only be resolved by finding a wiser man if one existed and thus proving the Oracle wrong.

He first approached a statesman, thought to be wise by many and, as Socrates wryly remarked, "wiser still by himself." By questioning him, he discovered that he was, in reality, not wise at all. The victim of the inquiry was not amused by it, and neither were his friends, but Socrates had found his answer. The statesman did not know and was ignorant of his true state, whereas Socrates, though he too did not know, knew that he did not, and so, in this respect at least, was wiser. Driven by the god's pronouncement, Socrates went from man to man, proceeding next to the tragic playwrights and lyric poets to try to find a man wiser than himself. Here too, however, he met with failure. The poets could not explain their own poetry as well as any casual bystander could. It must, he concluded, have been inspiration rather than wisdom which enabled them to produce their works. They too, however, labored under the delusion of thinking themselves wise. The craftsmen, the last objects of his investigation, were in no better case. Because they were skillful in what they did, they believed that they were wise in other matters, and Socrates was forced to conclude that, by virtue of his recognition of his own ignorance, he was wiser than any of those he had questioned.

So far as is known, Socrates never committed any of his thought to writing. What we know of his philosophy comes to us filtered through the dialogues of Plato, a few comments by Aristotle, the *Memorabilia* and *Symposium* of Xenophon, and the satirical treatment of the philosopher in Aristophanes' *Clouds*. How much of what emerges is attributable to Socrates himself and how much to the writers portraying him is a question which is unlikely ever to be answered with certainty, but it is not improbable that a reasonably faithful portrait can be found in the works of Xenophon and Plato, both of whom knew the philosopher and wrote of him in a day when his memory would have been fresh in many Athenian minds.

### The Gadfly

"The unexamined life is not worth living," Socrates maintained, and he regarded himself as a gadfly, appointed by God to sting Athens, which was like a great lazy horse, out of its intellectual and moral lethargy.

"What is justice?" he would ask someone who had just used the word, and on receiving a stock answer, he would commend his companion for his astuteness.

"However," we can imagine him adding, with the air of one struck by an afterthought, "I have just one or two little questions which you can surely answer, so that we may be completely satisfied."

The questions would completely demolish the original

214

definition, and the process would be repeated with variations again and again, always with increasing refinement of the concept, until an acceptable definition emerged or until it became evident that the dialogue was not going to resolve the issue.

To convince one's associates of their ignorance is not a guaranteed road to popularity, and it is a tribute to the Athenian respect for freedom of thought that Socrates, living through periods of external peril to the state, compounded by internal turmoil, managed for many years to pursue his persistent inquiry into the nature of truth without interference by the government or persecution by his fellow citizens. To be sure, his refusal to compromise his character occasionally threatened his security. As a member of a committee of the *Prytaneis*, he courageously refused to collaborate with his fellow committeemen in their attempt to force an illegal joint trial of a group of commanders charged with cowardice after the naval battle of Arginusai, in 406 B.C., for their failure to collect the bodies of their fallen comrades. Some two years later, during the reign of the Thirty Tyrants, he had further occasion to show his courage in his refusal to take part in their plot to arrest and execute Leon of Salamis in order that they might seize his property.

There were, indeed, many Athenians who thought Socrates a dangerous man. Among the young, however, who had serious reservations about their elders' too-confident answers to important questions, he achieved great popularity, and, indeed, boys of tender years were among his admirers, as is evidenced by his conversation with young Lysis in the dialogue of that name. It was this influence which was responsible for the troubles which led to his death.

It is not difficult to imagine a youngster who had recently been the object of his attention hurrying home to practice his version of the dialectic on a conventional and apoplectic father who would terminate the conversation by shouting, "You've been talking to that Socrates again!"

### Trial and Execution

In the year 400/399 B.C., after the restoration of the democracy, matters came to a head. One Meletus was induced by a politician named Anytus to bring charges against Socrates of failure to worship the gods of the state—or, as Meletus rashly maintained under cross-examination, failure to believe in any gods at all—and of corrupting the youth of Athens. The prosecution demanded the death penalty, though it is unlikely that they or anyone else in Athens dreamed that it would ever come to that. The charges were somewhat vaguely defined because the specific instances which might have provided some substance for the accusations—both of them connected with the career of Socrates' erratic protege Alcibiades—had both been made inadmissible as evidence by a general amnesty. This circumstance rendered the case so flimsy that it would have been difficult to imagine such a trial in free Athens had the times through which the state had passed been less uncertain and troubled. In all probability, the purpose of the indictment was to force Socrates into voluntary exile, but, as might have been expected by anyone who knew his character, he scorned such a course and appeared for trial.

Plato's *Apology* is undoubtedly a reasonably accurate representation of his eloquent if somewhat abrasive defense. On the first allegation, he tricked Meletus into basing his allegation of atheism on the assertion that Socrates had held the sun to be a stone and the moon earth. "Are you trying Anaxagoras?" Socrates asked. The theories of the Clazomenaean could, he said, be heard by anyone with a drachma to buy a ticket in the orchestra of the theatre. Moreover, Meletus, in maintaining that Socrates, while teaching new "spiritual things," was nevertheless an atheist, was guilty of a self-contradictory allegation. It is, the defendant pointed out, as impossible to believe in "spiritual things" without believing in spirits as to believe in "horsey things" without believing in horses, and no one who believes in spirits can be a complete atheist.

As for the charge of corrupting the young, Socrates led the rash young Meletus into contending that everyone in Athens except Socrates made the young better and that Socrates alone corrupted them. If such were the case, Socrates said, it would certainly be different from the case with regard to horses, which are made better by a skilled horse trainer rather than by the general public. At any rate, it would be absurd for him to corrupt the youth intentionally, as Meletus charged, for by so doing, he would be promoting a society dangerous to himself. If, on the other hand, it were done unintentionally, he could not legitimately have been brought to trial for it.

Despite the dialectical ingenuity of Socrates' defense and the flimsiness of the case against him, he was found guilty by a slight majority of the five hundred or so citizens composing the jury. The prosecution proposed the death penalty, and it was up to Socrates to suggest an alternative. The artful course would have been to recommend a sentence substantial enough to satisfy the court but moderate enough to be borne. Socrates, however, maintained that if the penalty were to reflect his deserts, it should be something good. Perhaps, he suggested, it would be appropriate to provide him with free board in the town hall, like a winner in the Olympic games. In this, he insisted, he was not being frivolous. He could not think of another penalty which would be suitable. The slavery of prison would be intolerable, and he had no money to pay a substantial fine. Banishment might satisfy the court, but if civilized Athens could not tolerate him, where else could he go? As for living in exile and remaining silent, that would be to disobey the god's command. Perhaps, he conceded at last, he might manage a fine of a mina – or, he noted, Plato, Critobulus, and Apollodorus had offered to stand surety for thirty minas. That, then, was the penalty he would propose.

A defiant statement of this sort was a far cry from the usual attempts to influence the jury by pathetic appeals and the introduction of weeping families into the courtroom. By the time Socrates had finished, the court was so angered that the death penalty was voted by a larger majority than the judgment of guilt, and Socrates was led off to prison to await execution.

A sacred ship was on its annual voyage to Delos, commemorating Theseus' freeing of Athens from the obligation to send a yearly sacrifice of seven youths and seven maidens to Knossos. During its absence, no execution could occur in the city. Socrates' friends used the delay to arrange an escape which would undoubtedly have had the full cooperation of the authorities. Socrates, however, stubbornly refused to sanction their enterprise. He had enjoyed the benefits of Athenian citizenship and had served the state to the best of his ability. To repudiate this relationship because the government was treating him badly would be to abandon the principles on which his life had been based.

The fatal day arrived, and Socrates spent his last hours with his friends, proving to his satisfaction, and apparently to theirs, the immortality of the soul. The discussion ended, he retired to another room to bathe himself so that it would be unnecessary to wash his body. Then he received his three sons and the women of his family, among them certainly his wife, Xanthippe, for whom he undoubtedly felt strong affection, in spite of the well publicized masculine jokes about her which caused her, with questionable justice, to be regarded as a shrew. A cup of hemlock was prepared, and Socrates, rejecting the suggestion that he postpone his fate as long as possible, drank it down, chided his friends for their weeping, walked about to set the poison to working, and then lay down and covered his face. When the effects of the draught were felt in his body, he uncovered his face and addressed his friend Criton. "We owe a cock to Asklepios," he said. "Pay it without fail." The words— a request that a sacrifice be offered in his name to the god of healing— were his last.

### Socratic Thought

What can be said with reasonable certainty about Socrates' philosophy? We have seen that his theory of knowledge challenged the relativism of the Sophists by its claim that the process of dialectic is a road to truth rather than mere opinion. In the light of this claim, the ignorance professed by Socrates can be seen only as a starting point for inquiry and, as Socrates himself said, the condition of the wisest man in comparison with God.

While he held common knowledge to be attainable in mathematics and science, Socrates' greatest interest lay in the field of ethics. Philosophy was to serve as an instrument for infusing human life with meaning and value. For Socrates, material possessions and pleasures, while not necessarily discounted as ornaments to the good life, were not themselves the measure of good, and he did not regard their loss as intrinsically evil. A confiscation of all he had, he said following his conviction, could do him no harm, and earlier in the *Apology*, he had made the startling statement that eternal law prohibits a better man from being harmed by a worse. The reason is clear enough in the light of Socrates' conception of human good. Death, banishment, imprisonment, and the like are not in themselves evil, for they cannot make one worse than he is. Good and evil are states of character and not of external circumstance.

Closely related to Socrates' conception of good is his much-discussed identification of virtue with knowledge. Often assailed as an over-intellectualized ethical formula, the equation becomes somewhat more palatable if one keeps in mind precisely what

Socrates thought knowledge to be. To know something is not simply to be able to assert propositions about it. Such propositions can be learned by indoctrination, and it must be remembered that real knowledge cannot be put into a man. One may "know," in the sense of being able to speak the words, and even to assent to them in some sense, that an act is wrong and still decide to perform the act. To know it in the Socratic sense, however, is, at the very least, to apprehend it with such clarity that it is as indisputable as an axiom in geometry. No one could entertain seriously the proposition that on a Euclidean plane surface a parabola is the shortest distance between two points, and, similarly, no one can seriously accept a proposition which runs counter to a clearly seen ethical principle. Knowing, for Socrates, involves an intimacy with and commitment to truth which in some sense identifies the knower with the known. To know the good in this way is to be good. Considered in this light, the contention that knowledge is virtue may still be questioned, but it is not *prima facie* silly, as it would be if knowledge were thought of as not involving the added Socratic dimension. Certainly Socrates suggested that there is an identification of virtue with *eudaimonia*— true happiness or well-being—and it may have been inconceivable to him that a man could ever act in a way which he clearly sees to be inimical to his real interest.

In the absence of writings by Socrates' hand, it is impossible to reconstruct his metaphysical system with certainty. We must suppose that Plato, in his development of the doctrine of ideas, was at the very least propounding a theory which he regarded as consistent with his master's conception of reality, and it is not unlikely that he found the essence of his system in the actual conversations on which the dialogues were based.

It is, however, to Socrates' life and death that we must look if we would gain an understanding of his significance in the history of Western thought. In fulfilling his conception of himself as a divinely commissioned gadfly, he was one of the foremost contributors to the flowering of thought which produced the greatest intellectual adventure the world has known. In the manner in which he faced his trial and execution, he inspired Plato to make sure that his influence would not die with him and he set a pattern for those in subsequent generations who would elect to retain their loyalty to their society while recognizing a higher allegiance to a transcendent truth. All in all, Socrates was fully deserving of Crito's characterization of him as "a man, we should say, who was the best of all his time that we have known, and moreover, the most wise and just."

# Chapter 20

# *The Ascent from the Cave*

Plato was born in Athens, or perhaps on the nearby island of Aegina, about 428 or 427 B.C. His father, Ariston, and his mother, Perictione, were both members of distinguished Athenian families. By tradition, he was a descendant of the god Poseidon, and, more plausibly, he numbered among his kin the great lawgiver Solon, who gave Athens her constitution. Early in life, he lost his father and was undoubtedly brought up in the house of his stepfather, Pyrilampes, a friend of Pericles. Given the name *Aristocles* at birth, he acquired the nickname *Plato* (*Platon*, "Broad") in recognition of his athletic physique, though it could equally well have been a tribute to his far-ranging interests. He is said to have studied painting and written poetry in several modes, but he centered his attention on a political career, considered appropriate for a young man with his aristocratic background. His life was changed, however, by his contacts with Socrates—contacts which were close enough for him to have been one of the good friends who offered to stand surety for the thirty-mina fine and to have been absent from the prison at the time of Socrates' death only because of a sickness which kept him at home.

Shaken by the tragedy and turned from the contemplation of a political career by the violence of the oligarchy which followed the collapse of Athenian power in the war against Sparta and by the injustice of the democracy which succeeded it, Plato took refuge in Megara with the philosopher Euclid, and somewhat later he apparently engaged in extensive travels and the writing of the early dialogues. It is known with certainty that at the age of forty he visited southern Italy, where he became a friend of one of the most remarkable men of his age, the Pythagorean Archytas. A statesman, a military man, a philosopher, a mathematician, a musician, an engineer, and an inventor, Archytas was one of the universal geniuses who appear at rare intervals in human history. It is unfortunate that a treatise which Aristotle wrote on his work did not survive. If it had, we might know more about such achievements as his pioneer work in aeronautical engineering—not to mention his distinction as the inventor of the baby's rattle. He was noted as well for his noble and benevolent nature, and Plato saw in him the ideal statesman described in the *Republic* as the philosopher-king.

It was while he was enjoying the company of the Pythagoreans in Italy that Plato received an invitation to visit Sicily, which, among other attractions, offered the opportunity of seeing Mount Aetna and boasted some of the finest cuisine in the world. The invitation was arranged by the brother-in-law of the tyrant Dionysius I, a young man name Dion, but was extended by the ruler himself.

Dionysius was in many ways a remarkable man. An able ruler, he had made Syracuse a military power second to none in the Hellenic world and had attracted to his court military engineers who had substantially advanced the science of warfare. He also fancied himself as a patron of the arts and even wrote poetry himself, albeit such bad poetry that it is said to have been hissed when it was read at the Olympic Games. Despite his very real talents, he was a parvenu and an unscruplous demagogue, whose rise to power exemplified everything in politics which Plato found most intolerable.

The philosopher was well received upon his arrival in Syracuse, but he and the tyrant were poles apart in temperament, and it was not to be expected that a man of Plato's background would meekly endure the sort of indignities his host was capable of visiting on those who ventured to disagree with him. The two men had words and, so the story goes, Dionysius handed Plato over to Pollis, the Spartan ambassador. Pollis sent the philosopher to Aegina, a state allied at the time with Sparta, to be sold as a slave. There a friend from Cyrene, one Anniceris, happened to see him in the slave market, bought him, and sent him back to Athens.

The long war was ending, and Athens was embarking on a relatively peaceful and prosperous era. Plato had independent means and was at liberty to do with his life whatever he pleased. What he decided to do was to teach, but there was no school in which a man of his standing and ability could exercise his talents. Undaunted, he proceeded to found what may with justice be called the first university in the Western world. Outside the city on the road to Eleusis, he owned a house and garden bordering on a park and playground named after a local hero named Hecademus, or Academus. Here he incorporated his school as a religious association dedicated to the Muses and named the "Academy." The institution acquired new buildings, and students from many parts of the Greek world traveled to Athens to study with Plato and the other masters who came to be associated with him. There they were taught mathematics, astronomy, logic, physics, biology, and, most importantly, philosophy. All these, and not merely "practical" subjects such as rhetoric, were, in Plato's view essential to an understanding of the timeless truths which a statesman must know. And the fundamental mission of the Academy was the production of statesmen who could govern their countries wisely.

In 367 B. C., it is said, his old enemy Dionysius entered a tragedy of his own composition entitled *The Ransom of Hector* in an official competition in Athens. Syracuse was at the height of her power at the time, and Athens needed allies. These circumstances may have had something to do with the fact that the judges awarded the first prize to the royal playwright. Word of his triumph was dispatched to Syracuse, where Dionysius read it and promptly died.

Dionysius II, the son of the old tyrant, succeeded him. A man of about thirty and not without ability, he had, nevertheless, been given little training to fit him for his duties, and his Uncle Dion asked Plato to return to Syracuse to supervise the young ruler's education. Plato accepted the invitation, doubtless hopeful that he might inaugurate something akin to the sort of government envisioned in the *Republic*. For a time, the court of Syracuse was awash with mathematics, but in time, Dionysius and Dion had a falling-out, and Dion left the city. Plato, after some difficulties in taking his leave occasioned by the admiration he had inspired in Dionysius, returned to Athens, arranging, however, to continue his young ruler's instruction by correspondence and promising to return to Syracuse when conditions might be more favorable. He failed in his attempts to effect a restoration of the tyrant's friendship with Dion, who took up residence in Athens, but in 361 B.C., Plato did make good his promise to return to Syracuse. This visit, however, like the first two, ended in frustration, for he failed in his effort to have his friend Dion recalled and was unsuccessful in his attempt to gain approval for a confederation of Greek cities to oppose Carthagenian expansion. He departed for Greece in 360 B.C., again after some difficulty, and lived in Athens until his death in 347 B. C., leaving a legacy of a large number of literary and philosophical masterpieces in dialogue form, of which some thirty-eight survive.

## The Line and the Cave

Plato's theory of knowledge was undoubtedly derived from Socrates, and the dialectic, which served the master so well, was, for the pupil too, an instrument not merely for presenting what is known, but for the discovery of truth. The Sophists were right, so far as Plato was concerned, in their assertion that one man's opinion has as much claim to authenticity as another's. To be sure, granting any sort of objective reality, one proposition based on opinion may happen to be true and another false, but in the absence of some method of validation which goes beyond opinion, any such truth value is simply coincidence and has no status as knowledge. Nor can sense perception be the basis for anything beyond opinion, for each man can validate only what he perceives as true, and no man is in a position to vouch for any real correspondence between what he experiences and an objective reality lying beyond the senses.

But was Protagoras right in claiming that nothing can be known which transcends sense experience and personal opinion? Plato maintained that he was not. The assertion that his theory is true is a claim which is destructive to the theory, for by Protagoras' own argument, a man who judged it to be false would be saying something equally true. This fact reduces the Sophist's position to nonsense, for if the theory were true, it could never be known to be true.

The senses present nothing more than a Heraclitean flux, which can only be considered as appearance. True knowledge must be of an unchanging reality, and it must be certain. Particular things change. The principles behind them do not. The number of sheep in a meadow may vary from time to time, but the mathematical principle by which two of them and two more of them must necessarily make four of them never changes. The apprehension of that principle is knowledge. We may draw "circles" of varying degrees of accuracy, but our judgment of their circularity, even aided by the finest instruments, must always be approximate. A true circle cannot exist in nature, but our knowledge of its qualities is precise. It is with this circle that the geometer deals, and the drawings he uses to illustrate his work are only imperfect imitations. It is this discrepancy between the object of experience and the universal it suggests which led Plato to assert, "The things which are seen are not known, and the things which are known are not seen."

In the celebrated example of the Divided Line in the sixth book of the *Republic*, Plato sets out graphically, if a trifle obscurely, his conception of the degrees of knowledge and opinion and of their proper objects. The vertical line he describes may be represented in this way:

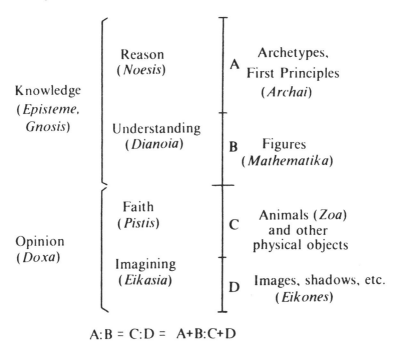

$$A:B = C:D = A+B:C+D$$

The overcoming of ignorance demands an upward movement from *doxa* (opinion). The lower part of that section of the line is designated as *eikasia* (imagining) and, on the psychological side, represents the process which has as its object *eikones*, which Plato described as "shadows" and "reflections," but which may be taken to include images in general. *Pistis* has as its object the animate and inanimate things which are usually judged to be "real" rather than imaginary. One might say that the person who does not distinguish between hallucination and sensation is inhabiting the realm of *eikasia*, whereas the hard-headed "realist" who believes only what the "physical world" presents to him is relying on *pistis*. Neither possesses true knowledge.

The upper section of the line represents genuine knowledge (*episteme*). *Dianoia* (understanding), represented by the lower sub-section, contemplates *mathematika*, items such as true circles and spheres, which can be known by the mind but not apprehended by the senses. This is the realm in which all points on the circumference of a circle, considered as an intelligible particular, really are equidistant from the center. The highest place on the line is reserved for *noesis* (reason), which has as object *Archai* (Forms, or first principles). Through the dialectic, one passes beyond the use of "images," such as those which the mathematician uses to facilitate his thinking about pure numbers and figures, and apprehends the Ideas directly. In this division, we find ourselves directly confronted with Plato's theory of the Forms or Ideas as ontological principles, to be discussed later.

The second famous image by which Plato illustrated his theory of knowledge is his allegory of the Den or Cave in the seventh book of the *Republic*. He described a group of human beings imprisoned in a cave from birth, chained by their necks and legs so that they can never see anything but the wall of the cave farthest from the entrance. Behind them, at some distance and higher up is a fire, and between the fire and the prisoners is a raised way bordered by a low wall, which serves as a screen of the sort used by puppet showmen. Passers-by on the road hold up statues of animals and other objects which project above the top of the wall. The light of the fire casts the shadows of these things on the far wall seen by the prisoners, who, never having known anything else and having no way of seeing one another or any of the objects behind them, think the shadows to be the real world. Similarly, when the bearers on the raised way utter sounds, an acoustical trick of the cave reflects the vibrations from the opposite wall, causing the prisoners to suppose the echoes to be sounds made by the shadows.

But suppose, Plato continued, one of them were released and made to turn around. The firelight would dazzle him, the objects would be indistinct, and he would disbelieve anyone who told him that he was nearer to reality than he had even been before. As he became accustomed to the firelight, however—corresponding to the light of the sun—the objects casting the shadows would be seen for what they are, and the shadows and the condition of the prisoners would be understood more clearly. If he were then dragged up a steep and rough ascent, out of the cave into the sunlight—

representing the realm of *episteme*—he would be blinded and at first incapable of seeing. Then, however, as he became accustomed to the brilliance, he would not only understand shadows and images, but would see distinctly the things of the world and the heavens—symbolic of intelligible objects. Lastly, he could look at the sun—the Idea of the Good—which imparts light and intelligibility to all other things.

If he then went back into the cave, he would, with "his eyes full of darkness," find it difficult to compete with his fellows in their competition for honors in judging shadows. They would laugh at him for going up sighted and coming back blind, and if he tried to free them as he had been freed, they would kill him if they could lay their hands on him.

## *The Doctrine of Ideas*

In view of the balance between the ways of knowing and the objects known, as depicted in these two illustrations, it can be seen that Plato's epistemology was closely allied with his metaphysics, and especially with his doctrine of Ideas. It should be stressed at this point that his thought was flexible and that it underwent a number of changes during his lifetime. With regard to many matters, he provided more questions than answers, and he had little of the systematic rigidity evident in some who have claimed to be Platonists. The language he used in reflecting on the nature of reality was often figurative or mythic, and even when it was intended more literally, it unavoidably dealt with categories for which no unequivocal vocabulary existed. It remains to this day, then, subject to a variety of interpretations, most of which have had able champions. All this being recognized, however, there still remains a basic structure of metaphysical thought which may safely be called Platonic.

It has been noted that the objects of *episteme*—of true knowledge—do not exist in the world of sense. There we have only particular things, and each thing is in many ways unlike every other. Nevertheless, we find real resemblances among the items of experience which impel us to categorize them—to apply a single generic term to a variety of instances. Plato called the universals thus named *Ideai* or *Eide*. These "Ideas" are not just the psychological contents of particular minds, but are, rather, real intelligible essences, having a being not dependent on the existence of specific items included in a category. Circularity is real, whether or not there are things which are roughly circular. More debatably, "horseness" is not contingent on the existence of individual horses. In fact, the reverse is true.

The Ideas are not in space and time. Circularity is not itself a big circle projected on some cosmic screen. It cannot be said to be any*where* because the word *where* has no meaning when applied to intelligible essences. Plato sometimes used figurative phrases like "the heaven above the heavens" in describing the abode of the Ideas, but there is no reason to suppose that he was suggesting a spatial location for them. Similarly, being eternal, they have no temporal dimension. They neither come into being nor cease to be, and they do not change. The fact that they have a reality independent of particular things does not mean that they must be thought of as being in a separate spatial or temporal frame.

The soul, which Plato described in the *Phaedo* as unitary and eternal, in becoming incarnate in a body, has become alienated from the contemplation of the Ideas, which are the proper objects of its knowledge. Philosophy is the discipline by which it "recollects" the truths which have been concealed or distorted by the changing world of sense and passion. In the *Meno*, Plato described how Socrates, by question and answer, elicited the Pythagorean theorem from an illiterate slave boy to demonstrate that the child implicitly possessed mathematical knowledge of which he only had to be made aware. Through the Dialectic, Plato said, the soul can rise ever higher until it can contemplate the *Archai*, the first principles, and, at last, the Idea of the Good, that ultimate reality which he called "Beauty" in the *Symposium* and which, according to his pupil Aristotle, he also identified as "the One."

Why is a soul impelled to make the ascent? In the *Symposium*, Plato, in a Socratic presentation combining mythic language and rational discourse, suggested that the answer is to be found in the nature of *Eros*, or Love. Eros, "the child of Poverty and Plenty," according to a prophetess with whom Socrates said he talked, is the basis of all desire and striving. If one says that he loves what he now has, what he really means is that he desires the continued future possession of it, which, of course, is something which he does not have now. Love may have many particular objects, but what one ultimately desires is the Good, or, more precisely, the permanent possession of the Good. As the perfect attainment of the goal is not possible in this life, the philosopher is always, in a sense, preparing for death, but the other-worldliness of Plato's philosophy should not be exaggerated. A sensitive reading of the dialogues provides ample evidence of Plato's appreciation of the world of experience— an appreciation based in part on the fact that sense objects are reflections of real essences.

The precise nature of the relationship between particulars and universals was, however, one of the problems with which he had to wrestle most diligently throughout his career. Two formulas were used to describe the relationship: imitation (*mimesis*) and participation (*methexis, metechein*). The former suggests a separation of the Ideas from the things which imitate them, whereas the latter represents particular objects as *sharing* in the higher reality so that the Ideas are in some manner immanent in things. Although Plato used both formulations during the same periods of his career and did not clearly subordinate one to the other, his tendency to use metaphorical language and his account in the *Timaeus* of the origin of the physical universe lends itself more readily perhaps to the formation of images suggestive of a process of *mimesis*—images which have played a role in provoking much of the criticism to which the doctrine of Ideas has been subjected.

The *Timaeus*, a complex work, tells the "likely story" of how God the Builder, whom Plato called the Demiurge (Greek *Demiourgos*, "Public Craftsman") constructs the physical universe to conform as closely as possible to the pattern established by the ideas. Matter, as we usually understand it, is not the basis of physical reality. Without the intervention of the Demiurge, the world would be, as the Book of Genesis describes the primal condition, "without form and void," a mere "matrix" or "receptable" or "space," which has potentiality for being acted upon but has no properties of its own. The Demiurge, using the Forms as archetypes and acting through a subordinate being called the World Soul, projects into this space geometric figures which, taken in combination, constitute the surfaces of what we call physical reality. The phenomenal world, then, is a changing reflection of the changeless realm which is the eternal abode of the Ideas, the Demiurge, the World Soul, and the souls of men. How the timeless soul, imprisoned in a corporeal shell, ought to act individually and politically in a world of flux will be the subject of a later chapter.

# Chapter 21

# *The Union of Form and Matter*

In the fourth century before the Christian era, Macedonia was a wild and rough country, lying to the north of the highly developed city-state culture of the Greek mainland. There, in Stagira, an Aegean coastal town settled by Greek colonists, Aristotle, the second of the two greatest Greek philosophers, was born in the year 384 B.C. His father, Nichomachus, was a distinguished physician who claimed descent from Apollo through the patron god of medicine and was a member of the guild of the "Sons of Asklepios." While Aristotle was still a child, his family moved to Pella, the swampy capital of the country, where his father accepted an appointment at the court as physician to King Amyntas II. While there, the boy probably became a friend of Amyntas' son Philip, some two years younger than Aristotle. After several years in the capital, Nichomachus and his wife died, and their son returned to Stagira as the ward of a kinsman.

At the age of seventeen, he was sent to Athens, where he was enrolled in Plato's Academy. It was the year in which Plato, then sixty, was invited to Syracuse for the second time, but his stay there was brief, and during most of the twenty-year period which Aristotle spent at the Academy as student and teacher, he was directly under the influence of the master. By the time of the young Macedonian's arrival in Athens, Plato had moved in his thought to a finer logical analysis of the Ideas, and the sciences—especially mathematics and astronomy—were being cultivated at the Academy. Aristotle, son of a physician, found the mathematical approach to learning less congenial than the biological, but he had a lively interest in almost everything, and Plato provided him with a solid groundwork for his logic and his metaphysics. Plato's political thought, after his traumatic experiences with practical statecraft, had progressively become more empirical, and the realistic views expressed in the *Laws*, which was probably written after his third journey to Syracuse, influenced Aristotle's own political theory.

The difference between the older philosopher and the younger has been exaggerated by later commmentators, as often as not for polemic purposes. Undeniably there were temperamental traits which led the two men to approach the fundamental problems with which they were both concerned from somewhat different points of view, but they seem to have remained close friends during the years of their association, and Aristotle's earlier writings— now unfortunately lost—were dialogues in the Platonic style.

With Plato's death, in 347 B.C., his nephew Speusippus became director of the Academy. Aristotle, to whom Speusippus' thought may not have been congenial, left Athens, accompanied by Xenocrates, another of Plato's pupils, and traveled to Assos, in Asia Minor, at the invitation of the ruler of the region, an able man of humble origin named Hermeias, who had been given the title of "Prince" by the occupying Persians. A former student at the Academy, Hermeias had kept up a lively interest in philosophy and cultivated a Platonic circle at Assos. Aristotle taught and wrote there for three years, in the course of which he married Pythias, the ruler's niece and adopted daughter.

About 344 B.C., he moved to the island of Lesbos, where he spent two years studying natural history, with special emphasis on marine biology. He also concerned himself with the Pan-Hellenism of his childhood friend Philip, who had become King of Macedon and was busily engaged in a diplomatic and military campaign to unite the Greek states in a league which could challenge the power of Persia. Hermeias appears to have entered into negotiations with Philip on this matter, and in the course of the contacts between the two countries, Aristotle was invited to Pella to become the tutor of Philip's thirteen-year-old son Alexander. He accepted the invitation in 342 B.C. and spent the next seven years in his native land. Shortly after his arrival in Pella, he received the melancholy news that his good friend Hermeias had been tortured and crucified by the Persians, saying with his last breath, "Tell my friends and companions that I have done nothing unworthy of philosophy." Hermeias' fate undoubtedly strengthened Aristotle's Pan-Hellenic sentiments and had its influence on the education he gave the young prince.

Philip was assassinated in 336 B.C., and Alexander ascended the throne. Before pursuing his father's plans for invasion of Persian-held lands across the Hellespont, he found it necessary to secure his position at home and in the Greek world generally. His preoccupation with that enterprise officially brought an end to a course of study which may virtually have been terminated before

Philip's death. Aristotle, out of a job, lived for a short time in Stagira and then went back to Athens.

Xenocrates, his old companion in the emigration to Assos, was now director of the Academy, but Aristotle decided to found a school rather than return to his old position. In a suburb of the city, there was a park dedicated to Apollo Lykeios. Aristotle set up his school in the vicinity and named it the *Lykeion*, or *Lyceum*. Chartered as an organization (*thiasos*) dedicated to the Muses, the new institution, like the Academy, grew into a complete college, with its own dining hall, library, and lecture rooms. Aristotle conducted many of his morning courses with advanced students while strolling about in the *Peripatos* or "Walk" on the grounds, a practice which led to the name "Peripatetic," popularly and later traditionally used to refer to the school and, by extension, to the Aristotelian philosophy. For the next few, years, Aristotle headed the school, using his encyclopaedic store of knowledge in his lectures and in the treatises based on those lectures, which dealt authoritatively and creatively with virtually every aspect of the learning of his day.

During those years, Alexander had made himself master of a vast empire which, short-lived as it was destined to be as a political entity, would shape the future course of Western history, bringing to an end the era in which the Hellenic city-state was the basic model for social organization and inaugurating what is known as the Hellenistic period. Aristotle, protected by the Macedonian regent who had been left in charge of the affairs of the subjugated Greek states, was not forgotten by his former protege, who sent him scientific specimens acquired during the military expeditions. When Alexander died in 323 B.C., however, his old teacher's position became precarious in a new wave of anti-Macedonian feeling. Charged with impiety, Aristotle chose to flee Athens rather than stand trial, "lest the Athenians should sin twice against philosophy." He went to his mother's home in Chalcis, on the island of Euboea, and died there the following year. In addition to a daughter he had by his marriage to Hermeias' niece, he left a son named Nichomachus, born after his wife's death to a young woman named Herpyllis, with whom he enjoyed a happy if unofficial relationship. The generosity of his nature, evident during his life, was further demonstrated by his will, in which friends, relatives, and slaves were materially benefited by legacies of money, security, and freedom.

He left the world too a substantial inheritance in the form of a collection of treatises which, if they lack the poetic quality of Plato's dialogues, are nevertheless equally significant in the history of Western thought.

### The Framework of Reason

Aristotle's six treatises on logic, known collectively to later commentators as the *Organon*, have been among the most influential works ever written. As a charter for correct thinking, they were regarded as authoritative even during the early centuries of the Christian era, when the other works of Aristotle were unavailable to European scholars. Logic is the instrument by which investigation is conducted in the sciences, or "inquiries," which Aristotle defined and classified with greater precision than any of his predecessors. He was not the first to reason validly, of course, but in a very real sense, he was the father of formal logic in the West.

Reasoning begins with the determination of categories, or the kinds of predicates which can be asserted of subjects. These include substance or essence (*ousia*), quantity, quality, relatedness, place, time, position or posture, possession, action, and passivity. *Ousia* is complicated by the fact that the word refers both to the subject about which an assertion is made and the "whatness" which is asserted of it. In the second sense—that of essence—it can be incorporated into logical propositions, specifically the premisses and conclusions of syllogisms.

The syllogism was, for Aristotle, an instrument for establishing true knowledge by proceeding from *archai*—first principles determined by observation and induction—to truths derived from them with logical necessity. Thus, if the premisses "All M is P" and "All S is M" can be established as true of any sets of objects which can properly be designated as S, P, and M, it must necessarily follow that the conclusion "All S is P" is true. This is an instance of valid deductive reasoning, in which the premisses cannot be true and the conclusion false. In establishing the first principles used as premisses in the particular sciences, Aristotle maintained, we use induction, a process involving the examination of particulars to discover the universals embodied in them. All science is supported by these two pillars of logic.

As for the sciences themselves, Aristotle established a classificatory system which, with some modification, is still in use.

There is first a distinction between the theoretical or contemplative (*theoretikos*) sciences and the practical (*praktikos*) ones. The theoretical sciences include "first philosophy" (*prote philosophia*), mathematics, and the natural sciences (*physike*), which are physics, biology, and psychology. The practical sciences are ethics and politics, which, for Aristotle, are both subsumed under the general heading of *politike*. These disciplines are concerned with matters which involve human choice and questions of value.

## Form and Matter

In the *Metaphysics*, Aristotle addressed himself to the problem with which Plato had struggled for so long—that of the relationship existing between individual things and the universals which enable us to assign them generic names. He strongly criticized the Platonic notion of *mimesis* as an inadequate explanation of the nature of real resemblance. Suppose we say that John and Sam can both be called men only by virtue of the fact that each of them resembles the Idea of man. How then, is the resemblance between either man and the Idea to be explained? The assumption that resemblance between any two items calls for a third to account for the relationship must inevitably lead to an infinite regress.

To avoid the difficulty, Aristotle had to find a way to assert the reality of universals without separating them wholly from the world of particulars. Plato had moved cautiously in this direction with his concept of participation. Aristotle, with a bold leap, asserted that in nature, form is never found without matter or matter with form. Forms are real, but their reality is found in particular things. Form and matter exist in a sort of hierarchical system. Insofar as something is acted upon, it is matter with respect to that which acts—that which gives it its "whatness." Insofar as it is active principle, imparting qualities to that which is below it, it is form. For Aristotle, as for Plato, there could be no clear concept of matter undetermined by form, because no predicates could be applied to it. It is matter, however, which makes an object the particular thing it is rather than another having similar predicates. It is the basis of individuation.

The *ousia* of a thing, thought of as the subject which has predicates but cannot itself be predicated, is an entity which persists through changes. A block of stone in being made into a statue has many of its qualities altered without losing its identity, but every change occurs in a manner which is compatible with the essential nature of that which is changing. The block of stone does not change into a cream puff, and an acorn does not grow into an apple tree. In the acorn, there is a *potentiality* for becoming an oak, and the oak is the *actuality* of an acorn. Anything in the natural world falls short in some measure of the full perfection of kind implied in its definition. Its full actual character, or *entelechy*, however, draws it toward its ideal fulfillment. The processes by which change occurs may, of course, be quite complex. There are internal and external factors involved in the transformation of the acorn and its nutrients into the mature tree, just as there are in the production of a statue, one difference being that in the latter the processes involve a great measure of human agency. If Aristotle is right, however, the fundamental principles must be the same in both instances, for change is never merely random, and every sort of process involves a goal (*telos*) toward which the complex motion tends.

Aristotle described causation as involving four factors. First, there is the material cause—the stuff (*hyle*) which is acted on to produce the change in question. In the case of a statue, the material cause may be a block of marble, which, of course, has a form of its own but not the form it will have at the end of the process. Left to itself, though, the stone has many possibilities which will never be realized—among them, the finished statue. But suppose that Praxiteles, passing by the quarry, sees the stone and perceives it as being eminently suitable for the realization of a vision he has of a statue of Hermes and the Infant Dionysus. This vision introduces the formal cause into the process.

Still, there is no statue. The sculptor must collect his tools, take his measurements, and chip away at the marble until the figures he has envisioned emerge from it. These physical elements constitute the efficient cause. But the account of the process is still incomplete. There remains the determination of the reason for which the statue is made—the final cause or purpose (*telos*) behind the whole process. This causal account is applicable not only to human artifacts, but to the entire world of nature.

The difference between the Aristotelian idea of causality and that given by mechanistic philosophies is obvious. In the latter, all process is explainable in terms of material and efficient causation and, in many forms of materialism, is randomly determined. In Aristotle's system, there are rational and telelogical factors, with movement from potentiality to actuality determined by final and formal causes as well.

### The First Cause

Motion must be eternal, and so there is a perpetual chain of efficient causes. The ultimate answer as to why process occurs at all cannot be found in some uncaused *event* in the past which initiated a sequence of subsequent causes. Every event, to be sure, is necessarily contingent on antecedent events, but this fact does not make it any less incumbent on a philosopher to consider the question as to why anything at all should exist. Efficient causes are in time, but eternal motion in time must have an eternal cause. According to Aristotle, there must be some ultimate reality having the power to impart motion while remaining unmoved. Such a mover cannot be material and so must be pure form. He is pure actuality, and his activity consists in thinking, unmarred by uncertainty, passion, or desire. Such thinking is pure self-contemplation—"thought thinking thought." The unmoved mover is God, and that part of the *Physics* which deals with him is appropriately referred to as "theology." God in Aristotle's thought, is not the capricious chief of the society of Olympians, and he does not providentially govern man or nature in just the same way as he is said to in the Hebrew Scriptures, or even in Plato's *Timaeus*. He is, rather, the final cause who draws all things to himself by the perfection of his nature.

### Plants, Animals, and Men

Aristotle's remarkable grasp of the entire spectrum of the science of his day made him a leading authority in a number of individual disciplines. In some of them, he failed to arrive at the best possible conclusions, as was the case when he put the earth at the center of the universe and surrounded it with concentric spheres containing the sun, the moon, the planets, and the fixed stars, or in his contention that heavy bodies by their nature fall faster than light ones. He was not nearly so dogmatic in his speculations, however, as those who, centuries later, were to elevate him to a status of infallibility in scientific matters which, ironically, would retard the modern development of the very scientific approach which he did so much to foster, and many of his own conclusions in matters of science were remarkably prophetic of later developments. His rational account of nature rested on a solid respect for empirical investigation, evidenced most strongly, perhaps, in his researches in the fields of biology and psychology.

He classified living things into three fundamental categories: plants, the lower animals, and men. The life of plants, he observed, is characterized by the processes of nutrition, growth, and reproduction. The capacity for sustaining these processes is what distinguishes a living plant from a dead one, and Aristotle referred to it as *soul (psyche)*. In living things, it is form related to the matter which it animates. Animals, in addition to the sort of vegetative and nutritive soul possessed by plants, have the power to see, hear, taste, smell, and feel. They can take in the forms of objects without absorbing their matter and so are said to have sensitive souls. Men, while sharing both these levels of process, are capable of deliberation and reason. Aristotle referred to this capacity as the rational soul and defined man as a "rational animal." This function of humanity is the highest in nature and so is closely akin to the divine, but human knowledge is discursive and partial.

Aristotle's thought was more empirically oriented than Plato's. His basic concerns, however, were not greatly different from those of his teacher, and it is, perhaps, the course of wisdom to see their systems as complementary rather than antithetical. If Plato seems to have the ascendancy in our time as a result of the emphasis on mathematics and theoretical physics, it may well be that future development in the biological sciences will bring about a new appreciation of Aristotle's organic approach to reality. Certainly his ethical and political views, to be considered in a later chapter, have much to say to our age.

# VIII.
# THE ATHENIAN
# VISION OF SOCIETY

# Chapter 22

# *The Greek Polis, Cradle of Democracy*

The ethical and political thought of Plato and Aristotle, the two foremost philosophers of antiquity, cannot be seen in proper context without some consideration of the development of the institutions which provided the environment in which their theories were formed.

Those institutions took shape in a geographic setting vastly different from the fertile river valleys which gave birth to the great monarchies of Mesopotamia and Egypt. To be sure, the island kingdom of Crete, from which the Hellenes derived much of their culture, had the geographic unity and security which made a centralized government possible, but its political system was not readily adaptable to the more rugged Greek mainland. With the collapse of the Minoan kingdom, a system more feudal in character became the typical form of social organization throughout the Greek world. The culture described by Homer was composed of tribes ruled by chiefs holding the title of king (*basileus*). Only on rare occasions and for special purposes such as the conduct of a war would some measure of the sovereignty exercised by the various rulers be relinquished to a common leader, who might then be accorded a higher title, rather like that given to the ancient Irish "high kings." Thus, in the *Iliad*, Agamemnon, the leader of combined forces of the Greeks in the Trojan War, was called *Basileuteros* and *Basileutatos*.

In his own district, each of the kings held his place at the summit of a class of nobles (*aristoi*). Those closest to him and accompanying him into battle were known as companions (*hetairoi*). Below the ruling class were the *demioergoi*, freehold farmers and craftsmen, and, on a still lower level, the *thetes*, freemen who worked for hire. Slavery does not seem to have been the highly developed institution in Homeric Greece that it was to become in the classical period. The *boule*, or council, had its origin in the group of selected sub-chiefs (*gerontes boulephoroi*) who advised the king on matters of public policy. Even at that time, the people of the lower classes played a part, even if not an especially active one, in the process of government, being summoned on occasion to the *agora*—the marketplace—to hear and perhaps endorse the decisions of their ruler and his council. From quite early times, there was, among the people of the Hellenic tribes, a recognition of the dignity and worth of the free man in a free society.

The idea of kinship was also an important element in the social life of the early Greeks, and by the eighth century B.C., real or fancied blood ties were deeply imbedded in their political institutions. The topography of the Greek mainland, with its small valleys ringed around by mountains, made relatively small unions more practical than larger ones. Where strong bonds of kinship existed among the families of a region, the typical social organization was the *genos* or clan. Where those bonds were weaker, it was the *phratria* or brotherhood, which came to involve some of the moral and emotional ties of the clan by virtue of the tendency of its members to create for themselves a genealogy linking them together in descent from a common ancestor, who was accorded religious veneration. The *phyle*, or tribe, was the characteristic larger unit, and a group of tribes, more or less loosely federated, was known as an *ethnos*.

## The City-State

The *polis*, which was to become the dominant political institution in the Greek world, did not originate in any great tendency of the people to live in cities. Whatever early progress there may have been toward the growth of a metropolitan culture was given a serious blow by the Dorian invasion, in which many of the old centers of population were destroyed and their surviving inhabitants dispersed. But the looser organization which followed the conquest still required some sort of fortified center of power where the populace could take refuge in an emergency. Such strongholds were frequently held by tribal kings and probably served not only as fortresses but as centers of trade. The stage was thus set for the emergence of the city-state, based more on political compact than on ties of blood. The impetus for such a development was especially strong among the Ionian refugees on the coasts of Asia Minor, Italy, Sicily, and later France. There, with hostile neighbors in the interior and the sea at their doorstep, the colonists, who in many instances had no tribal homogeneity, found the sort of contract on which the *polis* was based the only practical solution for the problems they faced in founding new communities. With the reestablishment of commerical and cultural relations with the mainland, the pattern set by the exiles influenced the course of the development of the city-state in Greece itself.

It was in the Ionian cities of Asia Minor too that the sharp differences between their own political system and that of the Persians, their enemies and at times their overlords, was most evident. Herodotus, (c. 484-425 B.C.) the "Father of History" and the most celebrated traveler of his day, spent his youth and early manhood as a resident of his native Halicarnassus, at that time under Persian domination. His subsequent travels and historical investigations intensified his commitment to the Greek city-state, even at its worst, as infinitely preferable to the absolute monarchies of other lands. He wrote admiringly of Cyrus, the great sixth-century king of Persia, but his accounts of the barbaric cruelties of other Persian monarchs gave graphic expression to the Greek aversion to the sort of absolute power which places its holder beyond the restraint of law or reason. "A tyrant," he wrote, "violates women, kills men without trial. But a people ruling—first, the very name of it is so beautiful; and secondly, a people does none of these things."

"You know perfectly well what it is to be a slave," he quoted a Greek reply to a Persian urging submission to Xerxes. "Freedom you have never tried, to know how sweet it is. If you had you would urge us to fight for it not with our spears only, but even with hatchets."

Certainly the passion for freedom burned brightly in the Hellenic spirit and fired the respect for the individual which was embodied in the ethical systems of Plato and Aristotle. It was not to be expected that the political forms of the Greek *polis* would always embody the highest aspirations of the *politai*—the citizenry—and, indeed, they did not. However, the very idea of the city-state involved the theory that the ultimate sanction for any form of government a particular society might adopt was the will of the citizens. In the *polis*, the Western concept of the citizen was born and came to maturity.

In some areas of Greece, such as Elis and Thessaly, the tribal pattern survived with little significant alteration. In others— Arcadia and Boetia, for instance, a sort of federal union of their constituent cities emerged. By the beginning of the classical period, however, the city-state was well established as the dominant political institution on the Greek mainland.

## Forms of Government

The change in governmental pattern was a gradual one. As the citadels developed into full-fledged cities and the interests of the states became more diverse, the power of the nobles began to grow and that of the kings to wane. Though they often kept the title of *basileus*, monarchs whose role had been analogous to that of a patriarch of an extended family, found their authority being stripped away by their associates until they were at last merely the first among equals and the transition from monarchy to aristocracy was, in effect, complete. But this form of government too was, in the long run, inherently unstable. The aristocratic age for which Pindar felt such nostalgia produced an ethos which at its best won the admiration of poets and philosophers, but the system, like all political systems was undermined by the failure of the wielders of power to live up to their own code and by the growth of a prosperous merchant class as the result of the geographic expansion of the Greek world and the growing use of coinage as a medium of exchange. The increasing wealth of some was at the expense of the impoverishment of others, especially the small farmers, whose ill-treatment was lamented by Hesiod in his *Works and Days*. The efforts of the nobles to hold on to their power resulted in an administration of law in a self-serving manner, and the resultant social disorder led to far-reaching changes in the political structure of the city states.

In some of the states adjustments were made in the laws so as to permit men of humble birth who had acquired substantial amounts of property to participate in the processes of government along with the nobles who had inherited wealth. The qualification for the exercise of the franchise and the holding of office was thus shifted from one of blood to one of possession, and the form of government which emerged was oligarchical rather than aristocratic. The use of the term *oligarchy* to designate political systems based on property qualification was common among Greek writers, but the word often had a wider reference to states governed by minorities of any sort. Thus the distinction between oligarchy and other forms of social organization, especially aristocracy, was not always easy to define. In practice, oligarchies generally relied on *boulai* or councils, composed of selected members of the privileged classes, for the actual work of government.

Democracy involved an even greater broadening of the base of power. The people (*ho demos*) held the reins of power and exercised it through the actions of the many (*hoi polloi*) rather than the few. Directly or indirectly, public policy was determined by majority rule. In practice, Greek democracies were seldom pure expressions of the popular will. In some of them, assemblies composed of all the citizens exercised certain judicial and administrative powers but elected as magistrates men who met property qualifications for holding public office. In others, the requirements were broad enough to permit the election of almost any adult male of the citizen class. In some of its applications, democracy was so indiscriminate that minor offices were filled by lot. Thus, though the principal seat of authority in the typical democratic state was the assembly, many of its powers were delegated in a manner prescribed by law to duly designated officials. Apart from their occasional indulgence in sweeping constitutional reforms, the Greeks exhibited considerable distrust of changes in the structure of law, and so the assembly rarely exercised any direct legislative powers, leaving to those entrusted with judicial authority the task of adjusting the law to individual cases. This emphasis on the primacy of law laid a solid foundation for the Western conception of constitutional government, and those occasions in the history of the Greeks where it became so weakened that the will of the majority could override legal restraint brought democracy into such disrepute that Aristotle found it necessary to use a different term, *polity*, to refer to the legitimate rule of the many in accordance with reason. The danger of this sort of corruption was inherent in the exercise of power by a large popular assembly, in which demagoguery might be more effective than statesmanship in influencing public policy. Always, there was the ominous possibility that a rabble-rouser of exceptional ability and persuasiveness could use a public crisis to end the democracy and establish himself as a tyrant.

Whether instituted as the successor to a democracy, an aristocracy, or an oligarchy, the typical tyranny was inaugurated by popular support and maintained by force. The freedom-loving Greeks, while deploring the tyrant as a lawless man ruling in his own self-interest, were not immune to the threat he posed to the political institutions they found more congenial, and the mainland city-states bred a number of tyrannies, beginning early in the seventh century B.C. and ending with the overthrow of Hippias of Athens in 510 B.C. In the colonial cities, tyrants came to power from time to time in later centuries. Some of them, like Dionysius I of Syracuse, were men of considerable ability and imagination. Untrammeled by law or tradition, they engaged in extensive programs of public works, established new colonies, and, like the later Medici, gained renown as patrons of the arts. Some actually governed with benevolent concern for the material well-being of their people, but the Hellenic aversion to the tyrant's defiance of legal and moral restraint normally insured that his reign would be of brief duration. Even when power could be maintained long enough to be transferred to a successor, the absence of constitutional legitimacy made his situation precarious, and few tyrannies were able long to survive the death of their founder. The great thinkers of Greece unanimously condemned such governments as the worst which could be conceived. Throughout the classical age, the principal political conflict in most of the city-states was waged between the advocates of oligarchy and those of democracy, and legitimacy—the recognition by the people of the right of the government to exercise authority—was highly prized.

## The Spartan State

Two constitutions—the Spartan and the Athenian—strongly influenced the political theorists of the fifth and fourth centuries before Christ. The relations between the two states was a complex mixture of mutual admiration, suspicion, fear, and outright detestation. There is no body of Spartan literature to testify directly to the Lacedaemonian side of the picture, but there is ample testimony to the Athenian respect for the discipline of the Spartans, combined with a contempt for their culture, and it may reasonably be accepted that the reverse must have been true of these Spartans whose sensitivity had not been so diminished by their harsh regimen that they were incapable of appreciating an Athenian poem or a civilized dinner party.

The Spartans had not always been hostile to the arts and, indeed, had at one time been especially proficient in the art of music. Their decision to divest themselves of the ornaments of their culture came as a result of an insecurity stemming from the sort of society in which their Dorian ancestors had entrapped themselves when they invaded the Peloponnesus and subjugated the native population. The ruling class, descendents of the Dorian stock were the *Spartiatai*, the citizens. These descendents of the original inhabitants who had retained their freedom were the perioeci (*perioikoi*), the "dwellers around," inhabiting the mountains and coastal regions. As the Spartiates were forbidden to engage in trade or industry, the perioeci, who carried on those functions, were essential to the economic life of the state. They served in the armed forces, where they were eligible for positions of command, and those who lived on their own lands paid tribute to the Spartan kings. They had no political rights and no protection against the arbitrary actions of their overlords. Spartiates and perioeci were sometimes collectively designated as Lacedaemonians (*Lakedaimonioi*). At the bottom of the social scale were the Helots (*Heilotes*), serfs who were bound to land owned by the Spartiates. They paid their masters rental for the land they tilled, and members of Helot families served as domestics in the city. Their men were expected to accompany their masters in war, and if they acquitted themselves bravely, they might receive their freedom. To an even greater degree than the perioeci, however, they were denied civil rights, and a Helot suspected of sedition could be killed by the secret police, the *krypteia*, with complete impunity.

In the early years of Sparta's expansion a military operation against Messenia resulted in a decisive victory which greatly increased the size of the Spartan state and made Helots of the Messenian people. Faced with a ratio of perhaps ten to one of perioeci and Helots over citizens, the Spartans turned their backs on literature and the fine arts and converted their nation into a permanent military garrison. It may have been during this period that the constitution attributed to Lycurgus attained its final form.

The durability of that constitution was attributed by some writers of antiquity to its balance of powers, involving elements of monarchy, aristocracy, and democracy. Even at the royal level the balance was maintained. Not content with one king, the Spartans had two, and neither could act over the veto of the other. So opposed were the Spartans to innovation, that it was generally regarded as a healthy state of affairs when the two kings were in disagreement. They performed the city's religious sacrifices, served as chief justices, and commanded the army in war. The principal governmental power resided in the *gerousia*, a senate composed of kings and twenty-eight citizens sixty years of age or older, elected *viva voce* by the Assembly or *appela*. That Assembly consisted of all Spartiates who had attained the age of thirty. They met each month on the day of the full moon and heard proposals from their public officials, which they then approved or disapproved by voice vote or, if necessary, by formal division. Although sovereignty resided formally in the *apella*, the constitution was amended after Lycurgus to permit the *gerousia* to override the larger body if it judged the *apella* to have acted "crookedly." There were also five ephors, representing an institution surviving from pre-Lycurgan days. Elected annually by the Assembly, they served as a check to the power of the kings, and ultimately they were given almost absolute authority.

In Sparta, the state was supreme, and the individual citizen was expected to dedicate his whole life to the public good. At birth, he had to pass a state inspection to avoid being thrown from a cliff on the face of Mount Taygetus. At the age of seven, he was taken from his parents and placed in a military school, under the supervision of a *paidonomos*, a master of boys. He was taught to bear hardship and privation without complaint and made into a skilled soldier with a magnificent physique and minimal literacy, spending his time through early manhood in the field, in barracks, and in public messes. If he remained unmarried past the age of thirty, he was subject to public humiliation and deprived of the franchise. From thirty to sixty years of age, he had to eat the main meal of the day in a public mess hall, where the food was of the simplest variety. If, in spite of the rigors of his life, he managed to grow fat, he faced censure or banishment. He dressed simply and was discouraged from the accumulation of wealth by an iron currency of such weight that its use, transport, and storage was difficult. He had few contacts with foreigners, for he was forbidden to travel abroad without governmental permission and was taught to share the Spartan distrust of visitors who might corrupt the state. His wife and daughters, though they spent more of their lives in the home than did the men, participated in public festivals, owned property, and, all in all, enjoyed a higher status and a greater degree of freedom than the women of any other Greek state.

### The Athenian State

If one side of the Greek spirit was best incorporated in the Spartan society, the other came to its finest flower in Athens, the

capital of a region known as Attica—from *aktika*, coastland—
which, according to Greek tradition, was originally brought
together into one political entity by the legendary Theseus. All the
landholders in Attica were citizens of the Athenian *polis*. Again
according to tradition, the period of monarchy ended in 1068 B.C.,
when King Codrus, to fulfill a prophecy that only the death of the
Athenian king at the hand of the enemy could save the state from the
invading Dorians, heroically entered the enemy's camp in disguise,
provoked a quarrel, and permitted himself to be killed. The
Athenians declared that no one was worthy to succeed him,
abolished the monarchy, and replaced the king with an archon,
chosen for life. The term of the archon was later reduced to ten years
and in 683 B.C. to one. The latter reduction was accompanied by a
division of the powers among nine archons. One, the archon
*eponymos* provided a basis for dating by giving his name to the year
of his service. A second was archon *basileus*, who, despite his kingly
title, was in practice merely the presiding official for the religious
observances of the state. A third, the *polemarchos*, commanded the
armed forces. The other six, the *thesmothetai*, were lawgivers. All
these officials were chosen from among the members of the upper
class, the *Eupatridai*, who governed Attica for almost five hundred
years. Upon completion of their term of office, they became life
members of the *boule* or Council, the governing body, which met on
the Aereopagus, the Hill of Ares.

Under the Eupatrid oligarchy, the populace was divided into
classes on political and economic bases. Politically there were the
*hippes* or knights, who, as owners of horses, could serve as cavalry
in war, the *zeugitai*, who served as heavy-armed infantry, and the
*thetes*, laborers who could fight only as light-armed infantry.
Citizenship was restricted to the higher classes and the higher
political offices to the knights. The economic distinction also
involved three ranks. The *Eupatridai*, the richest, were supported by
the labor of others. The *demiurgoi* or public workmen were the
tradesmen, merchants, professional men, and free laborers. The
*georgoi* were the Attic peasants.

In Athens, as in other parts of Greece, the seventh century B.C.
produced drastic economic changes. The land had for the most part
fallen into the hands of a few rich men, and the dispossessed
landowners, driven by debt and poverty, were, in many instances,
reduced to serfdom. Meanwhile, in the city, a powerful and well-to-

do middle class was replacing free laborers with slaves and rendering free labor not only unprofitable but degrading. Many members of the working class found themselves reduced to the direst poverty, and some were sold into slavery for debt. The situation was further complicated by the growing tension between the ruling class and the newly rich merchants, who were resentful at their exclusion from public office. Public discontent stemming from all these conditions and rivalries among the ruling houses laid the ground for an abortive try at tyranny which at last led to the appointment about 621 B.C. of a *thesmothete*—a lawmaker—named Draco. He devised a legal system which made some of the prosperous merchants eligible for high office and, even more constructively, substituted public law for the widespread private vengeance. In order to gain acceptance of his reforms, however, he had to prescribe penalties so severe that the word *draconian* still has a harsh ring. His code had no effect on the economic injustices of the time, and, as the seventh century neared its end, Athens found itself on the verge of revolution.

In 594 B.C., Solon, a man of the most distinguished ancestry and a reputation for great personal virtue, was elected archon *eponymos* and given dictatorial authority to deal with the state's social problems and establish a new constitution. He cancelled all debts and mortgages, abolished slavery-for-debt, and made sweeping currency reforms.

Solon's new constitution was a complex one and of necessity involved compromises which caused the lawgiver himself, when asked whether he had given the best laws, to reply, "No, but the best that they could receive." He applied the sanctions of law impartially to all freemen, but divided the citizenry into four economic classes, based on annual income. Members of the upper classes were eligible for higher public offices and military rank than those of the lower. On the other hand, a graduated income tax altogether relieved the lowest class from taxation and imposed the highest rate on those with the greatest income.

Retaining the Council of the Areopagus, he created a Council of Four Hundred, manned by a hundred members from each of the four historic tribes of early Attica. To give a democratic flavor to the constitution, he instituted an *ekklesia* of all the citizens, which was empowered to elect the archons and to exercise a considerable measure of control over them. All citizens were also made eligible for selection by lot to the *heliaea*, the six-thousand-member body from which the courts were selected before which most cases were tried.

As Lycurgus' constitution embodied the Lacedaemonian spirit, so Solon's proved to be a durable expression of the more liberal Athenian mind. It survived the dictatorship of Peisistratus, who ruled Athens with intelligence and humanity in the sixth century, showing respect for the reforms which Solon had established. It acquired new dimensions of freedom and equality under the auspices of the democracy which, in 507 B.C., brought an end to the twenty years of turmoil that followed the death of Peisistratus. Forty-four years later it provided the foundation for the Periclean Golden Age.

Pericles, for almost thirty years, was the most influential man in the government, wielding his power not through the tyrannical use of force, but through annual democratic sanction. Under his leadership the base of eligiblility for the office of archon was further broadened, and the remaining judicial powers of the archons were transferred to the popular courts. More important than any changes he made in the structure of government, however, were the ways in which he used constitutionally prescribed methods to foster those attitudes and activities which expressed the historic values of Athens. Those values, while not excluding the martial virtues dominant in the Spartan ethos, were a far more complete expression of the classical conception of humanity.

The best of human institutions are subject to corruption and decay, and Pericles' Athens was no exception to the rule. Flushed with imperial success, she became more like the nations she despised. The long Peloponnesian War, begun with self-assurance, ended in crushing defeat and a self-doubt from which Athens never fully recovered. By the time Plato and Aristotle were committing their political theories to writing, Pericles' *polis* was only a shining vision of a vanished age of gold, but much of what they were trying to recover in the *Republic* and the *Politics* was imbedded in that vision.

The vision was always better than the day-to-day reality. But a vision must be transcendent if it is to inspire greatness, and it may well have been the Spartan self-satisfaction with their success in living up to their own limited image of themselves which ultimately brought about their own decay and insured that their fame would live only in the writings of other people. The Athenians had faith in a higher vision and, in daring to aspire to it, they achieved the civic greatness which Pericles described so eloquently in the course of his funeral oration honoring the soldiers killed during the first year of the war between Athens and the coalition of Sparta, Corinth, and Thebes.

"Our government is called a democracy," he said, "because power resides, not in a few people, but in the majority of our citizens. But every person has equal rights before the law; prestige and respect are paid those who win them by their merits, regardless of their political, economic, or social status; and no one is deprived of making his contribution to the city's welfare.......... In our public dealings we have respect for our officials and the laws which protect the helpless and those unwritten laws whose violation is generally regarded as shameful.

"But we do more than this. We have provided for the happiness of our people many creations: athletic games, contests of various sorts, festivals throughout the year, and beautiful buildings to cheer the heart and refresh the spirit as we see them every day. Also we enjoy imported goods from all over the world, which add to the attractive variety of our life.

"As far as preparing for war is concerned we are much better off than our enemies. Our city is open to the world, and we have no regular deportations to keep foreigners from learning what might be of use to an enemy. For we have confidence in our native resourcefulness rather than in mere military strength. Our enemies have a rigid system for cultivating courage from their youth onward, but we, doing pretty much as we please, are as well prepared as they when danger arises ........

"We love beauty without extravagance, and wisdom without weakness of will. Wealth we regard not as a means for private display but rather for public service; and poverty we consider no disgrace, although we think it a disgrace not to try to overcome it. We believe a man should be concerned about public as well as private affairs, for we regard the person who takes no part in politics not as merely uninterested but as useless. We reach decisions on public policy only after full discussion, believing that sound judgment, far from being impeded by discussion, is arrived at only when full information is considered before a decision is made.

"To sum it up, I claim that our city is a model for all Greece and that here more than anywhere else a man can become independent in spirit, versatile in accomplishment, and richly developed in personality."

The spirit of the Greek city-state at the height of its development was never more effectively summarized, and the passage of two thousand four hundred years has not diminished the power of the words to express the ideals of freedom and justice as the proper ends to be sought by political institutions.

# Chapter 23

# The Republic: Man Writ Large

For Plato, the Good was the Form of Forms, but, as we have seen, it could equally well be called *the One* or *Beauty*, and the concept of it tells us nothing specific about the good man or the good state. For knowledge on that score, it was necessary not only to examine concepts of a lower order, but also to devote some attention to the empirically ascertainable conditions of life in society. What is the good for man? This is the question to which moral and political philosophy must attempt to find an answer.

Plato held that for the attainment of the highest good, there must be a harmonious development of the various ingredients of life under the guidance of the rational intellect, for, like Socrates, he held that happiness is dependent upon virtue, and virtue cannot exist without knowledge.

The Platonic psychology posits three parts of the human personality, though the term "parts" must not be taken too seriously, in view of the unitary nature of the soul. The word "faculties" has sometimes been used and perhaps better conveys the meaning of *metos* as applied in this context. The lowest of the three is the appetitive faculty (*to epithymetikon*), the seat of hunger, thirst, and other physical cravings. Above it is the spirited part (*to thymoeides*), the seat of daring and the desire for adventure. Highest is the rational faculty (*to logistikon*), which ideally governs the other two and keeps them in harmony.

In the *Phaedrus*, Plato presented the image of a chariot drawn by two horses. The charioteer represents the rational element of the soul and strives to keep the vehicle on a steady course. One horse, the spirited element, is nobler than the other and more closely akin to reason. It is, therefore, more easily controlled. The other, symbolizing the appetitive faculty, is proud, insolent, and governable only by the use of whip and spur. This, Plato held, is the problem with which every human being is faced. The three functions of the soul cannot be in harmony unless the two lower parts are firmly under the control of the rational faculty. When a proper condition of balance is established by such subordination, each part of the soul is able to achieve the virtue proper to it.

In the *Republic*, Plato examined the several virtues. Temperance (*sophrosyne*) is the virtue appropriate to the appetitive faculty, operating together with the spirited under the rule of reason. Fortitude, or courage (*handreia*) is that of the spirited part, when, unlike mere foolhardiness, it is evidenced by rationally dictated actions. The rational part of the soul must, of course, be autonomous, and the virtue resulting from its proper self-governance is wisdom (*sophia*). When all the parts of the soul are working together in harmony, a fourth virtue emerges: justice (*dikaiosyne*). This condition is the good for man.

Such a position is antithetical to the Sophistic view, challenged by Socrates in the *Gorgias*, that human good can be defined in terms of power or pleasure. Power, ungoverned by reason can be self-destructive, and a life involving nothing more than pleasure, while it might be a good life for an oyster, is inappropriate for a human being. If pleasure were the sole good, Socrates suggests, the perpetual scratching of an itch might be the highest state of human well-being. He does not, however, reject pleasure in proper kind and degree as an ingredient of the good life.

Callicles, a Sophist of some note, argues in the same dialogue that the "popular" morality which he sees Socrates as supporting has no ground in nature, but only in convention. Nature, he maintains, really favors the rule of the strong over the weak. Popular morals emerge when the weak band together and by force of numbers determine right and wrong on the basis of their own preferences. If this is the case, Socrates asks him, in effect, have not the weak become the strong and therefore entitled to rule by Callicles' own criterion? Forced to defend the right of the hard and ruthless sort of man whose cause he favors, Callicles maintains that he ought to rule because he is wiser. Socrates asks if he should not rule himself as well as others. No, says Callicles, he should be ruled by his desire for pleasure. Under Socrates' cross-examination, however, he is forced to admit that some pleasures are intrinsically superior to others and that their quality must be judged by reason. Pleasure, therefore, is not the ultimate good.

Plato's idea of moral good does not exclude punishment which aims at the good of the offender, but it is in agreement with the Christian ethic in specifically prohibiting the returning of evil for evil. Insofar as a man is just, he is never at liberty to try to do hurt to another, that is to say, to make him worse than he is.

## Man in Society

A genuinely human life is not lived in isolation, and Plato saw the state as a macrocosm of the human person, having the same faculties and requiring the same virtues to function properly as the individual. In fact, Socrates suggests in the *Republic*, the anatomy of justice, which is the proper end of man or state, can be explored more easily in the macrocosm than in the microcosm. The simplest society, in which the needs of the inhabitants are met by common effort, shows a need for some degree of specialization, and as needs become more varied, a greater diversity of occupation is required. As the hypothetical city serving as a model in the *Republic* becomes larger and more luxurious in its tastes, the satisfaction of its appetites and the necessity of defending its possessions lead it into conflict with other states. This circumstance produces the need for a special class of men skilled in the art of war—a class which, at this stage of the discussion, is given the name of guardian.

Now there are two classes—the artisans, who satisfy the state's appetites, and the guardians, whose duties require that they be endowed in superior degree with the spirited faculty. Their high temper, however, must be matched with gentleness of spirit when they deal with their own people. Like well-bred watchdogs, they must be able to discriminate between friend and enemy, and this means that a guardian must be a lover of wisdom (*philosophes*). The sort of wisdom needed for guardianship in human society can be acquired only by proper education.

The curriculum recommended by Plato for that education begins with music—which, in Greece, embraced literature as well as music proper. Plato's remarks on this subject have often been criticized because he proposed a censorship which would bar the works of the epic poets and tragedians from the educational system, not for any lack of artistic merit, but because they tell falsehoods about the divine nature, attributing to the gods deeds which everyone ought to regard as shameful. Plato's suggestion was especially startling to the Greeks, for he began his blacklist with the names of Homer and Hesiod, who held a central position in Hellenic education. Plato, himself a consummate artist, never underestimated the power of art, but he held that it must serve a moral purpose. Poetry, therefore, should describe the actions of virtuous people in such a way as to cultivate similar actions on the part of the citizens of the state. Similarly, song and melody, the other part of music, must be carefully regulated. Lydian tunes should be banned because they are suitable only for relaxation or dirges, and Ionian airs are unsuitable because of their association with drinking parties. Only Dorian and Phrygian airs are acceptable in the ideal state, for only they stimulate the heroic virtues.

The second important discipline in the earliest stage of education is gymnastic, interpreted broadly enough to provide for the prescription of a simple regimen of physical activity and diet suitable for the production of warrior-athletes.

### The Rulers

Having provided a formula for producing properly qualified citizens to perform two of the three principal functions of a society, Plato turned his attention to the third—that of governing. As the spirited faculty is more closely akin to the rational, and as the rational faculty must govern, it is obvious that the rulers of the state should be chosen from among the best of those who have proved themselves as guardians. The determination of their qualifications can be made only when they have reached a sufficiently advanced age for their abilities to have developed fully. At that time, citizens who have demonstrated outstanding wisdom and proved that they see the interests of the state as synonymous with their own are named as rulers of the Republic. They now are recognized as "perfect and complete" Guardians, and other members of the class from which they come are called "Assistants" or "Auxiliaries." The fully developed state, then, has in it three sorts of citizens: artisans, Auxiliaries, and Guardians.

Membership in the two higher classes is not accompanied by material advantage. In fact, the Guardians and Auxiliaries live far more austerely than the artisans. They may not own private property or make use of gold and silver, lest they be led, out of concern for their possessions, to neglect their duty to the state. It is important for the Guardians to perform their own supervisory function without the distractions which would be occasioned by activities appropriate to another class, for in the state, as in the soul, only when the appetitive, spirited, and rational parts are in harmonious relationship can a condition of justice exist.

The aristocratic features of Plato's Republic are further mitigated by its flexibility. One's position in the society is not rigidly determined by birth, for some of the children of the Guardians may not have the talent or the inclination to follow in their parents' footsteps and so may be called upon to serve the state in a humbler capacity, and children of artisans may, if they prove qualified, become Guardians. To be sure, Plato held that heredity plays an important role in determining competence, and he suggested that marriages and the conception of children in the two upper classes be controlled by the state for eugenic purposes. The decisive factor in the determination of one's position is to be the degree in which one attains wisdom, and the instructional system thus becomes, in a sense, the most important institution in the society.

Music and gymnastic are, as we have seen, the solid core of the elementary curriculum, and a competent performance in these disciplines is presumably a prerequisite for the higher schooling required for guardianship. The training is to be open to men and women alike, for although the sexes differ in the roles they play in bringing children into the world, the difference is not one which disqualifies women from holding the highest positions in the society. Plato concluded, in fact, that there is no occupation in the Republic which should be reserved strictly for women and none to which only men should be admitted. The traits which qualify individuals for activities of all sorts are found in both sexes, but women are, in general, somewhat weaker than men.

The remark about the relative weakness of women might seem to cast doubt on the seriousness of Plato's commitment to equal rights, but he was explicit in his rejection of that distinction as a criterion for inequality of opportunity.

"Then are we to impose all our enactments on men and none of them on women?" Socrates asks Glaucon in the Fifth Book of the *Republic*.

"That will never do," Glaucon replies.

"One woman has a gift of healing, another not; one is a musician, and another has no music in her nature?"

"Very true."

"And one woman has a turn for gymnastic and military exercises, and another is unwarlike and hates gymnastics?"

"Certainly."

"And one woman is a philosopher, and another is an enemy of philosophy; one has a spirit, and another is without spirit?"

"That is also true."

"Then one woman will have the temper of a guardian and another not. Was not the selection of the male guardians determined by differences of this sort?

Glaucon's answer is in the affirmative, and Socrates concludes that women should be "companions and colleagues" of the men they resemble in temperament and ability.

Similar rights entail similar responsibilities, and women too must undergo the prescribed education, learning "music" in all its forms and exercising naked in the gymnasium. Women of the guardian classes—using the term in its original broad sense—must share in all the functions of guardianship, including war, though due to their relative weakness, their assigned duties can be less arduous. The state is to prescribe holidays in which "brides" and "bridegrooms" chosen by lot are brought together for the procreation of the number of offspring needed to keep the city from becoming too small or too large. The prospective parents are to be selected from among men between twenty-five and fifty-five years of age and women between twenty and forty. No guardians are to be permitted to become aware of the identity of their own offspring. They are to call all children born between the seventh and tenth month after the day of their marriage sons or daughters, and those children will call one another brothers and sisters. Any children not born under proper public auspices must be "disposed of," and defective children, even though properly conceived, are to "put away as is proper in some mysterious, unknown place."

Healthy, legitimate children are handed over to selectᶜd guardians of both sexes and placed in public nurseries, where they live a communal life until, at the proper age, they begin their instruction in music and gymnastic. Those who show the necessary aptitude continue their education by being taught mathematics and astronomy. Plato prescribed these two subjects not merely because of the practical need for calculation or out of interest in the stars, but in order that future guardians might have their attention directed to the realm of Ideas. The study of mathematics, Plato said, "leads the soul forcibly into some upper region and compels it to debate about numbers in themselves; it nowhere accepts any account of numbers as having tacked on them bodies which can be seen or touched." As for astronomy, just as an intricate model of the heavens is only an imitation of the celestial bodies, so those bodies themselves only reflect a transcendent reality which is the true object of the astronomer's contemplation.

Having been properly prepared through the strenuous education provided for them, those candidates for Guardianship who have successfully demonstrated their excellence, begin the study of dialectic at the age of thirty. They continue in this noblest of disciplines for five years, after which "they must be taken down again into that cave, and compelled to rule in the affairs of war and the other offices of young men that they may not be behind the others in experience." If, after a fifteen-year apprenticeship in statecraft, they still exhibit the intellectual qualities and moral character required of a ruler, they must, at the age of fifty, be led to the contemplation of the source of the light which illuminates the soul. Looking to the Good as the guide for their conduct, they must be willing to serve the state in positions of high public trust. Though they will be at liberty to devote most of their time to philosophy, they must, when their turn comes, share with the other Guardians the responsibility of rule, not out of ambition or the desire for pleasure, but because it is their duty. Then they will be expected to educate a new generation of Guardians to take their place, after which they will be a liberty, on leaving this life, to make their way to the Islands of the Blest, confident that they will receive their civic reward in the form of monuments erected to their memory and sacrifices offered in their honor."

Men who have attained such a height of philosophical insight have their minds fixed on higher matters than politics and can be persuaded to take their turn in active service as rulers only as a matter of duty and in grateful recognition of the education given them by the state.

Is a society such as that described in the *Republic* feasible in practice? Plato, presenting his model as an ideal by which any state must be judged, recognized that it might not be realizable "exactly and in fact." However, something approximating it might be possible on one condition.

"Until philosophers are kings," he wrote, or the kings and princes of this world have the spirit and power of philosophy, and political greatness and wisdom meet in one, and those commoner natures who pursue either to the exclusion of the other are compelled to stand aside, cities will never have rest from their evils,—no, nor the human race, as I believe,—and then only will this our State have a possibility of life and behold the light of day." Later on in the *Republic*, he added a further condition for the establishment of an actual state which would approximate his ideal by suggesting that philosophers who wished to try it would find it necessary, upon taking power, to send into the country everybody other than themselves who had passed the age of ten years and bring the remaining children up in accordance with the educational pattern which he had prescribed.

### The Decline of the State

As all existent things are subject to destruction, even a state patterned as closely as possible on the ideal set forth in the *Republic* can give way to inferior forms of government. The first step in the process occurs when disputes develop between rulers—the lovers of wisdom—and the Auxiliaries—the lovers of honor. When the latter prevail, the result is a timocracy, a government in which the spirited function is dominant. Having diluted the rule of reason, the guardians are now subject to further factionalism. Some, who are drawn to moneymaking and property-holding, begin a struggle for power with those who hold to the older tradition of virtue, and the timocrats begin to acquire private possessions at the expense of the former owners, who become their tenants and servants. By the time the process has run its course, the state has become an oligarchy—a government of property owners in which the many have no share. The state then becomes ruled by its appetites. The state is then set for crisis, for "a city of that sort is not one but two by necessity, a city of the rich and a city of the poor, living together and always plotting against each other."

The desire of the oligarchic rulers to become ever richer leads them to encourage intemperance in those whose property they wish to acquire and there appear among the poor a large number of dispossessed and disfranchised victims of the oligarchs, bitter against the men who brought about their ruin. The inevitable result is revolution, and the people who are left in the state after the killing or banishing of those oligarchs who refuse to accept the new order, establish a democracy—a rule of the many in which, to the greatest extent possible, each citizen does what he likes. The essential thriftiness of the oligarch is replced by the prodigality of the democratic man, who has no rule of life other than to satisfy whatever desire may be dominant at any given time. On occasion, he drinks heavily and plays the flute. Then he drinks water and tries to lose weight. He applies himself to gymnastics and then turns to a life of careless idleness. He may, for a whilc, attempt to assume the role of a philosopher. Then he may try his hand at politics, making speeches based solely on impulse. He may take a turn at being a soldier or a man of business. His life is devoid of discipline or order, but blissfully unaware of his regrettable condition, he regards himself as the most fortunate of men.

From democracy, the path goes downhill to tyranny. The passion for liberty produces a city in which parents fear their children and teachers their pupils. The old imitate the young, and even domestic animals share in the license which characterizes their master's lives. The populace, in its rejection of the slightest suggestion of servitude, loses all respect for law. Three classes emerge in such a state. The first and most powerful consists of the "drones," idle and extravagant men who find in a democracy an opportunity for the exercise of power which is denied them in an oligarchy. "The fiercest part of them talk and act," Plato said, "while the others swarm round the platform and buzz." A second and more orderly group is busy making money and becoming the richest segment of the society—an attainment which makes them the natural source of "honey for the drones." The third class, the "people," is potentially powerful by virtue of numbers, but without the political influence of the drones or the money of the rich. The politicians, from time to time, take wealth away from the rich and, while keeping most if for themselves, distribute the remainder among the "people." The plundered rich, driven to defend themselves, will be called "reactionary oligarchs" and accused of plotting against the people. Driven to excesses by the position in which they find themselves, they become truly oligarchic, and the state becomes riddled with "impeachments and sentences and lawsuits."

A "protector" inevitably arises among the common people, who leads them by fraud and violence into an assault on the rich. Such a man must become a tyrant or perish. To protect himself from plots against his life, he asks the people for a body-guard, and, with the force thus acquired, he consolidates his power. At first he is all smiles, friendliness and promises, freeing the people from their debts and redistributing land. But when he had vanquished outside enemies or made terms with them, he still must stir up wars, so that the people will continue to need him as a leader and be so occupied with working to stay alive and pay their taxes that they will be unlikely to plot against him. Anyone who has a free spirit or is suspected of having one must be disposed of in some fashion. The dictator cannot tolerate anyone brave, magnanimous, rich, or prudent. "A blessed necessity binds him," Plato said, "which commands him to have worthless creatures about him for the most part, and to be hated by them too, or else to live no longer." He augments his bodyguard with drones and freed slaves, and he squanders the city's wealth to keep himself in luxury and feed his growing army. The transition from the Republic through the stages that lead a society at last to tyranny is then complete.

## The Statesman and the Law

In a later work, the *Politicus*, Plato argued that in a truly ideal state a philosopher-king, untrammeled by constitutional restrictions, could make law as he went along to fit individual situations. Since he would be guided by wisdom alone, his summary legislation would completely satisfy the requirements of justice. Such a monarch, though, would have to have divine knowledge, and so any realizable state must make do with a government in which Law is sovereign and in which the rulers are as bound by it as are their subjects.

In the *Laws*, probably his last major work, Plato addressed himself more specifically than in the *Republic* to an examination of the actual conditions under which an acceptable form of government might be instituted and preserved. He had not abandoned the ideal proclaimed in the earlier work, but he had, through years of sometimes harsh experiences, learned his way around the cave.

The state, he insisted, must be a real polity and serve the needs of all the citizens, unlike tyrannies, oligarchies, and democracies, which serve particular groups at the expense of others in the society. As in the *Republic*, he saw the character and ability of the governors as a paramount consideration, and, as in the *Politicus*, the governors were held to be responsible to the law. Plato proposed a state which, as described in the *Laws*, contains a number of elements difficult to reconcile with the Athenian idea of freedom, but which he regarded as essential to the protection of the society. The currency he envisioned, for instance, would have no international use, and, except for military service, citizens would be forbidden to travel abroad until after the age of forty, and then only with state approval and on condition that they teach the young on their return that foreign institutions are inferior to their own. Men between fifty and sixty years of age might be dispatched to foreign countries, however, to see if there might be something in some of them worth adopting. Education for boys and girls would be provided by the state. Religious festivals would be prescribed, and laws would be passed against atheism and heresy. There would be a "Nocturnal Council." which, in spite of the somewhat sinister sound of its name, would be composed of citizens educated in dialectic and would be charged with guarding the constitution and seeing to it that the state would follow the path of reason. Slaves would have certain protection in law and citizens would be enjoined to treat them justly, though not with the familiarity common in Athens in Plato's day. Wars would be conducted only in order that peace might ensue.

Few critics could be found in Plato's day or in our own who would suppose that his ideal state as described in the *Republic* could provide a detailed model for an actually existent state on earth. Fewer still, faced with the intricacies of modern statecraft, would regard the small and isolated city-state described in the *Laws* as one which could profitably be imitated. Nevertheless, his enunciation of principles by which states may be judged to be just or unjust is far from irrelevant to our concerns, and his strongly delivered warning that true statecraft must be grounded in something beyond passion and power is one which is needed in every age.

# Chapter 24

# *Man, the Political Animal*

The term *good*, as used by Aristotle in his Nichomachean *Ethics*, is not first applied to a suprasensory reality and then, by derivation, to particulars. Such a good could serve no ethical use, he held, for it would be pure form and devoid of the content required for practical moral action. The goals for an individual or for a society must be found through inquiry into the good for man, or, even more specifically, for a particular man. The realizable good is that end toward which all action are directed. If there is one such aim, it will be the human good sought, and if there are many such ends, they will all be goods.

Now many goods are clearly instrumental. A good flute is one on which good music can be produced. But is music a good? Here again, the answer must be found by reference to some end which is realized by music. So we have a series of items which serve the dual role of means and end—means as related to that toward which the action is directed and end as related to the actions which have been directed toward its achievement. With reference to instrumental actions, we can easily see that practicality constitutes a criterion for evaluation. But any action imaginable is practical for achieving some sort of end. Overindulgence in strong drink, for instance, is quite practical for the production of alcoholism, and so the question of whether or not it is a good thing hinges on the further query as to whether that condition either serves a useful purpose or is a good in itself. If the answer to both disjuncts is in the negative, then an excess of strong drink is not good. If, on the other hand, some action produces a condition which conduces to some further result which, in turn, leads to something else, and so on, and if all the stages in the process are called "good," we are forced to fix the principle on which an evaluation of each is made, not in any point in the series which is a means to any other end, but in that final term which is never a means, but only an end in itself.

In human life, happiness, or well-being (*eudaimonia*) may reasonably be regarded as such a final end (*telesis*), Aristotle maintained. All qualities and activities of life seem to be regarded as worthy only if they contribute to happiness, whereas it would be regarded as frivolous to ask why one wants to be happy. The very notion of happiness involves not merely finality, but self-sufficiency.

But what specifically is happiness, or good in the human sense? It must be defined in terms of function. The good for an eye is its capacity for seeing well. The good for a flute-player is the ability to play the flute well. Just so, the good for man must be found in the exercise of his proper function as a man, whatever that function may be.

Now man, it will be recalled, is not merely a consumer of nutrients, and so his good cannot be defined in terms of preservation of life alone. Nor is he simply a sentient creature, although he shares the senses with other members of the animal kingdom. Unlike them, however, he can obey a rational principle and exercise reason (*logos*). A man's proper function, must, then, be an activity of the soul in conformity with reason. To be a good man is to perform that activity well. Moreover, a temporary or sporadic exercise of that function would not qualify a man as good or happy. For that distinction, the course of his whole life should be measured by the yardstick of reason and must predominantly tend toward *eudaimonia*. "One swallow," Aristotle commented, "does not make a spring, nor does one fine day."

Happiness, in the Aristotelian sense, is not attainable by members of sub-human species. Plants fulfill their natural function by drawing nutrients from the soil which enable them to become healthy members of their species. "Happiness" could be ascribed to the lower animals only on the basis of hedonic criteria which would not have met Aristotle's requirements, and even children could be called "happy" only by virtue of the hopes their elders have for them. Only adult human beings exercise reason and choice, and on their level, the good cannot be hedonically determined.

The end of man, then, is the life of reason, and human happiness, rather than being reducible to pleasure, may be defined as activity of a virtuous variety. But reason itself has two aspects: the cognitive and the practical. It follows that virtue (*arete*) is of two sorts—the intellectual and the moral. Intellectual virtues are acquired through teaching and moral virtues through habit (*ethos*). Good in the moral sense lies in the time-honored Greek virtue of moderation (*sophrosyne*), defined as a mean falling between two extremes, an extreme of excess and an extreme of deficiency.

## Moral Virtue

It is not difficult, of course, to cite examples of applications of the doctrine of the mean by the practical reason, especially in the morality of bodily appetite. Virtue in eating, for instance, obviously lies somewhere in the area between gluttony and self starvation. But the mean must be determined with a sufficient degree of precision to insure the best possible health. As the amount of food or drink of particular kinds which may safely be consumed may vary greatly from individual to individual, the attainment of temperance may require a grasp not just of the general characteristics of mankind, but of the specific traits of the person in question.

Similarly, the virtue of courage can be seen as lying in a mean— in this case, between cowardice and foolhardiness. Friendliness lies between obsequiousness and sulkiness, self respect between vanity and humility, and truthfulness about oneself between boastfulness and mock modesty. The overt character of an action is not the sole determinant of its ethical significance. The motive for which it is done is an integral part of the deed itself. There are, for example, instances of standing-in-the-face-of-the-enemy which, in an external sense, would be judged to be courageous but which lack the motive of true courage. There is the so-called courage of the citizen-soldier who holds his ground in battle because of desire for recognition or fear of criticism. There is that of the professional soldier who might flee in a really perilous situation but who stands firm in a particular battle because his military insight enables him to see that the situation in question is not really very dangerous. The man of passionate disposition will stand if he is sufficiently enraged for his fear to be driven out by the stronger emotion. An optimistic man will fail to evaluate the real danger facing him because he cannot believe that disaster can really befall him, and the ignorant man simply may not recognize the danger. All of these men may act identically, but their motives are, in descending order, divergent from courage. True courage stems from a motive in which the character of the agent and the pleasure he derives from noble action are stronger determinants of his conduct than are the external aspects of the situation in which he finds himself. Right habits may be cultivated in youth which later dispose a man to courageous actions whether or not they bring extrinsic reward. "It makes no small difference, then," Aristotle remarked, "whether we form habits of one kind or another from our very youth; it makes a great difference, or rather *all* the difference."

External circumstances may, of course, contribute to happiness or, in some measure, detract from it. Other things being equal, it is better to have money, position, good friends, and the like, than to be without them. The essence of happiness, though, lies not in the circumstances in which a life is lived, but in the personal moral qualities which give that life meaning. The traits of character which Aristotle saw as desirable reflect the highest Greek conception of the responsible citizen of a city-state. In addition to temperance, courage, wisdom, and justice, he examined such virtues as liberality, magnificence, friendliness, and pride.

This last trait, in the sense in which it was described in Aristotle's system, is not that kind of flaw which leads to *hubris*. It is, rather, the quality which enables a man who is genuinely worthy of great things to recognize the justice of his claim to honor. Such a man is not fond of dangers, but will face great danger without flinching. He would rather give benefits than receive them. He is not given to admiration and has a short memory for wrongs done him. Neither a gossip nor a flatterer, he has a slow step, a deep voice, and a "level utterance" which testifies to his lack of excitement. It must be stressed that the doctrine of the mean as applied to such virtues does not mean that their posessor ought to be only moderately virtuous. The end toward which the mean of conduct is directed is an extreme of virtue, and Aristotle clearly stated that certain modes of behavior admit of no mean because the names given them—murder, adultery, and the like—are terms which recognize the extreme character of the actions so named.

The mean is not a mathematically determinable point midway between the extremes. It may vary from person to person or from situation to situation. Then too, there are general traits of character in which the mean is farther removed from one extreme than from the other. Cowardice, a deficiency, is more opposed to courage than is rashness, an excess, whereas profligacy, an excess, is more opposed to temperance than is "insensibility," a deficiency. "Accordingly," Aristotle advised, "whoever aims at the mean should first of all strive to avoid that extreme which is more opposed to it, as in Calypso's advice to 'keep the ship clear of the foaming surf.' For of the two extremes one will be more of an evil, the other less; therefore, as it is hard to hit the exact mean, we ought to choose the lesser of two evils and sail, as the saying goes, in the second best way, and this is accomplished most successfully in the manner stated." If Aristotle was mistaken in attributing to Calypso the advice given Ulysses by Circe to avoid the loss of all his crew to Charybdis by risking the loss of some of them to Scylla, his point is, nevertheless, clear. Moral situations involve dilemmas entailing a calculation of the probable consequences of alternative courses of action. The reference to the "second best way," an allusion to the necessity of using oars to propel a ship when there was insufficent wind, serves as another reminder of a strongly practical element in Aristotle's ethics. Where perception is involved, he acknowledged, reason cannot determine precisely at what point a deviation from the mean actually occurs, and conduct which is blameworthy may not be recognized as such until the excess or deficiency is considerable. Persons who display too little anger, for instance, are sometimes praised as gentle, while those who show too much may be regarded as manly.

The difficulty of judging, however, does not invalidate the principle, for, "So much is clear: that in all departments of conduct it is the indeterminate disposition that is laudible; but that we must sometimes incline toward the excess, sometimes toward the deficiency, since in this way we shall most readily hit the mean and thus attain to worthy conduct."

Aristotle was more concerned than Plato with the problem of moral responsibility, a concept which, for him, was inextricably associated with the distinction between voluntary actions—those which flow from the agent's own character—and involuntary actions—those "which take place under compulsion or owing to ignorance." A compulsory action is one which stems solely from external causes, as, for example, one which results from the forcible administration of a drug given the agent. Some actions are, to be sure, difficult to classify in this manner. A tyrant might, for instance, command someone to perform an ignoble deed to avoid having his family put to death. Such an action is voluntary in the sense that the principle governing it is an internal one and the decision to act or not to act within the control of the agent. It is, however, involuntary "in the abstract," in that it is the sort of behavior which would not be chosen in the absence of the threat.

Aristotle recognized the uncertainties involved in bestowing praise, blame, or pardon, when faced with actions of this sort. There are some things which one ought not to do, even under threat of painful death. On the other hand, "there are circumstances so painful that nobody could withstand them." Then too, there are actions which are judged to be involuntary not because of external compulsion, but because of the agent's ignorance of the true nature of what he is doing. Whether an act is just or unjust in the moral sense depends not only on the external character of the act, but on whether it is voluntary or involuntary in origin.

### Intellectual Virtue

As distinguished from the moral virtues, the intellectual virtues are not determined by reference to a mean, but rather in the attainment of truth. The soul discovers truth by virtue of five faculties: apperceptive intelligence (*nous*), scientific understanding (*episteme*), art or technique (*techne*), sagacity (*phronesis*), and wisdom (*sophia*). Apperceptive intelligence involves the intuitive grasp of principles. Scientific understanding, in accordance with Aristotle's conception of science, has as its object that which is necessary and eternal. Art (technique) is "a trained disposition to produce in accordance with correct calculation." Sagacity, as distinguished from mere cleverness, involves the presence of right principles in the making of moral decisions, and, requiring as it does, long years of experience for its development, is not found in young men. Wisdom is a union of apperceptive intelligence with scientific understanding in concern for the most exalted matters. In the exercise of intellectual virtue, man finds his greatest happiness. "If happiness is activity in accordance with virtue," Aristotle said, "it is reasonable that it should be in accordance with the highest virtue; and this will be that of the best thing in us." The "best thing" must be that aspect of human nature which is most akin to the divine, and that, or course, is contemplation.

If the supreme happiness is to be found in the exercise of the higher faculties of the intellect, it is nonetheless true that certain external circumstances are essential conditions for the attainment of true felicity. It is, then, necessary for an individual to pay serious attention to the environment in which his actions are performed, for the lack of friends or money "takes the lustre from happiness."

Human good, then, is not readily attained in solitude. The desirability of friendship is rooted in the fact that man is by nature a communal animal. Even prosperity loses much of its value if there is no one with whom to share it. Friendship, according to Aristotle, is of three kinds, founded on the love of man for the useful, the pleasant, and the good. The first two varieties—friendships of utility and friendships for pleasure—are a secondary sort and are readily dissolved, for the friend is not loved for his own sake, but simply as a source of advantage or amusement. The third sort, perfect (*teleios*) friendship is more enduring, resting in the bond of virtue existing between two good men who, because of the excellence of their characters, wish each other's good. Such a friendship, in addition to being absolutely good, incorporates within itself the merits of the lesser kinds of friendship as well, for it is a source of utility and pleasure to both the participants.

## The State

From the concept of man as communal in nature, it is a short step to the recognition of the necessity for the existence of a state, for in view of the reliance of human beings on the rational faculty, they cannot depend on instinct to provide them automatically with the sort of social organization found among bees or other gregarious animals. The power of speech in man enables him to distinguish specifically between expediency and inexpediency, justice and injustice. Man alone is required to take into account through conscious deliberation the nature of good and evil in laying out the pattern for his society. In consequence, man must be defined not merely as a social animal but as a political animal. In view of the fact that he cannot live a full human life in isolation, the state does not exist merely by arbitrary convention, but as a creation of nature, logically prior to the individual. In his *Politics*, Aristotle examined the concept of the state and developed his political theory. Like Plato, he thought in terms of the Greek city-state, but recognizing the impossibility of realizing an ideal state in practice, he devoted the major portion of his treatment to a consideration of the best sorts of states which could exist under given sets of circumstances.

What sorts of governments are possible? For Aristotle as for Plato, there are three options. The control of a state may be vested in one person, a few persons, or many persons. Each sort of government has a true and a perverted form.

The good form of rule by one person is monarchy, an institution which may exist in different forms, the purest of which is the absolute role of a king over his subjects in the way a father and husband ruled the Athenian family. Such a monarchy is good, however, only when an individual is so clearly superior in virtue to all other citizens that it is reasonable for them to conform to his judgment. Moreover, for a hereditary absolute monarchy to be desirable, it would be necessary for generation after generation in the same family to be pre-eminently virtuous. Monarchy has disadvantages apart from the problem of succession, for even the monarch, if he is wise, cannot dispense with the general principles embodied in the law, and an assembly of interpreters of the law, acting collectively, is likely to be wiser and less corruptible in the application of the law to individual cases than is a single man.

Unlike monarchy, which is merely fraught with risks, tyranny, the perverted form of one-man rule, is intrinsically bad, for the tyrant recognizes no law higher than his own will to which he is subject and rules his equals and his betters with regard to nothing more than his personal advantage. Echoing Plato's harsh judgment of governments like that of Dionysius I, Aristotle condemned the arbitrary power of a tyrant as abhorrent to all men.

The pitfalls of rule by the few are similar to those of rule by one man. The discussion of aristocracy, its legitimate form, is unfortunately quite limited, possibly due to Aristotle's feeling that truly aristocratic governments were no longer a live option in the Hellenic states of his day. It is clear, however, that in order to be acceptable to Aristotle, a "government of the best" would have to be composed of men whose eminence consisted in the possession of superior virtue and who therefore had the best interests of the state at heart. There can, of course, be no guarantee that such *noblesse oblige* would motivate a privileged class based on heredity, wealth, or political advantage. As for an aristocracy of merit, even Plato had expressed doubts about the possibility of establishing his Republic and had admitted that even if it were practicable, it might be difficult to defend against the sort of degeneration which can push a state down the slippery slope to dictatorship.

The reverse side of the coin, oligarchy, is the rule of the rich in their own interest. Although it, like aristocracy, is thought of as government by the few, it would, in Aristotle's view, be proper to classify a state as an oligarchy even if the class of rich rulers constituted a majority of the populace. In fact, Aristotle appears to have classified any state as in some degree oligarchic which has a property requirement for participation in government, even if the amount specified is small. In such states, as in others where great families acquire hereditary power, the lines of demarcation between oligarchy and other political forms are difficult to establish with any precision. What is most dangerous about government by a rich and noble class, however established and however broadly based, is that it tends to be a rule by men rather than a rule of law.

Rule by the many also has two forms, polity and democracy. In branding democracy as the perverted member of the pair, Aristotle must have offended many Greeks for whom the word had favorable associations. It must be remembered, however, that for Aristotle, as for Plato, the history of Athens after Pericles offered very little proof that majority rule would invariably produce good government. There are, to be sure, in his system of classification, various kinds and degrees of democracy, some of which—to wit, those with property qualifications—are hard to distinguish from oligarchies. Some avoid democratic excess by adherence to law rather than popular whim, but in others, the decree of the people overrides the law. In the latter case, the many become sovereign and wield absolute power collectively. The ultimate result is the democratic counterpart of tyranny. What the flatterer is to the tyrant, the demagogue is to the *demos*, exercising power in the popular assembly through the support of the people who have succumbed to his blandishments. The rule of law collapses, and the whims of groups pursuing their own selfish interests become supreme.

A polity is based on rule by the middle class, which ought, in a healthy state, to be numerous and to have more power than the rich and poor combined or, in any event, than either of the other classes singly. The middle class, represents a mean between the extremes of wealth, which tends to spoil its possessors, and poverty, which tends to degrade them. Men of moderate means are not as likely to have despotic or servile tendencies and can, therefore, be more safely entrusted with authority.

Ideally, Aristotle thought, monarchy ought to be the best form of government and tyranny, "which is the perversion of the first and most divine. . . . necessarily the worst." Aristocracy is the next best form theoretically, and oligarchy is slightly less objectionable than tyranny. Polity, which is, in principle, less desirable than either of the other "true" forms. in practice proves to be the best form possible for most states, and democracy is less objectionable than either of the other "perverted" forms.

Throughout Aristotle's discussion of the several forms of government, his concern for law is evident. "The rule of the law . . ." he held, "is preferable to that of any individual." The function of magistrates is not to make laws, but simply to apply the general principles of the law to particular cases. Aristotle's respect for law was not, of course, indiscriminate, for bad men with power can issue bad decrees with the force of law. What he had in mind was something like the concept of Natural Law, which was to become a continuing theme in Western ethical and political theory. The laws which ought to govern a state have their origin in the nature of reality itself, and, as Aristotle declared, "he who bids the law rule may be deemed to bid God and Reason alone rule, but he who bids man rule adds an element of the beast; for desire is a wild beast, and passion perverts the minds of rulers, even when they are the best of men. The law is reason unaffected by desire . . . ."

How did Aristotle reconcile such an eminently civilized political theory with his acceptance of an economic and social system based on slavery? The surprising thing, perhaps, is not that he failed to condemn the institution, but that it had been called into question in his time to a sufficient degree for him to think it necessary to discuss its moral implications. "There are people who consider owning slaves as violating natural law," he wrote, "because the distinction between a slave and a free person is wholly conventional and has no place in nature, so that it rests on mere force and is devoid of justice."

To this view, Aristotle opposed his own theory that some men are by nature slaves, who find whatever human fulfillment their limitations permit by making possible the leisure which enables those superior to them to attain a higher level of life. When it came to justifying the actual slavery found in the Greek states, he faced formidable difficulties. Obviously, it could be defended only to the extent that it could plausibly be maintained that the individuals who actually composed the enslaved population were "natural slaves." In view of the fact that membership in that class was actually contingent on fortunes of war and that many slaves were of as distinguished lineage as their masters—and, in not a few instances, of overlapping lineage—Aristotle was never able to show that "slavery by law" was grounded in "slavery by nature." This difficulty, however, which he honestly acknowledged, was not enough to make him an abolitionist, and indeed, he was less of an egalitarian than Plato, holding not only to the idea of natural slavery but also to the notion that men are by nature superior to women.

### Man and Art

A consideration of man individually or socially is incomplete without some attention to his relation to art, and Aristotle was less delinquent than Plato in his treatment of the subject. His principal contribution in the *Poetics* consists of an extensive discussion of the dramatic poetry about which his teacher had such serious reservations. Aristotle treated it with far greater respect, not only recognizing its literary merit but maintaining that the works of the great tragic playwrights are more "scientific" than history in exhibiting the necessity of the events described, given the context in which they occur and the character of the persons in the drama. Poetry draws attention to universals rather than particulars. "By the universals," Aristotle wrote, "I mean how a person of a certain type will on occasion speak or act according to the law of probability or necessity." Art is, to be sure, imitation (*mimesis*), but it strikes through the particular to the universal.

With regard to the effect of art on the individual, Aristotle advanced his theory of catharsis. A tragic drama presents situations which arouse pity and fear, but these emotions induced by the situation of the characters in the play purge the spectator of the similar emotions which may be excessively present in his personal life. This function determined for Aristotle the form which a proper tragedy must take. A wholly virtuous man must not be reduced from prosperity to adversity, for that produces only shock, as does the case of a bad man moving from adversity to prosperity. Nor is catharsis induced by the spectacle of the downfall of a complete villain, for he is too wicked to excite pity and too unlike most men for his plight to arouse fear. The character must be a mean between two extremes—a better than ordinary but not completely virtuous man—and his tragic fate must be due to some "tragic flaw" (*hamartia*) rather than to vice or depravity.

The form and content of tragedy exercise their appeal through two fundamental instincts deeply imbedded in human nature. One, the instinct of imitation, is satisfied in drama when the spectator has the thrill which comes from recognizing in the action of the play something which he knows to be true in his own experience. The other is the instinct for harmony and rhythm, which finds its expression in the special way in which language is used in poetic drama. Aristotle recognized dactylic hexameter as the most appropriate form for a narrative poem. "Nature herself . . .," he said, "teaches us the proper form of verse to select."

Aristotle had profounder influence on the formation of Western thought than any other Greek thinker with the exception of Plato. Even during a period of history lasting for several centuries when many of his writings were inaccessible to Christian scholars in Europe, his thought survived among Islamic peoples and, in the thirteenth century, emerged as the dominant force in Catholic philosophy on the Continent. It is of contemporary importance not only in its fullest expression in modern Scholasticism, but at the core of the thought-forms in terms of which modern man still formulates his most essential questions about his own nature and the world in which he lives.

# IX.
# EXPRESSIONS
# OF JEWISH
# THEOLOGY

# Chapter 25

# *Apocalyptic and the Way of Hope*

Theology is the product of reflection upon religious experience, belief, and practice. The theology that is produced by such reflection may be either good or bad. It may serve to edify religious people and institutions if it is informed, skillful, and constructive; or it may be useless and even destructive if it is naive, narrow, or negative. Whatever its quality may be, theology is probably an inevitable result and companion of religious life because the rational faculty of man insists upon understanding his experiences; and experiences that are found to be true and valuable are then given structure, form, and expression so that they may be preserved, shared, and repeated.

Although the ancient Hebrews did not produce the kind of philosophical speculation which arose among the Greeks, it was inevitable that they should begin to think about their religious experience and thus to develop what may properly be called theology. We have already observed that process in operation, even from the beginnings of Hebrew existence. The fundamental elements of theology were set in place in the Mosaic era, and those elements were, indeed, precisely the factors which formed the diverse constituents of Israel into the Covenant People of Yahweh. That early theology was immature, of course, and it had to be corrected and deepened by succeeding ages. We have seen how the sages, the priests, and especially the prophets, of Israel contributed unique dimensions of morality and universality to the original cultic faith so that , by the end of the Babylonian Exile, the teachers of Judaism began to claim that Yahweh is the only God and that obedience to his Torah is the only adequate righteousness.

The loss of nationhood, the dispersion among the *goyim*, and the continuing calamities and failures which befell the Jewish people all forced the kind of serious thinking which results in profound and structured theology. In addition, the Jews could not escape the impetus which was brought to bear on their theological reflection by the challenge of other faiths and cultures. Therefore, because of internal religious development and external challenge, as well as because of other individual and historical conditions, the centuries immediately following the Exile, and on through Roman times, witnessed the growth and maturing of a theology among the

Jews which provided the fundamental principles of Judaism and Christianity, and hence of subsequent Western culture.

Those centuries between the fall of Jerusalem to the Babylonians and the fall of Jerusalem to the Romans were times of never-ending troubles for the Jews. The glorious hope for restoration and well-being which had shone so brightly in the poetic oracles of Second Isaiah soon began to fade. The dedicated remnant who returned to Judah, led by the Davidic heirs-apparent, Sheshbazzar and Zerubbabel, and the priest, Joshua, found only ruin, poverty, and division. The ancient cult was revived and the Temple was rebuilt, but they met only minimal expectations. The Persians, even though patronizing and tolerant masters, remained unmistakably in absolute political control. More than a century after the initial return of a few from exile, when the governor, Nehemiah, attempted to protect and rebuild Jerusalem, and when Ezra, the scribe, forced a Torah-centered reformation, the community of the faithful remained poor and weak, with no evidence of great promise or blessing from Yahweh. The centuries slowly passed as hope itself grew dim. Thoughtful Jews increasingly asked profound and searching questions of their faith, stubbornly refusing to give in to apostasy. Had God abandoned his people? Is there a meaningful future for Israel? Is death the end for everyman? What can be said for the purpose and justice of the God of the Covenant? What is the faithful Jew to do in the face of the powerful and attractive ideologies which the surrounding cultures present as alternative answers to the questions of existence?

The books which comprise the third division of the Jewish Scriptures, the Kethubim, contain, in large measure, the theological reflections which resulted from such questions. In addition, the so-called non-canonical Jewish literature of antiquity should be consulted in an effort to discover the developing theology of post-exilic Judaism. We observed in chapter 4, above, that much of the ancient Jewish literature which was refused canonicity has been preserved in two major collections known as the *Apocrypha* and the *Pseudepigrapha*. Recent years have also brought to light the Dead Sea Scrolls. This material, apparently the library of the separatist Jewish community at Qumran, was written around the first century B.C. and thus is highly significant for the study of pre-Christian Jewish thought.

The remainder of this chapter and the two that follow will be devoted to three major expressions of Jewish theology which may be found in that sizeable body of canonical and non-canonical Jewish literature. First we shall see how hope survived in a variety of forms of eschatology, especially in terms of an increasing apocalypticism. Then we shall examine the ancient Jewish Wisdom literature, writings which most resemble Greek and Roman philosophical inquiry and speculation. And, finally, we shall observe the literary artistry of the Jews as they struggled with the particular problem of conviction versus compromise, while they continued to find themselves a threatened minority in a pagan world.

## The Dominance of Apocalypticism

The vision of a new age beyond the history of this world was a major antidote to the despair which increasingly infected the Jewish spirit during the disappointing centuries following the Exile. That vision was characteristically cast in the genre of apocalyptical writings. Prophecy declined and ceased; apocalypticism became a replacement. Available evidence suggests that the canon of prophecy had become fixed by 200 B.C. From that time forward others spoke for God or claimed to reveal his will, and prominent among those who did so were the unknown authors who used pseudonyms from the past and spoke at the end of history, as they believed, concerning the imminent new age of God, the Kingdom of the Most High and his saints that was dawning.

We have suggested that the apocalyptic mode of expression had its origin as early as Amos, the first written prophecy, from the eighth century. The visions of coming judgment in the last three chapters of his book may surely be so understood. And by the time of Ezekiel, at the beginning of the Exile, such imagery had become so prominent that he has been designated as "the father of apocalypticism." Nevertheless, prophecy also continued following the Exile, as may certainly be seen in the work of Second Isaiah, Haggai, Zechariah, Obadiah, Joel, Malachi, and in post-exilic portions of other books. Prophecy gradually grew silent and apocalypticism increasingly became dominant. The primary cause would seem to be a disillusionment with an unrealized hope for repentance and restoration, and the pessimism that pervaded the Jewish mind regarding this world and its history.

Probably because of its pessimism about a doubtful future and its bizarre, easily misunderstood language, apocalyptic literature did not find ready acceptance into the canon. Most that has survived is to be found in the Apocrypha, the Pseudepigrapha, or elsewhere in non-canonical literature. The only wholly apocalyptic book in the Hebrew canon is Daniel, and it was included, in all probability, because it was written about a renowned prophetic figure and claims to be a prophecy from a time much earlier than its actual composition. There are, of course, apocalyptic sections of other canonical books, as we have seen, especially in Ezekiel, Isaiah 24-27, and Zechariah. However, the genre received its purest expression in the *Sibylline Oracles*, the *Ethiopic Book of Enoch*, the *Assumption of Moses, Fourth Esdras,* the *Syriac Apocalypse of Baruch,* and possibly the *Book of Jubilees,* the *Testament of the Twelve Patriarchs,* and other ancient writings associated with the names of Enoch and Baruch.

Earlier, in chapter 16, we noted that apocalypticism was one of the major aspects of Judaism which developed because of the "new situation" resulting from the Exile and dispersion among the nations. There we briefly described apocalypticism as it may be contrasted with prophecy. Here, as we study the period of apocalypticism's profuse blooming and widest use, we must observe the phenomenon more carefully and directly in order to assess its essential nature and permanent influence.

First, what may be said as to the source and origin of apoclyptic? A great deal has been written on this question in recent years by many scholars representing a wide variety of opinions. Prominent among them are Hilgenfeld, Schweitzer, H. H. Rowley, Ploger, von Rad, Kasemann, and Schmithals. All of them suggest that the movement and literary genre arose in Judaism because of the impetus that came from one of three sources: the extremely dualistic religion of the Persians, known as Zoroastrianism or Parseeism; the religio-philosophic world view associated with the central concept of *gnosis,* which was essentially Hellenistic, though eclectic in content; or the indigenous piety of the Jews themselves as it was developed under the influence of the cessation of prophecy, the pressures of the social and political situation, and the inevitable amalgamation of cultures due to the dispersion among the *goyim.* Strong arguments have been offered in support of each position, and it is probably correct to say that the choice depends in large measure on the prior opinion concerning the essential nature of apocalypticism. What are its usual characteristics, and how is it distinctive from other literary forms and fundamental stances regarding reality?

Probably the most obvious characteristic of apocalyptic is its pseudonymity, as the titles of the books show. They were written by unnamed authors during the centuries just before or just after the rise of Christianity, but they claimed to have been written by such ancient persons as Moses, Enoch, or the great, mysterious Sibyl

Such a claim not only gave prestigious authority to the writings but also enabled them to appear to predict the events of history which occurred after the pretended author, though well before the real author.

A second trait of apocalyptic is its use of signs, visions, and dreams as means of God's disclosure. The prophetic revelation is usually auditory; the apocalyptic is typically visual. We have noted that as early as Amos, the prophet said, "the word of Yahweh came to me," or, "Now hear the word of Yahweh." But even Amos began also to say, "He showed me, and behold I saw...." The difference in communication became more pronounced in Ezekiel, and the dream or vision became almost exclusive after the canonization of the prophetic works. After the time of Ezra, the Word of Yahweh was found either in the written Torah or in the recorded oracles of past prophets. Furthermore, it is worthy of note that the *Word had come to* Moses and the prophets in the midst of their lives and times; but the apocalyptists were usually translated in dream or vision *to another time and place,* often of a super-mundane order. Revelation had been intrahistorical. Now it became suprahistorical.

A third characteristic of apocalyptic is its objective view of history. The seer stands within history and yet also above it in his understanding, judgment and interest. He sees the whole of history, having received his purview and evaluation by dream or vision from the God who is above and apart from history. He believes that history is coming to a close and that a new age, created by God and of an entirely different nature, is about to begin. The world is doomed and time shall soon be no more. Nature is of no value, associated with sin and death. There is no possibility of repentance bringing restoration. The gods of this age and this world, Satan and the demons, must be resisted at any cost, and their realm cannot be redeemed but must be escaped.

Furthermore, closely associated with this view of nature and history is a fourth characteristic of apocalyptic, its constant emphasis upon eschatology (the doctrine of the end, of last things). The seer not only looks with disdain and despair upon history; he sees the dawning of a new day in which the saints of the Most High will live in victory and peace, unthreatened by evil, suffering, or death. Such a belief requires, of course, new ideas about the consummation of this world and the survival of the righteous. Therefore, grandiose schemes may be found in the apocalyptic writings about the final struggle between the forces of evil and the forces of good, the signs of the end, the catastrophic victory over evil and the destruction of the world, and the ultimate salvation of the righteous by such hitherto unthought means as rapture to another realm or the resurrection of the dead.

Finally, apocalyptic is, paradoxically, almost always both pessimistic and optimistic. Its pessimism is extreme with respect to man, nature, and history; but its optimism knows no bounds concerning the power and ultimate victory of God. The apocalyptist sees all of history as an increasingly tragic struggle between sin and righteousness, between Satan, the ruler of this age, and God, the Creator of the age to come; and there is no possiblity of real progress in this order of being. Nature has been cursed and corrupted since Adam, and it must be either destroyed by a cosmic catastrophe or radically transformed by the recreative power of God. All men are depraved and helpless; they would be totally lost except for the providential grace of God, who will redeem his chosen ones out of the fiery judgment which is to consume the cosmos and bring an end to history. But that very grace of God is the essential certainty which the apocalyptist proclaims. He sees beyond the despair of this age, in spite of all its ample causes, and he provides courage and hope by the assurance that God will intervene to overcome the power of evil, guaranteeing final felicity to those who remain faithful and righteous.

Thus apocalypticism was an appropriate medium for theological expression to the Jews during their long era of frustration and persecution under the Persians, the Greeks, and the Romans. It spoke to their need as perhaps no other genre could. The apocalyptists borrowed, of course, from the imagery and insights of both Persians and Greeks, and hence there are parallels between apocalypticism on the other hand and Zoroastrian dualism and Hellenistic gnosticism on the other; but it is probably most accurate to see the origin of apocalyptic in terms of the religious response of the Jews, bolstered by an invincible faith, to a continually threatened existence.

As we have seen, the book of Daniel is the only apocalyptic work to be included in the Hebrew canon of Scriptures. Even it is not altogether typical of the genre, since the first half contains a series of stories about the faithful and obedient Daniel and his companions. Furthermore, it is significant that Daniel was not included among the prophets, having been written after that portion of the canon was "closed," and it was placed among the Kethubim in the Septuagint. Modern scholarship has concluded, on the basis of both internal and external evidence, that the book was composed during the Maccabean Revolt against the Hellenistic Syrians, probably early in 164 B.C. It has been designated as "the Manifesto of the Hasidim" because it expresses the unyielding attitude of those pious Jews who rejected Hellenistic paganism, even at the risk of death, and won a brief independence for a Jewish homeland—a feat unmatched again until the twentieth century.

Daniel serves well as an example of the nature and purpose of Jewish apocalypticism. It is divided into two equal parts of six chapters each. The first part contains six exemplary stories about the prophet Daniel, who supposedly lived as a faithful and uncompromising Jew during the last days of the Babylonian and the early years of the Persian empires. He demonstrated faithfulness and fortitude against all trials and temptations, always receiving the protection and blessing of God. He escaped even the lion's den without harm, and his three pious friends were not so much as singed although thrown into an overheated furnace! The message was unmistakable: the persecuted and martyred Jews should not succumb to the paganism that the Hellenists were attempting to force upon them, for Yahweh would bless them as he had promised.

The last six chapters present five visions which Daniel saw, in true apocalyptic fashion. The visions revealed by symbols the history which was to come (from the point of view of the prophet in Babylon in the time of Belshazzar, or later in early Persian times), including the period of the Persian Empire (538-332 B.C.), the conquest by Alexander the Great (332-323), the rule of Palestine by the Ptolemies in Egypt (323-198), and the terrible time of the Syrian Seleucids right down to the Maccabean Revolt (168-165) and the death of the persecuting Antiochus IV Epiphanes (165). With the last vision (chapter 12) the prophet was instructed to seal in a book the record of what he had seen, and to wait for the final consummation which was soon to come. He was promised that "at that time your people shall be delivered, every one whose name shall be found written in the book. And many of those who sleep in the dust of the earth shall awake, some to everlasting life, and some to shame and everlasting contempt" (12:1-2). That is the first clear reference in Scripture to a resurrection of the dead, including both the righteous and the wicked.

288

## The Future of Israel

A stubborn hope for the future continued to be expressed among the Jews during the centuries following the fall of the nation in 586 B.C., in spite of defeat, dispersion, and every indication that restoration would remain impossible. And their hope took forms other than that of apocalyptic eschatology. The belief that Israel would somehow be restored as a unified people, and even as a powerful state, was periodically renewed, and, as time passed, the idea of political revival came to be associated with apocalyptic ways of thinking. Two particular forms of this hope for national restoration which are found prominently in the literature, both canonical and not, should be noted here: the revolutionary and the messianic.

The yearning for liberty never fully dies in mankind, even after its most brutal denial and crushing defeat. That spirit of continuing struggle for freedom is to be found at every stage of Jewish history, as we have already observed it from the Exodus to the Exile. No sooner were the leaders of Judah taken as captives to Babylon, along with their king, Jehoiachin, in the first deportation of 597 B.C., than they began to plot escape and revolt. That audacious expectation was certainly behind the letter which Jeremiah wrote to the exiles from Jerusalem, in which he urged them to resist such vain suggestions (Jer. 29). Nevertheless, rebellion against the Babylonians was fomented in Judah under the last king, Zedekiah, in spite of every warning by Jeremiah; and we have seen how Nebuchadnezzar and his legions finally retaliated, in 586, by pillaging Jerusalem and destroying the nation, it appeared, root and branch.

Still the indomitable spirit and faith of the Covenant People of Yahweh would not die, in spite of all expectations to the contrary. During the early years of the Exile, Ezekiel saw visions and dreamed dreams of national resurrection (chapter 37) and cultic revival (chapters 40-48). And, when Babylonia was defeated and annexed by the Medes and Persians under Cyrus, the hope for return and glorious restoration was expressed with unbounded, lyrical joy by the great prophet of the Exile, Second Isaiah. When only a pitiful remnant finally did return to the wreckage of Jerusalem, led by Zerubbabel and Joshua, and when the Temple was rebuilt, such as it was, in 516 B.C., the prophets Haggai and Zechariah apparently encouraged the leaders to reassert national independence by restoring the Davidic kingdom. Although the details of that event are cloudy, the known facts seem to suggest that the Persians did not look with favor on such dreams, to say the least. Attempts to achieve political freedom were apparently so thoroughly inhibited that they are not recorded in the sparse record of Jewish existence during the remainder of the Persian period and even until the conquest of Palestine by the Seleucids in 198 B.C. The work of Nehemiah and Ezra, under the Persians in the late fifth century, involved permissible religious reforms and social improvement and did not, as far as the record shows, cause or intend any political rebellion.

However, the banked fires of freedom burst forth again with consuming heat when the house of Hasmon led a guerrilla struggle for freedom against the Syrians, leading to the establishment of a Jewish commonwealth under the Maccabees in 165 B.C. The holy day, Hanukkah, has been celebrated ever since by the Jews of all nations, commemorating that achievement of blood-bought liberty, symbolized by the Rededication of the Temple in December, 165 B.C. The theocracy which was intended soon gave way, however, to the corruption and internecine fighting of the Maccabean Kingdom until freedom was lost again with the coming of the Roman legions under Pompey in 63 B.C.

The evident motivation behind this long history of rebellion against all foreign domination was more than mere patriotism. For that matter, we have seen that the Hebrews were from the beginning a mixed multitude derived from various ethnic strains; and they had been united into a single state only briefly under David and Solomon. Their bond was rather one of religious ideology cemented by the Covenant with Yahweh, and expressed externally by devotion to the Torah. Without that cohesive faith they became immediately fragmented and were easily absorbed without distinctive identity into the ethos around them. However, their faith and destiny had been given new form by the glorious achievements of David, especially as those achievements were re-interpreted by Isaiah and other prophets in the times of the decline and fall of Israel and Judah. Then the so-called Royal Theology was created, and that religio-political doctrine has been a major force in Jewish life through all subsequent ages. The promise of Yahweh through the prophet Nathan to David, that David's "house" would endure forever (II Samuel 7:1-16), was made the heart of a dream that would not die. The Jews of the post-exilic era, especially, looked back to the golden age of David and then looked forward to the fulfillment of that promise in a golden age of the future.

The word "messiah" is a Hebrew word meaning "anointed one." From no later than the period of the Judges, priests and prophets had ceremonially anointed the heads of national and religious leaders, pouring ointment upon them to symbolize the gift of *ruach*, the empowering Spirit of Yahweh (Greek: *charisma*). After the rustic days of Saul and the early David, when power, wealth and sophistication grew among the Hebrews, the kings were probably anointed at dramatic coronation ceremonies. Thus, after the nation ceased to exist, the hope of the Jews for restoration included the vision of a new David, reigning with peace, prosperity, and grandeur over a reconstituted Israel. The "son of David," the Messiah, would rule in Zion, bringing to realization the new golden age which had been promised. It was a powerful motivation which often fueled the fires of political rebellion and sustained an invincible hope. For the pious Jew, the future of Israel was as certain as the promise of God.

## A Future for the Individual

The theology which developed among the Jews during the post-exilic era included not only ideas concerning the future of Israel, both as a people and as a nation, but also ideas about the possible future of every individual. The Jews began to give serious attention to the question of life after death, apparently for the first time, as far as the record shows.

Pre-exilic Hebrew religion does not appear to have been concerned to any significant degree with the possibility of individual survival after death. In fact, for the Hebrews a socially isolated individual was as unthinkable, or unthought, as a biologically isolated individual, *sui generis*, was impossible. Every person was considered to be inextricably a part of his family, his tribe, and, perhaps, the Covenant People. There was no notion of pre-existence, and there were only vague allusions as to what happens to a person when he dies. However, two significant, though undeveloped, ideas may be found in the literature. First, solidarity with family, tribe, and people does constitute an important kind of immortality. Ancestors continue in the land of the living through their descendants, and many children are a blessing because, among other things, they provide continuity into the future. This conception explains why barrenness was dreaded as a curse; and it reveals the ultimate terror of a judgment like that of Elijah upon Ahab in which the prophet declared that Yahweh "will utterly sweep you away" (I Kings 21:21).

The second teaching concerning the after-life was in terms of the idea of *Sheol*. The etymology of the word is uncertain, but it appears to be derived from either *sha'al*, "place of inquiry," or *sho'al* "hollow place." Thus Sheol meant the Grave, the Underworld, or the dark and forbidding realm of the dead. At any rate, all go there, and the going is to be dreaded and mourned. There are frequent suggestions that Yahweh has no control over Sheol. Those who have gone there are mere "shades," probably implying a shadowy unreality, a reflection of what was. Thus to be a "shade" in Sheol is to be a "has been." The same attitude of dread is found in Homer concerning Hades.

These undeveloped ideas proved to be unsatisfactory in the reflective theology of the post-exilic era. Several factors made further thinking on the subject necessary. First, the disappearance of tribe and nation, and often of family, led naturally to greater emphasis upon the individual. Second, new cultural influences caused a revision of thought with respect to death and the afterlife just as foreign ideas affected every other aspect of Jewish life and faith. The Persian religion involved highly advanced teachings about immortality, a final judgment, and rewards for the righteous and punishment for the wicked. Furthermore, when the Jews came into contact with Hellenistic religion and philosophy, after the conquest by Alexander the Great, they found an attractive and detailed body of opinions concerning the nature of man and, especially, the immortality of the soul. And, third, reflection upon the central Jewish Doctrine of Two Ways, which was enshrined in the Torah and the Deuteronomic History of the Former Prophets, led to serious questions about its adequacy. Life and history appeared to contradict so simplistic a view: the righteous are not always blessed, and the wicked seem more often to prosper than to be punished. Nevertheless, since God must be just, can it be that the scales will be balanced in some later existence? The Jews began to believe in an afterlife when the rewards and punishments will surely be meted out, and Yahweh will be justified.

The question of the afterlife, of a future after death for the individual, was thus raised and seriously debated among the Jews in the post-exilic era. However, the issue is only barely mentioned in the canonical Scriptures; most of the claims are found in the Apocrypha and Pseudepigrapha, especially the latter. And the few references in Scripture occur in the latest writings, especially those of an apocalyptic nature. The clearest passages are found in Isaiah 26:19, a late apocalyptic addition, and in Daniel 12:1-2, to which we referred earlier. Other references, such as Job 19:25-27 and Psalm 73:24, are of questionable meaning relative to belief in an afterlife.

Judaism has never developed a normative teaching about eschatology, particularly with respect to the immortality of the soul. There are at least two reasons for this theological hesitancy. First, the primary concern has always been with morality and the practical application of religion to this life. Judaism has avoided any form of dualism by being doggedly monotheistic; it has thus emphasized the essential goodness of the creation and the responsible joy that is possible in life. Asceticism and otherworldliness are contrary to the spirit and world view of Judaism. Second, the Jewish view of the nature of man, based upon Scripture, finds it difficult to conceive of an immortal soul, separate or separable from man as a whole. The *nephesh* is not some ethereal spiritual entity, possibly pre-existent, as in much Hellenistic thought; rather it is the whole man, the inspirited flesh, which is made vital by the presence of the gift of God, the *ruach* (spirit). Therefore, following the direction of the Hasidim and their successors, the Pharisees, Judaism has generally believed that any possible afterlife will involve a resurrection of the whole person, by the recreative power of Yahweh, at the Last Day and for the New Age.

# Chapter 26

## *Wisdom and the Way of Meaning*

We have said that theology is the product of reflection upon religion. Reflection is the use of the rational faculty, the mind of man. As a rational activity, reflection objectifies that which was originally subjective, immediate, and experiential. Reflection seeks understanding and, therefore, to some degree, uses the methods and categories of philosophical analysis and construction. Thus the development of a conscious theology in Judaism during the post-exilic period required also the beginnings of philosophy among the Jews.

Nevertheless, the Jews did not create the kind of formal philosophy that was produced with such profound grandeur among the Greeks. Apparently the Jews were not interested in logical systematizing or rigorous speculation about the possibility and ways of being and knowing. Both their fundamental assumptions and their approaches to the problems of existence were different. In modern terms, the Jews were existential rather than ontological. Thus they produced practical wisdom rather than speculative philosophy. To the Torah of the priest and the Word of the prophet among them, there was added the Wisdom of the sage (cf. Jeremiah 18:18 and Ezekiel 7:26).

It is instructive to note the distinctive fundamental assumptions and approach to the problems of existence which characterized Judaism in contrast with Hellenism. Obviously, for example, the Jews were monotheists and the Greeks were polytheists, and the Jewish God was the source of strict moral demand while the Greek gods were so immoral that they became an embarrassment to their human creators. The Jews thought of Yahweh in personal terms; therefore, consciously and without apology, they used grossly anthropomorphic language when describing his nature or speaking of his relation to the creation and history. They believed and taught that the will of Yahweh is the ultimate source of everything that exists and that his will also determines or permits everything that happens. The Greeks, on the other hand, believed that an inscrutable Fate (*Moira*) is supreme, even over the gods, and therefore is the determinant of both what really is (the object of ontology) and what ought to be (the object of ethics). The essential difference in stance may be seen, indeed, in the fact that the verb is basic in the Hebrew language whereas the substantive is basic in the Greek. That may suggest that the Hebraic mind perceived *action* as primary and thus saw truth as it was revealed to the eye of faith in the events of history; but the Greek mind perceived *being* as primary and thus conceived truth as it was grasped by the mind through disciplined reason. Hence it is fair to say, though it is a generalization, that the ancient Jews were existentialists and the ancient Greeks were ontologists. Therefore, the Greeks wrote Philosophy and the Jews wrote Wisdom.

## Jewish Wisdom Literature

There are three books of Wisdom in the Hebrew canon: Proverbs, Ecclesiastes, and Job. Significantly, they are in the Kethubim, the last division of the Jewish Scriptures. Some students of the Bible, especially in the early Christian church, also considered the Song of Solomon and many of the Psalms as belonging within the genre of Wisdom. In the same way, the books of Esther and Ruth, and the first half of Daniel, have been interpreted as Wisdom writings, probably because of their didactic intent.

In addition to these books in the Hebrew canon, several books of the Apocrypha belong to the category of Wisdom. The two major ones are the Wisdom of Solomon and Ecclesiasticus, or the Wisdom of Jesus the Son of Sirach. To these may be added, according to how they are interpreted, the books of Tobit and Baruch, and the additions to the canonical book of Daniel. Although the books of the Apocrypha were not included in the Hebrew canon, they are found, except for II Esdras, in the Septuagint, the Greek translation of the Hebrew Scriptures which was begun in the period of the Ptolemies (c. 250 B.C.). Most of them came to be accepted as canonical by the Roman Church and the Orthodox Church (with some variation), but they have not been counted as Scripture by Protestants.

Perhaps the most remarkable feature of the Wisdom literature as a whole is its radical contrast with the other books of Scripture, especially the Torah and the Prophets. For one thing, Wisdom has its source in reason, based upon the thought and experience of the sages; its product, therefore, is wise counsel. On the other hand, revelation is the source of the precepts of the Torah and the oracles of the Prophets. Moses and the prophets claimed to be spokesmen for Yahweh, presenting his Commandment and Word, not their own. Second, the dominant theme throughout the Torah and Prophets is *heilsgeschichte*, the sacred history of Israel as she has been called, judged, punished, and redeemed, so that she might be God's instrument in the salvation of all mankind. But, as we have said, Wisdom contains theological reflection of various sorts; it is not concerned with the history of Israel or the events of the future. Wisdom seeks timeless truth and value.

A third difference between Torah and Prophecy on the one hand and Wisdom on the other is the latter's lack of concern for the institutions of religion, or the cult, or even the nation itself, which are matters of greatest regard and anxiety for the former. Wisdom is essentially an individual possession or goal, and when two or more seek wisdom in dialogue, or a larger group is instructed, the emphasis remains on the inner life of prayer or reflection. Further, this absence of specific concern with the Covenant People points to a fourth distinctive characteristic of Wisdom: its universality and frequent relation to the thought and literature of other ancient peoples. The particularity which marks the Torah and the Prophets, seen in their Covenant theology and central concern with Israel, is almost invisible in Wisdom.

The Wisdom literature is a part of the wider humanistic heritage of the ancient world. Its authors borrowed freely from many sources, and their interests, thoughts, and forms are similar to those of their contemporaries in other nations. The subject of the sage was the meaning and value of human life, even when examined from the specific stance of Jewish faith. Instances of the same concerns may be found in the writings of many cultures, some of which are known to have been antecedent to the Hebrews. For example, the close similarity between Proverbs 22:17-24:22 and the Egyptian "The Teaching of Amen-em-ope" seems to suggest not only a common interest but also a possible dependence of the Hebrew work on the Egyptian. The same kind of relation has been noted between the very old Egyptian "The Instruction of King Meri-ka-re" and passages in Proverbs and elsewhere in the Scriptures. Furthermore, there are provocative parallels between "A Dispute over Suicide," an Egyptian writing from the third millenium B.C., and "The Babylonian Theodicy" (1400-1000 B.C.), on the one hand, and the book of Job, on the other. Numerous other examples could be cited to demonstrate that the Wisdom writings of Judaism were part of a general phenomenon.

## Prudence and Skepticism

The two main types of Wisdom literature are the "prudential" and the "reflective." The first represents the sifted good sense of the ages or, perhaps, the weighty advice of a sagacious person who has learned from experience. The second is usually more contemplative and philosophical, revealing the profitable result of mental and spiritual struggle with the problems of human existence. The book of Proverbs is an example of the first type and Ecclesiastes of the second. Both have proved their value by the profound influence they have exercised in subsequent Western culture.

The book of Proverbs is a collection of earlier collections of wise epigrams, insightful observations, and moral conclusions. It preserves an accumulation of practical wisdom gleaned through most of ancient Hebrew history, some retaining evidences of Egyptian, Canaanite, and Babylonian influence. The whole collection has been attributed by tradition to Solomon, since his name had become an eponym for wisdom; and he was, apparently, a patron of literature and art during his time, in spite of his disastrously foolish policies which led to the division and ultimate downfall of the nation. Some parts of Proverbs very probably did have their origin in the time of Solomon, or they were collected and edited then. But other parts show marks of a later setting.

The book is divided into three main parts, and, in addition, there are two smaller appendices attached to each of the second and third parts, as well as a final conclusion. The first collection, chapters 1-9, is entitled "the proverbs of Solomon, son of David, king of Israel." It is thought to be the latest section of the book, judging from its forms as well as content. The second division, 10:1-22:16, is headed simply "the proverbs of Solomon." Added are two smaller collections, 12:17-24:22, apparently based upon the ancient Egyptian work, "The Teaching of Amen-em-ope;" and 24:23-34, called, simply, "these also are sayings of the wise." The third main division, chapters 25-29, bears the superscription "these also are proverbs of Solomon which the men of Hezekiah king of Judah copied." It also has two small attachments, chapter 30, "the words of Agur son of Jakeh of Massa," and 31:1-9, "the words of Lemuel, king of Massa, which his mother taught him." The conclusion to the book, 31:10-31, is an acrostic in praise of the "good wife."

Several particular aspects of the book of Proverbs deserve special notice. First, its essential Hebraic nature, even a kinship to

Torah and prophecy, is shown by its recurring theme that "the fear of Yahweh is the beginning of wisdom" (cf. 1:7; 9:10; 15:33). Second, in places the book suggests that Wisdom is much more than the accumulated experience of thoughtful men, but that, indeed, it is the pre-existing, personified agent of creation which still seeks the attention and discipleship of mankind (cf. 8:1-31; 1:20-33). This idea became especially significant as it came to be interpreted by the first century Jewish philosopher, Philo, and in relation to the Christian conception of the pre-existent Word in the Gospel of John. Third, the national sensibility, based upon interpreted experience, indicates a new tendency toward philosophy in Judaism, as we have seen with respect to the Wisdom literature as a whole. This development reveals a new era in Jewish religion, characterized by emphasis upon thought rather than experience, the mediate rather than the immediate, the celebration of the past instead of the expectant opening of the present.

A fourth feature noteworthy in Proverbs is its depiction of the intimate relation between wisdom and morality. The book is replete with admonitions, especially to the young, to seek wisdom and to heed instruction in order to be righteous, godly, and blessed. There is a constant equation made between wisdom and goodness, on the one hand, and foolishness and evil, on the other. Further, a fifth aspect of the book is its steadfast devotion to the dubious Doctrine of Two Ways, which we have observed already in Deuteronomy and the Former Prophets. Perhaps the fundamental theme of the book of Proverbs is its repeated assumption that the wise and righteous person will surely receive the blessing and reward of God, but, just as certainly, the foolish and wicked will remain punished by poverty. Such an easy ethic seems obvious, especially to the pious; but the godly who still suffer find it a false logic, untrue in experience and adding to their suffering. That problem also became a concern for the wise, as we shall see.

The prudential counsel of Proverbs is balanced by the reflective skepticism of Ecclesiastes. The title of the latter is the Greek Septuagint translation of its Hebrew name, Qoheleth, which is in turn derived from the noun, Qahal, meaning "assembly" and frequently used with reference to the Covenant People or the Remnant. Thus Qoheleth is "the Preacher," one who addresses the faithful of Israel. The identification of the speaker as "the son of David, king of Jerusalem" (1:1), is to be understood as a typical association of Wisdom with Solomon. However, the book appears to have been composed late in the period of the wisdom schools, probably during the time of the Ptolemies. It provides a direct challenge to the Doctrine of Two Ways, and to all simple piety, by claiming with funereal monotony that no certainty about the meaning of life is to be found anywhere, either by wisdom or by revelation.

Qoheleth, like Esther and the Song of Solomon, was almost denied inclusion in the canon when the rabbis made the final decision near the end of the first century after Christ. Its acceptance was no doubt due to its popular usage, its attribution to Solomon, and probably also because it had been made palatable by orthodox editorial additions (cf. 2:26; 8:11-13; 12:9-14). The book has been read traditionally in Judaism as the Festal Scroll for the Feast of Tabernacles in order to remind the worshippers of the seriousness, the transience, and the mystery of life. More than any other part of the Scriptures, it teaches the utter bankruptcy of all human effort, including speculative wisdom.

The doleful theme of Qoheleth is stated at the beginning and repeated at the end: "Vanity of vanities, says the Preacher, vanity of vanities! All is vanity" (1:2; 12:8). The whole book is a rambling discourse on the theme, and the absence of perceptible structure may have been intended as an illustration of the meaninglessness of human existence. The author claims that he has sought "by wisdom all that is done under heaven" (1:13), but he has found no value that will last. He has tried pleasure and wisdom, wealth and fame. He has indulged in every possible experience, but all have failed. Time carries away every possession and, inevitably, death comes to all. Since time is the condition of existence, and death is the ever-present mark of finitude, the only way of meaning and value open to man is the fullest possible enjoyment of the temporary pleasures of life. The best advice, then is to enjoy youth while it is at hand, live a moral life in order to avoid pain, and make the most of the brief light and life that are given.

The book seems to betray some aquaintance, or at least similarity of interest, with the philosophy of Heraclitus, Stoicism, and Epicureanism. It dwells on the constant flow of all things, the wisdom of living according to nature, and the relaxing appeal of hedonism. However, Qoheleth remains Hebraic in his stance. He is no atheist. He believes in God and constantly refers to him, and he speaks as a faithful agnostic. He does not doubt the existence of

God, but he is convinced that the knowledge of God and of his ways is beyond the capacity of man. Thus man is foolish to seek for a meaning which is beyond him or to think that his life has ultimate consequences (cf. 3:11; 8:14). The wise man is the one who accepts the conditions of his existence and comes to terms with them, avoiding the sin and misery which result from the attempt to escape creatureliness.

The wisdom of Qoheleth and the correctness of its inclusion in the canon are manifested by its influence on subsequent religion and philosophy. It has served as a reminder of human finitude, showing that man's vision must remain limited, "under the sun." But it has also signified the wisdom of accepting life as it is, with its balance of pain and pleasure. Qoheleth counseled a faithful agnosticism, a courageous and possibly joyful living in the moving stream of time while avoiding the anxiety that comes from demanding more understanding than is proper to man. Such wisdom has provided a source of strength in Judaism, making it a religion of world-affirming joy even in the midst of continuing tragedy. It is the wisdom of gratefully accepting the gift of life without knowing all the answers.

## Wisdom and Theodicy

The theological and philosophical reflection which is the content of Jewish Wisdom literature could hardly fail to deal with the most intractable of all questions in human existence, the problem of evil, or *theodicy*. What satisfactory, rational explanation can be given for the fact of evil? The term "theodicy" is composed of the Greek words for "god" (*theos*) and "right" (*dike*) and therefore means the vindication of the rightness, or justice, of God, particularly in the light of the existence of evil in any form.

The problem of evil is a timeless and universal one. The fact that the Wisdom writings are so prominently concerned with it, from various angles, demonstrates again the universally humanistic nature of this literature. Similar treatments of the problem may be found in the extant writings of the ancient Egyptians, Babylonians, and Greeks, as we have noted earlier. It is especially significant that the Jews became acutely aware of the problem and began to reflect upon it in their literature just at the time during which they first came into contact with Hellenistic thought. The Greeks approached the question in several ways. The idea of *Moira*, for example, which played an important role in the Homeric material, represented the belief that there is a "fixedness" in all reality, a Fate, which is contravened only at great peril. The Furies, or Erinyes, were conceived as avenging spirits who pursue all who commit evil. Nemesis was the goddess of retributive justice. And the Greek poets and philosophers alike carried on a long debate over the relation of nature and morality. Behind all the forms of discussion were the questions of accounting for evil and avoiding it.

However, in addition to cultural influences, there were two other factors which forced theodicy to the center of Jewish attention. First, there was the painful experience of continued dispersion and political domination. The question could not be avoided: if Yahweh is the almighty creator, the Lord of nature and history, and if he is truly righteous, then why does he not defeat all evil and redeem his people? And, second, the problem was greatly intensified by the peculiarly Jewish doctrine of universal monotheism. There would be simple answers to the problem of evil if one believed in many gods, as all the other nations did, or if one accepted an ontological dualism, as in the religion of the Persians or in most of the philosophy of the Greeks. But, if there is only one God, and he is both all powerful and altogether good, why does evil exist, and why does it persist? The problem is perplexing when considered, reflectively by the mind; it becomes excruciating when faith is threatened by loss, pain, and death.

The problem had been raised already in historical form in the brief prophecy of Habakkuk. That little book was written about the time of the decisive battle of Carchemish, in 605 B.C., when the Babylonians defeated the cruel and hated Assyrians and their Egyptian allies. Although the Hebrews were delighted to witness the demise of Assyria, Habakkuk raised the question of how Yahweh could use a wicked, pagan nation such as Babylonia as his instrument of retribution, which was the claim of other prophets, including Jeremiah.

> Thou who art of purer eyes than to behold evil
> and canst not look on wrong,
> why dost thou look on faithless men,
> and art silent when the wicked swallows up
> the man more righteous than he? (Hab. 1:13)

The prophet failed to discover an answer. He apparently found contentment in patience and faithfulness, accepting the limitations of human understanding (cf. Hab. 2:1-4).

The problem was expressed frequently in terms of personal experience, as, for example, in Psalm 73. The poet was deeply disturbed by his observation that the wicked seem always to prosper, whereas the righteous continually suffer. He confessed that his faith was seriously challenged, and he had begun to doubt that faithfulness is profitable. The Doctrine of Two Ways was again called into question, as by Qoheleth. However, the Psalmist, like Habakkuk, apparently found sufficient assurance in faithful worship, suggesting further, in debated and cryptic words, that a better solution might yet come (Ps. 73:24).

The most beautiful and satisfactory answer to the problem was given, in profound theological terms, by the book of Job. Scholars of the Bible and literary critics through the centuries have heaped extravagant praise on this book, some judging it to be the most nearly perfect book ever composed. It is undeniably the greatest product of Jewish Wisdom, and its grandeur is exhibited both in the intricacy of its literary structure and in its Promethean struggle with God. Job shows theology at its highest reach, and the book's greatness is seen precisely in its revelation that theology cannot reach high enough to understand the ways of God or to bring man into his presence.

The book of Job is a fascinating study in literary criticism. No one knows who wrote the book (it is *about* Job, not *by* him), or when or where it was composed. The best guess is that it was written in Palestine, possibly east of the Jordan or in the Negeb, in the late Persian or early Hellenistic periods. It is clearly not a unity, and the various parts may have originated over a long span of time. There are three divisions. The first, chapters 1, 2, and 42:7-17, is a prose story, similar to several from other cultures, about a good man who was severely tested but remained faithful and finally received great reward. The second part is the major portion of the book, a magnificent poetic drama found in chapters 3-31 and 38-42:6. The poetic author apparently used the familiar prose story as his prologue and epilogue, splicing his dramatic composition between the two. Finally, a third author added the Elihu speeches, chapters 32-37, attempting to correct the unorthodox theology contained in the poetic drama.

The poetic drama presents a formal dialogue, first between Job and his three friends and then between Job and God. After Job's introductory lament (chapter 3), full of misery and longing for the release of death, each of the three friends speaks three times, with increasing impatience and harsh accusation; and Job replies to every speech, alternating in mood between touching self-pity and shrill self-defense. The drama is heightened as the friends cease being comforters and turn to prosecution. They display amazement and indignation at Job's apparent self-righteousness, and they both beg and command him to repent of his obvious sinfulness and submit to the healing forgiveness of God. The three friends present the strongest possible case for the doctrine of retributive justice, the Two Ways of normative Judaism.

However, it is evident from the beginning of the dialogue that Job's real debate is not with the three friends but with God. Their arguments are the best that traditional theology can offer, and Job answers them with equal skill. The debate comes quickly to a dead end, thereby illustrating the final impotence of reason in its arrogant attempt to rise above itself and to discover a wisdom that is more than human. That is precisely what causes Job's greatest pain and frustration. He can argue successfully with his human opponents, reminding them often that he is at least as good and wise as they are. But he is admittedly unable to meet God on equal terms. God is hidden from human view, and his ways are inscrutable to reason. If God is unfair, and Job fearlessly claims that he is, there is nothing man can do about it, in the nature of the case.

Thus, as the dialogue proceeds, Job turns increasingly from concern with the so-called friends, whose words wound and whose weal is woe; he sits in degredation on his ash heap, bereft of family, wealth, and friends, miserable with sores without and aches within, and yet dares to challenge God to explain the tragedy and apparent meaninglessness of human existence. He refuses to accept the silent mystery accepted by Qoheleth. Job demands that God answer the probing questions of man. Yet, even as he asks, he despairs of satisfaction, for he acknowledges his creatureliness and impending death.

> My spirit is broken, my days are extinct,
> the grave is ready for me (17:1).

The only possible vindication that can come to him will be too late. For he suggests, in a powerfully defiant passage which has been too frequently misinterpreted, that after his death, when his affairs are finally settled, he will be vindicated.

> For I know that my Redeemer lives,

and at last he will stand upon the earth;
and after my skin has been thus destroyed,
then without my flesh I shall see God,
whom I shall see on my side,
and my eyes shall behold, and not another (19:25-27).

The language does not yield messianic interpretation or provide a testimony to immortality. Job is rather expressing his invincible hope that his advocate (Hebrew, *Go'el*) will somehow, ultimately prove his innocence and expose the unfairness of his suffering.

The climax of the drama comes when God speaks. The voice comes out of the overpowering whirlwind of the natural creation. God still does not speak directly to Job, Person to person, since that is impossible. There can be no equality between the Creator and the creature. Yet, the voice is heard, and it meets the challenge. Job is simply told that he cannot have the knowledge he demands and desires, because he is not capable of receiving it. *Finitum non capax infinitis.* With a good bit of tension-relieving humor, the poet even has God demonstrate to Job that he is unable to comprehend natural things, let alone the supernatural (chapters 40, 41). Thus Job, and everyman, must remain content with faithful righteousness, accepting the goodness and grace of God as they are revealed to him. He may deny and reject God if he will, but at his peril; or he may live with the mystery of creatureliness, penetrated only by faith, while receiving the rewards of grace.

The book of Job advocates the Wisdom of accepting the inscrutable reality and goodness of God:

Therefore I have uttered what I did not understand,
things too wonderful for me,
which I did not know. . . .
I have heard of thee by the hearing of the ear,
but now my eye sees thee;
therefore I despise myself,
and repent in dust and ashes (42:3, 5).

# Chapter 27

# Heroism and the Way of Preservation

The post-exilic era brought the Jews into ever-widening contact with other religions and philosophies, some of which appeared to be more attractive and challenging than their own religion of Yahweh. The Jews were a small minority in the Persian, Hellenistic, and Roman worlds, and the pressures to conform were enormous. It was inevitable, therefore, that the question of conviction versus compromise became increasingly one of the most prominent in their theological reflection.

The ancient Jewish discussion of this problem can provide valuable instruction for modern man, especially in the twentieth century, since this period has been designated appropriately as the "Age of Ideology." The answers to the questions that arise out of reflection on this issue have practical and permanent consequences for both individuals and social groups, including nations. How is truth to be distinguished from error? That is the question of authority. Do persons have the right to be wrong, especially when they are weak and controllable or potentially dangerous to society? That is the question of freedom. Should unpopular minorities be allowed to hold views, to propagate them, and to behave according to their beliefs, when the majority disagrees and has the power to proscribe and to prohibit? That is the question of justice. How firmly should one stand by his convictions, especially if his standing appears to be stubbornly eccentric and results in suffering for himself and disaster for others? That is the question of integrity. These and similar issues were faced by the Jews in the ancient Greco-Roman world, and both the questions and the varying responses received sharp focus in many of the canonical and non-canonical books of Jewish literature. That is another reason that the literature is a valuable source for modern study.

The problem of compromise was more constant and crucial for the Jews than for any of their ancient contemporaries for two obvious reasons. First, the peculiar nature of their religion caused them to be inherently distinct from all their neighbors. They were monotheists in a vast sea of polytheism. Their moral standards were a great deal more stringent than any others of antiquity. And the rituals and ceremonies of their faith, which they believed were required by their God, made them highly visible in the world of paganism around them. Second, the Jews were a small minority, except, of course, in portions of the homeland, and even there they were ruled and oppressed by pagan foreigners. To be a Jew was to be strangely different, in the eyes of all other people, and therefore the Jews were separate, suspected, despised, and often persecuted. The result was that they were forced to choose either assimilation or isolation. Many chose assimilation, adopting the language, dress, and even the religion of their fellow-countrymen wherever they lived in the dispersion; they thus ceased to be Jews, losing all that set them apart as a unique people. But others remained tenaciously faithful even when the choice condemned them to isolation and frequent suffering. Thus began the long history of "Jewish quarters," or ghettos , as well as pogroms and expulsions.

### The Threat of Extinction

The existence of the Covenant People, Israel, has always been maintained by the slender thread of faith, and that thread has often been almost severed. That is why prophets regularly reminded the people that they had come into being only by the providential grace of God and that their well-being continued to be conditional and precarious. The Hebrews, who were not "a people," had been made to be a people by being called out of Egypt and led safely through the wilderness and, finally, into the land of Canaan, by the mighty hand of God. Moses and the prophets warned the people that their Covenant with Yahweh was conditioned upon their continued faithfulness. Their status was artificial, based upon the grace of Yahweh and their responsiveness to that grace; their status was not like that which other peoples claimed, wherein, as the offspring of their gods, they were assured a natural relation of guaranteed blessing. To abandon Yahweh meant death and oblivion for Israel; she was constituted by the Covenant and without it she ceased to exist.

The threat of extinction was not new to the Jews in the post-exilic era, although it was greatly intensified then because of the loss of nationhood and the dispersion among the pagan *goyim*. That threat may be seen as the motivating theme underlying the ancient traditions, both oral and written, which were finally combined and edited to form the Torah and the Former Prophets (the Deuteronomic History). The Yahwist Epic (J), probably composed in the Solomonic era, was essentially a theological apologia for Yahwism, intended as an ideological defense against the idolatry which threatened the young nation. The Elohist Epic (E) served a similar purpose in the Northern Kingdom, Israel, after the people were divided by tribalism, idolatry, and political tyranny. The second edition of the Torah, Deuteronomy (D), was clearly published by Yahweh loyalists, prophets and priests together, in an attempt to save Judah, the remaining portion of the Covenant People after the demise of Israel, against the overwhelming encroachments of Assyrian and Egyptian religious beliefs and practices in the seventh century B.C. And all three of these bodies of tradition were edited and enlarged by the priestly leaders (P) of the Jews during and after the Babylonian Exile in order to provide a "portable Temple," an anchor for survival in the Covenant, even under the conditions of the dispersion.

The Former Prophets, as we observed in chapter 16, are best interpreted as a theology of history, describing the blessings and curses that were brought upon the Hebrews from the time of Moses to the last days of Judah, in an inexorable demonstration of the Doctrines of Two Ways. That survey of tragic history said plainly to the Jews of the dispersion that the way of steadfastness would bring blessings and final vindication, but the way of compromise led inevitably to death. The past was depicted as a roller coaster of moral experience, with glorious heights of prosperity in times of faithfulness and righteousness as well as frightful depths of deprivation in times of apostasy.

In that history, the religious leaders of Judaism in the continuing dispersion of the post-exilic era inspired their people to remain faithful by holding before them the exemplary heroes of the past. The ancient traditions of Israel's initial conquest of Canaan were gathered around the central figure of Joshua, the successor of Moses; he was described as a loyal Yahwist who led the People of the Covenant in a rapid, military defeat of the Canaanites and then, at the end of his life, assembled the tribes of Shechem and required of them a pledge of allegiance to Yahweh alone. The stories of the separate tribal heroes, known as the Judges, were edited and recorded in such a manner as to provide an unforgettable lesson concerning the dangers of idolatry and the certainty of deliverance. And the whole, long history of the united and divided monarchies, from Saul to David to the Babylonian exile, was recorded and repeated for Jews everywhere, so that they might know their heritage and use its unmistakable examples of the power of their God and the value of faithfulness to him.

## The Maccabean Crisis

There is no way to know what portion of the Jews abandoned the faith and became assimilated in the cultures around them after the Babylonian destruction of Judah and during the several centuries that followed that decisive event. The scant records that have survived indicate that large numbers, probably a majority, were absorbed into the pagan milieu of Egypt and Mesopotamia, disappearing into the masses just as the former citizens of Israel had done when they were deported by the Assyrians in the eighth century. There is evidence of apostasy and syncretism among the Jews who fled to Egypt, and the record suggests that relatively few of those in Babylonia chose to return to the land of their fathers when the opportunity was provided by Cyrus and his successors. Nevertheless, many did remain faithful, both in Egypt and in Persian lands, and we have noted how they faced the new situation by creatively retaining the essentials of their faith even as they gave it new form and expression. In fact, as we have seen, the old was so radically transformed that it became a new thing: the Hebrew religion of Moses and the pre-exilic prophets became the Judaism which has survived until the present, providing a major source of Western culture.

However, although the threat of extinction by apostasy and assimilation did not completely and finally succeed, a new crisis was created in the early second century B.C. by the Hellenistic overlords from Syria which brough Judaism as close to the edge of oblivion as it was ever to come before the Nazi genocide of the twentieth century. Where voluntary compromise with paganism had failed, fire and sword almost had their way. The cause of that crisis lay in the political and cultural developments which occurred following the defeat of the Persians by Alexander the Great, beginning with the battles of Granicus (334), Issus (333), and Gaugamela (331).

After the early death of Alexander (323), the huge and diverse territory which he had conquered was divided among his generals. The largest number of identifiable Jews lived in the old homeland and in Egypt, both controlled by Ptolemy Lagi and his successors, who apparently continued the lenient policy toward Jewish religion which had been practiced by the Persians. However, that favorable condition began to change after 198 B.C. when Phoenicia and Palestine were annexed by the Seleucids, the successors of Alexander who ruled over the vast areas of Syria, most of Asia Minor, and the heartlands of Persia stretching eastward all the way to India. The Seleucids increasingly attempted to force Hellenistic uniformity upon the Jews, and resistance mounted. Finally, during the reign of Antiochus IV (175-163 B.C.), the struggle came to a climax. Pressed by the rising power of Rome in the west, by the Ptolemies in the south and by the Parthians in the east, and angered by intrigue, corruption, and insurrection among the Jews of his realm, Antiochus instigated policies first to control Judaism. By the end of 167 B.C., the practice of Judaism was proscribed, the altar of Zeus was set up in the Temple in Jerusalem, and Jews were compelled to participate in the hated and idolatrous ceremonies of Hellenistic religion.

Jewish resistance exploded in an apparently hopeless guerrilla war unto death. The leaders were from an ancient priestly family, the house of Hasmon. The patriarch, Mattathias, soon died and the leadership was taken up by his son, Judas, known to history as "Maccabeus," the Hammer. Judas and his brothers were eventually able to recapture Jerusalem from the distracted Syrians, and the Temple was cleansed and rededicated, in December, 165 B.C., with a glorious celebration, the Feast of Lights ("Hanukkah"). The religious zealots, including the Hasmoneans, who led the struggle for religious liberty were known as the Hasidim, "the pious ones." Thus Judaism was saved again from the very real danger of oblivion, and a relative political autonomy was established for the first time since the Babylonians destroyed the Kingdom of Judah. The so-called Maccabean commonwealth survived until the Roman general, Pompey, occupied the area in 63 B.C.

### The Examples of the Heroes of Faith

The period from Cyrus to Pompey covers nearly five hundred years. During that long stretch of history, Judaism was formed out of the rich heritage of past Hebrew religion and in response to the cultures surrounding its people. It was also tested and hardened by fire. We have observed how the Hebrew Scriptures came into existence and received their final form at least in part because of that historical process of preservation, formation, and purification. And it has become clear that the sacred books were in large measure composed of inspiring accounts of the past, recounting the lives and works of the judges and kings, priests and prophets, who were heroic examples of faithfulness. The records were finally accepted as sacred Scripture precisely because they conveyed the Word of Yahweh from the past to the present, calling every generation anew to keep the Covenant and to be the righteous People of Yahweh.

Much of the latest literature of the canon, especially in the Kethubim, presents the theological reflections of Judaism in terms of additional hero stories. That is particularly true in the considerations of the problem of preservation—how the pious Jews should be related to other people, cultures, and religions. The writings which have survived, within the canon and outside, are not of one mind with respect to this question. Hence there remains the unsettled issue of particularism versus universalism, or, in another phrase, the ever-recurring problem of conviction versus compromise. Judaism even-handedly portrays magnificent and classic examples on both sides of the debate.

The books of the Torah and of both the Former and Latter Prophets have been shown to lend strong support to the argument for Jewish uniqueness and separation. That position received even more explicit statement in the later books of the Kethubim, especially in the Chroniclers' History and in Esther and Daniel. Ezra-Nehemiah, part of the ideologically-oriented Chroniclers' History, depicts the crucial struggle against assimilation and amalgamation which occupied the weak community of faithful Jews in Jerusalem and Judah during the Persian period. Both the Persian-appointed Jewish governor, Nehemiah, and the reforming scribe, Ezra, required a harshly narrow separatism of the people (cf. Ezra 9-10 and Nehemiah 9 and 13). They refused to accept the help or friendship of the Samaritans, the mixed population of the old Northern Kingdom, Israel; and they forced the people of Judah, both those who had remained there during the Exile and those who had returned, to put away their foreign wives and children. No Ammonite or Moabite was to be allowed in the assembly (Nehemiah 13:1). The intention was to preserve the purity of the faith, to guard against contamination by pagan influence. Believing such a stringent policy to be both necessary and the will of God, Nehemiah repeated his proud prayer for reward: "Remember me, O my God, for good" (13:22, 31).

The much-debated book of Esther, whose place in the canon has been seriously challenged since ancient times, is a fascinating, secular book which probably achieved acceptance by becoming associated with the feast of Purim, the annual Jewish celebration of cunning victory over pagan enemies. It is a short novel, with its setting at Susa, one of the capitals of Persia, during the reign of Ahasuerus (Xerxes I, 486-465 B.C.). Some scholars believe that it was based upon some actual persecution of the Jews in Persia, though others contend that it reflects the pogrom of Antiochus IV which led to the Maccabean revolt. The plot involves the ingenious way in which Mordecai, a Jew of Susa, was able to use his cousin, Esther (her Jewish name was Hadassah), to thwart the plans of the Persian Haman, a high official, who intended to liquidate all the Jews of the Empire. Esther, who had become Queen, was enabled to protect her people and even to bring about the destruction of all their enemies, especially Haman and his family. In the background of the struggle is the ancient failure of King Saul—supposedly an ancestor of Mordecai—to kill King Agag and the Amalekites—Haman is called "the Agagite" (cf. 1 Samuel 15). Mordecai and Esther finally accomplish what Saul had failed to do, thus heroically demonstrating the glory and duty of Jewish separation from all the pagan *goyim*.

We have discussed the Book of Daniel earlier (in chapter 25) as an apocalyptic work responding to the threat to Jewish existence which led to the Maccabean war against the Syrians. Often designated "the Manifesto of the Hasidim," it was an urgent call to faithfulness even in the face of death. In a series of six stories which comprise the first half of the book (chapters 1-6), Daniel and his fellow Jews, especially the famous Shadrach, Meshach, and Abednego, are portrayed as heroes of steadfastness who are rewarded by the protection and blessings of God. Thus, again, the Hasidic faithful were teaching the Jews under threat at home and in the dispersion that they must remain apart and refuse to compromise, even in the lion's den and fiery furnace of pagan persecution.

In the same vein, two books of the Apocrypha contain stories of heroes (and heroines) who remained faithful to their Jewish belief and practice in times of great danger, only to be preserved and rewarded by the power of Yahweh. *Judith* bears many similarities to Esther, and it has remained a favorite story to Jews and Christians alike; but it was not accepted into the Jewish canon. That may have been due to its survival in Greek (though some believe it to have been composed in Hebrew); or it may have been due to its flagrant historical confusions (with Nebuchadnezzar called king of *Assyria*, after the Jews had returned from exile and rededicated the Temple!). Nevertheless, it supported Jewish resistance to apostasy by its gory tale of Judith's salvation of her people by the decapitation of Holofernes. The book of *Tobit* is also a hero story about a faithful Jew and his family who received the favor of God. It recounts the guidance given to the devout Tobias and his wife, Sarah, by the angel, Raphael, as they escape Nineveh with Tobias' father, Tobit, and forsee the destruction and restoration of Jerusalem.

These are examples from post-exilic Jewish literature, both canonical and non-canonical, that illustrate the attitude of narrow ethnic and religious particularism. The stirring accounts of heroes of the faith were designed to stiffen Jewish resistance to compromise and assimilation; and the further result was a widespread conviction that Israel alone was the elected, favored People of God, a chosen race with an exclusive claim to God's care and ultimate redemption.

However, an alternate view also received emphatic expression among the Jews. The Torah's account of Yahweh's commission of Abraham, the archetypal hero of them all, specified that "all the families of the earth" are to be blessed by the blessing of Abraham and his descendants (Gen. 12:1-3). When the Israelites arrived at Mt. Sinai, following the exodus from Egypt, just as the Covenant was being sealed, Yahweh proclaimed to his people that "all the earth is mine," and Israel is to be "a kingdom of priests" (Exodus 19:5, 6). Priests have the primary function of representing the people they serve to God for reconciliation and worship; thus Israel was given the vocational responsibility of bringing all mankind to the true God. Further, the note of universal concern was frequently sounded in the oracles of the prophets (cf. Micah 4:1-4; Isaiah 11:9; Jeremiah 1:5 and 46-51). Nevertheless, as might be expected, universalism as a religious philosophy could hardly be expected until the Hebrew faith broke out of the narrow tribalism and nationalism of pre-exilic times into the wider world of the Diaspora. There the threat of death by apostasy and assimilation was matched by the challenge of a broader life through missionary witness.

It is sufficient here to take note of three other parts of the Jewish Scriptures which bear powerful witness to the wider vision of Yahweh's concern and purpose through Israel. First, there are the matchless poems of Second Isaiah, which were discussed earlier (chapter 18). Standing at a crossroads of the ancient world and watching the rising and falling of empires, the great nameless prophet of the Exile dared to claim that Yahweh said:

> Turn to me and be saved,
> all the ends of the earth!
> For I am God, and there is no other (45:22).

And Second Isaiah stretched the self-understanding of the Jews by teaching them that the intentions of their God went far beyond the mere restoration of Israel.

> I will give you as a light to the nations,
> that my salvation may reach to the end
> of the earth (49:6).

The book of Ruth was probably written for the precise purpose of counteracting the narrow conception of Yahweh's will expressed in works such as Esther and Ezra-Nehemiah. Ruth is a lovely story set in the time of the Judges, though the evidence indicates that it was written in the post-exilic era, probably in the fifth or fourth centuries B.C. It tells about a Moabite girl, Ruth, who remained faithful to her Hebrew mother-in-law, Naomi, even when both had become widows. Unlike her sister, Orpah, Ruth went with Naomi when she returned from Moab to the homeland of Judah; and there she accepted the Hebrew religion and eventually married Boaz, a wealthy citizen of Judah, a kinsman of her first husband, and bore him a son, Obed. The climax of the didactic story is reached at the end: Obed "was the father of Jesse, the father of David" (4:17). The book is thus a powerful and delightful polemic against religious bigotry and particularism. If David was the ideal king, the forebear of the coming Messiah, and the architect of the Temple, how could anyone dare to suggest that "no Ammonite or Moabite shall enter the assembly of Yahweh; even to the tenth generation none belonging to them shall enter the assembly of Yahweh forever" (Deut. 23:3)? According to that law, and the policies of Nehemiah (13:1), David, whose great-grandmother was a Moabite, would not have been permitted to enter the Temple! The book of Ruth is thus a brilliant *argumentum ad absurdum.*

Finally, the little book of Jonah, strangely included among the Prophets, in the Book of the Twelve, presents an unforgettable statement against narrow-minded religion. Unlike other prophetic books, Jonah does not contain oracles but is rather a short story about a prophet. It appears to have been composed after the Exile, but no later than Sirach and Tobit, both of which presuppose it; and, interestingly, its author chose as the chief character of his story an obscure prophet of the eighth century B.C., Jonah, the son of Amittai, who apparently supported the expansionist policies of the hated Jeroboam II, King of Israel (II Kings 14:25)! It has been suggested that the book is based upon a striking passage in Jeremiah:

> Nebuchadrezzar the king of Babylon has devoured me,
> he has crushed me;
> he has made me an empty vessel,
> he has swallowed me like a monster:
> he has filled his belly with my delicacies,
> he has rinsed me out. . . .
> And I will punish Bel in Babylon,
> and take out of his mouth what he has swallowed.
> (Jeremiah 51:34, 44)

Although Jonah, unfortunately and frequently, has been both ridiculed and defended as a great "fish tale," it conveys the central message of universal, moral religion—that the one God, the Creator and Redeemer, is equally and fully gracious toward all mankind, and that the recipients of his grace are thereby privileged and obligated to be his agents of reconciliation in the whole world. The book, therefore, represents the highest point of prophecy. With subtle artistry and psychological acumen, it does not inveigh against the dominant particularism of contemporary Judaism; rather, it effectively leads its readers to see the unexpected success of the reluctant prophet who led even the despised Assyrians to repentance. There can be only one answer to the rhetorical question which concludes the book: "And should I not pity Nineveh, that great city, in which there are more than a hundred and twenty thousand persons who do not know their right hand from their left, and also much cattle?" (3:11)

# X.
# STRUCTURES FOR LIVING IN GREECE AND ROME

# Chapter 28

## *The Way of Reserved Judgment*

Alexander's conquests, in bringing an end to the political effectiveness of the Greek city state, created a new environment for philosophical speculation. In spite of the influence of Aristotle, Alexander was a true internationalist who believed that many diverse peoples could be successfully consolidated into a single political entity without prejudice to institutions and customs which the Greeks had always regarded as greatly inferior to their own. For a short time, he was master of an empire which, had he lived, might have provided a model for political unity as effective as the one which would later be created by Rome. His untimely death shattered that dream, but the splintered remnants of his empire were still organized along lines which rendered the *polis* obsolete as an ultimate object of political allegiance. As the young conqueror lay on his deathbed, ravaged by drink and fever, his generals asked him to whom he was leaving his empire. "To the strongest," he replied.

No single man proved strong enough to hold the empire together. For more than two hundred years, the territory conquered by Alexander was divided among several dynasties and often rent by war. After some conflict, Macedonia, Greece, and Thrace came under the domination of the Antigonids, a dynasty founded by a son of Philip known as Antigonus "Cyclops" or Antigonus "Ophthalmos" as a result of the loss of an eye. Antigonus was ambitious to make himself ruler of all Asia, but, thwarted by his equally ambitious rivals, had to settle for a more modest achievement. The Asian territory came under the control of the Seleucids, a line of kings founded by Seleucus, the son of one of Alexander's generals named Antiochus, whose name was preserved in that of Antioch, the capital city founded by his son. Ptolemy, son of a Macedonian nobleman, founded the dynasty which ruled Egypt from Alexandria as successors to other royal houses, domestic and foreign.

The change in the political outlook had the paradoxical effect of simultaneously expanding and contracting the range of philosophical concern. One the one hand, the breaking down of the intellectual and emotional walls which had bound individuals to the city-states forced a recognition of wider horizons than had seemed natural even to men of such broad interests as Plato and Aristotle. On the other, the world became so amorphous and complex after the fragmentation of the empire that many thinkers were tempted to withdraw altogether from participation in political life. These tendencies shaped the major philosophical movements which developed in the period between the death of Aristotle and the rise of Christianity.

Even in times of rapid change, the legacy of a great past has considerable durability. In Athens, the Academy and the Lyceum continued for a while to preserve the educational traditions of their founders. Theophrastus of Lesbos, Aristotle's successor at the Lyceum, carried on the Peripatetic work in the sciences and wrote four hundred volumes dealing with a variety of subjects. An eloquent and popular teacher, he had a reputation for benevolence and affability which may have been as much responsible as his scholarship for raising the Lyceum to its greatest height of popularity. A state decree in 307 B.C. mandated governmental approval in the selection of heads of the schools, and about the same time, Theophrastus was indicted on the shopworn charge of impiety. He left Athens, and so did great numbers of his students. The loss in trade created such an economic crisis for Athenian merchants that, within a year, repeal of the decree and withdrawal of the indictment permitted Theophrastus to return to the city, where he continued to direct the affairs of the Lyceum for almost twenty more years. After his death, the fortunes of the Lyceum declined, and Alexandria became the new capital of science in the Hellenistic world.

At the Academy, Xenocrates of Chalcedon, Plato's old friend who had accompanied Aristotle to Assos, kept his position as head of the institution until his death in 314 B.C. A man of conspicuous virtue, he refused all fees for his teaching and became quite poor. As an expression of his disapproval of Macedonian hegemony, he refused the citizenship offered him, but his poverty was too great for him to be able to keep up the payment of the heavy taxes levied on resident foreigners. Threatened with loss of his freedom, he was saved by Demetrius of Phalerum, who provided the money due the state. Essentially loyal to Plato's teaching, he placed more emphasis than his master on arithmetical unity and plurality, identifying ideal numbers with arithmetical numbers in Pythagorean fashion. He was especially concerned with ethics and regarded philosophy as valuable primarily for its ability to cultivate the happiness which comes from the possession of virtue. Xenocrates' successor Polemon was little concerned with metaphysics, but, in general, he accepted Plato's ethical philosophy. Crates, who followed Polemon in 270 B.C., continued the mode of teaching practiced by his predecessors, but the winds of change were blowing strongly in Athens, and that phase of the school's history now called the "Old Academy" was drawing to an end.

### Pyrrho

The new tenor of thought was essentially a reversion to the sort of doubt which Socrates had tried to replace with the approach to knowledge which undergirded the systems of Plato and Aristotle. That approach now seemed to many critics to be as unproductive of certainty as the sort of speculation on which earlier metaphysical systems had been based. Their doubts led to the widespread popularity of a form of skepticism taught by Pyrrho of Elis and bearing his name.

Pyrrho was born in Elis, in Southern Greece, about the middle of the second quarter of the fourth century B.C. He studied with Anaxarchus of Abdera, who had accepted the view implicit in the atomism of Democritus that no perceptions or value judgments can be verified by any standards transcending those of individual opinion. He joined Alexander's expedition to the East, where he studied with the Indian philosopher's whom the Greeks called gymnosophists (*gymnos sophistes*, "naked philosophers"), also known as *Hylobioi* from the practice followed by some of them of living in forests as hermits. He was impressed by their way of life and, presumably, even more by their lack of dogmatism and freedom from enslavement to metaphysical abstractions. On his return to Elis about 330 B.C., he became a teacher of philosophy, living a life of cheerful poverty. He was widely known for his teaching but, out of modesty, refused to commit his thoughts to writing. They were, however, incorporated in the *Silloi* of Timon of Phlius, three books of satirical verse on Greek philosophy. The fullest surviving account of Pyrrhonic skepticism is in the *Outlines of Pyrrhonism* and *Against the Mathematicians*, written by Sextus Empiricus a century or so later.

Sextus approached his subject systematically with a definition of skepticism as the Pyrrhonists saw it. "Skepticism," he said, "is an ability, or mental attitude, which opposes appearances to judgments in any way whatsoever, with the result that, owing to the equipollence of the objects and reasons thus opposed, we are brought firstly to a state of mental suspense and next to a state of 'unperturbedness' or quietude."

The definition has several features which help to clarify the precise nature of the claims made by the Pyrrhonists and distinguish them from the sort of dogmatic skepticism put forward by Gorgias. It is not, in the first place, a doctrine but rather an "ability, or mental attitude." By so defining it, Sextus and, presumably, Pyrrho, relieved themselves of the necessity of defending a truth claim, specifically a virtually indefensible truth claim such as "Nothing can be known." An ability is something which one may or may not possess. An attitude is something which one may or may not adopt. The question thus is not whether the position of the school is true but whether it is advisable to act on it if one has the ability.

It is advisable? The Pyrrhonists held that it is and gave a clear account of the reason. "The originating cause of Skepticism is, we say, the hope of attaining quietude," Sextus said. "Men of talent, who were perturbed by the contradictions in things and in doubt as to which of the alternatives they ought to accept, were led on to inquire what is true in things and what is false, hoping by the settlement of this question to attain quietude. The main basic principle of the Skeptic system is that of opposing to every proposition an equal proposition; for we believe that as a consequence of this we end by ceasing to dogmatize."

The quietude thus sought is, like Aristotle's *eudaimonia*, the rational end of human effort, "that for which all actions or reasonings are undertaken, while it exists for the sake of none," as Sextus put it, or "the ultimate object of appetency." It is only in matters of opinion, however, that the Pyrrhonist aims at quietude. In "things unavoidable," his goal is "moderate feeling." The quest for a resolution of conflicts of opinions, and the choice of one over the other introduces a condition of imbalance. This is especially the case with questions of value. "For the man who opines that anything is by nature good or bad is for ever being disquieted: when he is without the things he deems good he believes himself to be tormented by things naturally bad and he pursues after the things which are, as he thinks, good; which when he has obtained he keeps falling into still more perturbations because of his irrational and immoderate elation, and in his dread of a change of fortune he uses every endeavour to avoid losing the things which he deems good. On the other hand, the man who determines nothing as to what is naturally good or bad neither shuns nor pursues anything eagerly; and, in consequence, he is unperturbed."

The happiness or quietude which follows the proposed abdication of judgment was held to be arrived at by something akin to indirection. By way of analogy, Sextus cited the case of the painter Apelles, who, while painting a horse, found himself unable to represent the animal's foam. Giving the attempt up as a bad job, he threw at the painting the sponge on which he wiped his brushes, and the mark it made turned out to be precisely what was needed. In the same way, Sextus suggested, the Pyrrhonists sought peace of mind by trying to resolve the conflicts which arise in making judgments about the objects of sense and thought. When the attempt failed, they simply suspended judgment and "found that quietude, as if by chance, followed upon their suspense, even as a shadow follows its substance."

Some experiences, he admitted, do not admit the sort of suspense prescribed. The Skeptic, like anyone else, is disturbed by "things unavoidable," such as hunger, thirst, and ill health. Even in these situations, however, he has an advantage over those who are disturbed not only by the raw experiences themselves, but by the conviction that the conditions experienced are by nature evil. In declining to assert that conviction, the Pyrrhonist avoids a part of the discomfort and has as his goal the facing of the remainder with "moderate affection."

Reservation of judgment, then, does not mean that the Skeptic refuses to make positive statements about the direct data of experience. What he renounces is dogma, defined as "assent to one of the non-evident objects of scientific inquiry." It is out of a determination to avoid inconsistency in his position that the true Pyrrhonist refrains even from asserting the truth of his own philosophy in any metaphysical or ontological sense. The criterion to which he appeals as a ground for decision and action is that of appearance, which, for the individual, is not subject to dispute. Appearance presents him with four sources of guidance for his conduct. The "guidance of Nature" comes through sensation and thought. "Constraint of the passions" refers to hunger and thirst. "Tradition of customs and laws" prescribe standards of good and evil. "Institution of the arts" provides grounds for activity in practical and creative pursuits. "But," Sextus reminded, "we make all these statements undogmatically."

How does one suspend judgment? By setting  things in opposition: appearance to appearance, object of thought to object of thought, and object of thought to appearance. A tower may appear round from one point of view and square from another. No judgment is made as to its "real" shape. Or the argument that the ordered movement of the heavenly bodies proves the existence of Providence may be countered by arguing that Providence does not exist because the good suffer and the evil prosper. Or objects of thought may be opposed to appearances, as in Anaxagoras' counter to the observation that snow is white: "Snow is frozen water, and water is black; therefore snow also is black." Some of the appearances or objects referred to in the oppositions are simultaneously present. Others can be opposed because they are not, as when a theory which may appear perfectly sound at one time may be supplanted by an opposing one, by no means self evident at that time but destined to seem so in the future. The Pyrrhonists concluded that it is always inadvisable to assent to theories which may at the moment seem valuable, and so they enjoined distrust of all theories.

The "equipollence" which resulted from their investigation of opposing claims, they defined as "equality in respect of probability and improbability to indicate that no one of the conflicting judgments takes precedence of any other as being more probable." This equality justifies the "suspense," which is "a state of mental rest owing to which we neither deny nor affirm anything." This, in turn, produces the desired "quietude," the "untroubled and tranquil condition of the soul."

For Pyrrho, the founder of the movement, the discipline was a personal success. Adapting to the West the attitude he had admired in the East, he conformed himself cheerfully to the political and religious practices of his native Elis and died at the age of ninety, so popular among his fellow citizens that they honored him with a law exempting philosophers from taxation.

### The Spread of Skepticism

In 269 B.C., Arcesilaus, a native of Pitane in Aeolia, succeeded Crates as head of Plato's school and launched it on that phase of its history known as the Middle Academy. Like many other thinkers of the period he apparently regarded his philosophy as grounded in the teachings of Socrates and Plato. Rather than contenting himself with Socrates' profession of ignorance, "I know that I know nothing," he asserted, "I am ignorant even of my ignorance" and "Nothing is certain, not even that." While both these statements invited the infinite regress the Pyrrhonists were trying to avoid, Arcesilaus apparently was able to avoid the difficulties of dogmatic skepticism by shifting his emphasis to his advocacy of the "withholding of assent" (*epoche*). Actions generally regarded as having moral significance could, in his view, be justified by showing them to be "reasonable" (*eulogon*). He was Platonic only in his attacks on sense perception, probably reminiscent of the early dialogues. In his refusal to recognize any sort of knowledge which could provide the certainty and unchangeableness lacking in the realm of opinion, he turned the Academy away from Platonism and inaugurated a period of skepticism which reached its peak in the second century B.C., when Carneades of Cyrene instituted the Third or New Academy.

Coming to Athens about 193 B.C., he turned logic, the primary weapon of the rival school of Stoicism, back on the Stoics themselves, especially Chrysippus, its chief logician. Having studied with Stoics himself, he delighted in confronting them with a Sophistic dilemma: "If my reasoning is right, well and good; if it is wrong, give me back my tuition fee." While adding little to the theoretical account of Pyrrhonism, he practiced its tenets with devastating effect, using one day's lecture to support a theory and the next to oppose it and doing both so convincingly that even if he had a preference himself, his students could never detect it. All conclusions he held to be equally unsound, and he held that daily life must be based entirely on probability and custom.

During the latter part of the third century, Rome, a city to which most of the Greek world had, during the classical age, paid relatively little attention, had become a great political and military power, expanding her influence over large areas of the fragmented portions of Alexander's empire. By 155 B.C., Roman domination of the Greek mainland was so far advanced that when Athens, still nominally a free city, made an unauthorized raid on neighboring Oropus, the Romans were in a position to levy a fine of five hundred talents on the city. The Athenians, hoping to get the penalty canceled, decided to appoint three of their most distinguished philosophers to go to Rome to plead their cause. They selected Diogenes the Stoic, Critolaus the Peripatetic, and Carneades, the head of the Academy. Carneades, though he had studied under Diogenes, seems to have been the most conspicuous member of the delegation. On two successive days in Rome he delivered two lectures on justice, one for it and one against it. On the third day, the elder Cato, never a man to suffer gladly frivolity of that sort, had the delegation expelled from the city. The Romans had encountered Greek philosophy before that time, but perhaps never such outrageous dialectic, wielded with such devastating impact, in their own respectable republican city. Its effect on youthful minds is suggested in an attack written later by Polybius, a Greek historian who spent much of his life with the Romans, on the "excessive love of paradox" which had "brought all philosophy into disrepute." The philosophers of the Academy, he complained, "have implanted such a passion in the minds of our young men that they never give even a thought to the ethical and political questions that really benefit students of philosophy, but spend their lives in the vain attempt to invent useless absurdities."

Unfortunately, Carneades left no writings, but his influence on the Graeco-Roman world through his teachings was enormous, and he is due a considerable measure of credit for the fact that Pyrrhonic Skepticism gained a permanent and reputable place in Western philosophy, not so much, perhaps, as the complete and self-sufficient way of life envisioned by its early advocates, but as a method of inquiry which, by showing the limits of sense and reason was instrumental in opening new avenues of epistemological inquiry. In that role, it would one day play an indispensable role in the development of what we call modern thought.

# Chapter 29

# The Way of Pleasure

Among the members of Socrates' circle of friends was a man named Aristippus, a native of the North African city of Cyrene, which gave the name *Cyrenaic* to the school of which Aristippus was the founder. Like other philosophers who claimed to be following in Socrates' footsteps, Aristippus took from his master's teaching the element with which he was most sympathetic and elevated it to the status of a principle on which an entire system could be based. He found that element in Socrates' remarkable ability to enjoy living and his admission that pleasure is a legitimate part of the good life.

A part? Aristippus could find no other aspect of human experience that has any value at all, and so he came down on the side of psychological hedonism—the theory that everything that is done, no matter what the ostensible motive may be, is done out of desire for pleasure or aversion to pain. After all, even the thrill of heroic conduct in battle or the delights of philosophical discussion have their worth in the pleasure they give the hero or the philosopher. Of what less intrinsic value is the pleasure of a well prepared meal to the gourmet or a vintage wine to the toper? Aristippus concluded that there are no "higher" and "lower' pleasures. There are only greater or lesser amounts involved in different experiences, and what may be pleasurable for one individual may not be for another. Although it is the course of wisdom to show a reasonable respect for law and public opinion, a wise man will, as far as possible, preserve his freedom to govern his life by a hedonic calculus aimed at obtaining the greatest possible amount of pleasure.

Knowledge is elusive, and the pleasures of philosophical pursuits are pale compared with those of the senses. The value of reason lies not in itself but in its usefulness as an instrument to secure greater enjoyment for its possessor. The truly wise man will employ it in the quest for a continuous series of the intensest sorts of pleasures. Nor should he be overly concerned about long-range consequences. The future is uncertain, and he cannot know whether or not he will be alive tomorrow to enjoy pleasure or suffer pain. To live wisely is to fill each present moment with the maximum quantity of enjoyment possible. To sacrifice a present pleasure for a future one is to give up the real for the unreal.

After Socrates' death, Aristippus spent some time in travel before founding his school in his native city. Wherever he went throughout his life, he was well liked for his good looks, ready wit, refinement, and kindliness. When he had money, he spent it lavishly. When he did not, he could rely on his charm to lift him from poverty. He went to a gymnasium in Rhodes, after a shipwreck had left him without funds, and so delighted the Rhodians with his conversation that they gave him and his companions royal treatment. The incident led him to remark that "parents should give children wealth able to swim ashore with them after shipwrecks." Like the Sophists, he unabashedly accepted pay for his teaching, and, unlike Plato, he could accept gracefully insults from a tyrant who could provide him with the benefits he valued. When Dionysius I spat in his face, he remarked smilingly, "A fisherman has to tolerate more wetness than this to land an even smaller fish." Reproached for kneeling before Dionysius, he said he was not to blame if the tyrant's ears were in his feet. In general, however, he practiced the independence he preached and was far from deferential to the rich.

His virtues showed him to have been a better pupil of Socrates than his philosophy of egoistic hedonism would suggest, and his genuine respect for nobility of conduct occasionally broke through his pleasure-seeking facade. He named his daughter *Arete* (Virtue) and when he was facing death in 356 B.C., at the age of eighty-five, he said that his greatest legacy to her was his teaching that she should "set a value on nothing that she can do without." Quite apart from his reservations about his own position, though, he served philosophy well in pointing out the importance of each present moment. His weakness lay in his reluctance to recognize that today's pleasures and pains are the result of yesterday's decisions and that tomorrow, when it arrives, will be today. That recognition came later in a maturer form of hedonism.

### Epicurus

Epicurus was born on the island of Samos in 341 B.C. His father, Neocles, was an Athenian, who had been a resident of Samos for about ten years. The boy became interested in philosophy at the age of twelve, and seven years later, he spent a year in Athens studying at the Academy. He traveled to Asia Minor to join his father at

Colophon and later taught for a while at Mytilene and Lampsacus. The inhabitants of Lampsacus, wishing to honor him, bought him a house and garden on the outskirts of Athens, thinking that his teaching ought to have the prominence that only Athenian residence could give it. He moved to his new home in 306 B.C., at the age of thirty-five, and lived there the rest of his life, using the house not only as a residence, but as a school.

In his acceptance of students, he showed a complete indifference to traditional social barriers. Athenian matrons who had the courage to attend his lectures found themselves associating with citizens, freemen, slaves and courtesans on a basis of complete equality. One of his pupils, a hetaira named Leontium, became his mistress, the mother of his child, and the author of several books. A law-abiding citizen, Epicurus stayed clear of politics and showed a marked preference for a quiet life in his garden in the company of his students and friends. He though less of the gourmet fare of the banquet table than of the simpler delights of bread, cheese, and wine. The charge of his enemies that his temperance was forced on him by a digestive disorder induced by his prior gluttony was probably quite untrue. He had a general reputation for kindness and a wealth of friends and admirers. He somehow found time to write three hundred books, but only a few letters and fragments of one book have survived.

Agreeing with Aristippus that pleasure is the only good and pain the only evil, Epicurus was far more concerned than his cheerful predecessor with the fact that intense pleasures often engender even more intense pains. Tonight's alcoholic revel is followed by tomorrow's hangover, and a lengthy series of such revels may ultimately produce the horrors of delirium tremens. Far more attainable than a condition of perpetual strong pleasure is the sort of tranquility—*ataraxia*, the absence of that which disturbs—sought by Pyrrho. The quest for that tranquillity was the substance of Epicurus' philosophy and his life. Over his garden entrance was the inscription, "Guest, you shall be happy here, for here happiness is esteemed the highest good."

Epicurus apparently saw no necessity for positing a transcendent reality like that of Plato to provide a ground for tranquillity. The senses provide all the data directly available to us concerning the nature of the world, and our feelings are the source of information about our own natures. Reason can legitimately construct a model of the universe (*to pan*) on the basis of what is given in experience. If such a model is desired, the best one is that given by Democritus. Reality is wholly composed of bodies (*somata*) and space (*topos*), for though the senses do not show us immediately the "things which are obscure" about the world, they suggest that it is composed of physical bodies, and "if there were no space (which we call also void and place and tangible nature), bodies would have nothing in which to be and through which to move, as they are plainly seen to move." Bodies are either compounds or the simple elements of which the compound bodies are made. The elements are indivisible atoms (*atoma*) and are unchangeable, for when a compound body is dissolved, things must either pass into non-existence, which the atomists, like the Eleatics, held to be impossible, or their elements must be "incapable of being anywhere or anyhow dissolved." The universe must be infinite, for anything which is finite has an extreme limit, and that limit could only be determined by reference to something else. The universe—the sum total of everything—cannot be determined by reference to anything else, and therefore, it must be infinite. Moreover, infinity must be predicated both of the number of the atoms and the extent of the void; for if there were a finite number of atoms in an infinite void, the atoms, not having "supports or counterchecks" to keep them collected in one area, would have spread throughout infinity, and the world as we know it would not exist. If, on the other hand, the atoms were infinite in number, their extension would be infinite, and no finite void could hold them.

The atoms are of different shapes, for atoms of one shape could not account for the varieties of experienced objects. The number of atoms sharing any single shape is "absolutely infinite," whereas the variety of shapes is only "indefinitely large." Similarly, though they differ in size, they are not of all sizes, for if they were, they could not all be invisible. They are in continual and eternal motion, and all of them move at the same velocity, for the void offers no resistance to their motion. The formation of objects could not, then be explained in terms of heavier atoms overtaking lighter ones in their fall through space. Epicurus introduced instead a spontaneity in the atoms which enables them to swerve from their paths and become entangled with other atoms. When complex things have certain forms, the atoms composing them can only "oscillate in one place," whereas other atoms "rebound to a considerable distance from each other." There are an infinite number of worlds, some resembling our own and some quite different.

Epicurus accounted for perception by positing images (*eidola*)—extremely thin outlines or films, given off by solid bodies and resembling them in shape. These images, traveling at enormous velocity, are transmitted through the sense organs to the souls of sentient beings. The experiences thus produced are the source of our knowledge. The soul is a corporeal object composed of fine parts and dispersed over the whole body. The atoms composing the soul, being round and smooth, do not hold together unless protected by the more solid body. So long as the body preserves a reasonable degree of integrity, the soul remains sentient. When body and soul are separated, all awareness is gone, for the soul is no longer present to impart sentience to the body, and its own atoms, becoming scattered, are incapable of further sensation. Sensations, concepts, and feelings, are the criteria of truth, and all these are, of course, reducible in some way, to material processes.

The atomistic metaphysics of Epicurus served primarily as a framework for his ethics, which, as his way of life illustrated, was based on a particular version of hedonism, directed toward the achievement of a life as free of disturbance as possible.

What are the disturbing things which must be avoided? The chief of them, Epicurus maintained, is fear, and no fear can be greater than fear of the gods, who spy on men, take vengeance on hapless mortals who offend them, and blind their devotees with the dark dogmas of religion. All these terrors, he held, are based on misunderstanding. The gods exist, to be sure, but they themselves are material beings—Epicureans, dwelling apart in the spaces between the worlds—and so should not inspire terror. "A blessed and eternal being," he wrote, "has no trouble himself and brings no trouble upon any other being; hence he is exempt from movements of anger and partiality, for every such movement implies weakness." Gods of this sort do not meddle in the affairs of men.

Another source of disquiet is the fear of death, and in dealing with this too, Epicurus employed his materialism as an antidote. "Death," he said, "is nothing to us; for the body, when it has been resolved into its elements, has no feeling, and that which has no feeling is nothing to us."

*The Anatomy of Pleasure*

Rid of the two principal sources of anxiety which make for an unquiet life, the Epicurean is supposed to be in a position to devote himself to a consideration of the sort of regimen which, by reducing pain to a minimum can assure that such pleasures as are compatible with *ataraxia* can be enjoyed in sufficiently great degree to insure a favorable hedonic calculus. In such an enterprise, the essential virtue is prudence, which Epicurus described as "a more precious thing even than philosophy."

Some desires, he held, are natural, and others are unnatural. Of those which are natural, some are necessary, and others are unnecessary. The desire for a sufficient amount of food or sleep is natural and necessary. The desire for foods which, without relieving the pangs of hunger, merely introduce variation into the pleasures of the table is natural but unnecessary. Unnatural desires, all of which are unnecessary, are those which are simply products of "illusory opinion," such as the desire to have a statue erected in one's honor. Natural desires can also be attributed to illusory opinion when they are of the sort which do not result in pain when they are not gratified. Fortunately, Epicurus thought, the natural and necessary desires are far easier to satisfy than those which are unnatural or unnecessary or both. Their objects are more readily come by, and they do not produce the inordinate craving that is found in desires which have no natural limit, such as those which drive an alcoholic, a drug addict, or a slave to ambition.

The wise man, then, does not encourage desire when the failure to achieve its object would not result in real pain. He accustoms himself to simple food and drink, is satisfied to live in modest quarters, and delights in fresh air, good books, and the company of friends. He is not ruled by envy or ambition and abstains from politics. For all his attractive traits of character, he lives by a philosophy of escape. If he praises justice, it is because it is "something found expedient in mutual intercourse" and not an ideal for which he could reasonably imperil his tranquillity.

In 270 B.C., after years of peace and quiet teaching in his garden, Epicurus was struck down by a painful and, at last, fatal illness, which he bore with grace and fortitude, writing to his friends that the extremity of his suffering was countered by his delight in thinking of his talks with them. He left his property to the school and a legacy of teaching to his disciples to which they remained remarkably loyal, despite the widespread misunderstanding of

Epicureanism as a philosophy of gluttony and license. The legitimate body of instruction commanded a substantial following for several centuries, attaining at least as great a popularity in Rome as in Greece.

## Later Epicureanism

Titus Lucretius Carus was the greatest of the Roman Epicureans. Except for the fact that he lived during the first century B.C., nothing certain is known about his life, but he left the world the most eloquent of all the surviving expositions of the metaphysical doctrine associated with the ethical teachings of the school. In that work, a poem entitled *De Rerum Natura (Concerning the Nature of Things)*, Lucretius demonstrated great fidelity to Epicurus' philosophy and honored the master with a glowing tribute.

"When human life lay groveling in all men's sight," he wrote, "crushed to earth under the dead weight of superstition whose grim features loured menacingly upon mortals from the four quarters of the sky, a man of Greece was first to raise mortal eyes in defiance, first to stand erect and brave the challenge. Fables of the gods did not crush him, nor the lightning flash and the growling menace of the sky. Rather, they quickened his manhood, so that he, first of all men, longed to smash the constraining locks of nature's doors. The vital vigor of his mind prevailed. He ventured far out beyond the flaming ramparts of the world and voyaged in mind throughout infinity. Returning victorious, he proclaimed to us what can be and what cannot: how a limit is fixed to the power of everything and an immovable frontier post. Therefore superstition in its turn lies crushed beneath his feet, and we by his triumph are lifted level with the skies."

There is, in these lines, a suggestion of the tragic and the heroic. Certainly, the Epicureans did not deserve the unfortunate reputation they were later to acquire as the result of a popular confusion of their philosophy with grosser forms of hedoism. Their position is, however, shot through with logical difficulties, some of which are intrinsic to any form of philosophical materialism, while others stem from the special nature of their ethical doctrine.

The Epicureans dealt with the problem of accounting for experience by admitting that sensations exist, not, to be sure, as properties of individual atoms, but as somehow emergent in complex biological structures. To give themselves a theory of knowledge, they had to rely on other questionable assumptions about the ability of the insensate atoms to produce something out of nothing. They were declared to be the source not only of sensations but of concepts and feelings.

With regard to questions of value, they were somewhat more cautious. Having admitted sensation and feeling, they might, with equal ease, have smuggled into their system a variety of the psychological ingredients which went into the making of other ethical systems. Without doing even greater violence to their atomism, however, they could not have found in any number of these a convincing metaphysical ground for a normative ethic, and so they settled for the economy of a pleasure-pain calculus.

As a basis for moral conduct, such a calculus has serious flaws. If one's own pleasure is the sole ground for preferring one mode of conduct over another, it is difficult to arrive at a convincing reason for benevolent activity unless it can be shown that it will produce a greater amount of pleasure for the person who engages in it than would be produced by any alternative course of action. Efforts to demonstrate that such is the case are seldom persuasive unless it is maintained that the pleasure derived from doing good for others is a moral pleasure resulting from an appreciation of the goodness of the conduct. But this is to give the game away. The Hedonist is obliged to say, "It is good because it is pleasant." He is not at liberty to turn around then and say, "It is pleasant because it is good."

Indeed, the notion of "pleasure" is not a very clear one in Epicureanism. Is there really some common ingredient in all the varied experiences valued by human beings which can be extracted and measured quantitatively? When one is faced with the question of whether he ought, at a given time, to engage in a highly unethical business transaction which will make him rich or to accept with good grace of life of poverty and discomfort, can the conflict really be resolved by calculating which course of conduct is likely to be productive of the greater amount of pleasure and the lesser amount of pain? Epicurus, like other hedonists, appealed to social sanctions. "Injustice is not in itself an evil," he said, "but only in its consequence, viz. the terror which is excited by apprehension that those appointed to punish such offenses will discover the injustice." One can never be sure, he went on to say, that he will not be found out, and this fact was presumably the reason for his contention that "the just man enjoys the greatest peace of mind, while the unjust is full of the utmost disquietude." But surely there are many instances in which the probable pains involved in actions done in conformity to social compact far outweigh those likely to be incurred in breaking it. If the Hedonist tries to get around the problem, as the Greek and Roman Epicureans seemed at times on the verge of doing, by accepting such a broad definition of "pleasure" that it includes all possible kinds of value, including moral value, he must then either advocate immoral acts where they are likely to be productive of a greater quantity of pleasure of a different kind or give up the merely quantitative approach in favor of a qualitative one which recognizes the intrinsic superiority of some sorts of pleasure over others. This, however, is to abandon a strict Hedonism and to embrace a value philosophy which needs a firmer support than can be found for it in Epicurean metaphysics.

# Chapter 30

## *The Way of Reason*

If Aristippus was guilty of going to one extreme in exaggerating Socrates' favorable attitude toward pleasure, Antisthenes did equal violence to the master's teaching by deriving from it a philosophy which repudiated pleasure altogether. The son of an Athenian citizen and a Thracian slave girl, he served in the army, studied with Gorgias and Prodicus, and established his own school. Then he heard Socrates and became a disciple, if an incomplete one. He was genuinely impressed by Socrates' conception of virtue, but decided that the secret of its attainment lay in an asceticism far more fanatical than the moderate indifference to possessions which would have been justified by Socrates' teaching and example. He lived a life of voluntary poverty and dressed in rags. "I can see your vanity, Antisthenes, through the holes in your coat," Socrates once told him. After the master's death, he began giving free lectures on his philosophy of hardship in the Cynosarges (Dogfish), a gymnasium that did not exclude men of mixed birth. Whether his school got its name *Cynic* from this circumstance or from the general view that to be a loyal member of the school one had to live a "dog's life" is not clear.

A young man named Diogenes came to Athens, driven into exile with his father from his native Sinope and now impoverished. Doubtless delighted to find a teacher who could see mendicancy as a mark of virtue, he asked to be accepted as a pupil. Antisthenes turned him away but he persevered and was at last accepted. So enthusiastic was he about the way of virtue taught by Antisthenes that he soon outstripped his teacher in flamboyant asceticism and, more than any other man, became the archetypal Cynic. To show his contempt for comfortable lodging, he resided for a while in a tub belonging to the temple of Cybele at Athens. He lived the life of a beggar and, going farther, tried to imitate the lower animals in every way possible, sleeping on the ground and showing no respect for the rules of privacy prescribed by social convention. For a while, he permitted himself the luxury of a wooden bowl for food and drink. Then seeing a little peasant boy drinking out of cupped hands, he threw away the bowl. Like the Hebrew prophets, he enjoyed dramatizing his message, as was illustrated by his practice of carrying around a lantern "looking for an honest man." He combined a mind well honed for controversy with a ready and rowdy wit. Seeing a courtesan's son throw a stone in the direction of a crowd, he admonished him, "Take care lest you hit your father."

While on a voyage to Aegina, he was captured by pirates. Sold in Crete to a Corinthian named Xeniades, he was asked his trade. "Governing men," Diogenes replied. Xeniades made him master of his household and tutor to his sons, and the philosopher lived cheerfully and outrageously as a slave in Corinth, becoming one of the most famous men in the Greek world. Late in his life, probably while he was attending the Isthmian games, where he was accustomed to lecture, he was lying on the ground one day soaking up the sun, when young Alexander, flushed with the early successes of his career of conquest, came and stood beside the philosopher, casting his shadow over him.

"I am Alexander the Great King," the monarch said.

"I am Diogenes the Dog," the Cynic replied.

"Ask of me any favor you wish," Alexander said magnanimously.

"You might move out of my sunlight," Diognes told him.

"If I were not Alexander, I would be Diogenes," the ruler declared, on which note, the conversation apparently ended. It is an interesting postscript that the two men are said to have died on the same day in 323 B.C., Alexander in his thirties and Diogenes in his nineties. The Corinthians put a marble dog over the philosopher's grave, and his native city of Sinope, proud of the exile at last, erected a monument in his honor.

The Cynics had little interest in metaphysics. Nature was not for them a puzzle to be solved but a model for conduct. Their only interest in religion lay in its inducement to a life of virtue, by which, of course, they meant a life free of the bondage of luxury. In this, men must treasure virtue for its own sake and not depend on extraneous rewards from the gods, who apparently do not govern the universe in such a way that the good prosper and the evil suffer. Commenting on the offerings in Samothrace dedicated to the gods by shipwreck survivors, Diogenes observed that there would have been more of them if they had been offered by those who were lost instead of those who were saved.

They thought it wrong for one man to injure another. How then should one defend oneself? "By proving honorable and upright," Diogenes replied. To be sure, some of their prescriptions for virtue shocked the upholders of conventional morality. They frowned on marriage and favored free love as more "natural." Their views of law bordered on anarchy, and Diogenes thought Prometheus no hero for bringing fire to mankind but rather a criminal deserving of his punishment. To maintain his consistency, he tried to discipline himself to eat his meat raw. All in all, the Cynics were picturesque and provocative examples of the sort of rebels who in every age challenge the very foundations of civilization and demand a return to a simpler and more primitive way of life. By the end of the third century, the school had passed from the stage of history, but their influence survived throughout the Graeco-Roman world and, through the teaching of two of Diogenes' disciples, Stilpo and Crates, established a foundation for the development of Stoicism.

## The Early Stoics

Citium in Cyprus, a place of mixed Greek and Phoenician culture was the original home of Zeno, the founder of the Stoic school, and his ancestry is said to have reflected the mixture. He became quite rich as a merchant, but appears to have been impoverished when he arrived in Athens about 314 B.C. after a shipwreck. He became a student in the school run by the Theban Crates, who had given up a considerable fortune to become a mendicant Cynic. Zeno was highly impressed by the Cynic's doctrine and way of life. His first book advocated the abolition of private property, money, laws, marriage, and religion. In time, however, he came to see that Crates' ethic could not successfully be applied to a whole society, and so he broadened his philosophy by studies with Stilpo of Megara and with Xenocrates at the Academy.

*In 301 B.C.* he began his own school in the *Stoa Poikile*, the Painted Porch, a colonnade of the Agora, amid the rich murals of the sack of Troy painted more than a century and a half earlier by Polygnotus of Thasos. So it was that his followers acquired the name of Stoics, or "Porchers." He became a friend of the Macedonian king Antigonus II, but declined an invitation to live on the monarch's bounty in Pella, preferring Athens and the Stoa. He so won the respect of the citizens that the Assembly honored him with a citation, a statue, a crown, and the "keys to the walls."

When Zeno died, probably at about the age of ninety, his work was carried on by Cleanthes of Assos, who was, in turn, succeeded by Chrysippus of Soli. Chrysippus set himself the task of systematizing the Stoic teachings and turned out more than seven hundred books as notable for their dullness as for their clarity. Only fragments of his writings have survived. After Chrysippus, Stoicism became widely disseminated throughout the Greek world through the efforts of a number of able teachers, including Boethus of Sidon, Panaetius of Rhodes, Diogenes of Seleucia, and Zeno of Tarsus.

For the Stoics, philosophy was so completely identified with the virtuous life that they defined the three principal divisions of the philosophy of the time—logic, physics, and ethics—as the most basic "virtues." Logic, for them, included their theory of knowledge, which was based on sensation and denied the existence of universals except as conceptual abstractions. As did the empiricists of a later age, they held that the mind at birth is a blank tablet and that objects stamp impressions on it like a seal on wax. True perceptions are distinguishable from false ones by their greater intensity or their greater persistence. For knowledge, however, there must be more than experience, which may be distorted by emotion or desire. Reason is, in man, the final arbiter of truth.

Human reason has its ground in the very nature of the universe. Though the Stoics maintained that everything is material, they were certainly not materialists in the mechanistic sense, for they regarded the world not as a blind and meaningless dance of atoms but as a living fire, shot through with intelligibility and purpose. The ultimate ruler of the universe is the *Logos Spermatikos,* the Primal Reason, the soul of the world. The indebtedness of the Stoics to Heraclitus is obvious, and they were largely responsible for the emphasis which came to be placed on his concept of the Logos. By the time of the Stoa, the concept of monotheism had undergone sufficient development for Cleanthes to feel free to address the Stoic God by the name of the Olympian Father of Gods and Men.

Thou, O Zeus, art praised above all gods:
many are thy names and thine is all power for ever.

The beginning of the world was from thee: and
with law thou rulest over all things.

Unto thee may all flesh speak: for we are thy offspring.

Therefore will I raise a hymn unto thee:
and will ever sing of thy power.

The whole order of the heavens obeyeth thy word:
as it moveth around the earth:

With little and great lights mixed together: how
great art thou, King above all for ever!

Nor is anything done upon the earth apart from
thee: nor in the firmament, nor in the seas:

Save that which the wicked do: by their own folly.

But thine is the skill to set even the crooked
straight: what is without fashion is fashioned and
the alien akin before thee.

Thus hast thou fitted together all things in
one: the good with the evil:

That thy word should be one in all things:
abiding for ever.

Let folly be dispersed from our souls: that we may repay
thee the honor wherewith thou has honored us:

Singing praises of thy works for ever: as
becometh the sons of men.

Though Stoicism has frequently been called pantheistic because of its insistence on the indwelling of God in the totality of things, the spirit of Cleanthes' hymn to Zeus is as theistic as that of the Hebrew Scriptures. Certainly the Stoic attitude toward God was as religious as it was philosophical. He is not only the rational ground of natural process, but a providential God who orders all things and who, out of love for men, acts for their well-being. He is Spirit (*Pneuma*), and the souls of men too are fiery breath or *pneuma*, present throughout the body as the divine Spirit is present throughout the universe. The universe goes through a cyclical history, returning to pure fire in a cosmic conflagration at the end of each cycle, and then goes through the whole process of creation, development, and dissolution again. Individual souls, surviving the death of their bodies, become absorbed into God at the conflagration, only, according to one Stoic theory, to be re-created in the next cycle.

As man is a microcosm reflecting the macrocosm, the way of virtue for human beings lies in rational conformity to the mind of God. The wise man sees that the only real freedom comes through the recognition that, in the economy of nature, all things are determined for good. Even the lowly bedbug, Chrysippus held, has a place in the order of things as an incentive to early rising. Evil does not reside in objects or events but rather in the way in which one permits himself to be affected by what happens. Everything really good or evil, then, is subject to human control. External circumstances may be gratifying or painful but are morally "indifferent." It is necessary to free oneself from domination by pleasure and pain if one wishes to live virtuously. This involves the cultivation of *apatheia*, an absence of feeling complete enough to free one from concern about one's circumstances. The good Stoic does not worry about poverty, personal loss, sickness, or death. Seeing all events as ordained, he nevertheless subscribes to a stern code of moral responsibility for his own conduct, and he is equally demanding that others do their duty. Zeno once beat his slave for stealing, and the slave, hoping to turn his master's philosophy against him, protested, "But it was fated that I should steal." "And that I should beat you," the philosopher serenely replied. The Stoic is virtuous for the sake of virtue. By submitting himself to God and living in accordance with reason, he achieves a personality of such intrinsic worth that it cannot be crushed by ill fortune or corrupted by good. He is master of himself, and if his duty to others does not require him to continue to live, he may take his own life when it seems good to him to do so. While living, he dutifully plays the role which God has seen fit to assign him.

As God is the common father of all, all men are brothers, and so the human community is in reality a *Cosmopolis* or universal city, of which everyone is more truly a member than he is of any more limited community. In this worldwide brotherhood, all persons are equal in intrinsic worth. The decree of fate that makes one an emperor and another a slave only determines the sort of duties incumbent on each. The Stoics, unlike the Epicureans, saw no virtue in an undisturbed life in a walled garden. Theirs was a philosophy of the marketplace and the political arena. That their thought achieved such wide acceptance was in part due to the fact that they saw that political arena in terms of a broader allegiance than had been demanded by the old city-state. They provided the most persuasive theoretical support for the expansion of the Alexandrian world and, to an even greater extent, for the later claims of Rome. In this connection, it is likely that their most enduring contribution to Western thought was their conception of Natural Law. The vision of a universal rational mind which imposes obligation on human minds attuned to it by virtue of their own rationality established a standard by which the "positive laws" of states could be judged. The idea that a government which fails to acknowledge that standard forfeits its legitimacy was to play an important part in European and American history.

## The Way of Virtue in Rome

There was that in the Roman republican temperament which responded favorably to the rigors of the early Stoic ethic. One of their most celebrated heroes of legend was Mucius Scaevola, who, during the siege of Rome in 509 B.C., was captured in an attempt to assassinate the Etrusan king, Lars Porsena. To demonstrate to the enemy that it would be useless to try to extract information from him by torture, he thrust his hand into a brazier and held it there impassively while it was being consumed by the flames. The admiration the Romans felt for Mucius and for other men and women in their history who had shown conspicuous ability to endure pain and adversity with equanimity found philosophical justification in Stoicism, and in the second century B.C., it began to acquire a substantial following in Rome. To be sure, Cato the Elder, one of the leading statesmen of the city was suspicious of Greek philosophers, but his own way of life was in many ways a model of Stoic *apatheia*. In later centuries, a Roman form of Stoicism would have its own luminaries such as Epictetus and Marcus Aurelius, but in the time before the rise of Christianity the principal impact of the Stoa in Roman life was manifested in its influence on thinkers who incorporated significant Stoical elements into philosophical systems which were syncretistic on eclectic in nature.

Under Roman auspices Stoicism lost many of the extreme elements which had linked it to its Cynic parentage. The concept of Cosmopolis was appealing to men who could justify the spread of Roman power by appeal to a sort of divine sanction for the attempt to bring the actual world into conformity with the ideal one through the establishment of a world-state composed of many peoples. Other principles of the Stoa, however, required modification or reinterpretation. *Apatheia* as conceived by an educated Roman influenced by Stoicism was likely to be a much less absolute quality than it had been for Zeno or Cleanthes. The all-or-nothing attitude which had, in effect, denied that virtue could be attributed to anyone who had not achieved it perfectly gave way in practice to a more tolerant standard of judgment. Again, while not denying that "good" or "bad," strictly speaking, could refer only to moral virtue or its absence, the Roman man of affairs insisted that among the morally indifferent things, some are "advantageous" as compared with others and therefore really to be preferred. With these reservations, he could accept whole-heartedly the Stoic emphasis on the virtues dear to the Roman heart and avail himself of the justification for practicing them in a wider context than that provided by the early history of the city.

Marcus Tullius Cicero combined Stoic, Platonic, and Aristotelian forms of thought in an especially effective way. Born in 106 B.C., he lived through the last days of the Republic and the civil turmoil which accompanied its collapse. Well prepared for a public career by an excellent education in his boyhood, Cicero, as a young man, studied philosophy in Athens and Asia under a variety of teachers representing the major schools of the Greek world.

Cicero agreed with the Stoics that the good life is one lived in conformity to Nature, but he rejected Zeno's idea that an enormous chasm separates those things which have moral significance from those which do not. "To maintain that the only Good is Moral Worth," he said, "is to do away with the care of one's health, the management of one's estate, participation in politics, the conduct of affairs, the duties of life; nay, to abandon that Moral Worth itself." Even Zeno had not taken his position seriously, Cicero argued, for, although he had declined to call health, prosperity, and comfort goods and their opposite evils, he had not hesitated to call them "things preferred" and their opposites "things rejected." There is, then, only a verbal difference between the Stoics' position and that of Aristotle and the other students of Plato, who had stated unequivocally that things in accordance with nature are good and those contrary to nature are bad.

Cicero did not deny, however, that moral value is distinguishable from other forms of good, and his definition of moral worth anticipated the one given by Immanuel Kant eighteen hundred years later. It is "that which is of such a nature that, though devoid of all utility, it can justly be commended in and for itself, apart from any profit or reward." Actions performed out of anticipation that some pleasure will follow from them are not moral in the strict sense, for "virtue driven to duty by pleasure as a sort of pay is not virtue." Man can be moral as the lower animals cannot by virtue of the fact that Nature, in endowing him with reason has given him the taste for association with his kind, the desire for the contemplation of truth, and the capacity to apprehend the dignity and grandeur of the rational life. These three kinds of goodness combine in a fourth: the principle of restraint and order which Nature exhibits in the beauty of moral character as in the beauty of external form. The moral law is all-pervasive, for "no phase of life, whether public or private, whether in business or in the home, whether one is working on what concerns oneself alone or dealing with another, can be without its moral duty."

Justice restrains men from illicitly harming one another and leads them to use public property cooperatively for common ends, while maintaining the right to hold private property. That right, however, rather than being grounded in nature, has its origin in long occupancy, conquest, or legal transfer. Justice demands that punishment be limited to that sufficient to bring offenders to change their ways and deter others from doing wrong. It requires humane treatment of all men, from the highest to the humblest, for "there is no difference in kind between man and man." It forbids not only the doing of wrong but the failure to shield others from the infliction of wrong.

Cicero made an explicit distinction betwen man-made laws, which may vary, and natural law, which is eternal and unvarying. "We cannot be freed from its obligations by senate or people," he wrote, "and we need not look outside ourselves for an expounder or interpreter of it. And there will not be different laws at Rome and at Athens, or different laws now and in the future, but one eternal and unchangeable law will be valid for all nations and all times, and there will be one master and ruler, that is, God, over us all, for he is the author of this law, its promulgator, or its enforcing judge."

Statesman though he was, Cicero was unable to arrest the decline of the Roman Republic, and upon its collapse, he was put to death in 43 B.C. by order of the men of the Second Triumvirate. It is, however, significant that many of his most thoughtful works were written toward the end of his life, when he could see the fabric of his society disintegrating. By giving eloquent expression to his faith in a transcendent ground of private and public good which outlasts the destruction of men and institutions, he contributed significantly to the strength of the foundation on which the moral and political thought of the Christian era would rest.

# XI.
# JUDAISM
# IN THE
# ROMAN WORLD

# Chapter 31

## *The People and the Book*

During the long history of the Roman Empire, nearly all of the Jews lived within its territory, whether in the Jewish homeland, in Egypt, or in Mesopotamia. In early Roman times, most of them remained in those eastern portions of the Empire; but as the centuries passed, many migrated toward the West, to Asia Minor, Greece, and Italy, or along the northern coast of Africa to Gibraltar and thence into Spain. Thus Jewish life and destiny became historically associated with the beginnings of Western civilization, of which it has been a major component since. Some Jews turned south and east—to Arabia, Yemen, Persia, Afghanistan, and India; but Judaism has continued to be, in the main, a part of Western culture.

Jewish life in the Roman Empire was sometimes peaceful and happy, but more often it was difficult, and frequently perilous. We have observed how the distinctives of Jewish belief and practice caused the Jews to be obviously different from their pagan neighbors, wherever they dwelled. The result was continual separation, suspicion, hatred, and persecution. In addition, the occasional attempts by the Roman government to force unity in the Empire by uniformity of culture, especially religion, led to inevitable resistance and rebellion by the stubbornly monotheistic Jews. Tensions increased, as might be expected, and the Jews were in constant trouble with Rome from the day that Pompey occupied Jerusalem, in 63 B.C., until the final destruction of the nation, the city, and the Temple, in 135 A.D.

The Romans were actually welcomed into the Maccabean Commonwealth because the Hasmoneans, who had led the initial revolt against Syrian rule and paganism, had themselves deteriorated into a self-perpetuated dynasty of power-hungry rulers. The people discovered that the priestly family who had been chosen to protect Judaism against the inroads of Hellenistic idolatry soon became themselves the patrons of Hellenism, changing their role from High Priest to King and even adopting Greek names. The result was political and religious corruption followed by sectarian division and civil war. Thus Pompey and his Roman legions were invited to provide stability. The Romans installed Hyrcanus II, a descendant of Mattathias ben Hasmon, as High Priest, but state policy was placed in the hands of a trusted servant of Rome, Antipater the Idumean.

Herod, the politically astute and morally degenerate son of Antipater, was made king of Judea and Samaria by the Roman authorities in 40 B.C. His position was confirmed and enlarged by Augustus Caesar in 37 B.C., and he continued to rule the whole area, including Galilee, Perea—east of the Jordan River, and Idumea, until his death in 4 B.C. Known to history as Herod the Great, he served his Roman masters well in spite of his ruthlessness and brutality at home. He managed to keep the peace, for the most part, and he provided security for Rome on her eastern frontier. He also engaged in vast building enterprises throughout the land, and, in spite of the hatred of the Jews because of his Idumean ancestry, he supported their religious practices and even began the rebuilding of the great Temple in Jerusalem. Just before the death of Herod, a child was born in his domain to a poor family of Galilee. The child was given the Aramaic name, Jesus.

Augustus approved the will of Herod, which directed that three of his sons should succeed him, except that the Emperor would not permit them the title of king. Archelaus, the eldest, was appointed ethnarch of Judea, Idumea, and Samaria; Antipas was named tetrarch of Galilee and Perea; and Philip became tetrarch over a large, semi-Jewish territory north and east of Galilee. Archelaus was as tyrannical as his father, but not as cunning, so that Rome soon found it expedient to banish him (in 6 A.D.); but the other two brothers were able to continue their rule until their deaths. Archelaus was replaced by a series of military governors called "procurators." There were 14 of them in the succession, the most famous being Pontius Pilate (26-36 A.D.). The last procurator, Florus, was so inept and harsh that he provoked the rebellion of 66-70 A.D., which ended with another dispersion of the Jews and the sacking of Jerusalem. The Roman general Vespasian, began the campaign to quell the revolt, but, when he was called to Rome to become Emperor, his son, Titus, brought an end to the Jewish national existence. That epoch-making event is memorialized by the Arch of Titus, which still stands in the Forum of Rome, bearing artistic witness to the looting of the Temple and the humiliation of the Jews. When the remnants of the people attempted another revolt in 132 A.D., encouraged by their religious leaders and led by a self-styled "Messiah," Bar Cochba, the Emperor Hadrian crushed them with such finality that Jews were forbidden to enter the new, pagan city of Aelia Capitolina, built upon the ashes of Jerusalem, and the practice of Judaism was proscribed.

## A Religion of the Laity

Like most of the religions of history, Judaism and its antecedent Hebrew religion had maintained a distinction between priests and laymen. The Hebrew cult apparently began at Sinai (cf. chapter 5, above), with the usual trappings of priesthood, vestments, altar, and sacrifice; and the main body of the people stood apart as unworthy and unclean, dependent upon those who were ordained to effect reconciliation with their God through prayers and offerings. The portable Tent of Meeting was replaced by the Temple of Solomon, and the powerful role of the official priesthood was evident throughout the nation's history. The Deuteronomic Law of the Central Sanctuary, symbolizing the people's one God, Yahweh, made priest, altar, and Temple even more essential for the preservation and practice of religion just before the end came with the Exile. We have observed that one of the chief motivations for the return from the Exile was the prospect of rebuilding the Temple so that lawful worship could be resumed. However, a majority never returned. The Temple was indeed rebuilt, such as it was (516 B.C.), only to be burned and reconstructed several times again; and the grand complex begun by Herod the Great was destroyed, with "not one stone left upon another," in the war with Rome. The cult, including the priesthood, disappeared in that final calamity.

Nevertheless, since it was born in the Exile and largely developed in unclean lands, Judaism from the beginning was not dependent upon the Temple or the priesthood. It was of necessity a religion of lay people. Its creators were prophets and sages, its sacrifices became prayers and psalms, and its holy places were the home and the synagogue. The ancient struggle in Hebrew religion between priests and prophets ended with prophetic victory, and that is one reason that the prophets interpreted the sufferings of national defeat as not only the punishment of Yahweh but also his method of purification and redemption. The narrowness and corruption of institutional religion were no longer possible, but the religion of morality and spirit was released for universal proclamation and acceptance among the nations.

It is not difficult to trace the historical transition of the religion of the Jews from priestly control to lay dominance to final hierarchical disappearance. The loss of the Temple, and the Exile, made such a development both inevitable and necessary. The process was continued by the ever-wider dispersion of the Jews among the nations, and by the consequent fulfillment of the religious needs of the people by the creation of the synagogues as a gathering of the faithful for instruction and worship. Further, both late Scripture and Tradition (e.g. Nehemiah 10:2-29; 8:4-7; 9:4-5; Psalms 50:5; 89:20; 132:9, 16; Abot 1) provide ample evidence that a new group of lay leaders arose to preserve the holy books, to interpret them to teach the people, and to guarantee the survival of the ancient covenant faith, even in the face of death. Among these lay leaders were the groups known to history as the *Levites*, who were gradually separated from the priests and given secondary roles; the *Psalmists*, who edited ancient liturgies and composed new ones for the expression of faith and constancy; the *Soferim*, the "bookmen" who edited, transmitted, and interpreted the Scriptures; "the Men of the Great Synagogue," a traditional group of one hundred and twenty men who were apparently the forerunners of the Sanhedrin; and, probably most important, the *Hasidim*, "the pious ones," or "saints," who came into prominence at the time of the Maccabean War as stubborn defenders of the faith against paganism. From the Hasidic movement came the *Pharisees*, led by "rabbis" and "tannaim," the major preservers and teachers of the Scriptures and Traditions. Some of these groups overlapped; but the significant point is that they were all composed of the laity.

Two major events brought about the final demise of the priesthood in Judaism. The first was the treasonous identification of the priestly caste with the sources of political power during the despised foreign rule by both the Syrian Hellenists and the Romans. The people who were concerned with the spirit and morals of prophetic religion, led by the Hasidim, became increasingly disaffected by the open hypocrisy and corruption of the hierarchy. That spirit had already been attributed even to God himself by the post-exilic author of what is called Trito-Isaiah:

> Thus says the Lord:
> "Heaven is my throne
> and the earth is my footstool;
> what is the house which you would build for me,

and what is the place of my rest?
All these things my hand has made,
and so all these things are mine,
    says the Lord.
But this is the man to whom I will look,
he that is humble and contrite in spirit,
and trembles at my word.
He who slaughters an ox is like him who
kills a man;
he who sacrifices a lamb, like him who
breaks a dog's neck;
he who presents a cereal offering,
like him who offers swine's blood;
he who makes a memorial offering of frankincense,
like him who blesses an idol.
These have chosen their own ways,
and their soul delights in their abominations;
I also will choose affliction for them,
and bring their fears upon them;
because, when I called, no one answered,
when I spoke they did not listen;
but they did what was evil in my eyes,
and chose that in which I did not delight."
(Isaiah 66:1-4)

The second event, of course, was the catastrophic destruction of the nation, including its Temple, by Titus in 70 A.D. The priests had become so concentrated at the Temple that they could not survive without it. They were lost for all time amid the ashes and debris of ancient Zion. Judaism arose from those ashes in a new form; it was henceforth to be a religion of the laity. The altar was gone; now the center of faith and worship was the Book.

### Keepers of the Tradition

The Jewish faith was guarded, enlarged, and transmitted through the centuries by a series of dedicated and learned men. They were given differing titles, and they did their work in a variety of places. The most familiar title for them is "rabbi," meaning "master," or "teacher;" and they usually did their work in association with a synagogue or academy. During the years following the destruction of Jerusalem, most of them lived in either Palestine or Babylonia, though they later accompanied their people wherever they went in the Diaspora. They were the Fathers of Judaism and therefore major contributors to the foundations of Western culture.

A list of these keepers of the Tradition might well begin with Simeon ben Shetah. He was a member of the Sanhedrin, the Jewish High Court, in Jerusalem during the last days of the Maccabean Commonwealth; his sister was Alexandra Salome, the widow of Alexander Jannaeus, who was Queen from 86 to 67 B.C. Simeon was identified with the Pharisee party, in opposition to the priests, and he was able to exert considerable influence upon government policy through the good offices of his sister. He was responsible for the enlargement of educational opportunity among the people; he also aided the cause of justice by improving the methods of trial and punishment. Simeon emphasized the Scriptual requirement of fairness and mercy. Thus he helped to promote the application of religious principles to every aspect of Jewish life.

Through one of Simeon's disciples, Joshua ben Perahyah, the leadership in such practical teaching passed to Shemaya and Abtalyon, who were apparently Babylonian converts to Judaism; and a follower of Abtalyon was the famous rabbi, Hillel, one of Judaism's greatest teachers. Hillel was the leader of a school in Jerusalem in the time of Herod the Great. His influence was so important among the people that it was said, "When Torah was forgotten in Israel Ezra restored it; when it was forgotten again, Hillel came from Babylonia and established it again" (Talmud, Sukkah 20 a). His genius was in his giving humaneness priority of value over privilege, custom, or law, even the Torah.

The school of Hillel was opposed by the school of Shammai, another teacher of Jerusalem who was known for his strict interpretation and application of the Torah and the traditions of the past. It is worthy of note that the two men remained friends even while disagreeing on basic religious precepts; they thus helped to establish the spirit of freedom and toleration that has remained a democratic characteristic of historic Judaism. Hillel was honored for his indefatigable study and gentle patience, and he taught that human life is more important than Torah, in spite of the fact that Torah was given by God as the expression of his will. Probably his most famous teaching was the rule, "Do not do to your neighbor what would be hateful to you were it done to you. This is the whole Torah, all else is commentary" (Talmud, Shabbat 31 a).

Tradition teaches that Hillel had eighty disciples. One of them was the founder of the Academy of Jamnia, Johanan ben Zakkai. Reportedly a friend of the Roman General Vespasian, he was smuggled out of Jerusalem in a coffin as the city was under siege, in 69 A.D., and he was allowed to gather some of the Jewish scholars in the city of Jamnia (Jabneh), where the study of the Torah continued. By this historically significant act, Rabbi Zakkai and his colleagues saved Palestinian Judaism from oblivion in the ruins of the Temple. He continued to lead the faithful remnant in Jamnia until his death, about 80 A.D., and his work pointed the direction for the development of the future religion of the Jews. Zakkai distrusted religious enthusiasts, who had so often brought disaster; rather, he made the study of Torah, and living by its regulation, the center of true religion. Under his direction the Jewish calendar began to receive its fixed form, and the discussions were begun among the rabbis which led to the closing of the canon of Scriptures. When asked how proper worship could continue without the priestly sacrifices in the Temple, Rabbi Zakkai taught that the most worthy sacrifices are deeds of love.

The leader of the new Sanhedrin and Academy in Jamnia who followed Zakkai was Gamaliel II, the son of a great rabbi, Simon ben Gamaliel, who had led in the disastrous revolt against Rome. Continuing the reforming and creative work of Zakkai, Gamaliel II helped to reshape the nature of the oral tradition by which the Scriptures were interpreted and applied. He also revised the *seder* of the Passover and made it no longer necessary for Jews to follow the Scriptural requirement to slay a lamb for the paschal meal. The Academy took the further decisive step of declaring that the new sect of Christians, considered by the Romans to be a Jewish movement, was heretical. The Emperor Nerva, who followed the last of the Flavians, Domitian, achieved a temporary peace with the troublesome Jews by recognizing Gamaliel as "Patriarch," the official leader and representative of his people.

Rabbi Akibah ben Joseph led the Academy during the perilous reign of the Emperor Hadrian (117-138 A.D.). He began the great age of scholarship which was to save and characterize Judaism for many centuries to follow. In a manner similar to Socrates and his followers in ancient Greek philosophy, Akibah taught that ignorance is the primary source of sin, and that knowledge can lead to virtue and reality. Moreover, just as the magisterial philosophers had emphasized the transcendent and moral dimension of the knowledge they sought, so Akibah believed that learning leads to truth and righteousness as they are found in the revealed teachings from God in the Torah. As a result, academies and study flourished among the dispersed Jews, and every synagogue became both a place of prayer and a school. Unfortunately, Rabbi Akibah was imprisoned, tortured, and killed by the Romans because of his support of the final rebellion led by Bar Cochba (132-135 A.D.).

The greatest of the Palestinian Patriarchs was Judah Hanasi (the Prince), who was born at the time of the catastrophic Bar Cochba revolt and died in 217 A.D. He was a man of wealth and wisdom as well as great knowledge, and he enjoyed the support of his own people while gaining the friendship of many Romans, including the Stoic Emperor-philosopher, Marcus Aurelius. Judah recognized the need for a thorough editing and recording of the vast interpretation and commentary which had been developed by the scholars over the centuries, much of which was retained only in the memories of the teachers and disciples. The recent threats to Jewish survival, such as the pogrom of Hadrian, made urgent the task of preserving the traditions of the Fathers, along with the Scriptures. Thus Judah Hanasi was a leader in bringing to a close the age of the Oral Torah, while initiating the age of the Talmud. The work of creative teaching continued among the Jews in Palestine until the Academy was closed in 425 A.D., at the insistence of the Christian Patriarch of Jerusalem; then the vital centers of Jewish study passed to Babylonia and, ultimately, to Europe.

### The Creation of the Talmud

The creative leaders of Jewish piety and scholarship whom we have just described, from Hillel to Judah Hanasi, along with their innumerable colleagues, are known as the *Tannaim*. The word means "teachers," although *tanna*, toward the end of the period, came to designate merely one who memorized and recited the Oral Torah. However, beginning with the work of Judah, another category of religious scholars arose who are called the *Amoraim*, "interpreters." Most of them lived among the large and prosperous communities of Jews in the generally peaceful lands of ancient Babylonia, beyond the reach of an increasingly hostile Rome, whether pagan or Christian. The Amoraim composed the *Talmud*, "instruction," containing a huge compilation (2½ million words on 5894 pages) of all the recognized traditions of the Fathers. (There are, in fact, two Talmuds: the Palestinian, completed with the closing of the Academy in 425, and the Babylonian, concluded around 500 A.D. The latter has been of greater significance.)

The Scriptures, having been "canonized" by the rabbis at Jamnia by 90 A.D., were called TeNaKH, from the names of the three parts: Torah, Nebi'im, and Kethubim. A collection of commentary, *Midrash*, had grown between the time of Sirach (c. 200 B.C.), and Judah Hanasi (c. 200 A.D.). This material was in the form of sermons, allegories, and folklore. Alongside the Midrash there developed a more scholarly body of commentary, entitled *Mishnah*, "review," or "repetition." All of this was organized, edited, and recorded by Akibah and Judah, along with their disciples; and there was added, finally, a new body of material called *Gemara*, "completion." This made up the whole Talmud, although it was again eventually divided into two types of literature, called *Halachah* and *Haggadah*. The former term means "the Way," and signifies rules for living by the Torah; the later designates "narrative" and contains various stories, parables, and illustrations to make religious truth easier to understand and apply.

The Talmud should not be conceived as an enormous tome of abstract and speculative theology. Like the Judaism which produced it, it is intensely practical. That is shown by the topics under which the Mishnah is organized. There are six Orders of the Mishnah, each being subdivided into Tractates (books), Chapters, and Paragraphs. Their titles are as follows: (1) *Zeraim* (Seeds); (2) *Moed* (Appointed Days); (3) *Nashim* (Women); (4) *Nezikim* (Damages); (5) *Kadashim* (Holy Things); and (6) *Taharot* (Purifications). Taken together, they encompass the whole life, providing guidance for the solution of every conceivable problem of individual or social living.

In summary, the Jews both suffered and prospered during the long period of Roman domination. They bore the pains of frequent persecution, and they lost nation, cult and Temple. Many were martyred and many more were driven to the edges of the map in a search for survival and freedom. But in spite of their suffering, their religion gained strength and depth. Their priests disappeared and they became, in the words of the Torah, "a kingdom of priests and a holy nation" (Exodus 19:6). As the People of the Book, they transmitted its truth to the nations.

# Chapter 32

# *The Practice of Holiness*

The practice of religion by the Jews in ancient times is an interesting subject for study in its own right. However, it has added significance because of its continuing influence upon the familiar institut·ons and celebrations of modern Western civilization. For example, we divide the ceaseless flow of time into convenient segments of weeks, months, and years. Our calendar arrangement is the result of many factors, especially the contributions of the ancient Romans and Babylonians. However, the religious practices of the Jews also were decisive in the making of the calendar. It is sufficient evidence of that truth simply to take note of the increasing prominence of the weekend as a time for change of pace, recreation, and worship, all the direct or indirect result of the Jewish seven-day week culminating in the Sabbath.

Our division of the year into twelve months, with constant reference to the changing of the moon, may be traced to the lunar calendar of antiquity, including the particular place of the new moon in Jewish liturgy. Many of our annual celebrations of historical events and natural recurrence have their origins or models in Jewish practice, such as Passover and Easter, Yom Kippur and Good Friday, Shabnot and Pentecost, Sukkot and Thanksgiving. And the treatment by family and society of the crucial events in the life of the individual—birth, religious maturity, marriage, death— reveals marked similarity to the customs of the ancient Jews.

Furthermore, it is a truism that the church is the daughter of the synagogue; and the family resemblance remains. Both the organization and function of the synagogue were carried over in the beginnings of the church, as would be expected in the light of the fact that the leaders of the early churches were Jews, and most converts, for a generation, came out of the synagogues. Thus synagogue and church alike, throughout their history, have made central the reading and explanation of the Scriptures, prayer, praise, the instruction of the young, ministry to the hurt and needy, and the preservation and extension of the community of faith. With their teachings, rituals, and moral influence, synagogue and church stand in contemporary society as constant reminders of the heritage received from the religious practices and institutions of the ancient Jews.

## Holy Ways and Days

Religion is related to every aspect of life, according to ancient Judaism. It is not merely for holy days and holy places. Nevertheless, recognizing that values which become commonplace are easily overlooked, the Jews appointed special times and places for emphasizing and celebrating the particularities of faith. They developed methods of worship that would guarantee the primacy of religion among the people.

We have seen in earlier references that the Temple in Jerusalem was the center of religious practice until it was destroyed by the Romans. There the priests presided over the system of ceremonies and sacrifices that were required by the Torah. However, we have also noted that the conditions of the Exile and dispersion, made final by the loss of the Temple and the nation, transformed Judaism into an essentially lay religion. The sacrifices of the Temple became the prayers of the synagogues, and the role of the priests was superseded by the instruction and leadership of the scholars and rabbis. The new leaders continued to encourage and guide the practice of private religion, with its attendant moral code, by individuals and families, of course; but, since the group has always been the center of concern in Judaism, rather than the individual, the creators and custodians of the faith formulated over the centuries a complex system of worship and celebration. Most outstanding in this system were the communal prayers, the Sabbath, and the annual cycle of holy days.

Scripture and tradition provided for the religious observance of every major stage in the life of an individual, observances in which the family and community played significant parts. The most important events, naturally, were birth, inclusion into the Covenant People, marriage, and death. The birth of a child brought great rejoicing, both in the family and in the community. If the child were a girl, the father had the privilege of reading the Torah in the synagogue and offering a special blessing for his wife and daughter. If the child were a boy, he was formally included in the People of Abraham by the ceremony of circumcision, on the eighth day of his life (cf. Leviticus 12:3). That ritual was considered so sacred and necessary that it was performed even if the eighth day fell on a Sabbath or other holy day. The honor of performing the circumcision was reserved, in ancient times, for a special person, a *Mohel*, who was respected for his piety; and the ritual included precise prayers of thanksgiving and blessing. When the boy reached the age of puberty, he was qualified to be counted among the required ten to compose a synagogue; he then became "Bar Mitzvah," son of the commandment.

In Judaism, marriage has always been considered to be ordained by God the Creator. The solemn yet joyful contract is sealed by the acceptance of religious obligations, and the sanctions of God add strength to the union. In ancient practice, betrothal usually preceded marriage by approximately a year; it was a binding relationship. The marriage ceremony itself involved the family and friends as well as the couple. Usually, the groom brought his bride under a canopy, called a *Huppah*, which symbolized their home. Sometimes the two were united simply by exchanging gifts, perhaps rings. The contract was made legal by the reading of the *Ketubah* by the rabbi, in which the man and woman made their vows in the presence of witnesses. These religious ceremonies and sanctions have continued throughout history, becoming woven into the fabric of Western culture; and it may be noted that the religious emphasis has been a major factor in the remarkable stability of Jewish marriage and the home. Here is a potential source of great value.

Sickness, death, and mourning have always been surrounded and assuaged, in Jewish custom, by the aid and comfort of religion. We have noted earlier that ancient Judaism was at best uncertain about the possibility and nature of an afterlife for the individual. Religion therefore was practical and world-affirming. Nevertheless, since death is the inevitable fate of every person, the Jew came to it with faith in God and sustenance from his family and friends. The last words were an affirmation of faith, the *Shema* (Deut. 6:4,5), and the body was prepared with dignity for an immediate burial. Grief was openly and honestly expressed—a sound psychology—and mourning and memory were not neglected. Thus, from birth to death, Judaism provided for the application of religious teaching and practice in the life of the individual.

The practice of holiness in Judaism has always been centered in prayer, and prayer has been an activity of the community at least as much as of the individual. In fact, individual prayer is made with the consciousness of being part of the whole community of the People of God. The Jew is a Jew because he is within Israel; and the life of Israel is sustained by prayer. That is made abundantly clear throughout the Scriptures and in the Tradition; and the life of prayer is encouraged and guided by a system which has been handed down from the earliest times of the saints (Hasidim) and rabbis.

The basic formula of prayer is the *Berakhah*, the blessing: "Blessed art Thou, God, our King, King of the world" (cf. Psalm 119). It is repeated in all prayers, and there are three main, daily prayers which should be made, along with the affirmation of faith, the Shema. They are the *Shaharit* (Morning Prayer), the *Minah* (afternoon Prayer), and *Maarib* (Evening Prayer), each following closely the structure of Psalm 19. In addition, the *Mussaf*, a special prayer derived from ancient Temple usage, is repeated on the Sabbath and other holy days. And on the most solemn and holy day of the year, *Yom Kippur*, the closing prayer is called *N'eelah*. Finally, the *Kaddish* (sanctification), a prayer of ancient origins, is always used to open and conclude public worship. It is essentially an affirmation of reverence: "May His great name be blessed for ever and ever."

Worship in prayer, by the community assembled or by the individual as a part of the community, has been prompted by the use of three visible instruments: the *Tallit*, the *Tefillin*, and the *Mezuzah*. All had their origin in scriptural requirement (Numbers 15: 37-41 and Deuteronomy 6:8-9). The Tallit is a prayer shawl, or stole, which symbolically wraps the worshipper in the will and awareness of God. The Tefillin are the small leather cases containing pieces of parchment with Scripture written on them; they are bound upon the arms and head by leather straps, encircling the hand and mind with God's command to love. And the Mezuzah is a small scroll of Torah, encased within a leather container and affixed to the doorpost of the home, reminding the faithful of identity and duty as children of God. These have been called "visual aids" to faith and worship.

The Sabbath is probably the most obvious symbol of Judaism. It remains to the present in Western culture a significant legacy of ancient Judaism, whether celebrated still by Jews as the seventh day, or by Christians on the first day, or even by Islam on Friday. At least a weekly observance is retained for rest if not for worship. The origins of Sabbath-keeping are lost in the distant past, though it may be safely assumed that the seventh day is related to the four phases of the moon. It has been kept with care and solemnity since the beginnings of Hebrew religion, and its remembrance is commanded in the fundamental Torah, the Decalogue (Exodus 20:8 and Deuteronomy 5:12). Ancient Judaism developed a strict pattern for the keeping of the Sabbath. It included preparation of home and spirit, worship in the synagogue, cessation of all labor, the joyful partaking of special food, and happy fellowship with friends. Body and mind were restored by the relaxing break in the wearing round of work and duty, and life was enriched by the proleptic experience of the presence of God and the hosts of heaven. The Sabbath provided discipline, renewal, and hope. It served as a regular reminder that Yahweh, the God of the Covenant, is both Sovereign Creator and gracious Father, holy and accessible. Thus to keep the Sabbath was to keep the faith.

The Sabbath comes every week, but there are other holy days that come but once a year. Listed in the order of the ancient Jewish calendar, the following seven deserve special attention:

1. *Rosh Hashanah* (New Year's) comes in the Fall, in September or October, and signifies the new beginning of the moral life as well as of the year. It stands at the beginning also of the most solemn season of the year, the Days of Awe, the ten high holy days, which culminate in Yom Kippur. Rosh Hashanah is announced by the blowing of the ram's horn, the *shofar*, which calls the people to *teshubah*, repentance. The total period of self-examination and renewal lasts ten days—two for Rosh Hashanah, one for Yom Kippur, and seven between. The season is marked by special prayers and the repeated praise of God.

2. *Yom Kippur* (Day of Atonement), as indicated, brings to completion the Days of Awe. It is the Sabbath of Sabbaths, the holiest day of the year. No food or drink are taken during its passing, and the worshipper gives the most serious attention to his relation with God and with his fellowman. The story of Jonah is recited for Yom Kippur, reminding all of the universal mercies of God.

3. *Sukkot* (Booths), sometimes called the Feast of Tabernacles, follows immediately after the Days of Awe. It lasts for seven days and commemorates the providence of God which supplied food, water, guidance, and protection for the Hebrews during the sojourn in the wilderness of Sinai after the Exodus from

Egypt. Thus it has become a festival of thanksgiving, a time for gratitude for the past and for the annual harvest. Faithful Jews through the centuries have built a *Sukkah*, a shelter of branches, in the home or in the synagogue, as a place for meditation, breaking bread, and giving thanks. The influence of this festival is obvious in the American Thanksgiving Day celebration.

4. *Hanukkah* (Dedication), as we have seen earlier, is a winter festival commemorating the rededication of the Temple after its liberation from the Syrian Hellenists in 164 B.C. This holy day is the only one of the seven that is not commanded in the Scriptures. However, it is described in the Apocrypha (I Maccabees), and it brings to mind the miracle of God's redemption of his people at a particularly crucial time in their history. Hanukkah is therefore a joyful festival, a time for blessing, feasting, and games. The light of happiness shines brightly from the candles of the nine-branched candelabrum, celebrating victory and the decoration of the ancient Temple.

5. *Purim* (Lots) is the merry festival, coming at the end of winter in February-March, which is perhaps least religious and most jingoistic. It is based upon the story in Esther of the turning of the tables against Haman the Agagite after he had plotted the destruction of the Jews in Persia. Though largely a secular event, it has a place in religion at least by its assurance that good must ultimately triumph over evil; and one may therefore be excused for the glee that comes in being on the side of the angels. The name apparently comes from the "lots" used by the wicked Haman as he planned his ill-fated pogrom.

6. *Pessah* (Passover) is celebrated after the spring equinox. It is the Birthday of Israel. Along with Shabuot and Sukkot, Pessah was a pilgrim festival in ancient Palestine, when the people were commanded to go to the Temple in Jerusalem for special worship (cf. Deut. 16:16). The eight-day festival begins with the *Seder*, a solemn meal and religious service that is kept in the home, where the Haggadah of the Exodus is told and the experience of the escape from Egyptian bondage is repeated. The meal includes roasted lamb (in place of the former sacrificed lamb), *matzah* (unleavened bread), wine, and bitter herbs. A chair is left unoccupied at the table, with the hope that the prophet Elijah may appear to announce the New Age. It is a celebration of freedom and hope.

7. *Shabuot* (the Feast of Weeks) is the feast of revelation, getting its name from the fact that it comes fifty days after Pessah (Leviticus 23:15f.). It recalls the giving of the Decalogue to Moses on Mt. Sinai, where, according to tradition, the Word was translated simultaneously into all the languages of mankind. This festival is celebrated as Pentecost (Greek, "fifty") by Christians, in memory of the coming of the Spirit and the universal proclamation of the Gospel in the early church (Acts 2).

### Religious Parties

Like all living things, Judaism from its beginning has been characterized by growth, change, and diversity. We have observed, for example, the conflict between priests and prophets, reaching back into the pre-exilic times of Hebrew religion, and continuing during and after the Exile. We have also noted the variety of responses to the ever-increasing contact with other religions and cultures, especially with respect to the ideologies of particularism versus universalism which are reflected even in the Scriptures. Such diversity of belief and practice eventually led to the rise of identifiable religious "parties" among the Jews, especially among those who remained in the homeland. Josephus named four "philosophies," and other groups may be seen to have existed even if little is known about them. The three parties of greatest significance were the Sadducees, the Pharisees and the Essenes. There were, in addition, the Therapeutae, the Zealots, the Sicarii, the Herodians, the Boethusians, the Covenanters, and others.

Several known factors led to the conscious evolvement of the Sadducees, Pharisees, and Essenes, which apparently occurred during the second century B.C., under the threatening rule of the Seleucids or at the beginning of the Maccabean period. First, some of the Jews, especially the aristocratic and powerful, were eager to accept the foreign domination which was the source of their position, wealth, and security. They cooperated with the Hellenists and the Romans, and they advocated and adopted many elements of the culture of their rulers. However, such acquiescence was repugnant to the pious and the poor. They bore the burden of foreign cruelty and heavy taxation, and they resisted compromise because they believed it was God's will that they be separate and free. Second, the old struggle had, as we have seen, developed in Judaism into a distinction between the interests of the hierarchy of the Temple, on the one hand, and the laity-led worship of the synagogues, on the other. And, third, the question of the understanding and application of the Torah received a variety of answers. Some insisted on a conservative and literal interpretation, rejecting all innovation and enlargement; others believed that it was necessary to interpret the Torah anew in every age according to the needs of the day and the growing learning of the scholars.

The Sadducees were the party of privilege. They were the priests, the aristocratic families, and the merchants who profited by maintaining the status quo. Most modern scholars believe that the name of the group was derived from Zadok, the high priest of David (II Samuel 8:17, 15:24 ff.) and Solomon (1 Kings 1:34 ff.), whose descendants ultimately came to rule the Temple and the Sanhedrin. The Pharisees, on the other hand, were pious laymen among the Hasidim who originated as a party when John Hyrcanus, the Maccabean High Priest-King (135-104 B.C.) excluded laymen from the Sanhedrin and branded them *Perushim*, "Separatists," because of their resistance to Hellenism and their criticism of the corrupt priesthood. Taking the name as a badge of honor, the Perushim (Pharisees) opposed the priests and foreign paganism, developed the synagogues as their primary institution, and gained the support of the common people. The Essenes are not mentioned in either the New Testament or the Talmud, but they are known from descriptions in the works of Josephus, Philo of Alexandria, and the Roman historian, Pliny. Many recent scholars have suggested that they were the monastics who lived in the valley of the Jordan River and by the Dead Sea, at such places as Qumran, and that they were therefore responsible for the recently discovered library of remarkable documents known as the Dead Sea Scrolls.

The differences between the teachings of the Sadducees and the Pharisees are best understood in the light of their opposing views regarding the Torah and its interpretation. The Sadducees were strict constructionists, insisting upon a literal interpretation of the written Torah and rejecting the authority of the Oral Tradition. On that basis, they did not accept the recently developed idea of the resurrection of the dead, and they did not believe in angels and other spiritual beings. However, they were willing, apparently, to adopt the Hellenistic belief in the immortality of the soul. On the other hand, the Pharisees sought an ever wider application of the Torah in every passing generation. They were therefore the creators and transmitters of the Oral Torah which was ultimately to become the

Talmud. In line with that evolutionary hermeneutic, the Pharisees believed in angels and demons, and they accepted the apocalyptic idea of the future resurrection (cf. Mark 12:18 ff. and parallels).

Since the Sadducees were the party of the priests and, according to the Deuteronomic Law, the priests were restricted in their liturgical duties to the Temple in Jerusalem, when the Temple was destroyed by the Romans, the Sadducees ceased to exist as a party. However, the Pharisees, as we have seen, were found wherever there were synagogues, and that came to be the case throughout the Roman Empire. Thus, the Judaism which survived the rebellions against Rome was essentially Pharisaism.

The Essenes were similar in many ways to the Pharisees. The main difference between them was that the Essenes believed that the only viable way to holiness is withdrawal from the world of ordinary affairs, whereas the Pharisees attempted the way of holiness in the midst of the world. The Essenes established monastic communities in areas apart where they could seek to obey Yahweh in study, prayer, ritual and labor. But the Pharisees lived among the people, interpreting and teaching the Scriptures, guiding the synagogues, and attempting even to spread the knowledge of God by the winning of proselytes to Judaism.

The *am ha-aretz*, the people of the land, were often referred to as "sinners," not because they were morally inferior to the others so much as because they were not able to attend to the requirements of life and at the same time give the necessary attention to study and ritual. Neither could they engage in the revolutionary activities of the Zealots and Sicarii (assassins). But they generally followed the leadership of the rabbis in the practice of holiness, and in that practice the essential faith of Moses and the prophets survived and prepared the ground out of which sprang the religious heritage of the West.

# XII.
# THE ADVENT OF
# CHRISTIANITY

# Chapter 33

# The Matrix of the New Way

Christianity came into the world at the time when Rome had become the center of an empire which had turned the Mediterranean Sea into a waterway which the Romans could, with complete accuracy, call *Mare Nostrum*—"Our Sea." The history of the development of the Christian West is inextricably bound up with that of the political and cultural institutions which cradled the new faith and provided the environment in which it grew to maturity. Those institutions had a variety of sources, but it was through Rome, the great assimilator, that the streams merged into a single channel.

In the eighth century B.C., while the early Olympic Games were inaugurating the Hellenic period in the Eastern Mediterranean area, three villages on the Tiber in Italy were being consolidated into a single city-state. The sixth century—the age of the Milesian philosophers and the return of the Jews from Exile—saw the rise and fall of the Tarquin kings and the establishment of the Republic. The subsequent political development of the city had much in common with that of the Athenian *Polis*. An aristocratic system, which initially vested power in the hands of a class of particians who dominated the Senate and the magisterial offices, gradually gave way, through confrontation and compromise, to one in which the populace at large played a far more important political role. In the fifth century, the plebeians won the right to elect officers known as "tribunes of the people," whose persons were sacrosanct and who were empowered to protect citizens against illegal arrest and prosecution. Their authority was expanded as the plebeians gained a greater voice in government. In 452 B.C., a delegation was dispatched to Athens to study Solon's constitution, and in the following year, the *decemviri*, a body of ten men temporarily appointed to replace the consuls, began work on the codification of the laws. In 450 B.C., they had the completed code inscribed on the celebrated Twelve Tables and posted in the Forum. Not long after that, at the demand of the plebeians, the *decemviri* were deposed, and traditional offices of the consuls and tribunes were restored. In 449 B.C., the Valerio-Horatian laws reaffirmed the rights of individual citizens and provided that actions of the plebeian assembly should be placed before the Senate and, if ratified by that body, should become law. Four years later, the *Lex Canuleia* legalized marriages between patricians and plebeians. In 367 B.C., after ten years of agitation initiated by G. Licinius Stolo and L. Sextius, the Licinian Rogation opened the consulate to plebeians, and L. Sextius became the first member of that class ever to be elected consul. Little by little, the remaining powers of the patricians to control the government were worn away until, in 287 B.C., the plebeian assembly won the right to have its decrees recognized as law. These changes were made, interestingly enough, without diminishing the dignity and prestige of the Senate, which, throughout the history of the Republic and the Empire, embodied for the Romans their ideal of political legitimacy. To this day the letters "SPQR" (*Senatus Populusque Romanus*) on Roman inscriptions pay tribute to the durability and effectiveness of a government based on the shared power of the Senate and the people. When Pyrrhus, king of Epirus, in response to a request made in 280 B.C. by the Greek city of Tarentum in southern Italy, directed a serious foreign challenge to Roman domination of the Italian peninsula, he sent his minister Kineas to Rome to negotiate with the Senate. Kineas reported back to his sovereign that he had seen an "assembly of kings."

## Hellenes and Phoenicians

When Pyrrhus after a series of costly victories—"Pyrrhic" victories which resulted in a final defeat—left Italy, he said to his officers, "What a wrestling ground, my friends, we are leaving for Rome and Carthage." His remark was prophetic. The Greek kingdoms of the Hellenistc world lacked the unity to challenge successfully the growing power of a state which Greeks and Romans alike feared and hated.

For centuries, the Hellenes and the Phoenicians had been in competition for control of the lands bordering the Mediterranean. Greeks, sailing out of cities established during the early days of the migration from the mainland, had voyaged to the west and established new colonies in Sicily and Italy (*Magna Graecia*), the southern coast of France, and the eastern coast of the Iberian Peninsula. The Phoenicians, descendants of the Semitic settlers of the maritime cities at the eastern end of the Mediterranean, had migrated westward to the shores of North Africa, where natives of

Sidon founded the city of Leptis Magna and Tyrians established their "New City" (*Kart Hadash*, simplified by the Romans to *Carthago*). In time the Carthaginians became the dominant commercial and military power in the western Mediterranean. They controlled the Straits of Gibraltar, maintained colonies on Sardinia, Malta, the Balearic Islands, and the southern coast of Iberia, and challenged the Greeks for dominance in Sicily. The civilization of Carthage was a highly developed one, marred, however, by the sacrifice of great numbers of first-born children to the god Baal-Hammon.

Limiting the eastward expansion of Carthage on the northern rim of the Mediterranean was the great Greek city of Massalia (Marseilles) which, together with its colonial dependencies stretching from Monaco to Cape St. Martin in Spain, was bound to Rome by ties of friendship and commerce. Established about 600 B.C. by mariners from Phocaea in Asia Minor, Massalia, blessed with efficient government and humane laws, had become a major center for the shipping business and had established a prosperous trade with the Celtic tribes of the interior. The city was the chief Mediterranean terminus for the tin mined and smelted in Cornwall, shipped across the Channel to the Continent, and transported overland to its destination. It was probably the rumor of a Carthaginian sea route to the Tin Islands which led a Massalian scholar and navigator named Pytheas to undertake one of the greatest voyages in the history of exploration. In less than a year, he sailed to England, circumnavigated the island, explored a far-northern region called Thule, followed the coast of Europe as far west as the mouth of the Elbe, and returned to Massalia, somehow managing to elude the Carthaginian watchdogs at Gibraltar on the outward and inward passages.

### Hellenism in the East

In the East, at the time Pyrrhus withdrew from Italy, the shards of Alexander's empire provided such political cohesion as existed in the conquered areas. The cultural impact of the conquest, however, was probably as great as if the unity envisioned by Alexander had been maintained. Hellenic civilization made an indelible imprint on areas of the world where the Greek language had rarely been heard a century earlier. Antioch in Syria and Alexandria in Egypt became great metropolitan centers, where people of widely different cultures lived and worked and exchanged ideas. In Alexandria, a city dominated by Greek architecture, Greek engineering, and Greek learning, there were, nevertheless, many thousands of Egyptians and a Jewish community larger than the population of Jerusalem. The great Museum, a comprehensive center of learning founded by Ptolemy, had a library containing some five hundred thousand books and a vast array of facilities for research in many fields of learning.

There, about 270 B.C., Aristarchus of Samos advanced the theory that the earth rotates on its axis and revolves around the sun. A contemporary of Aristarchus, the mathematician Euclid, wrote the *Elements (Stoicheia)*, a textbook of Geometry used for two millennia. Asked by King Ptolemy if a less time-consuming way could not be found to learn the subject than by study of the thirteen volumes of the *Elements*, he replied, "There is no royal road to geometry." In the same century, Eratosthenes, a native of Cyrene and head of the Library at Alexandria, was informed that at Syene (Aswan), on the day of the summer solstice at noon, the sun would shine directly down the shaft of a well. Struck with the idea that he might use this fact as one of the data needed to measure the circumference of the earth, which he, in common with many other Greek men of learning, held to be spherical, he made an observation at Alexandria at the same hour and found that the sun cast a seven-and-one-fifth angle of shadow to the north, the fiftieth part of a circle. Syene and Alexandria were five thousand stadia apart, and so when Eratosthenes multiplied that distance by fifty, he concluded that the earth must be some two hundred and fifty thousand stadia in circumference. That figure—about twenty-six thousand miles—was far more nearly accurate than the later Ptolemaic one which was to lead Columbus to think he had found a westward route to China. These and other important scientific achievements were matched by milestones in other fields of Alexandrian scholarship. Aristarchus of Samothrace, in the course of his editing of the works of many of the greatest Hellenic poets, produced the most important annotated edition of the *Iliad* and the *Odyssey* ever published in antiquity, and the Jewish scholars responsible for the *Septuagint* made the Hebrew Scriptures available in Greek to interested Gentiles as well as to Jews who had no knowledge of the ancient language of their people. For some two hundred years before the beginning of the Christian era, many Jews in Palestine as well as those of the Diaspora became almost wholly Hellenized, and all levels of their society were affected to some extent by the prevailing Greek culture. Jewish scholars began to write in forms closer to those of Greece than to their earlier literary heritage, and there is evidence that the influence was mutual. Jewish monotheism could be seen by educated Hellenes who became acquainted with it under favorable circumstances as consonant with the highest concepts of Greek philosophy.

### Rome and the West

With the withdrawal of Pyrrhus, Rome was left in command of the Italian peninsula. To the north lay the kingdoms of the Ligurians and the Celts. Italy itself was nominally a confederacy of diverse peoples, enjoying local autonomy but bound to Rome by variously defined ties. In the unification of Italy, Rome showed the skill, patience, and tolerance which were to insure her imperial success on a larger stage. Greeks, who hitherto had paid little attention to the city on the Tiber, recognized that a new Mediterranean power had arisen, and other states began to seek alliances with Rome. The peril common to all of them was Carthage, now at the peak of her power and threatening to establish an absolute control over the seas between Italy and Gibraltar. In 264 B.C., war broke out between Carthage and Rome. For the first time in her history, Rome matched her well trained and intensely patriotic legions against a foe with superior naval power and an enormous mercenary army. Her efforts were successful, and at the close of the long conflict in 241 B.C. Carthage lost her Sicilian possessions, the nearby Lipari Islands, and a substantial financial indemnity. Not long after that, Rome acquired Sardinia and Corsica and established the groundwork for a colonial administration by electing praetors to govern those possessions and the ones acquired through the initial treaty. With her western front temporarily secured, she strengthened her position in the north by subduing some troublesome Celtic tribes and in the east by suppressing Illyrian pirates operating in the Adriatic. This latter expedition brought Roman officials into intimate contact with states of the Greek mainland. They were well received, and Romans were admitted to the Isthmian games in 228 B.C. In the meantime, Carthaginian generals, first Hamilcar and then Hasdrubal, expanded Punic control of the shores of Spain, and Hannibal, Hasdrubal's son, advanced up the western Iberian coast far enough to threaten to commercial interests of Massalia (called *Massilia* by the Romans). Ignoring a warning by an alarmed Rome, Hannibal, in 219 B.C., took the coastal city of Saguntum by siege and precipitated the second Punic War.

The struggle that followed threatened the very existence of Rome. Hannibal, a true military genius, marched toward Italy with a battle-hardened army which, in addition to the usual infantry and cavalry, had an elephant corps. He crossed the Rhone and turned north, bypassing Massalia. Crossing the snow-clad Alps in fifteen days, a feat which cost him almost half his army, he used the remaining force to win an unbroken series of victories, culminating, in the year 216 B.C., in his great triumph at Cannae, in southern Italy, where some fifty thousand Roman soldiers fell in battle. Rome's allies and dependencies deserted her in droves, and Philip V of Macedon allied himself with Carthage. After Cannae, however, Hannibal lacked either the ability or the will to follow up his advantage immediately, and the undaunted Romans began to turn the tide against the invader. He held on in Italy, threatening Rome itself but lacking the power to do more than hurl a defiant spear at the Colline Gate, while Roman forces were winning victory after victory against the Carthaginians in other parts of the world. Hannibal's brother Hasdrubal was defeated and killed while marching to relieve him, and a brilliant young Roman general named Scipio succeeded in driving the Carthaginians out of Spain. Hannibal was driven southward to Bruttium, in the toe of the Italian boot, and held out there while Scipio, having convinced the Senate that the war ought to be carried to Carthage itself, invaded Africa, where he was joined by Masinissa, a Numidian ally. Two battles resulted in Roman victories, and many Carthaginians wanted to negotiate a peace. More militant voices prevailed, however, and Hannibal was recalled from Italy to strengthen the defense. In 202 B.C., he met Scipio and Masinissa in battle, seventy-five miles southwest of Carthage on the plain of Zama. There the Romans and Numidians won the victory which earned Scipio the name "Africanus," and the Second Punic War was at an end. Hannibal went into exile, and a Roman-dictated peace treaty confined Carthage to Africa and deprived her of her navy, her elephants, and a large sum of money.

The victory settled the question of control of the lands of the western Mediterranean. Thenceforth Rome would determine its political structure. Some areas, like the whole of Sicily, were made into provinces. Others, like Massalia, remained independent states which were, in effect, clients of Rome. Even complete victory, though, could not quiet the fears of the Romans that Carthage would one day rise again. Cato the Elder achieved lasting fame for his habit of ending his speeches in the Senate on any and every subject with the words, *Ceterum censeo Carthaginem esse delendam*, "For the rest I vote that Carthage should be destroyed." His persistence was finally rewarded. In 151 B.C., Carthage was goaded into armed conflict with Rome's ally Masinissa, and the Romans declared war when the Carthaginians refused to destroy their own city. In 149 B.C., the Roman troops were back in Africa mounting a siege, and after three years of heroic defense by the despairing Carthaginians, the attackers breached the walls and, in a six-day house-to-house battle, in which men, women, and children chose death to surrender, took the city. The Roman commander, a grandson by adoption of Scipio Africanus, brought the Third Punic War to a close by burning Carthage, plowing the ashes into the soil, and sowing the furrows with salt.

## Rome and the East

Rome had been forced into war with Philip V of Macedonia when the monarch allied himself with Hannibal. The war with Philip had ended in 205 B.C., but Rome and the coalition of Greek states which had fought with her against Macedon were bound together by a common distrust of Philip. The growing friendship between Greeks and Romans was further enhanced by the popularity which Greek literature was beginning to enjoy in Rome. The works of the epic poets and dramatists were being read in Latin translation, and Hellenes and Romans alike were becoming aware that they had in common political, cultural, and religious traditions which distinguished them from other peoples.

As the Second Punic War drew toward its close, Philip entered into an alliance with Antiochus III of Syria which threatened Rome's Grecian allies. In 200 B.C., Rome declared war on Macedonia and within three years gained a decisive victory. Philip was stripped of all his territories in Greece, Asia Minor, and Thrace, and forced to become a client of Rome. The Greek states were declared free, but Rome's role as arbiter in Hellenic affairs was established.

The subsequent history of Roman hegemony in the East is too complex to permit more than the briefest discussion of those developments which were most significant in laying the foundations of the Western civilization of the Christian era. Antiochus III unwisely tried to appropriate the areas which Philip had lost and was soundly defeated. By 189 B.C. Rome had replaced Alexander's successors as the overlord of the eastern Mediterranean. Roman supremacy was not unchallenged. Macedonia unsuccessfully tried to regain some of its former glory, with the ultimate result that it became a Roman province. The restive Achaean League, angered at some admittedly severe Roman measures, overstepped the bounds of prudence and precipitated a disastrous war which brought devastation to several Greek cities and seriously diminished the liberties of the Hellenes. Left free in name, they were, thereafter, subject to most of the restrictions and obligations imposed on the provinces, with the added disadvantage of being under the general supervision of the Roman governor of Macedonia.

Throughout the East, the Romans faced similar complexities. The Hellenic culture, which had imposed itself with considerable success on the domain of Alexander, proved resistant to similar influence from Rome. Latin never became a popular language east of the Adriatic, and the general way of life of the region remained determinedly Greek. The Romans, however, with their enormous respect for everything Hellenic, were themselves assimilating the ways of their newly acquired subjects and were, indeed, in the last analysis, the restorers and preservers of Alexander's empire. More than that, they succeeded in insuring that the values of Greek civilization would survive in the West. The Roman administrators were, on the whole, patient and tolerant men, who rewarded cooperation with an honest respect for the institutions and customs of the subject peoples but who were capable of imperious firmness if their authority were challenged in matters touching the interests of Rome. In the second century B.C., the Seleucid king Antiochus IV Epiphanes considered himself free to invade Egypt following a dispute over Palestine. Rome had little visible presence in the area at that time, and it must have been something of a surprise to Antiochus when a Roman senator named Popillius Laenas, accompanied by a small retinue, entered his camp. Responding to an inquiry as to the reason for his presence, Popillius said that the Roman Senate was opposed to the Egyptian campaign and would like for Antiochus to withdraw. The monarch, who had spent some years in Rome as a hostage, knew that suggestions from that source were to be taken seriously. Wishing, no doubt, to save face, he replied that he would consider his answer. Popillius drew a circle around Antiochus with his staff. "Answer before you step out of that circle," he said. A century earlier, such impertinence would have cost him his head, but Popillius was a Roman, and the pattern of the new order was clear, even to kings. "I will go back to Syria," Antiochus said meekly.

## The Decline of the Republic

So, little by little, Rome tightened its grip on the Mediterranean world, bringing unaccustomed peace to areas whose inhabitants could remember nothing but war and often being hailed as liberators by people who had known nothing but tyranny. All the while, though, the fabric of life in Rome itself was undergoing changes which would ultimately bring an end to the Republic. Although the will of the popular assembly had been declared to be law, actual power had reverted to the Senate. That body, though in theory open to elected members of any class, was, in practice, in the hands of a sort of oligarchy composed of old patrician families and others privileged by wealth or newly acquired political power. The rich nobles, exposed to the broadening influences of Greek culture, were not always discriminating in their value judgments, and the beneficent influences of Hellenism were offset by a growth of luxury and moral license alien to the historic Roman concept of civic virtue.

From the latter half of the second century on, the Republican form of government suffered a series of crises from which it could not recover. The unsuccessful efforts of the Grachii to restore a considerable measure of popular rule and effect drastic agrarian reform revealed clearly the existence of an economic and social gulf between the classes which could not be bridged by the existing system of government. In the first century B.C., the Social War, the subsequent conflict between Marius and Sulla, and the election of Pompey and Crassus as consuls while their armies waited outside the walls of Rome evidenced the transfer of real authority from Senate and people to commanders of military forces. Such a development was, perhaps, inevitable in a society in which distinction was most readily achieved through service with the legions in maintaining the stability of a growing empire.

In 60 B.C., Pompey, Caesar, and Crassus formed the First Triumvirate. Crassus was killed in a battle with the Parthians in 53 B.C., and growing tensions between Pompey and Caesar ultimately resulted in Julius Caesar's crossing of the Rubicon with an army in 49 B.C. Pompey fled, and Caesar entered Rome as unquestioned master of the Italian peninsula. During the next four years, he succeeded in crushing opposition to his rule in the provinces. Pompey was killed, and, with no one else of his stature to lead the dissident factions, Caesar's power in the Roman world became absolute. As *imperator*, he governed with the brilliance which characterized all his activities, bringing order to the chaotic Roman society, strengthening the administration of the empire, and somehow finding time to introduce the most important calendar reform in Western history. On the fifteenth of March in 44 B.C., he was struck down by republican murderers, and for thirteen years the struggle of the Second Triumvirate (Antony, Lepidus, and Octavian) with its enemies and the civil wars which followed the dissolution of the Triumvirate spread bloodshed and chaos over the Roman world.

## The Roman Empire

Octavian, Julius Caesar's great-nephew, triumphed in the civil wars, and with the defeat of Antony at Actium in 31 B.C., no one was left to challenge his power. In 28-27 B.C., the government was re-established, maintaining most of the republican institutions but placing the nation under the leadership of Octavian as *princeps*. Under a grant of the *imperium* from the Senate, he exercised extraordinary powers, and he was formally given the name "Augustus." Rome had officially become an empire. Nothing could have been better calculted to facilitate the enormous task she had taken upon herself of governing the vast complex of nations which had fallen under her sway. The Emperor became not only the chief magistrate but the living symbol of Rome, and the later attribution of divine status to the holder of the office would add a religious dimension to her claim to be the legitimate custodian of a political cosmopolis. Some of the successors of Augustus would be personally unworthy and a few would be certifiable lunatics, but for the next few centuries Europe and the East would enjoy a time of unprecendented peace, prosperity, and efficient administration.

The people of the Empire were related to Rome in several different ways. Many inhabitants of places far distant from Rome were Roman citizens. Others were residents of provinces, of which there were two categories: imperial provinces, ruled by the Emperor through legates supported by armies, and senatorial provinces, governed in the traditional way by proconsular officials. Still others were citizens or subjects of political entities which retained a considerable measure of automony in internal affairs while being responsible to Rome for the conduct of relations with other governments which might affect the *Pax Romana*. There were barbarian cultures which kept their tribal structure under the watchful eyes of occupying legions, "allied" cities like Athens and Sparta, which Rome, out of admiration or gratitude, had honored by respecting their freedom in domestic affairs, and lastly, states governed internally by rulers holding royal or priestly titles.

This last situation was the one in which the Palestinian Jews found themselves at the close of the first century B.C. In 63 B.C., Pompey had asserted Roman suzerainty over the country and given the title of "ethnarch" to the high priest, Hyrcanus II. The political situation became highly confused, however, in the troubled times that followed. Hyrcanus II lost most of his power, and Antipater, a son of the native governor of Idumaea, was made a Roman citizen and appointed procurator of Judea. One of his sons, Phasael, was made governor of Jerusalem, and another son, Herod, was made governor of Galilee. These actions were not technically an imposition of foreign rule on the Jews, for the Idumeans had been conquered by the Maccabean priest-king Hyrcanus I and forced to embrace the Jewish faith. When Julius Caesar came to power, he treated the Jews with respect and granted them such privileges as exemption from military service and complete freedom of religion. In the turmoil following Caesar's death, though, Rome temporarily lost its control over the situation when the Parthians, in 40 B.C., invaded Palestine and appointed a Hasmonaean named Antigonus as king and high priest. Phasael killed himself, and Herod fled to Rome. There the Senate, with the sanction of Octavian and Antony, named him king of Judaea and returned him to Palestine, where, with the aid of Roman troops, he drove the Parthians out and, in 37 B.C., took Jerusalem from Antigonus. Realizing, no doubt, that Antigonus had been popular with many of his countrymen who referred to the Idumaeans as "half-Jews," Herod married a Hasmonaean princess named Mariamne.

Herod was an able administrator and a mighty builder. Whole cities were contructed under his supervision, and temples, palaces, gymnasia, and aqueducts sprang up all over the country. An enthusiastic Hellenist, he went to great lengths to promote Greek attitudes and customs among the people, earning the hatred of conservative Jews who clung to the ancient ways. To placate them while at the same time satisfying his love of grandeur, he built a magnificent Temple on the site of the one erected by Solomon, made of marble and ornamented with gold and precious stones. For all the qualities that caused him to be called "Herod the Great," however, he was a cruel, suspicious and lustful man, and these traits became more pronounced as he grew older, until he became a veritable monster. He had two of his sons strangled when he suspected them of plotting against him and later killed his oldest son Antipater. Numerous other murders were laid to his door, and he spent the latter years of his life alternating between paranoid fits of cruelty and luxurious self-indulgence with an Oriental harem.

It was in this empire, ruled by Augustus of Rome—and in this small country, balanced between East and West and governed by an aging tyrant—that Jesus of Nazareth came into the world.

# Chapter 34

## *The Christian Scriptures*

A new sect arose among the Jews of Palestine during the reign of the Roman Emperor Tiberius (14-37 A.D.). It originated in the work and teaching of Jesus of Nazareth, a Galilean Jew; and although the new sect was opposed and rejected by nearly all of the priests of the Temple (Sadducees) and leaders of the synagogues (Pharisees), it soon spread among many Jews of the homeland and in the Diaspora. The adherents of the new "Way," as it was first called, claimed that Jesus was the long-expected Messiah (Greek "Christos"). They did not consider themselves apostate from the faith of Moses and the Prophets; rather they believed that the Way of Jesus the Christ was the fruition and fulfillment of God's saving work among his Covenant People which had begun with Abraham. However, since Jesus and his followers were rejected by Judaism, they soon found it necessary and desirable to turn to the pagan Gentiles. Thus Christianity, as the new religion soon became known, was carried throughout the Roman Empire before the end of the first century.

### Uniqueness and Continuity

Christianity was a new religion precisely because it was centered in a specific series of historical events, especially the life, death, and resurrection of Jesus. The Apostles, the original followers of Jesus who were "sent out" after his death to be his "witnesses in Jerusalem and in all Judea and Samaria and to the end of the earth" (Acts 1:8), believed themselves commissioned to proclaim an event rather than to teach new ideas. Preaching (*kerygma*, proclaimed news) was prior to teaching (*didache*), although of course the latter became increasingly the complex and complementary sequel to the former, especially as the movement spread among the pagans who were not acquainted with the Jewish background of Christianity.

This characteristic of historicity has given Christianity uniqueness, setting it apart from every other religion and ideology, even its parent Judaism. Since the time of Jesus and the Apostles, Christians have claimed to be the "New Israel," the People of God anticipated by the Hebrew prophets (cf. Jeremiah 31), and the

Church has claimed that it is the continuation of God's work of judgment and redemption in the world as recorded in the Law and the Prophets. However, Christianity has also recognized the "scandal of particularity" in its essential insistence both that something unique and necessary occurred in the life and death of Jesus and that saving faith is related to that specific event. Christianity is thus tied to history, to a particular, recorded history, in a way which is not characteristic of any other world religion, even its kindred Biblical faiths, Judaism and Islam. That is why the record of that history, the Christian Scriptures, is so fundamental for Christian faith and practice.

Nevertheless, we must not emphasize the uniqueness of Christianity so much as to overlook its equally important continuity with regard to both Judaism and Greco-Roman culture. The Christian view that history is the arena of God's saving activity, the channel of God's disclosure of his nature, will, and purpose, is parallel to, and probably derived from, the understanding of history embedded in the Hebrew Scriptures. That is to say, the assumption concerning the significance of history for revelation and redemption is essentially the same in Judaism and Christianity; the difference lies in their views as to *what* history, and *which* persons and events within history, are authentic instruments of God's disclosure and saving work. In the same way, Christianity, from its beginnings, freely and gladly appropriated ideas, practices, and institutions from Greco-Roman culture for its own expression and development, as will be shown extensively in the second volume of this work.

These paradoxical characteristics of uniqueness and continuity, of separation and identity, may be seen in the earliest records of Christian beginnings. What are those records? What sources are available for an investigation into the origins of this new sect which arose within Judaism and then spread rapidly throughout the ancient world, claiming to be new and good news, yet borrowing so much from its Jewish background and its Hellenistic and Roman context, becoming finally the most powerful force in world history? That is the question to which we must turn our attention in the remainder of this chapter.

### The Records of Christian Beginnings

The Christian Scriptures, the collection of twenty-seven short and varied writings known as the New Testament, contain nearly all that is known about the beginnings of Christianity. That is a surprising fact, in the light of the stupendous claims made in that literature and in view of the subsequent impact of the faith. Furthermore, even those twenty-seven little "books" were not written contemporaneously with the beginnings; rather they were composed by advocates of the faith a generation or two, or even three, after the brief career of Jesus. Few, if any, of the authors were among the original followers of Jesus, and their writings made no pretense of objectivity but were designed to propagate a passionate faith. The books were written by several different authors, some known and some unknown, and they originated in a variety of places and times. The writers shared a common faith, but their understanding and application of it was not always the same. Their words were recorded for specific needs and occasions, and they certainly had no notion that what they wrote would eventually be considered sacred Scripture. In fact, the books were not even collected until many generations had passed, in the second, third, and fourth centuries.

In addition to the books which eventually composed the canon of the New Testament, there are, of course, a number of other writings from approximately the same time which give meager information about Christian beginnings. Their value is limited, however, since they add almost nothing to the canonical books and they are in some cases based on misinformation, fancy, or biased hostility. Nevertheless, they remain important if only because they bear witness from so early a time to the historicity of Jesus and to the rapid spread of the faith in the Roman world. These works may be considered in three categories: the surviving Christian writings from the century following the death of Jesus, the Jewish works of the same period which refer to Jesus and his followers, and the Roman sources.

A small number of extant Christian writings may be dated from approximately the first half of the second century. A larger number of other works of that period are known by later reference to have existed but have not survived. The so-called Apostolic Fathers are the most significant documents in this category, including the Letters of Clement, the Letters of Ignatius of Antioch, the Letter of Barnabas, the Shepherd of Hermas, the Didache, and a few other minor works. First Clement, written from Rome to Corinth about 96 A.D., is especially significant because of its early date, standard teaching, and clear knowledge of at least four of Paul's letters. It

384

was, in fact, included in the New Testament canon by some of the early churches. In addition to the Apostolic Fathers, about a dozen more or less complete "apocryphal gospels" have survived of some forty known to have been written. One of the oldest and probably the most important is the Gospel of Thomas, a book of mixed value containing about a hundred sayings of Jesus. All of this literature should be considered carefully in a thorough investigation of Christian beginnings, but such a consideration will reveal the wisdom of the Church in its decision to close the canon at the end of the Apostolic era, marking a definite line between the word and time of the original Christians, the witnesses, and the opinions of those who came afterward. Historical distance always contributes to the dangers of confusion and distortion.

The two contemporary Jewish sources which refer to Jesus and the new sect are Josephus and the Babylonian Talmud. Josephus (c. 37-100 A.D.) was a Jewish historian who took part in the tragic war between Rome and the Jews of Palestine (66-70 A.D.). Afterwards he settled in Rome, where he was apparently befriended by the Flavian family. He wrote several historical and apologetic works which have survived, including the *Jewish War* and *Antiquities of the Jewish People*,, both attempting to explain the Jewish cause to the Romans. Two passages in the *Antiquities* refer to Jesus in a complimentary manner, but modern scholarship has revealed that the references may have been interpolated by later Christian editors. The references to Jesus in the Talmud are clearly prejudiced, containing an attempt to discredit Christianity by slandering its founder.

Three Roman writers from the early second century reveal a bare and poorly informed knowledge about Christian beginnings. Pliny the Younger, the governor of the province of Bithynia, wrote a letter to the Emperor Trajan, around 112 A.D., asking for advice concerning how to handle the small and apparently troublesome sect of Christians. Tacitus, the celebrated Roman historian, referred in his *Annals* (c. 115 A.D.) to the Christians who caused difficulties in Rome in the days of the despised Nero (c. 64 A.D.), and Tacitus was aware that the Christians were followers of a Jewish leader named "Christus" who had been executed by the procurator Pontius Pilate during the reign of Tiberius. And, finally, Seutonius, author of *The Lives of the Twelve Caesars (c. 120 A.D.)*, like Tacitus mentioned the sect of Christians who were punished under Nero. He also recorded the expulsion of Jews from Rome by Claudius because they had stirred up trouble under the influence of a certain "Chrestus," probably a reference to quarrels between orthodox Jews and Christians.

The New Testament, which Christians have added to the Hebrew Scriptures to complete their Bible, is composed of twenty-seven varied writings. They may be better understood and conveniently studied if placed in five separate categories. The first group is the ten letters which have been traditionally attributed to the Apostle Paul: Romans, 1 and 2 Corinthians, Galatians, Ephesians, Philippians, Colossians, 1 and 2 Thessalonians, and Philemon. Many modern scholars question the Pauline authorship of several of these, especially Ephesians and Colossians; but it is generally believed that all represent a position associated with the thought of Paul—the so-called Pauline Circle.

The second group is composed of the four Gospels and the Acts, the latter included because it was written by the author of Luke and is really a second volume of the same work. Matthew, Mark, Luke, and John bear a marked similarity, of course, in that they all contain accounts of the life of Jesus, with which we shall deal in some detail in the next chapter. However, modern research has shown that it is a mistake to read these simply as biographies, since they are more properly and profitably understood as basic theological documents of the early church. We shall also observe, below, that there are striking and significant differences between them, particularly between the first three and the fourth. Further, it is important to note that the Pauline materials provide us with an earlier account of Christian beginnings, belief, and practice than the four Gospels. Paul had written his letters and had been dead for several years (c. 64 A.D.) before the first Gospel (Mark) was completed (c. 70 A.D.)

The third category of New Testament writings is generally known as the Pastoral Letters: 1 and 2 Timothy and Titus. Tradition has assigned these to Paul, and they are indeed written as if they were advisory letters from the Apostle to two of his younger associates. Nevertheless, close attention to their ideas and terminology seems to indicate a date later than Paul. Writing in the name of a famous person was a common and accepted practice in antiquity, as we have seen earlier; and the church polity, especially, of these letters requires a period after Paul.

Eight writings designated the General Letters make up the fourth group. They are Hebrews, James, 1 and 2 Peter, 1, 2 and 3 John, and Jude. These books are quite varied in length, style, content, and value; and some of them probably would not have been included in the canon had it not been for the ancient and popular belief that they were written by Apostles. Second Peter is the most questionable book in the New Testament, incorporating most of the earlier Jude, and it is believed to have been written in the second century. The longer book of Hebrews is actually not a letter but a remarkable and valuable homily, warning against apostasy in the face of persecution and providing a profound discussion of Christian theology against the background of Judaism. First Peter also deals with the problem of persecution, which became increasingly severe toward the end of the first century, and it contains original material for understanding Christian ethics.

The last book in the Christian canon, Revelation, belongs to a category by itself. The original title is the Apocalypse, and that is its true genre. We have discussed earlier, at some length, the development and significance of this type of literature in early Judaism, and it is therefore not surprising that Christians should take up the same means for facing persecution and despair and for presenting their eschatological ideas. Revelation is a powerful and dramatic call to faithfulness, probably written during the tragic days of Domitian's persecution (c. 95 A.D.); and in the language familiar to Jewish apocalypticism it presents the final struggle between good and evil, the last judgment, and the certain victory of God and his people over all enemies, including sin and death.

### The Canonization of the New Testament

When Jesus and his earliest followers spoke of "the Scriptures," they meant, precisely, the Law (Torah) and the Prophets (Nebi'im). The third part of the Hebrew canon, the Writings (Kethubim), was not yet fully recognized, though such books as Psalms and Daniel were already revered and used. Hebrew was no longer a living language, even in Palestine, and the Scriptures in their original language could be read only by the trained scholars such as scribes and rabbis. The main literary language of the first century, used throughout the Roman world, was Greek, the language of all New Testament books. The Hebrew Scriptures had been translated into Greek during Ptolemaic times (c. 250 B.C.), and that version, the Septuagint, was the Bible of the Jews of the Diaspora and of the early Christians. It contained not only the 24 books of the Hebrew Scriptures but also the books of the Apocrypha, most of them originally composed in Greek. The rabbis of the academy of Jamnia in Palestine, about 90 A.D., finally defined the Scriptures as composed of just the 24 books of the Law, the Prophets, and the Writings, and that has been the canon of Judaism ever since. Christians, however, continued to use the Septuagint, including some of the books of the Apocrypha, until Protestants, beginning with Martin Luther, returned to Jewish usage.

Many details concerning the process by which the New Testament canon was fixed are unrecorded and unknown. However, the basic facts can be ferreted out, and the general process may be fairly surmised. For example, the authentic letters of Paul, written near the middle of the first century and therefore providing the earliest Christian testimony, show that the life and teaching of Jesus were already widely known within 30 years of his death. A scrutiny of Paul's writings reveals a surprising amount of information about Christian beginnings, including specific events from the life of Jesus and a large number of direct and indirect quotations of the words of Jesus. The gospel story was already taking precise form, at least in the oral tradition (cf. 1 Cor. 11:23ff.), and it is possible that written materials were being composed and circulated among the churches (cf. Luke 1:1).

The letters which Paul wrote to various churches were certainly preserved by them and copies were shared with other churches (cf. Colossians 4:16). It is therefore safe to assume that collections of Paul's writings were gathered and studied, beginning even during his lifetime. The writer of Second Peter, early in the second century, referred to several "letters" of Paul and even classified them as "scripture" (2 Peter 3:16). And several of the so-called Apostolic Fathers show a considerable familiarity with the Gospels as well as other New Testament books.

The first conscious attempt to create a definite Christian canon, as opposed even to the Hebrew Scriptures, was by Marcion. He came to Rome around 140 A.D. from Sinope, in the province of Pontus, with an exaggerated Christian teaching about the uniqueness of the gospel, based upon a misunderstanding of Paul's doctrine of grace relative to the Law. In support of his claims, which were widely accepted, Marcion gathered 10 of the letters of Paul and Luke-Acts, all of which he expurgated of any sympathetic references to the Hebrew Scriptures and the teachings of Judaism. He was soon condemned and excommunicated from the Church, but he had made a permanent contribution by establishing a specific Christian canon.

Eusebius, the Bishop of Caesarea, composed his famous *Ecclesiastical History* about 320 A.D., and in that classic work he discussed the growth and status of the canon up to his time. Most of the process of inclusion and exclusion was by then completed, though Eusebius revealed that some doubt still prevailed concerning a few books, including several of the General Letters and the Apocalypse. However, consensus was soon reached, and before the end of the fourth century the canon of twenty-seven books for the New Testament was firmly fixed in both the East and the West. The extant Festal Letter of the year 367, by Athanasius, Bishop of Alexandria, specified exactly the twenty-seven; and the same canon was approved by synods at Hippo Regius (393 A.D.) and Carthage (397 and 419 A.D.). The canon of the New Testament has remained unchanged since that time.

What was the basis of the decisions as to which books were to be accepted and which were to be excluded? We should take note that the process of canonization was just that—a process, taking place over a considerable period of time and without formal consultation or authoritative fiat. The growth of the Christian Scriptures was a gradual and living movement, a response to spiritual insight and theological need. From the perspective of faith, within the Church and by the Christians, the process would be explained as the guidance of the Spirit of God, preserving the Word of Truth and providing permanent standards for faith and practice to the People of God; and from the perspective of objective history, either by the believer or by the non-committed, the process would be understood as the natural response of the Church to its evangelistic, educational, and apologetic needs, especially as time passed, the Church grew, and difficult challenges arose.

From either point of view, at least four related factors controlled the process of selection. The dominant one was doubtless the claim to apostolicity. If it was believed that a book was written by one of the original Apostles (including Paul), or by a companion of the Apostles, the book was accepted as canonical. After all, these were the faithful witnesses to the life and teachings of Jesus. No more dependable source could be found for a knowledge of the true Gospel or for a decision between disputed opinions. On that basis all four of the Gospels were included, in spite of their variations: Matthew and John were believed to have been composed by Apostles, and Mark and Luke were dependable companions of

Peter and Paul. In the same way, the disputed books of Second Peter, James, and the Apocalypse could not be finally excluded.

Again, consistency with the Rule of Faith was a factor in selection. Confessions of faith and incipient creeds are evident in the earliest records of the Church (cf. 1 Cor. 12:3; Rom. 1:3f.; 10:10; Matt. 16:16). Baptismal formulas were developed of necessity, and these rapidly grew into short, easily remembered and repeated creeds which were used for initiation liturgy, and for defensive definition of belief. The best known of these creeds, of course, is the Apostles' Creed, a summary of the essential faith which probably dates from the early second century. The churches could easily determine the sound doctrine of a document by testing its teaching by the Apostolic Faith. This became especially crucial in the second century as the various forms of Gnosticism became a threat. Since the Gnostics claimed to be the true Christians, possessed of a saving knowledge (*gnosis*) revealed only to the elect, it became necessary for the Apostolic teaching to be made explicit as a certain means of countering the claims of the Gnostics. The Apostolic writings and the Apostolic creed successfully met that precise need.

A third factor influencing canonization was long usage. A writing that had stood the test of time was not likely to be cast aside, especially if it met the foregoing requirements. The Christian books which had survived the generations and had been found "profitable for teaching, for reproof, for correction, and for training in righteousness" (2 Timothy 3:16) would inevitably take on the aura of sanctity and be preserved and accepted.

Finally, consensus was an important factor in the process of inclusion and exclusion. The early Church sought unity of mind and spirit in all of its decisions, and frequently actions were taken only upon that basis. Prayer and discussion were often used as a means to discern the will of God and to decide matters of dispute (cf. Acts 1:24; 13:2; 15:6 ff.). Thus the Church sought both unity and catholicity—oneness of faith and universality of fellowship. The method of holding synods and councils has continued through the centuries. The known record of the process by which the New Testament came into fixed existence, sketched above, provides an important illustration of that Christian practice by which decisions were made by agreement of mind and spirit.

# Chapter 35

## *The Lives of Jesus*

Jesus of Nazareth was the founder of the Christian religion and he is the center of the Christian faith. Nevertheless, as we have stressed in the preceding chapter, Jesus was also a human person who lived in a particular place and in a specific time. Therefore the discipline of historical study and the literary category of biography apply to him in the same way that they are applicable to every other event and person. Christians have insisted from the beginnings and throughout the history of the Church that Jesus was human, whatever other claims might be made about him, and that to deny his full humanity is both historically inaccurate and theologically heretical.

It is due to this historical character of Christianity that the Gospels are the beginning and heart of the Christian Scriptures. As we have seen, the Christian message begins with a story, the proclaiming of an event, and then goes on to interpret and extrapolate the consequences of that story for life and thought. The Gospels are not myths; that is not their genre. They do not contain stories about the gods and their relations with one another in some super-mundane realm, even though, as we have seen, such stories may be useful for the expression of religious truth. Rather, the Gospels give their major attention to a series of events which, from the perspective of all recorded history, occurred within recent times, even in a well-known time and place. Indeed, the events to which the Gospels testify were said to have happened during the lifetime of many who first heard and read the stories, not in some imaginary land and hazy, pre-historic period. Believers ever since have confessed faith in the man Jesus who "was crucified under Pontius Pilate," the first-century Roman governor of Judea.

However, the Gospel story, in spite of its apparent simplicity and clarity, is also paradoxical because of the meaning and purpose which lie behind the story. It both reveals and conceals. The reader understands what happened, and he may have no great difficulty in accepting the accuracy and authenticity of the report. But immediately he may begin to ask why the story was recorded and why these precise events were remembered. He may wonder what other incidents occurred along with those which were reported, why just these were transmitted, and in this particular form. After all, history is not the events of the past. It is rather the *record of some* remembered events of the past; and the record is the product of selection, memory, interpretation, and transmission. Thus the Gospels must be read as more than mere history and biography; they are also purposeful and meaningful theology, intended to convey truths of eternal value.

## The Gospel and the Gospels

One of the obvious questions that arise naturally from a reading or hearing of the story of Jesus of Nazareth is why there are four canonical Gospels instead of one. There is only one Gospel but there are four Gospels; and there are additional details from the story of Jesus which may be found in the writings of the Apostle Paul, preceding the Gospels, as well as in other parts of the New Testament. The answer to the question may be discovered by a study of the way in which the traditions were transmitted and finally recorded.

What is the essential *euangelion* (good news, gospel) which all the records report? The evidence indicates that Jesus lived during approximately the first third of the first century. Further, the records are concerned almost exclusively with the brief period of his active ministry, which lasted for possibly as little as one year and certainly not more than three and one-half years. Since he was born shortly before the death of Herod the Great, which occurred in 4 B.C., it is generally agreed that he was born in 6 or 5 B.C. and that he died about A.D. 28. He was born in Bethlehem of Judea, of Galilean parents whose lineage could be traced both to the royal house of David and to the priestly family of Aaron. He grew up in Nazareth, in Galilee, and very little is recorded concerning him until he was about the age of thirty, at which time he was baptized in the Jordan River by his kinsman, the new Jewish prophet, John the Baptist. Following that decisive event he began a popular career of teaching, preaching, and healing, mostly in his native territory of Galilee. Many of the Jewish leaders, especially the priestly class, opposed his work and claims; and, finally, when he visited Jerusalem for the celebration of the Passover, he was arrested, convicted of blasphemy, and executed by Roman crucifixion. His followers claimed that he arose from the tomb on the third day after his death, that he appeared alive to numerous witnesses during forty days, and that he ascended into the heavens as they watched on the Mt. of Olives, outside the walls of Jerusalem.

These are the barest facts of the Gospel story. They became the foundation for the message which the disciples of Jesus began to proclaim immediately after the ascension. Many other elements of the story were added to this foundation, and soon a fixed and formalized pattern began to appear. The basic facts as they were known and believed controlled the developing structure of the Gospel, of course, but the numerous details that embellished the framework were added in the oral tradition according to the needs of the growing community of believers.

Let us take note that this approach to New Testament study is largely the fruit of twentieth-century scholarship. It is called, in German, *formgeschichte*, the study of the history of the formation of the tradition, or Form Criticism. The method has been used also in the study of the Hebrew Scriptures, particularly the Psalms, as well as in the scholarly criticism of other literature. Among the chief originators and practioners of this useful method are the Germans Hermann Gunkel, Martin Dibelius, and Rudolf Bultmann; the Englishman Vincent Taylor; and the American F. C. Grant. Using this method, these and many other scholars have sought to penetrate behind the written Gospels and the recorded testimony and commentary of the other portions of the New Testament, in order, insofar as possible, to discover what the oral tradition was and how it was developed into the form in which it finally appeared in the written materials. The effort has borne much good fruit and produced more success than would have appeared to be possible.

One primary perception of Form Criticism has been that the Gospels are composed of small units (pericopes) of material which were probably separate and distinct in the oral tradition about Jesus during the earliest days of the Church. Each pericope was the result of the recalling and retelling of a particular incident or teaching from the life of Jesus in response to the evangelistic, teaching, or organizational requirements which constantly arose in the formation and growth of the Christian community. Frequently, no doubt, similar pericopes were used together when they would support or illustrate specific themes being discussed or rituals being celebrated. Such clustering of traditions, in oral form, was probably the first step taken in the process which finally produced the written Gospels. For example, when a Christian preacher or teacher was speaking concerning the Kingdom of God—the central theme of the teaching of Jesus—he would be expected to repeat some of the parables of Jesus on that subject. When new converts were being baptized, the story of the baptism of Jesus would be recalled. And when the Lord's Supper, or Eucharist, was celebrated, the familiar account of its institution would be retold (cf. I Cor. 11:23-26).

This primary period of oral tradition lasted for a full generation, that is, from the death of Jesus until the final writing of the Gospels during the last third of the first century. The accounts of the life and teachings of Jesus no doubt were clustered into indentifiable types. Scholars such as Vincent Taylor have defined the types as parables, pronouncement stories, miracle stories, sayings, wonder stories, paradigms, and others. The story of the Passion, composed of various sub-units, clearly became the longest and dominant portion of the tradition.

The collection of pericopes and of clusters of similar pericopes finally led, inevitably, to the composition of more or less complete accounts of the life of Jesus. The earliest one that we know was probably the Gospel of Mark, composed near A.D. 70. It may have had an earlier, briefer form. There appears to have been in circulation also, in more or less fixed form, a collection of the words or teachings of Jesus, sometimes referred to as the Logia. And, in addition, there must have been other identifiable collections of gospel material, each with its own special characteristics and concerns.

The final result of the whole process may be seen in the kerygmatic materials in the letters of Paul, in the four Gospels, in the similar materials of other parts of the New Testament, and in the less dependable references to the life and teachings of Jesus found in the non-canonical literature of the late first and early second centuries.

### The Synoptic Gospels

Matthew, Mark, and Luke bear a marked similarity, as distinguished from John. For that reason the three are called the Synoptic Gospels—they see the life of Jesus from approximately the same point of view. Yet they are different from each other; each has its own distinctive style and, to some degree, content. The result is what is known as the Synoptic Problem: how may we best account for both the similarities and differences between the first three Gospels?

The ancient and obvious answer to the question would seem to be that they are similar because they treat the same subject out of the same tradition and they are different because they were composed by different authors in separate times and places, each choosing his own materials and pursuing his own special purpose. That simple explanation is probably indisputable, but it does not exhaust the possible solutions. Additional opinions were expressed even by some of the early Fathers of the Church, such as Origen of Alexandria and Augustine of Hippo. The latter taught, for example, that Mark composed an abridged version of Matthew. And modern scholars have developed seveal theories which propose to solve the problem. All of the theories are based upon certain assumptions concerning the sources of the three Gospels, and how those sources were used by the three Evangelists.

The most widely accepted theory is based upon ideas first made explicit by B. H. Streeter, a British New Testament scholar, in his book *The Four Gospels: A Study of Origins*, first published in 1924. The theory has been altered and refined by many others since it first appeared; yet it supplies the most cogent explanation and satisfactory answer to the problem. In essence, the theory identifies four main sources behind the three Gospels. The four sources are designated as the Markan material, Q, M, and L. Mark, probably the first written Gospel, contains a brief account of the ministry of Jesus, beginning with his baptism and concluding with his resurrection appearances. Matthew and Luke both had access to Mark, at least in some early form, and they used it as the framework for their accounts, altering it to suit their materials and purposes. In addition, there was already in circulation a collection of the teachings of Jesus (the Logia) which may never have been in a universally fixed form. German scholars have called this collection "the Source" (*Quelle*), and thus it is designated "Q." The author of Matthew also took from the traditions available to him a variety known together as "M," Matthew's special source; and in like manner, Luke (cf. Luke 1:1-4) used a large number of pericopes which are found only in his Gospel and hence are called "L."

Thus there were four distinct sources, or collections of early Gospel material, which were used variously by the three Evangelists: Mark, Q, M, and L. The fact that all three have in common, to a considerable degree, the account of the ministry of Jesus found in Mark explains adequately the similarity between them; and the fact that Matthew and Luke appear to have used the common material designated as Q is a further explanation of their kinship. On the other hand, Matthew and Luke are clearly different from Mark and from each other because each uses distinctive sources found nowhere else.

This widely-accepted four-source theory provides an interesting study of the inter-dependence and composition of the Synoptic Gospels. However, it is only the basis for a further analysis of the content of the Gospels which can throw additional light on the intention of the authors as well as the faith of the early community. That is to say, a scrutiny of each of the four separate sources reveals that each has a radically distinctive character. They are like tessera of four different colors which were used to create three varied mosaics of the same face.

As we have said, Mark is the shortest of the Gospels, containing a terse narrative of the career of Jesus from the baptism to the resurrection. It frequently uses the word "immediately" to proceed rapidly from one scene to another, and the reader gets the impression that he is seeing a marvelous slide show, composed of clear and brightly colored pictures from the active life of Jesus, the whole designed as a call for acceptance and faith. There is relatively little sound—few teachings, discourses, and parables. The terminology and style suggest that the Gospel was written to be read and understood by Romans. The over-all purpose seems to be the evangelizing of Gentiles.

On the other hand, the "Q" material is almost entirely the sayings of Jesus, though a small amount of narrative is included also. The most familiar portion from this source is the Sermon on the Mount, a collection of the teachings of Jesus specifically concerned with the character and action of the disciple within the Kingdom of God. This special body of teachings is found in the form of a single address in Matthew 5-7, but the same material is varied and scattered in Luke.

The collection of pericopes found only in Matthew, and thus denoted "M," reveal a special concern with the Jewish background and identification of Jesus. He is presented as the promised Messiah, descended from both Abraham and David; and many events in his life are interpreted as the fulfillment of prophecy. Matthew begins with a genealogy of Jesus and then records three pericopes about the birth and infancy, all clearly designed to support the claim of authentic Messiahship.

Luke, on the other hand, is more Gentile-oriented and displays a universal interest. The special infancy narratives in "L" are different from those in "M," though both claim that Jesus was born of the Virgin Mary, having been conceived by the Holy Spirit. Luke also displays a particular concern with the poor, the outcast, and the sinner; and Luke has a special delight in reporting the parables of Jesus, including the ones about the Good Samaritan and the Prodigal Son, two of the best loved parables which are found in no other source. Luke contains one long section, 9:51-19:27, which records a series of events related to the final journey of Jesus and his disciples from Galilee to Jerusalem, by way of Samaria and Perea.

## The Gospel of John

The Gospel of John is so different from the Synoptic Gospels in both form and content that Christians have frequently considered the Synoptics to be more historical and biographical and John to be more spiritual and theological. The differences are indeed too obvious to be denied; nevertheless, there are many essential similarities also, and the historical basis of John is just as apparent to the careful reader as is the theological structure and purpose of the Synoptics. There are significant differences also between the Synoptics, as we have just observed, and all four Gospels are fundamentally the same Gospel, the Good News of what God has done in Jesus of Nazareth.

Unlike Matthew and Luke, John provides no account of the birth and childhood of Jesus. Instead, this Gospel begins with a discussion of the eternal Logos, whom it identifies with God himself. John lays his foundation for the telling of the life of Jesus by presenting a prologue about the pre-existent Logos, the source of light, life, and all creation; and then he proceeds, in the main body of his Gospel, to give an account of the earthly career of the Incarnated Logos. He claims that Jesus of Nazareth was a human being who lived and worked in a certain time and place, just as the Synoptics had reported; but he goes much further than they by claiming that this same Jesus was really the infinite made finite, the Son of God who "was made man" and dwelled among men, even dying as a slain lamb of sacrifice for the redemption of all mankind.

The structural differences between John and the Synoptics are many and striking. For example, the Synoptics imply that the ministry of Jesus lasted for only about a year, since they mention only one Passover during his active career; but John suggests that there were three Passovers and thus at least three years. Again, the Synoptics suggest that most of Jesus' work was in Galilee and that he met his death when he finally went to Judea and Jerusalem, presumably to celebrate the Passover and consciously to die. John, on the other hand, indicates that a large proportion of the ministry took place in Judea, to which Jesus went on several occasions prior to the last, fateful trip. The Synoptics place Jesus' attack on the Temple desecraters in the chronology of the last week, suggesting that such a direct challenge of the priests precipitated their decision to seek his death; but John puts the cleansing of the Temple at an early point during the ministry. John makes clear that the raising of Lazarus from the dead, which the Synoptics do not record, was the event which sealed the fate of Jesus. Further, John presents no parables of Jesus, although they abound in the Synoptics, especially in Luke. John rather records several long discourses of Jesus to the disciples and to others, grouping most of them as though they were delivered in the last days and hours of his life (cf. John 14-17).

On the other hand, the similarities between John and the Synoptics are so fundamental and numerous that they should not be overlooked. After all, John does give an account of the life and teachings of the same Jesus of Nazareth of whom the Synoptics speak. The character, the beliefs, the attitudes, the message of Jesus are essentially the same, as are the other personalities and the places of the drama. Furthermore, many of the incidents of the ministry are the same, even though usually in a different order: the baptism by John the Baptist, the cleansing of the Temple, the feeding of the multitude, the quieting of the storm, the anointing by a woman, the messianic entry to Jerusalem, the Last Supper, the arrest, trial, mocking, crucifixion, and resurrection. It is the same biography and historical account, though told in another style and with an alternate structure.

The literary structure and simple language of the Fourth Gospel are fitted perfectly to its central theme, the incarnation of the Logos, the temporal sojourn of the eternal. The little book is composed of two major parts, preceded by a brief prologue and concluded with an epilogue. The prologue (1:1-18), echoes the Torah ("In the beginning...") and relates the Christian message to the familiar Hellenistic concept of the Logos (cf. Heraclitus, Plato, the Stoics, Philo). Then it quickly introduces the heart of the Christian claim by the shocking assertion: "And the Logos became flesh and dwelt among us, full of grace and truth; and we have beheld his glory, glory as of the only Son from the Father" (1:14). It says that the Logos in the flesh was the man announced by John the Baptist. The remainder of the book is about him, Jesus of Nazareth—his deeds, words, and significance.

The first half of the Gospel, beginning after the short but determinative prologue, has been called the Book of Signs (1:19-12:50). That designation is derived from the seven mighty works, called miracles in the Synoptics, around which John recounts the public ministry of Jesus. John calls them "signs," meaning that they were dramatic actions of Jesus (cf. the Hebrew prophets) pointing to his identity and purpose. The truth is revealed through personality by both words and significant deeds. There is a noteworthy progression in the account of the signs, beginning with a challenge of the adequacy of ritualistic Judaism and reaching a climax in the raising of Lazarus, which provoked the enemies of Jesus to plot his death. The signs, which require careful analysis for a full appreciation of their meaning, are as follows: (1) the transformation of water into wine (2:1-11); (2) the healing of the son of an official in Capernaum of Galilee (4:46-54); (3) the healing of the cripple by the pool in Jerusalem (5:2-9); (4) the feeding of the five thousand (6:4-14); (5) the walking on the sea to meet the disciples (6:16-21); (6) the healing of the blind man in Jerusalem (9:1-41); and (7) the raising of Lazarus (11:1-53).

The second half of the Gospel is called the Book of the Passion (13:1-20:31). It tells of the last days in Jerusalem before the crucifixion, including several of the lengthy discourses to the disciples. Then it gives an account of the arrest, trial, and execution, supplementing the Synoptic record; and in a few puzzling cases John appears to disagree on some details of the story (e.g., was the crucifixion on the day of Passover or the day before?). John is particularly harsh in his accusation of guilt against the priests, and even against "the Jews" in general. He also presents a fascinating account of the confrontation between Pontius Pilate and Jesus. He brings the story to a conclusion, as do the Synoptics, with the central event of the resurrection and the appearances of the risen Christ to the women and to the disciples. The purpose of the book is stated in 20:30, 31, suggesting the intended conclusion: "Now Jesus did many other signs in the presence of the disciples, which are not written in this book; but these are written that you may believe that

Jesus is the Christ, the Son of God, and that believing you may have life in his name."

However, the final chapter (21) forms an epilogue, perhaps added as an afterthought by the original author or supplemented out of the tradition by an editor. It records a final appearance of Jesus to seven of the disciples "by the Sea of Tiberias" (Galilee) during which Jesus reminded Peter of his three-fold denial at the time of the trial and then commissioned him, and all of them, to continue his work of redemption.

### The Continuing Search

The four canonical Gospels provide most of what is known about the life and teachings of Jesus. A small amount of additional information may be gleaned from other sources, especially the writings of Paul, but most is repetitive or interpretative. The figure of Jesus has remained central in the faith of his followers through the succeeding centuries, but the memory and knowledge have been derived in the main from "the apostolic lives of Jesus," the canonical Gospels.

Although the history of Jesus was thus preserved and transmitted by the Christian community, and though the truths were constantly depicted by word, ritual, festival, and art, the historical interest was gradually replaced by a theological concern. The attention of the Church turned, even as early as the second century, to the meaning of Jesus Christ in doctrinal expression. Attempts were made by many of the great teachers to explain the Person and nature of Jesus the Christ. How was he related, ontologically, to the one God? What did it mean to refer to him as the Son of the Father? Was this a retreat to pagan polytheism? And, if he was in some sense the same being as the Father—as the Church finally declared at Nicea in A.D. 325—then what of his humanity? What about him was divine and what was human, and how were the "two natures" related and preserved? That question finally received an orthodox answer at the Council of Chalcedon in A.D. 451: he was fully God and fully man, one Person but in two natures. That has remained the normative Christology of Christendom ever since.

Thus through the Middle Ages and into modern times the tendency has been to accept the ancient lives of Jesus as a basis for faith and knowledge, but the major concern has been with dogma and mystical, sacramental experience. On the other hand, the

Crusades were in part the result of a renewed interest in the historical Jesus, the land where he lived, and the recovering of relics; and the Renaissance in western Europe involved a return to antiquity, to sources, to the historical and human. With the bursting forth of the Enlightenment in the 17th and 18th centuries, new questions began to be raised about the nature, accuracy, and meaning of the Gospels. Could modern, enlightened, reasonable men any longer believe the naive and primitive reports and opinions of the ancients, especially when they wrote uncritically on the basis of religious faith? Is it not necessary to search the records in order to remove the mythical, the unreasonable and the unscientific?

The result of such attitudes and questions has been the modern "search for the historical Jesus" and the tendency on the part of many to attempt to separate the historical Jesus from the dogmatic Christ of faith. One of the first to write a critique of the Gospels, with a view to expurgating the mythical and unscientific so as to find "the real Jesus," was the German scholar, Hermann Samuel Reimarus (1694-1768). He wrote a famous document known as "The Aims of Jesus and His Disciples," which was published after the death of Reimarus by the philosopher Lessing. A flood of similar attempts to update the Gospels followed, especially by such well-known critics as David Friedrich Strauss, D. F. E. Schleiermacher, Ernest Renan, and Wilhelm Wrede.

In 1906, Albert Schweitzer published his epoch-making *From Reimarus to Wrede*, later given the English title *The Quest of the Historical Jesus*, in which the great scholar reviewed the previous century's work and pronounced the search a failure. He persuaded most of his readers that it is impossible to go behind the record to see the face of Jesus in direct and accurate encounter. The mystery remains impenetrable. We must read the Gospels as best we can, but faith cannot finally be made dependent on the accuracy of historical information.

Since the Second World War a new attempt has been pursued to discover the historical Jesus. The effort has been made in various ways by such students of the New Testament as Rudolf Bultmann, Ernest Kasemann, James M. Robinson, Ernst Fuchs, Gunter Bornkamm, and Norman Perrin. They have developed new methods, such as *formgeschichte*, and new tools, such as the theories of structuralism. The task will probably never be completed and the challenge is constantly renewed.

The Lives of Jesus, the Gospels, remain as fundamental classics and sources of Western culture because their primary subject, the enigmatic figure of Jesus of Nazareth, has dominated the minds and spirits of ever-increasing multitudes since the days he walked upon the earth.

# Chapter 36

# The Philosophy of Jesus

Jesus of Nazareth was brought up in the province of Galilee. As a boy, he spoke Aramaic, the common language of the region, he apparently was able to read Hebrew, and it is reasonable to suppose that he knew some Greek. He was brought up in a home with other children. The only specific events of his childhood mentioned in the Gospels are the accounts of his birth and early infancy in Matthew and Luke and the story of his visit to Jerusalem at the age of twelve. After being found by his parents in the temple on that occasion, "he went down with them," according to Luke, "and came to Nazareth, and was obedient to them.... And Jesus increased in wisdom and in stature, and in favor with God and man" (2:51-52).

The Scriptures tell nothing more of his life before "the fifteenth year of the reign of Tiberius Caesar, Pontius Pilate being governor of Judea and Herod being tetrarch of Galilee, and his brother Philip tetrarch of the region of Ituraea and Trachonitis, and Lysanias tetrarch of Abilene, in the high-priesthood of Annas and Caiaphas" (Luke 3:1-2). At that precisely specified time, Jesus, by then a grown man, was baptized by John the Baptist, fasted in the wilderness, and began his public career. That career, a ministry of teaching and healing, described from different points of view by the writers of the four Gospels, apparently lasted about three years, during which the thought of Jesus was communicated to his disciples and the crowds that flocked to hear him. Like Socrates, he left no books, and we are dependent on later writings for all that we know of his philosophy.

The word *philosophy*, though freely applied to the work of Christian thinkers, is rarely associated with Jesus himself. The devout avoid such an association out of a feeling that is might suggest a reliance on human experience and reason on the part of a personage whom they regard as more than human. The less devout hesitate to contaminate the supposed purity of a speculative and independent intellectual activity by attaching its name to a body of "religious" teaching.

Neither of these objections has much substance. Whatever may be said of the person of Jesus from a theological standpoint, the Church has, throughout its entire history, affirmed that he was a man, growing in wisdom, tempted like other men, and subject to doubt. Every attempt to define his divinity in such a way as to diminish the fullness of his humanity has properly been rejected as heretical. Nor should he be considered simply as a "religious" figure. He was not an ecclesiastic, and there is not the slightest evidence that he was any more attentive to the rites and ceremonies of the faith of his people than were Socrates and Cicero to those in honor of the Olympians. He was religious in the sense that all philosophers are who recognize God as the source and center of all reality. He was philosophical in the sense that everyone is who is passionately addicted to truth and concerned with every aspect of human life.

A third objection might be urged that the teachings of Jesus cannot be classified as philosophy because they are not "systematic." If it is meant that they were not laid out in the manner thought proper for academic lectures or publication in scholarly monographs, the charge may be admitted, but it does not carry its point. Plato's "system" is embedded in accounts of informal conversations in which poetry, myth, allegory, and homely references to everyday experience abound. Aphorisms, having no explicit connection with one another, have been the stock in trade of many philosophers from Heraclitus to Wittgenstein. It is true that the work of some of the Greek philosophers was architectonic in character. Aristotle readily comes to mind as an example. But the underlying structure of Jesus' thought is no less evident because of his use of a rich variety of less formal modes of expression.

It has been suggested that a coherent account of his teaching is impossible because of our dependence on narratives written years after the fact by men with axes to grind. Especial weight has been given to the differences between the Synoptic Gospels and the Fourth Gospel, which some critics have treated as if it were nothing more than a biographical novel serving the author's didactic purpose. It should be evident to any fair-minded person, however, that all biographies reflect the personalities of the biographers and that in spite of the ways in which the Gospels differ from one another, they present a compelling and coherent picture of a personality greater than that of the writers. If John was more inclined than the others to stress Jesus' claim to identity with the source of truth, he was simply emphasizing an element of his teaching which was undeniably present in the oral tradition and acknowledged by the Synoptic writers. If one is more interested in the general nature of Jesus' philosophy, then, than in the minutiae of textual analysis, it is not unreasonable simply to take the accounts as seriously as they were taken by the first and second century Christians for whom they were written.

### Knowledge and Reality

Like other influential philosophical systems of the period, Jesus' teachings were, in the broad sense, ethically oriented, but the soundness of any moral position is dependent on its consistency with a defensible conception of ultimate reality and a reasonable account of the way in which it may be known.

The word *know* was often on Jesus' lips. To his Jewish followers, he promised, "If you continue in my word, you are my disciples, and you will know the truth, and the truth will make you free." The freedom promised was not the absence of external restraints, but liberation from the bondage of sin. The sort of new life envisioned in the promise is inseparably bound up with a certain sort of knowledge, the nature of which is suggested by Jesus' frequent references to light. Just as light in the physical world makes perception of objects possible, so there is a spiritual illumination which the writer of the Fourth Gospel called "the true light that enlightens every man" (John 1:9) and identified as the *Logos* of Greek philosophy, the rational ground of the world. The burden of John's book is that "the *Logos* became flesh and dwelt among us" (John 1:14) in the person of Jesus of Nazareth, and a number of statements are attributed to Jesus to show that he so identified himself. "I am the light of the world," he said, "he who follows me will not walk in darkness, but will have the light of life." And again, "I am the way, the truth, and the life." The light, however, is illuminating only for those whose eyes are open to it. "The eye is the light of the body," Matthew's Gospel reports Jesus as saying, "but if your eye is not sound, your whole body will be full of darkness. If then the light in you is darkness, how great is the darkness."

The sort of self-induced ignorance which defies enlightenment has moral implications. "This is the judgment," he said, "that light has come into the world and men loved darkness rather than light, because their deeds were evil." To illustrate the point, Jesus supplemented the metaphor of vision with that of audition. "He who has ears to hear, let him hear," he said, and it is clear that he was speaking of something beyond mere sensation, as the parable of the sower and the seed which preceded the remark makes clear. Any revelation of truth is dependent not only on the power of the revealer and the authenticity of the revelation but the quality of the recipient as well. Jesus' description of the state of those who close their eyes and ears to the truths of the spirit is reminiscent of the reaction of the occupants of Plato's cave when they are confronted with news of a sunlit world. If you throw pearls before swine, Jesus suggested in another vivid figure of speech, they will trample them and attack you.

Becoming sensitive to the realm of the spirit is a process of rebirth, he said in his conversation with the Pharisee Nicodemus; and when his disciples asked him who should be the greatest in the kingdom of heaven, he called a child to him and said, "Truly I say to you, unless you turn and become like children, you will never enter the kingdom of heaven." In Jesus' approach to knowledge, as in the other aspects of his teaching, those words, "the kingdom of heaven" or "the kingdom of God" provided the central theme. In representing himself as a embodiment of truth, he was careful to make it clear that he was not claiming arbitrary authority for the man Jesus. "How is it that this man has learning, when he has never studied?" the Jews asked. "My teaching is not mine, but his who sent me," Jesus explained. "If any man's will is to do his will, he shall know whether the teaching is from God or whether I am speaking on my own authority." In the same discussion, he enjoined his hearers, "Do not judge by appearances, but judge with right judgment."

Standing before Pontius Pilate in the praetorium, he again affirmed that truth is recognizable to those whose lives have prepared them to receive it. "For this I was born and for this I have come into the world, to bear witness to the truth," he said. "Every one who is of the truth hears my voice."

"What is truth?" the skeptical Roman asked, ending the confrontation.

Given a hearing, Jesus might have answered him as he had answered so many others, that the truth is discovered only by those willing to let themselves be made subjects of the kingdom of heaven. The only sin which cannot be forgiven—presumably because the one who commits it steadfastly refuses to recognize the need for forgiveness—is that persistent closing of the mind to truth which is what he must have meant by "the blasphemy against the Spirit."

Truth and knowledge are grounded in God, who is the creator and orderer of the universe. Like the Stoics, Jesus saw natural law as operating in the world on both the physical and moral planes. "When you see a cloud rising in the west," he said, "you say at once, 'A shower is coming'; and so it happens. And when you see the south wind blowing, you say, 'There will be scorching heat'; and it happens. You hypocrites! You know how to interpret the appearance of earth and sky; but why do you not know how to interpret the present time?" Moral law is just as certain and predictable as physical law, and both are subject to the providence of God. The physical world is not, however, designed to provide automatic reward for virtue and punishment for vice. God "makes his sun rise on the evil and on the good, and sends rain on the just and on the unjust." God is not the captive of laws operating outside of his control, but rather their author and administrator. Nothing in nature is too minute to be worthy of his attention. Sparrows are sold two for a denarius, but no sparrow can fall to the ground without God's knowledge and consent. A human being, who is of more value than many sparrows, can be confident that the hairs of his head are numbered and that he is an object of God's concern.

## The Kingdom and The Good Life

When Jesus was asked what he regarded as the great commandment in the Law, he replied, "You shall love the Lord your God with all your heart, and with all your soul and with all your mind. This is the great and first commandment. And a second is like it, you shall love your neigbor as yourself. On these two commandments depend all the law and the prophets." The entire system of ethical obligation, then, rests on a command to love. If it is interpreted as imposing an obligation to feel an emotion, one who attempts to keep the law is confronted by a virtually impossible task and is doomed to self-deception or an acknowledgment of failure. One can legitimately be commanded to act in certain ways, however, and actions, in turn, are productive of traits of character which may result in appropriate emotions. Jesus, in naming the love of God as the first essential, was recognizing that without a commitment of the heart, the soul, and the mind—the seats of feeling, will, and intelligence—to a trans-empirical ground of obligation, there can be no rational basis for a normative ethic.

The second commandment defines the sphere of moral activity. Jesus made it clear, by teaching and personal example, that the word *neighbor* was, for him, much broader in its extension than popular moral thought would have it, and he expanded the requirements of the injunction even further. "You have heard that it was said, 'You shall love your neighbor and hate your enemy,' " he said, "But I say to you, Love your enemies and pray for those who persecute you."

How can one love the unlovable? The answer is contained in the commandment. They are to be loved as oneself. One loves oneself properly by desiring what is really best for oneself, and true self-love is quite compatible with a hearty detestation of habits and character traits which deface the self. Love for oneself or for others, in the sense that it can be morally required, does not necessarily involve admiration, desire, indulgence, or even liking. What is demanded is an unflagging concern on the part of every human being for his or her own good and the good of others. That concern is the identifying characteristic of the kingdom of heaven.

What is the nature of that good? In essence, it is the happiness or well-being at which philosophy aims, and it has many ingredients. Some of them are associated with pleasure, for Jesus, while not condemning those who for good reason lived by a rigorously ascetic regimen, did not adopt such a mode of life himself or require it of others. He was keenly sensitive to beauty, and his obvious enjoyment of the pleasures of the table clearly caused some of his devout compatriots to question his sanctity. "For John came neither eating nor drinking," he said, speaking for his kinsman, John the Baptist, "and they say, 'He has a demon'; the Son of man came eating and drinking, and they say, 'Behold, a glutton and a drunkard, a friend of tax collectors and sinners!' Yet wisdom is justified by her deeds."

Recognizing the proper place of pleasure in life, he was, nevertheless, an uncompromising foe of hedonism. When the rich man in one of his parables stored up enough goods to last a lifetime and said to his soul, "Soul, you have ample goods laid up for many years; take your ease, eat, drink, be merry." God's response was swift and devastating. "Fool! this night your soul is required of you: and the things you have prepared, whose will they be?" Material things, Jesus thought, have their place, and God is aware that men need them, but they must not be made the main end of one's life. With what has been called an attitude of aristocratic carelessness, he held up the lilies of the field and the birds of the air as examples of species which enjoy the bounties of nature without worry about the future. "Therefore," he continued, "do not be anxious, saying, 'What shall we eat?' or 'What shall we drink?' or 'What shall we wear?' for the Gentiles seek all these things; and your heavenly Father knows that you need them all. But seek first his kingdom and his righteousness and all these things shall be yours as well. Therefore do not be anxious about tomorrow will be anxious for itself. Let the day's own trouble be sufficient for the day."

The physical world is a source of evil, then, only when it absorbs one's efforts to such an extent that higher concerns are neglected. Material things are useful servants but poor masters. "You cannot serve God and mammon," and it profits a man nothing "if he gains the whole world and loses or forfeits himself." The standards of the world are not the standards by which God judges. Tax collectors and harlots may go into the kingdom of God before the chief priests and elders, and the Pharisees, the most vigorous defenders of the complexities of the Law, are "blind guides, straining out a gnat and swallowing a camel!"

This last remark reveals a sense of humor frequently overlooked in treatments of Jesus' thought. The image of an ungainly beast like a camel being forced through an impossibly small opening obviously amused him, and he used it in another form when a rich young man came to him asking what it was necessary for him to do to have eternal life.

"Why do you ask me about what is good?" Jesus responded. "One there is who is good. If you would enter life, keep the commandments." The young man asked which commandments, and Jesus cited five of the ten delivered at Sinai and the injunction to love one's neighbor as oneself.

"All these I have observed," the young man said. "What still do I lack?"

"If you would be perfect," Jesus told him, "go, sell what you possess and give it to the poor, and you will have treasure in heaven; and come, follow me."

We are told that the young man left in sorrow and that Jesus remarked to his disciples that "it is easier for a camel to go through the eye of a needle than for a rich man to enter the kingdom of God."

The story is one of the prime examples cited in support of two theories designed to make Jesus' ethic less alarming. One holds that such an impossibly high standard must have been intended as an interim ethic for disciples expecting an imminent end of the age. The other holds more simply that his moral principles, while inspirational, are not intended for everyday application. With reference to the first, there is not the slightest evidence that his conception of the good life owed anything at all to any question he may have had about the probable duration of human history. The kingdom of God, as he described it in a host of similes and parables, is, in essence, present in the world as it is in heaven. For the second, it is clear that Jesus meant for his standards to be taken very seriously indeed. To be sure, they are impossibly high, in the sense that, as the rich young man discovered, in the world, no level of moral development that can be anticipated is so high that it cannot be higher, and every increase in moral sensitivity reveals shortcomings not previously recognized. Jesus removed all doubt on this score when he said, "You, therefore, must be perfect, as your heavenly father is perfect," setting a goal which is beyond human imagination.

Is everyone, then, doomed to suffer the fate of Tantalus, with admission to the kingdom of heaven a prize forever held just beyond the reach of those who hunger and thirst for it? This would, it seems, certainly be the case if men were under the necessity of becoming perfect merely by the exercise of their own wills. However much he may have alarmed his hearers, however, Jesus was clearly not preaching a gospel of perpetual frustration. "Who then can be saved?" his disciples asked him after hearing his discouraging remark about the camel and the eye of the needle. Jesus looked at them and said, "With men this is impossible, but with God all things are possible."

This acceptance by God of imperfect men is the good news which Jesus gave his followers. It in no sense excuses any relaxation of one's effort to move toward the required perfection. However inconceivable the ultimate goal may be, the next step required of anyone may be quite clear, and God is happy to accept that step as an earnest of one's intent. Jesus went around offering forgiveness and acceptance to an unlikely assortment of misfits, reserving his denunciation for those who were morally paralyzed by the conviction that they were already perfect. "Two men went up into the temple to pray," he said, "one a Pharisee and the other a tax collector. The Pharisee stood and prayed thus with himself. 'God, I thank thee that I am not like other men, extortioners, unjust, adulterers, or even like this tax collector. I fast twice a week, I give tithes of all that I get.' But the tax collector, standing far off, would not even lift up his eyes to heaven, but beat his breast, saying, 'God be merciful to me a sinner.' I tell you, this man went down to his house justified rather than the other; for every one who exalts himself will be humbled, but he who humbles himself will be exalted."

For Jesus, as for Aristotle, happiness is, in the last analysis, defined in terms of character. It is not a static state, but a state of purposive action. One's resources are to be put to use and not, as in the case of the unwise servant in the parable of the talents, left unused. Character is not a matter of ritual observance. Challenging the Jewish dietary laws, Jesus announced that men are defiled not by what goes into them, but by what comes out. Inner virtue and outward conduct go hand in hand, and the Pharisees were advised to "cleanse the inside of the cup and of the plate, that the outside also may be clean." The fulfillment of the law must be found in the inner life of the individual, and its outward observance must be flexible enough to serve human needs. Man was not made for the Sabbath, but rather the Sabbath for man. Certain sorts of outward action are specifically demanded, however, as expressions of the love for one's neighbor. The hungry must be fed. The thirsty must be given drink. The naked must be clothed. The sick or imprisoned must be visited. The stranger must be received.

In the "Sermon on the Mount," Jesus specified several classes of people who, by virtue of their possession of certain traits of character, may in some sense be considered as happy or blessed: the poor in spirit, those who mourn, the meek, those who hunger and thirst for righteousness, the merciful, the pure in heart, the peacemakers, and those who are persecuted for the sake of righteousness.

The poor in spirit may appear to be unlikely prospects for happiness until it is remembered that they are more likely to be those who hunger and thirst for righteousness than are those whose real needs are masked by riches of any kind. The happiness of those who are persecuted for righteousness' sake is clearly a result of the righteousness and not of the persecution. The merciful, the pure in heart, and the peacemakers are obviously entitled to admission to the ranks of the blessed. Perhaps the greatest source of puzzlement to many people is the inclusion in a list of the happy of those who mourn. At first glance, it may seem to be merely an evidence of Jesus' sympathy for human suffering. "They shall be comforted," he said of the mourners. But, in this context, a deeper meaning is suggested. If one tries to imagine a man or woman who moves merrily about the world completely unaffected by the misfortune of others and incapable of mourning when there is reason for grief, the result is not a picture of a happy man but of one so alienated from his own kind that, whether he knows it or not, he is the most unfortunate of men. Here, as in all of Jesus' teaching, true happiness is shown as consisting in being rather than in having.

In an all-too-limited space, it is possible to give only the barest suggestion of the wealth of philosophical wisdom which can be uncovered in the course of a careful reading of the Gospels. Jesus' teaching was timeless in its significance, and he avoided involvement in the revolutionary undercurrents in which many of his countrymen would have liked to entangle him. When an attempt was made to impale him on the horns of a dilemma by asking whether he thought it lawful to pay taxes to the Emperor, he asked to be shown a coin. "Whose likeness and inscription is this?" he asked. "Caesar's," his questioners answered. "Render therefore to Caesar the things that are Caesar's," he said, "and to God the things that are God's."

There were those, though, who saw his message as more revolutionary than that of the Zealots, and they ultimately succeeded in bringing him to trial. Under pressure from the Jewish authorities, the Roman procurator, Pontius Pilate, though unconvinced of his guilt, agreed to his execution, and he was crucified. Two days after his entombment, his body was missing, and in a surprisingly short time word was spreading throughout the Roman world that he had risen from the dead, transforming his dispirited followers into a force which no earthly power could suppress.

The Christian era had begun.

413

# Index

414

416

418